Albert A. Peña Jr.

 LATINOS IN THE UNITED STATES SERIES

SERIES EDITOR

Rubén O. Martinez, *Michigan State University*

EDITORIAL BOARD

Adalberto Aguirre Jr., *University of California–Riverside*
Robert Aponte, *Indiana University–Purdue University Indianapolis*
Teresa Cordova, *University of Illinois at Chicago*
Julie Leininger Pycior, *Manhattan College*
Rogelio Saenz, *University of Texas–San Antonio*

Albert A. Peña Jr.
DEAN OF CHICANO POLITICS

JOSÉ ANGEL GUTIÉRREZ

Michigan State University Press • East Lansing

Copyright © 2017 by José Angel Gutiérrez

∞ The paper used in this publication meets the minimum requirements of ANSI/NISO Z39.48-1992 (R 1997) (Permanence of Paper).

Michigan State University Press
East Lansing, Michigan 48823-5245

Printed and bound in the United States of America.

26 25 24 23 22 21 20 19 18 17 1 2 3 4 5 6 7 8 9 10

LIBRARY OF CONGRESS CATALOGING-IN-PUBLICATION DATA
Names: Gutiérrez, José Angel, author.
Title: Albert A. Pea Jr. : dean of Chicano politics / Jose Angel Gutierrez.
Other titles: Albert A. Peña Junior
Description: East Lansing : Michigan State University Press, 2017. | Series: Latinos in the United States series | Includes bibliographical references and index.
Identifiers: LCCN 2016040837| ISBN 9781611862515 (pbk. : alk. paper) | ISBN 9781609175337 (pdf) | ISBN 9781628953022 (epub) | ISBN 9781628963021 (kindle)
Subjects: LCSH: Peña, Albert A., Jr., 1917–2006. | Hispanic American politicians—Texas—San Antonio—Biography. | Hispanic American judges—Texas—San Antonio—Biography. | Hispanic Americans—Texas—San Antonio—Politics and government. | Politicians—Texas—San Antonio—Biography. | Judges—Texas—San Antonio—Biography. | San Antonio (Tex.)—Politics and government. | San Antonio (Tex.)—Biography.
Classification: LCC F394.S21153 P464 2017 | DDC 324.2092 [B]—dc23
LC record available at https://lccn.loc.gov/2016040837

Book and cover design by Charlie Sharp, Sharp Des!gns, East Lansing, MI
Cover image of Olga Ramos Peña and Albert A Peña Jr. and all images in the book are used courtesy of the author from his personal collection.

G green press INITIATIVE Michigan State University Press is a member of the Green Press Initiative and is committed to developing and encouraging ecologically responsible publishing practices. For more information about the Green Press Initiative and the use of recycled paper in book publishing, please visit *www.greenpressinitiative.org*.

Visit Michigan State University Press at *www.msupress.org*

To the *veteranos* of the Movimiento Chicano, early and first Chicano elected officials, community leaders, activists who like Albert A. Peña Jr. gave so much of their lives and worked in the trenches from South Texas, into the Midwest, Southwest, the Pacific Coast, and Washington, DC, so that all would benefit and gain access to political power. So many have passed from our lives and memories. See Appendix 1 for a partial listing. Also to the beneficiaries of that social movement, and the many struggles of the 1960s and into the 1980s, who continue today responsibly carrying on the work of group ascendancy for La Raza.

Contents

FOREWORD, *by Rubén Martinez* ix

PREFACE xiii

INTRODUCTION xix

PART 1. FAMILY AND FORMATION

CHAPTER 1. The Family and Young Albert Jr. 3
CHAPTER 2. Peña, the Sailor Man. 15
CHAPTER 3. Peña Jr., the Lawyer. 25

PART 2. THE MAKING OF A POLITICAL LEADER

CHAPTER 4. First School Desegregation Cases 33
CHAPTER 5. Barrio Presidential Politics 45
CHAPTER 6. *El Comisionado*, Our Man Downtown 61
CHAPTER 7. The Commissioner Years, 1957–1960. 69

PART 3. CHICANO NATION-BUILDING

CHAPTER 8. Viva Kennedy Clubs... 99
CHAPTER 9. PASO and Cristal's Los Cinco Candidatos..................... 117
CHAPTER 10. The Commissioner Years, 1965–1972........................ 157
CHAPTER 11. MALDEF: Peña's or Tijerina's?................................. 165
CHAPTER 12. Loss of Power... 179
CHAPTER 13. Politics of the Palace.. 187

PART 4. SECOND CAREER

CHAPTER 14. All Rise! Judge Peña Presiding................................ 205
CHAPTER 15. The End of Public Life.. 215
CHAPTER 16. Who Caused the Injury or Assault?........................... 229

PART 5. THE FINAL YEARS

CHAPTER 17. Second Retirement... 237

APPENDIX 1. In Memoriam.. 247
APPENDIX 2. Note on County Government................................... 249

NOTES.. 261
BIBLIOGRAPHY... 289
INDEX... 299

RUBÉN MARTINEZ

Foreword

BIOGRAPHIES PROVIDE WINDOWS THROUGH WHICH WE CAN VIEW AND DEEPEN our understanding of the times during which a person lived. Political biographies provide a dimensional window that brings into view the structures of political power and the struggles to alter and preserve them. A political biography of a Chicano leader focuses and sharpens our view further by shedding light on the political structures of domination and oppression, and the leadership approaches of those who sought to eliminate those structures. This book sheds light on all these levels by focusing on the life and leadership of Albert Peña Jr. (1917–2006), who was politically active from the post–World War II years through the first decade of this century.

Although the principal setting is San Antonio, Texas, the activities and leadership of Peña reached far beyond South Texas and the Southwest. Peña bridged the Greatest Generation with the roots of the Civil Rights Movement and the Chicano Movement by dedicating his efforts to electoral politics and to eradicating the barriers that excluded Mexican Americans and Chicanos from full participation in American society. His life spanned the Great Depression, World War II, the rise of labor unions and their influence, Keynesian economics and the rise of social democracy, struggles for civil rights, and the shift to neoliberalism (i.e., free market fundamentalism). Thus, his life bridged the social democratic order of the mid-twentieth century with the right-wing neoliberal order of the last forty years.

Peña ran for and held public office in Bexar County, where San Antonio is located, and used it to reduce social and political barriers while promoting the inclusion of Mexican Americans and Chicanos in exercising institutional power and influence. The author, José Angel Gutiérrez, who is no stranger to Chicano politics and struggles, knew and worked with Peña when he, himself, was a young activist. Peña became his hero, so it is not surprising that he presents a favorable view of that political fireball that was Pena Jr. But he is also willing to shed light on his human frailties, letting us know that our political leaders do not and never will walk on water; they are only human, exhibiting both extraordinary skills and strengths at the same time that they are characterized by weaknesses.

Overall, there are few biographies that focus on the political leadership of Mexican Americans and Chicanos within what one might consider the mainstream of U.S. politics, in contradistinction to the anticolonial struggles that characterized the Chicano Movement. Recent ones include *Taking on Giants: Fabián Chavez Jr. and New Mexico Politics*, David Roybal's volume on Fabian Chavez Jr., a major legislative leader in New Mexico politics, and *Edward R. Roybal: The Mexican American Struggle for Political Empowerment*, Frank Javier Garcia Berumen's work on Edward R. Roybal, a longtime legislative leader in the U.S. House of Representatives. The political careers of both of these leaders spanned the second half of the twentieth century. The political lives of many other Chicanos and Chicanas remain to be studied. For example, no major political biography has been written on Dionisio "Dennis" Chávez, the distinguished senator from New Mexico. Chávez was first elected to the state legislature in 1922, then to the U.S. House of Representatives in 1931, and in 1935 became the first Latino Democrat to serve in the U.S. Senate. He was among the first senators to denounce Senator Joseph McCarthy for his fearmongering, anticommunist tactics and activities, and later voted to censure McCarthy. Neither is there one on Joseph Montoya, who "succeeded" Chavez in the U.S. Senate. This volume on Peña adds to the body of knowledge on Chicano political leadership, and sets both a model and a standard for Chicano political biographies.

It does so by examining the civil rights efforts of Peña within a state that has a long history of exclusion and repression of Mexican Americans and African Americans. We learn of Peña's political battles, his accomplishments and failures, and the internecine struggles among Mexican Americans and Chicanos themselves. The volume can be read as a political playbook, as a history of Chicano political organizations in South Texas, and as a case study of Chicano political leadership. This book sheds light on all these dimensions as Gutiérrez draws us into the life and leadership of Albert Peña Jr., and it provides us with a deeper understanding of Chicano politics in South Texas, centered as they were in San Antonio, and how they linked to the broader civil rights struggles of Mexican Americans and Chicanos in the Southwest and the broader Civil Rights Movement across the country. The political life of Albert Peña Jr. allows Gutiérrez to shed light on the inner workings of electoral politics at a time when Texas politics were directly linked to the White House through President Lyndon B. Johnson and were the face, as it were, of political leadership on a national and international scale.

The barriers of exclusion that Peña confronted during his day are different from those Latinos face today, but they are not yet eradicated. For example, the poll tax is no longer in place, but right-wing legislators and judges, much like yesterday, are working actively to suppress the Latino electorate, this time through ID requirements, limited voting times, and other voter suppression tactics. Like Peña, Latino community leaders today confront a seemingly overwhelming system of domination and oppression. Yet, as Peña did within his day, they can hold a view and the values of a democratic society that can guide them through the maze of political maneuvers and manipulations that today reproduce the neoliberal order. The neoliberal order both uses and attacks the very institution that secures our civil rights, government. It uses government to dismantle government and seeks to replace it with market-based organizations under the pretext that the latter are more efficient and effective, even as history shows us that such is not the case.

The political pendulum's swing to the extreme right has reached its apex, however, and has begun swinging back to the center, and we do not yet know if it will swing past it. What we do know is that we live in a historical moment with great potential for overcoming and transcending neoliberalism—much as in Peña's time, when the Civil Rights Movement held the promise of a better society. Peña stayed local by choice and did what he could to make Bexar County, Texas, and the nation more democratic and inclusive. He serves as a model for contemporary Chicano and Chicana leaders to study, to emulate, and to adapt to their own lives and times. It took Gutiérrez a decade to complete the work, which makes a major contribution to the study of Chicano political leadership by combining research with an insider's political praxis. It gives me pleasure to see that the volume is now available to readers interested in Chicano leadership and the struggle for a better nation.

Preface

This biography has been a labor of love on my part for Albert A. Peña Jr. He was my hero and remains so in memory. When he passed in 2006 I felt guilty at not having completed the work in time. He used to tell me to hurry so he could travel the country and organize with his book. This effort has also been protracted and arduous, spanning more than a decade. I first interviewed Peña for my project *Tejano Voices* in 1996.[1] I knew then his story had to be memorialized in some way. Albert, with Dr. Rodolfo "Rudy" Rosales from the University of Texas in San Antonio (UTSA), visited me in 2003 while I attended a professional conference in that city and was interviewing yet another public official for *Tejano Voices*, former Texas state senator Joe Bernal.[2] Peña insisted I help Rosales write his biography.

This manuscript would not have been possible without the assistance of members of the Peña family, such as his brothers Richard and Antonio; sisters Belinda Dague and Madeline Davila, and her son, Richard "Guero Polkas" Davila; the grown children Albert A. Peña III and Belinda Dwyer from Josie Herrera, Albert's first wife; William "Bill" Peña and his mother Olga Ramos; and Albert's last wife, Frances Guerra, now deceased as well. And of course without the subject, Alberto A. Peña Jr., who made time to talk to me about his life over the course of the years, this manuscript would not be as complete. I also video interviewed many persons, others just audio, who are listed at the end of the manuscript. Dr. Rosales provided recorded interviews he had conducted, which I had transcribed and copied for use here. My copies will be on archival deposit at the Julian Samora Research Institute (JSRI) of Michigan State University. Dr. Rudy Rosales had interviewed peers and colleagues of Judge Peña, such as Rudy Esquivel, John Alaniz, Frank Valdez, Pete Torres Jr., Fred Vasquez, Jesse Herrera, O. J. Valdez, Matt García, Fernando Rodríguez, Rubén Munguía, Roy Sanchez, Felix Treviño, and Albert Peña Jr. himself. These stories are most valuable because many of these personages are deceased. Thank you, Rudy. Your early work of these recordings provides useful and important first-person narratives about Peña's life and times and those of his peers.

Judge Peña had the foresight—with the encouragement of Dr. Jesse Zapata, then provost of the downtown University of Texas–San Antonio campus, and Dr. Rudy Rosales—to deposit some archival material at UTSA's Institute of Texan Cultures (ITC) dealing primarily with his early political years while Bexar County commissioner. Judge Peña was so careless in the preservation of his papers that this deposit contains only limited material that is currently available to researchers and interested persons.[3] His various family members do have some memorabilia and documents. Olga has the most extensive collection of them all, including photographs that she still treasures and keeps. Son Bill Peña had some of the memorabilia Albert had in his office when he practiced law with Douglas Dilley; Bill also has passed away and these items are out there somewhere. I could gather photographs for this book primarily because Arnold Flores found many. Arnold Flores, also deceased, was among the last of Peña's trusted confidants, and his recollection of events, assistance in getting to other people, answering specific questions that kept coming up, gathering documents and photographs have been an invaluable source of information for this book. Thank you, posthumously, very, very much, Arnold. Walter Martinez, an associate of Flores with suboffices in Kingsville, carried parts of this manuscript and brought photographs from Arnold to me while I was there. Copies of the rough draft were made at their company in San Antonio for others to provide comments. Thank you, Walter. I also thanked Juan Patlan before he passed away for his help with the section on the Mexican American Unity Council and San Antonio's War on Poverty program.

Note on Research

The material utilized to produce this manuscript are primary sources consisting of various videotaped interviews with Peña Jr., two of his spouses, two sisters, and three adult children. These have been transcribed and are on deposit with Special Collections of the General Library at the University of Texas at Arlington. Other primary sources used were interviews with over a dozen persons with insight into and personal knowledge of Peña Jr.'s activities. These interviews were not transcribed due to lack of resources and time. Countless newspaper articles were utilized, as were his many, many opinion editorials published and speeches written out, some audio- and videotaped, and on deposit at the University of Texas San Antonio Archives at the Institute of Texan Cultures and the main City of San Antonio Library. I have left some material with the holdings of the Julian Samora Research Institute at Michigan State University.

I relied on these printed materials to make Albert come alive in the text. I assumed that if he spoke or wrote it at one time, I could quote him in proper context within these pages as if he would have said it again. Some quoted material is taken from these sources without specific citation due to several problems encountered during the collection, storage, and writing of this book. Secondary sources were utilized to fill in gaps of information not available from the primary sources: newspapers, books, reports, and magazines.

The major problem affecting citation was due to my eight changes in residence during 1996 to 2016 and the handling of documents by my students and other interested persons during this time period. The "yellow pasties" I placed on documents when I found and copied them invariably came off. The stamp on the back of the document as to its general location at the Institute of Texan Cultures during the writing in 2004 and 2007 was my only clue to the reference. I could not again return to the San Antonio archives and library to specifically identify box and folder for the reader. I apologize. To correct this deficiency, I have placed at Michigan State University all the last documents utilized for citations in this manuscript; they are in a series of folders labeled by year.

Peña also wrote hundreds of opinion editorials, some of which have been published in San Antonio's weekly, *La Prensa*. Many more are in his collection in the archives at ITC. The San Antonio Public Library also has some newspaper articles about Peña and some written by him. Some audio and video material that features Albert A. Peña Jr. has been preserved at the Institute of Texan Cultures and Our Lady of the Lake University's (OLLU) Mexican American Studies Program. I am leaving the video interviews conducted in the course of this research and copies of his editorials, essays, and newspaper columns with MSU's Julian Samora Research Institute, under the direction of Dr. Rubén Martinez.

These writings and speeches by Peña were invaluable in bringing his voice and opinion to the manuscript. I did not have to engage in much creative writing and license in this manuscript; there was little that Peña did not write or express an opinion about. I tried most unsuccessfully to raise funds among the many friends of Judge Peña to transfer his voice and image to current technology just before I departed from San Antonio on the first research and writing phase of this book in May 2004. I did manage to have transcriptions made of some of the Rosales interviews and made digital copies, particularly CD-ROM copies. Sister Carolina Flores at OLLU helped with the funding of this copying work and accepted responsibility for housing this portion of the Peña papers. The OLLU Center for Mexican American Studies has these transcripts, CD-ROMs, and a record of donors. In addition to other audio- and videotapes, some provided by Jaime Martinez and Arnold Flores, the many articles written by Peña were physically copied by Patricia Mejia and Laura Barbarena Medrano and are also on deposit at OLLU.

The staff at the Institute of Texan Cultures under the direction of Gerianne Schaad were most helpful during my initial visit in spring 2004 in retrieving boxes of archival material, storing my equipment after every workday, and opening the side door to start work early. Many thanks to Traci JoLeigh Drummond and Javier Garza for their selfless and tireless cooperation in retrieving for me material from the Peña archives day after day and copying relevant material. They were always in a jovial mood and disposed to helping me in my research.

Peña's many, many friends, relatives, and political collaborators, such as Herschel Bernard, Juan Patlan, Leo Alvarado, C. G. Sutton, Romulo Munguía Jr., Frank D. Wing, Rev. Claude Black, George Ozuna, Arnold Flores, Henry Casso, and Jake Johnson—all now deceased—Gil Murillo, Genaro García, Gail Beagle, Dr. William Elizondo, Tino Guerra, Tino Duran, Antonio Esparza, Joe Bernal, Eugene Coleman, Joyce Peters, Albert Bustamante, Mary Peña, Belinda Dwyer, Douglas Dilley, and Eleanor G. McCusker offered important information and insight. Marie (and Pic Schwarz, who prompted recall) and Virginia Escobedo provided information about the daily workings of Commissioner Peña and Judge Peña, respectively. They were the personal assistants to Albert A. Peña Jr. during his tenure in both roles. Many thanks to Joyce Peters and Federal District Judge Fred Biery for insightful information and phone numbers for people I needed to reach, and for their views on Texas politics in the Peña years, particularly from a liberal's perspective. On the occasion when I visited or just dropped in to see Judge Peña in his last years, Barbara de la Fuente, the office manager of the Frances Guerra Peña's insurance agency, where he often spent his mornings, was always helpful, cordial, and good for a laugh. She watched over Albert when Frances was not around the office. Upstairs from the office, Frances re-created his former law office at the Douglas Dilley firm, replete with plaques, photos, his gavel and nameplate, posters, and other memorabilia. But Albert would rather spend time with Barbara than watching television or sitting upstairs. I was present on several occasions when Albert sang to her, danced for her, and told stories, often with amazing clarity and recall.

There are many other persons whose help made this project materialize. At the University of Texas at Arlington (UTA), the University Faculty Development Leave committee members and the political science department chair, Dale Story, all worked to make possible a semester of leave for me during spring 2004. Dean Robert De Villar at Our Lady of the Lake University (OLLU) and political science department chair Richard Gambitta of the University of Texas at San Antonio offered office and parking space, equipment and supplies, and visiting scholar status to me during that period. I was fortunate to have been able to teach a graduate class at the Center for Leadership Studies at OLLU, under the direction of Dean De Villar, that paid the rent, gas, and food bills.

During 2007 I was treated very well by President Rumaldo Juarez of Texas A&M University–Kingsville (TAMUK), his executive assistant Darrell Lynn Pray, and Drs. Cecilia Aros Hunter and Leslie Hunter. TAMUK provided me a class to teach, an apartment to live in while there until mid-December 2007, and an office in which to write. The colleagues in the political science department headed by Dr. Mario Carranza were most cordial and supportive of my work. I really enjoyed the students in my class on public leadership that semester. Thank you Maria Jaramillo, political science department secretary for keeping track of my paperwork and calling me when I had mail.

While at TAMUK, I had an office in Baugh Hall, the office that housed the *Journal of South Texas* while under the editorial direction of Leslie Hunter. Both he and his wife, Cecilia Aros Hunter, were most helpful in facilitating my accommodation in Baugh Hall before they retired and moved to Arizona a few days before I arrived in Kingsville. Cecilia had invited me to participate in two events at TAMUK a couple of years before, which gave me the opportunity to meet with President Juarez and make my request for a visiting scholar appointment so I could visit and write this book. Elda Ayala Puentes, the day-to-day assistant at the South Texas Archives in Baugh Hall, was most helpful and delightful. She always found the supplies or equipment I needed, and knew who to call to make things happen. Lucas Faragoza and Alisha Davies, work-study students at TAMUK, were most helpful with hooking up my equipment and installing the latest software to help along my manuscript.

I thank Dr. Tatcho Mindiola of the University of Houston for his patience in waiting for me to finish this manuscript. When I was a visiting scholar in the Mexican American Studies Program, which he headed, he took enough interest in this project to energize me early on and occasionally prompt me to finish the manuscript. Both he and Lorenzo Cano provided preliminary commentary on the manuscript that improved it in many areas. Thank you. Rosalie Robertson, once again, for assisting me by editing a near final draft. Rosalie played a similar role for me and my coauthors of *Chicanas in Charge: Texas Women in the Public Arena* (AltaMira, 2007). She is simply terrific and promptly efficient.

My family also deserves acknowledgment for their support and patience during this three-pronged period: 2004, 2007, and June 2016. I have denied them quality time while I squirreled myself away in San Antonio to research—and later Kingsville and East Lansing, Michigan, to write and Brownsville to edit this manuscript. In Kingsville and Corpus Christi, the help of two lawyers with legal matters I was still involved in was very much appreciated: Delma Rios Salazar and Viviana Santiago Cavada, respectively. Delma let me use her office, equipment, and supplies, and Viviana collaborated on pending cases I had to work on while in Kingsville. Lastly, I would like to thank the staff at the Legal Center of José Angel Gutiérrez, P.C., for keeping up the good work while I was gone: Cecilia Lugo, Gloria Carrillo, and wife Natalia Verjat. Things have run so smoothly at the law office while I have been gone that perhaps it is best I stay away longer.

When the manuscript reached ready-for-submission status, I found a home for it at Michigan State University Press with the help of Dr. Rubén Martinez, editor of the LIUS series. He also deserves credit for helping to make this narrative a better read. He has a keen eye for necessary edits, which he dutifully completed despite his heavy workload as director of JSRI at MSU. He was a pleasure to work with, and it was even more gratifying to see the manuscript improve greatly due to his editorial suggestions. To the JSRI staff and student assistants, Jamie Wing, Devin Mazur, Jean Kayitsinga, Marcos Martinez, Temia Gaines, Samantha Martin, Eileen Stefansky, Barry Lewis, and Dr. Juan Coronado, postdoctoral fellow, who greeted me with contagious smiles and diligently copied, day after day, material on Peña necessary to tie narrative to endnotes—thank you all for the assistance given to me in this project.

Introduction

THIS BOOK IS ABOUT THE LIFE OF ALBERT A. PEÑA JR. OF SAN ANTONIO, TEXAS.[1] Reference is made in numerous books of his role in the politics of U.S.-born Mexicans. Peña's political involvement and impact have been a story waiting to be told. His story, and that of many other persons, organizations, events, places, and movements, has not been a subject in the field of biography. Academe, and publishers perhaps, are not as interested in biographies on the Chicano community as they are on whites or even blacks, First Nation natives, and other groups. Recently in 2014, Benjamin Márquez used an image of Albert A. Peña Jr. on the front cover of his book.[2] And a few years previously, in 2010, a full-bodied Peña with picket sign in hand graced the cover of another book about the War on Poverty and the Civil Rights Movement in Texas.[3] Yet, a political biography of this central character in Chicano politics remained missing from the growing body of such works. In both of these books, Peña figures prominently but not completely in these narratives on civil rights, liberal politics, and the War on Poverty.

By contrast, Ignacio M. García produced a biography on Hector P. García, the founder of the American G.I. Forum, and another, earlier prodigious work on the rise of the Viva Kennedy Clubs in the country.[4] Peña's political footprints are found in numerous pages of both works. Thomas Kreneck in the biography of Felix Tijerina, national president of the League of United Latin American Citizens (LULAC) and promoter of the Little School of the four hundred projects, mentions Peña's role as host to this organization's annual meeting in San Antonio.[5] Peña was then learning the exchange between leaders and followers during his early years as a newly licensed attorney; he was a follower of LULAC and American G.I. Forum leaders. Dr. Hector García frequently called on Peña for help in desegregating public schools near San Antonio.

Gilberto J. Quezada wrote a well-documented biography of Manuel Bravo, county judge for Zapata County, Texas, and political boss during the 1940s–1950s in South Texas.[6] No such study exists for an urban political boss such as Albert A. Peña Jr.

Many publications on Chicano history and politics, on topics such as the Political Association of Spanish Speaking Organizations (PASO); Crystal City, Texas; the Albuquerque Walkout of the Equal Employment Opportunity Commission; the Mexican American Legal Defense and Education Fund; the Southwest Voter Registration Education Project; and the National Council of La Raza, identify Peña in various roles as participant, leader, organizer, founder, and member. Photographs contained in major works on aspects of Chicano politics have memorialized Peña for his help in fundraising during the *Hernandez v. Texas* case of 1954, and in organizing the Viva Kennedy Clubs in the Southwest. More photographs have adorned walls in numerous offices of Peña with U.S. presidents and senators up to the Bill Clinton years. He was an important figure on the local, regional, and national political scene for many decades, but not researched in his own right.

Peña was a transactional and transcendental leader who changed the political culture of the Southwestern part of the United States.[7] In effecting this change, Peña organized persons of Mexican ancestry in the country from detached, inert nonvoters into political actors. He began programs that evolved into organizations and later became institutions. From his unglamorous post as county commissioner in an urban Texas county, he became a nationally known figure across the country and in the White House for decades. His vision for the national community of persons of Mexican ancestry, Chicanos, was not just over the horizon to the next elections but for the quality of life of the next generations. He became the national spokesman for the Chicano community at many forums. In 1991, the largest Latino advocacy network and civil rights organization, the National Council of La Raza, at its annual gathering in Houston, Texas, conferred on him and this author the Chicano Hero Award.

This book has three foci: biography, politics, and public leadership. Peña was the first person of Mexican ancestry to be elected, in 1956, to a major public office in urban Texas, that of Bexar County commissioner (San Antonio). The following year, in the border city of El Paso, Texas, Raymond Telles was elected mayor—the first person of Mexican ancestry in this office. Border cities and counties across the Southwest, however, had previously had persons of Mexican ancestry elected to public office. In 1960 Roy Barrera, also of San Antonio, was appointed secretary of state by Governor John Connally. Electing and appointing persons of Mexican ancestry to highly visible, urban governmental entities or state office was a new phenomenon and reflected the beginning of Chicano-led electoral politics. Peña led this new charge into public buildings and places.

Peña spent sixteen years on the Bexar County Commissioners Court winning election and repeated reelection. In the course of this period of time, with help from his second wife, Olga Ramos, he built a powerful urban political machine that helped elect many, many other persons of Mexican ancestry, from constables to justices of the peace, and even members of Congress—not to ignore the countless members of the city council and school boards in metropolitan San Antonio the co-leadership team of Olga and Albert also helped get elected. The effectiveness of Peña's political machine also helped win public office for others in other surrounding communities, such as Crystal City and Mathis, Texas.

Peña spent another fifteen years as an appointed official in the municipal courts of San Antonio as judge and later presiding judge. Despite the fact that he worked full-time while county commissioner or judge, he made time for grassroots organizing and travel across the country. He organized, founded, directed, and led many important organizations during the era of the Chicano Movement (late 1950s to late 1970s) that later became institutions and continue to this day. Peña led by example. He joined with others in countless protests, demonstrations, debates, group and student walkouts, labor strikes, consumer fights, product boycotts, press conferences, and rallies. On several occasions he single-handedly brought litigation to end segregation in South Texas. Throughout his life, roughly fifty-two of his eighty-nine years were spent as a doer, a transformational leader.

Politics of incorporation, according to Kim Geron, have multiple pathways, such as litigation, electoral activity, protest and demonstration, and building alliances and coalitions.[8] Albert A. Peña Jr. was an active, pivotal, central figure in building alliances and multiracial coalitions in San Antonio, South Texas, across the state and the country.[9] He was the first to effectively join in coalition with white liberals, labor leaders, blacks, and Chicanos in San Antonio. He also supported his wife's efforts at building a similar coalition among women Democrats in Bexar County.

Remnants of the Peña black/brown coalition remain in San Antonio, according to Arnold Flores, who reported prior to his death that the group still met monthly for lunch. Peña expanded coalition-building to the state level within the Democratic Party. While coalition-building is not a new practice among ethnic groups in the public arena, black-brown relations are a new subject matter. There are books that conclude such a coalition will not work, and others that it will and should.[10]

This book is also about the role of women in Chicano politics, especially Olga Ramos, the spouse of Albert A. Peña Jr. during his county commissioner years. In a coauthored publication, *Chicanas in Charge: Texas Women in the Public Arena*, and a subsequent work by Sonia R. García and various other coauthors, *Politicas: Latina Public Officials in Texas*, Olga Peña is featured and profiled. Peña's public life was greatly assisted by Olga Ramos Peña, and his last wife, Frances Guerra Peña, who cared for him until his death.[11] Olga and Frances were important coleaders and organizers with Peña during his lifetime.

I was hampered in this work by time constraints, personal issues, several residence relocations, lack of resources, and more importantly a paucity of prior studies. There are lacunae of information on Chicano politics and the role of Chicanos in Texas and U.S. politics. Generations of Texas public-school students since the 1930s were instructed on the white history of the state utilizing the most popular text for decades, *Texas History* and *The Story of Texas* (by the same author).[12] There are few biographies on Chicano public figures; perhaps a Chicano/Latino studies department will take that challenge and make it their primary focus. Hopefully, this preliminary work will begin to address that problem. And this work is but a small contribution toward documenting not only Peña's legacy but also his leadership skills, plus a new look at the events of the times. There is a need for biographies of Olga Ramos Peña, Arnold Flores, Juan Patlan, Raul Yzaguirre, and Mario Obledo, for example, and histories of organizations such as Loyal American Democrats (LAD), the Political Association of Spanish Speaking Organizations (PASO), the Mexican American Political Association (MAPA), the National Council of La Raza (NCLR), the older NCLR affiliates such as the Mexican American Unity Council (MAUC) in San Antonio and The East Los Angeles Community Union (TELACU), the Mexican American Legal Defense and Education Fund (MALDEF), and the Southwest Voter Registration Education Project (SVREP).

Significant events took place during Peña's lifetime that made notable history but have not been the subject of scholarly inquiry, and have only been somewhat documented by journalists and the electronic media: specifically, labor strikes—the Rio Grande Valley's La Casita Farms, Economic Furniture in Austin, Friedrich Refrigeration in San Antonio, Farah in El Paso—and the subsequent marches by farm workers to Austin and Washington, DC. The first march was catalytic and became iconic, yet little is known of the organizing, funding, participants, community response, and impact of these marches; the latter marched across the Right-to-Work Law states of the South into Washington, DC. The PASO/Teamster–sponsored electoral revolt in Crystal City in 1963 and the Mexican American Youth Organization (MAYO) and Raza Unida Party takeover in 1969 were studied by John Shockley and Armando Navarro, respectively.[13] The PASO involvement in Mathis, Texas, has been ignored, including the unresolved police murder of Dr. Fred Logan, who was providing medical care to indigent Chicano families during that time. PASO was also involved in the electoral activity of Beeville, Texas. The Raza Unida Party's other electoral victories in Washington, DC; La Salle County, Texas; the Texas cities of Cotulla, Carrizo Springs, Pearsall, San Juan, Anthony; and the Edgewood Independent School District have been mentioned in some works by Ignacio García and Armando Navarro but have not been independently examined by scholars. Douglas Foley with others published an anthropological study of Pearsall in Frio County, Texas.[14]

The hundreds of school walkouts by Chicano students across the country have not been studied or even quantified, except in the HBO film *Walkout*, about the Los Angeles school strikes, and a YouTube clip on the Edcouch-Elsa Walkout in 1968 narrated by Ed Rabel of CBS. Similarly, during the Vietnam War there were scores of Chicano antiwar protests, including the largest one in Los Angeles on August 29, 1968, during which noted journalist Rubén Salazar and others were killed by police and sheriff deputies. That movement and its counterparts have not been deeply studied. Raul Ruiz has authored a first book on that event.

Published biographies and autobiographies of Chicano leaders, institutions, events, places, organizations, and programs are sorely lacking. According to Arnoldo de Leon, the scholarly study of this community begun to take its place within the academy only since 1970.[15] This may be a primary reason for the lack of Chicano biography; but a second reason is also available. The various Chicano studies programs and departments, as well as other related departments and programs in universities across the country have not made biography of the Chicano community a central research focus. Thirdly, Chicano leaders and their organizations, programs, and institutions have neither taken the time nor allocated resources to the important work of documenting their personal and public struggle on behalf of the greater community. Similarly, the study of public leadership has been lacking generally in political science, and in the case of the Chicano community, specifically. Most notably, the disciplines of business and education have made giant strides in the study of public and organizational leadership. The military science departments are not far behind. In the social sciences, the study of public leadership has meant presidential studies, with few exceptions.

Chicano Biography and Public Leadership

There have been some notable biographical works since the 1970s on Chicanos and their efforts for group ascendancy. Chicano Movement figures such as César Chávez and Reies López Tijerina received most of the attention and continue to do so.[16] A lesser-known Chicano figure, Oscar "Zeta" Acosta, but nonetheless an icon, published two books in the 1970s: an autobiography and a biography of the Chicano people.[17] Both Arte Público Press and Bilingual Review Press began to publish biographies and autobiographies of significant public figures, primarily for a youth market.[18] Some academic presses, primarily in the Southwest, began to publish significant works, such as Rodolfo Acuña's *Pesquera* and Juan Gómez-Quiñones's *Sembradores: Magon* in the late 1960s. In 1971 noted scholar and activist Ernesto Galarza published his autobiography about his youth.[19] Carlos Larralde began pioneering work on Chicano biography with his two publications from the 1970s.[20] In the 1980s such publications as Mauricio Mazon's biography of the Zoot-Suit Riots emerged, as did Ignacio García's work on the Raza Unida Party augmenting the early work by Richard Santillan.[21] Armando Navarro's work on the Mexican American Youth Organization and also the Raza Unida Party were published the following decade.[22] The only biography on Hispanics with a focus on three major groups—Mexicans, Puerto Ricans, and Cubans (no group from Central America was included)—was written by Earl Shorris in 1992.[23] In his defense, the number of Central Americans in the United States had not yet reached the large numbers after the protracted Reagan wars in that region, which produced hundreds of thousands of refugees and millions murdered. Juan Gonzalez in his book *Harvest of Empire* very ably documents the history of migration not only from Central America but the Americas of Spanish-speaking peoples to the United States.[24]

Mario T. García produced two biographies on notable Chicano figures Bert Corona and Rubén Salazar, utilizing narrative and secondary materials, and in the late 1990s a book on a Chicano mayor.[25] His most recent publication is on the spirituality of César Chávez.[26] I also served as county judge in Zavala County, Texas, and published a political autobiography.[27] The story of the appointment and the life of the first Chicano federal judge was published in 1996.[28] Felix Almaraz has written an important biography of Carlos Castaneda, a significant Chicano scholar and mentor to a generation of protégés.[29] The noted cinematographer Jesus Salvador Treviño revealed his story in *Eyewitness: A Filmmaker's Memoir of the Chicano Movement*.[30] And after years in production, the life and times of Willie Velásquez, cofounder of the Mexican American Youth Organization and of the Southwest Voter Registration Education Project, was published by Arte Público Press. Regrettably, this book is detailed and most descriptive of events and happenings in the life of Velásquez, but totally absent of references. It is the author's story and not a substantive work, in my opinion.[31] Hector Galan—noted award-winning filmmaker, primarily documentaries—has produced a documentary based on the book entitled *Willie Velásquez: Tu Voz Es Tu Voto*. Most recently, I had two additional works published that add to Chicano biography: the translated and edited version of Reies López Tijerina's autobiography, and a youth-market biography on Severita Lara, the student leader of the 1969 Crystal City High School Walkout.[32] My wife, Natalia, and I coauthored a biography in 2013 of the forty-year-old Chicano organization the *Texas Association of Chicanos in Higher Education*, published by Arcadia Press.

While this brief overview is a partial list of publications, it is not an exhaustive compilation of work on biography, autobiography, and public leadership among Chicanos. Emilio Zamora and others compiled essays on public figures in Texas, as I have together with Michelle Melendez and Sonia Noyola.[33] A pioneering work by Américo Paredes, a folklorist—not necessarily biographical, but about a man, Gregorio Cortez, and his ballad nonetheless—was published in 1958.[34] Similarly, others have done work on Tomas Rivera, noted writer and educator.[35] And, a new genre of nonpolitical biographies and autobiographies have emerged with books on gangs, heroes, and heroines.[36]

In the changing times of the 1950s, Albert A. Peña Jr. began his life of political activism that lasted throughout the remaining years of the twentieth century and into the twenty-first. Albert died on July 3, 2006, just four and a half months shy of reaching eighty-nine glorious years of age. This is that story.

PART 1

Family and Formation

CHAPTER 1

The Family and Young Albert Jr.

DOLORES LA CHAPELLE, THE DAUGHTER OF AN ADVENTUROUS FRENCHMAN, was born and raised in the El Paso area in the late 1880s.[1] She never lived with her biological father and only met him on occasion. She learned from him during one of those rare visits that she had a brother and sister in Mexico City. Her mother finally moved the family to San Antonio, and Lolita, as she was affectionately called, soon met and married Antonio López, a very tall, handsome man. The Lópezes on the paternal side were originally from the Canary Islands, according to some family members, while others place the family in South Texas. The origin of the maternal side is also still debated by family members.

As early as March 29, 1896, Antonio López was a resident of Laredo, Texas. He was the son of Lorenzo Peña and Marcella Almendárez, according to Antonio Peña, the youngest brother to Albert A. Peña Jr. These branches of the Peña family tree were fourth-generation residents of a *rancho* near present-day Beeville, Texas.[2]

Young López had few domestic skills, and fewer social skills when it came to dealing with his young wife. He was very demanding and adamant about his food. If he didn't like what was served, with a swipe of his long arm he would clear the table onto the floor. Next he would take a swipe at Dolores and often manage to hit her if she did not move away in time. A neighbor learned of this abuse and advised her to grab a log from the wood stove and hit him next time he pulled that stunt. She took the advice and hit him back with the log and broke his arm. He never hit her again or cleared the table onto the floor.

The Lópezes started a family, and the first born was named Rosa; then the second was named Dolores, like her mother. Several other siblings were added to the family: Maria, Dora, Arthur, and "Rudy" or Rodolfo, the youngest. While in her late teens, daughter Dolores López met a dashing young man, Alberto Antonio Peña, who also was a newcomer to San Antonio.

The Peña family had relocated from Laredo when Alberto was five. His mother had gone blind when he was a young adult, and most of his earnings went to the family household because his father, Lorenzo, was not always around. Mama Peña used to tell her son, and later the grandchildren, many stories. One such story was that she would swim across the Rio Grande at the Eagle Pass/Piedras Negras crossing to visit her mother from time to time. Another was that she was a full-blooded Apache, related to the great war chief Victorio of the Eastern Chiricahua Apaches, also known as the Mimbreño Apaches, a subtribe of the Chiricahua Apaches. According to her oral tales, Victorio raided ranchos and townships in Mexico, West Texas, and New Mexico until he met his fate at the ambush in the mountains of Chihuahua laid by Lt. Colonel Joaquin Terrazas.

After one such raid, he was pursued by the Mexican military to his campsite. He was surrounded by Colonel Terrazas, leader of the Chihuahua state militia, in the Tres Castillas mountain range, some sixty miles inside Mexico from Fort Davis in West Texas. The Mexican soldiers massacred Victorio and his warriors on October 15, 1880, sparing only the women and children. The soldiers made them march south toward Coahuila, away from Chihuahua.[3] It is very possible that Mama Peña and her mother were among these survivors and fled along the border down to Nuevo Laredo, Mexico. Mama Peña made mention to grandson Albert Jr. that only she and another of her group and kin, Telesfora Mendoza, lived in San Antonio. Telesfora lived over in the *barrio de la Tripa* (stockyards) on Alta Vista and Trinity Streets.[4] Younger brother Antonio Peña, however, claims that Mama Peña "was in fact decended [sic] from the Kickapoo Tribe."[5]

Alberto Peña attended the San Antonio Vocational and Technical High School but did not graduate. He married young, but that first marriage did not go well and no children were born of that relationship. When Alberto first eyed Dolores López, as the family story goes, he knew this was his next wife-to-be. After a short courtship, Dolores accepted the marriage proposal and the Peñas settled down on California Street, off North Flores and Rowana.[6] Mother-in-law Dolores La Chapelle had to teach young Dolores how to make better *tortillas de harina* because Alberto insisted on fresh, handmade flour tortillas with every meal. Alberto Peña was a hardworking and hard-playing man. During the day he sold furniture at the Western Furniture store on Dolorosa and Flores streets and also worked as an "elevator boy."[7]

On weekends he promoted dances at two clubs he rented for the occasion, La Gloria and El Hidalgo in San Antonio's West Side. Often, to make ends meet, Alberto would barter dance tickets for chickens or car maintenance or yard work. When Dolores and he began to have children and the family grew, Alberto would use the same ploy and barter dance tickets for household help for Dolores. And the Peña family grew methodically like clockwork. It seemed that Dolores was pregnant every two years. The Peñas were very good Catholics. Alberto would attend early Mass at the San Fernando Cathedral daily, usually at 7 a.m., before reporting for work at the downtown furniture store.

Young Alberto Antonio Peña Jr. was the firstborn on December 15, 1917. Elder Alberto was delighted and announced to his wife that she could now have a daughter, but for every girl born there had to be a boy. He wanted matched pairs of boys and girls. Fortunately, the next child born was a girl, Madeline, on June 6, 1919. Unfortunately for Dolores, her third child was another girl, Belinda, born March 24, 1921. Alberto wanted another boy, but the fourth child was yet another girl, Irene, born on January 26, 1923. Alberto insisted on another son, and Richard was born two years later, January 11, 1925. The family now consisted of three girls and only two boys; there had to be another boy brought into the Peña family if matching was to occur. Dolores was harried and worn by having given birth to five children in eight years. The housework alone was overwhelming: making mountains of tortillas daily, washing cloth diapers by hand, cooking and feeding a family of seven.

Dolores was soon with child again, but this time the prognosis was twins. She dreaded another pregnancy and prayed for a pair of boys. Tragedy struck the Peña family when Dolores was eight months pregnant. While walking outside the home in the uneven, rutted, unpaved streets one early morning, she tripped, fell face forward hard on her stomach, and miscarried due to hemorrhaging. By the time she was taken for emergency care, the doctors could not save the babies. They opted for saving her life. The stillborn twins were a boy and a girl. The only respite Dolores got from this ordeal was two less children to feed and care for, for a few months. The other five children were increasingly more work than a mother could handle. Dolores was always exhausted and fatigued. It was not long before Dolores was pregnant again with Antonio. He was born on July 20, 1926. While this birth was a happy occasion, tragedy struck the family that same day. Grandmother Peña died the day little Antonio was born.

Young Albert Jr. was school-age by the time Richard was born, seven years and a month later, and so was Madeline by the time the twins were lost. Alberto made enough money somehow to enroll his children at St. Mary's Catholic School downtown. The tuition was nominal, but nevertheless with a family of eight there never was any extra money. Young Alberto Jr. first attended the Catholic school while in kindergarten, but the costs of more school-age children prompted Albert Sr. to enroll him at Stephen F. Austin Elementary and later in Hawthorne Junior High School. Alberto Jr. got his first suit from his dad for the eighth-grade graduation ceremony, and by this grade level his name had been changed to Albert by English-speaking teachers and peers.

Each morning, Alberto Sr. would motor down to the San Fernando Cathedral with kids in tow for Mass before school. Young Albert Jr. continued this religious practice long into his adult and senior life.[8] After school, the school kids would be dropped off at home for early dinner, chores, homework, and play before nightfall. The household rule was to be in bed by 8 p.m. every night. Young Albert Jr. had two major chores: help take out the garbage and help the younger siblings with their schoolwork. Since Albert Jr. was an avid reader and very bright, he had no problem doing his homework and tutoring his younger brothers and sisters. As the oldest male in the family, he had unearned privileges that irked his sisters Madeline and Belinda. They had to sweep, mop, wash diapers, hang clothes, iron, wash dishes, cook, clean, pick up, and clean the only bathroom in their modest three-bedroom home. The bathroom was the war zone, especially early in the mornings when all six children competed with the parents for access. The daily mess was for Madeline and Belinda to clean up, never Albert Jr. He was a boy.

In fact, Albert Jr. was all boy. He could not play with Richard (he was too little), with the little baby "Tony" (as he was called), or with the girls. He was outside most of the time while the girls were inside doing housework. Mama Dolores always needed help. When Grandma López would come over, she would help out as best she could, but usually just took the children to her home. Grandma Dolores López loved young Albert Jr. For some reason, Albert Jr. could never pronounce "Lolita" or "Mamacita" and instead said, "Chita," so the family members changed her nickname to Chita. When Grandma Peña came to visit, she had to be tended to, due to her blindness. She could not help Dolores. To the utter amazement of all her grandchildren, Grandma Peña knew each child by touching their faces and hearing their voices.

Richard was seven years Albert's junior, so Albert Jr. played outside alone or with the neighborhood kids. He had a bicycle and roamed the neighborhood and area. When the girls were allowed outside, Albert Jr. would teach them to ride the bicycle and play with pets he had. Albert Jr. always liked dogs and rabbits. He brought home a rabbit he found near the creek and it soon had four babies. He also brought home a bantam rooster with a broken leg. He and Madeline made a splint from Popsicle sticks for the rooster they nicknamed "Pajarito." On another occasion, Albert Jr. found a young man beaten to a pulp down by the drainage ditch and brought him home. Oscar, the young man, was frequently beaten by his father and swore he would not return to the family home. Albert Jr. convinced his parents to let Oscar Flores live with them. And he did for the next two years.[9] Early in life Peña demonstrated a deep compassion for other living creatures and their welfare. In adult life, that compassion grew into a moral code and philosophy of life grounded on justice, fairness, and equality for humankind. Each of his siblings developed the same fondness and care for little animals.

Albert Jr. grew socially and physically when he transferred from Catholic school to the public schools. He spent less time with the family and more time with his friends. Albert Jr. was not a large young man; on the contrary, he was small but fit. In high school he was nicknamed "Peanuts." His physical size did not deter him from sports or fights. He joined a "gang" of neighborhood young men that called themselves the River Side Cats, which was also the name of their city league football team. At other times the River Side Cats would also call themselves the "Moon Glows." The biggest challengers to the neighborhood turf were the "newsies," newspaper boys who delivered the papers in "their" streets.[10] Albert Jr. trained in boxing and competed in the city-sponsored boxing matches. He made the varsity football squad in high school. And he played city league football until he was twenty years of age. He played with the Triple Diamond Hill team for a year in 1937, then moved over to another team. Antonio Esparza, the quarterback for the Triple Diamond Hill team, recalls that Peña Jr. was not an outstanding player, but was very determined and unafraid of being hit and hitting larger players. For his size, Esparza said, "Peña was a toughie."[11] Mama Dolores would pack up all the kids to go watch Peanuts play Friday-night football at the high school or the city parks. This was the only night the eight o'clock curfew imposed by the dad was suspended.

When Albert Jr. was in high school, his teenage sisters were right behind him in grade level.[12] They wanted to go to dances and record hops where music was played by a disk jockey and the dancers shed shoes to twirl in socks. Albert Jr. didn't like dances because he did not know how to dance or want to learn. Madeline and Belinda, on the other hand, were dying to go to dances and meet boys. They practiced dance steps at home and were eager to go show off their stuff. Weekly they asked Albert Sr. for permission to go to a dance. And weekly Papa Albert would say no. Finally, in desperation, the sisters begged older brother Jr. to ask permission for all of them to go dancing. Reluctantly, Albert, the caring older brother, agreed to ask their father. Papa Albert acquiesced only because Jr. would chaperone his sisters. The dance was a turning point in Albert Jr.'s life. He discovered girls. While at the dance, he met a young woman, Mabel Murray, who also did not know how to dance. Albert Jr. and she talked all evening and for many more evenings after that, but never danced. She became Albert Jr.'s first girlfriend. Over time, Madeline and Belinda taught Albert Jr., Richard, and little Tony how to dance, but Jr. remained the clumsiest and most awkward of them all. Richard became a terrific dancer, much sought out by the girls.

As a teenager Albert, and his gang, would risk harm by going downtown late at night when he knew his father would not come home to impose the early night curfew. The River Side Cats would go to the Plaza del Zacate, which other people called "La Plaza del Menudo" because folks would eat *menudo, chicharrones, enchiladas, tamales, caldos, chili con carne,* and other Mexican foods at the tables set up for that purpose. If the boys ran into trouble they could count on Manuel Davila, who later married Albert's sister Madeline, to help them out. Manuel was tough and an accomplished street fighter. Augustine Garza was Albert's age and he too could be counted on to even the score with rivals. Later, Garza would be recruited to serve on the Mexican American Unity Council (MAUC) board of directors by Albert.[13]

In the 1930s, family members would play and accompany Lydia Mendoza in her singing of "La Golondrina." Lydia became a singing sensation and caused crowds to gather at the Plaza del Zacate.[14] Albert and his boys would hang out in the shadows of the Mercado to watch and listen. Most of the time they had no money to buy food. They also did not want to be seen by anyone who could recognize them and tell their parents should they sit at the tables to eat.

One particular night when someone had money, Albert and his friends ate at the Plaza del Zacate, and Albert got a stomachache before he reached home. As he walked home, the pain grew stronger and was becoming intolerable. He thought he was about to get a run of diarrhea. Keeping his pain from his mother and siblings, Albert retired to bed. He waited for the necessary dash to the bathroom next door, but it never came. Instead, he started running a temperature and sweating intermittently. The pain got worse until it was unbearable. Richard heard the moans and inquired, but Albert would not say anything except for more moans and doubling over with pain. He now was burning hot from the fever. Richard called his mother over to see what was wrong with Albert. Fortunately, Albert Sr. was home early that night, and the parents rushed him to the Santa Rosa Hospital emergency room. Younger sister Belinda had had her appendix removed when she was six, and the parents recognized the symptoms of acute appendicitis. Albert Jr. was taken in for immediate surgery. Since his appendix had already ruptured, the doctors—rather than make a wide incision—simply made another navel-like hole near his side to remove the body part and extract the toxic matter from the intestinal cavity. Albert

Jr. quickly recovered and was back to all his activities within a couple of weeks. He proudly showed off his other navel to his friends.[15]

Albert Jr. had started to help out his dad with the dance promotions for money. He would take and pick up the printed flyers announcing the dance and musical groups, first on his bicycle and later in the family car. His dad taught him how to drive at an early age. Albert would also distribute the flyers to local businesses and bars. At the dances, Albert would help ice down the drinks, check the coats and hats in the wintertime, and clean up the place after the dance. His dad would give him money for his help. As Albert took an interest in girls, he needed more money and his own car. Albert Sr. was burning the candle at both ends, working by day and on weekends and attending law school every night. He came home exhausted day after day for what seemed forever to Albert Jr. and the girls. Dolores didn't mind; if he wasn't home, she was just as happy.

His dad helped him purchase his first car when he was seventeen. Albert Jr. could now drive his mother to the grocery store, theater, parks, and church, and his sisters to dances. No other kid in the neighborhood had a car. He proposed to his dad to let him go visit Uncle Rudy, his mom's brother in Illinois, for the summer following his high school graduation. Albert Jr. wanted to see Chicago; besides, Uncle Rudy was his favorite *tío*. He took the train to Chicago and worked at odd jobs during the summer. Uncle Rudy refused to take any money for room and board; he was so proud of his nephew for graduating from high school and saying he was going on to college to become a lawyer like his father.

When Albert Jr. returned from Chicago, he had a surprise gift for his mother: a fistful of cash with which to buy her a washing machine with a wringer so she would no longer need to toil in the backbreaking job of scrubbing the clothes in the *tallador*, or wring her hands sore from twisting wet clothes for placement on the clothesline in the backyard. His mother was thrilled. Albert Jr. had always been a great son and loving older brother to his sisters. They worshipped the ground he walked on. He was like a surrogate father to them. In reality it was Jr. who spent the most time with them, not their father.

The Weber School of Law

John Kelly Weber was born in St. Louis, Missouri, in 1896. He was roughly the same age as Albert Peña Sr. Coincidentally, they both passed away within days of each other in the month of June, one year apart. Peña Sr. died first on June 23, 1963, at the age of sixty-seven, and Weber died on June 18, 1964, at the age of sixty-eight. The entwined lives of both men came together in San Antonio in the mid to late 1920s.

After his first military tour of duty in World War I as a second lieutenant, Weber was admitted to the University of Texas School of Law in 1919 and graduated in 1922. With his law degree in hand, he practiced law approximately three years in San Antonio. Sometime in 1925 Weber got the idea that San Antonio needed a law school and he began to establish one. Given the time, it was remarkable that Weber recruited and admitted working-class Mexican men into his law school. The Weber Law School operated for nearly twenty years until 1942 or so, when he was again called into military duty during World War II. From 1939 to 1942 he was also appointed special county judge by governor's decree to cases in which Judge Charles Anderson recused himself in Bexar County.

John Kelly Weber was sent overseas in 1943. He served in World War II and again in the Korean War. He was part of the legal team that drafted the Uniform Code of Military Justice during his second military tour of duty. In Korea he served as the chief of the Armistice Planning Commission and later as chief staff officer at the United Nations peace negotiations. He left the military with the rank of Colonel and various commendations, including the Korean Ulchi Distinguished Military Service Medal. Colonel Kelly Weber returned to San Antonio and practiced law until he died, but did not revive his law school.[16]

The Weber School of Law was the first to train and graduate significant numbers of lawyers of Mexican ancestry in Texas and the nation. Its twenty-year span of operation made it possible for working-class Mexicans to attend night classes and attain the goal of attorney. Apparently, Weber himself taught many, if not all, the law classes and was most competent. The Weber law students were taught and drilled in case law that would be found in the form of questions for the final attorney examination. Weber graduates passed the bar examination for the state of Texas without much difficulty.

The First Lawyer in the Family

In the 1920s, Albert Peña Sr. was selling furniture in downtown San Antonio's Western Furniture Store. Originally the store was located at the intersection of St. Mary's and Commerce Streets, and then later relocated to 114–116 S. Flores Street. He also promoted dances on weekends at La Gloria and other locations to make ends meet for his growing family. Peña Sr. daily heard horrible stories from his customers, dance patrons, and friends about the treatment of Mexicans in San Antonio. Since the Mexican Revolution of 1910, it seemed that life for Mexicans in the United States would always be entwined with life in Mexico; everyone had relatives or recent arrivals fleeing the violence across the border, only to meet face to face with rampant discrimination against Mexican people at the hands of Anglos.

During the 1920s and into the '30s, Alberto Peña Sr. heard gruesome testimonials from recent arrivals from Mexico. The treatment meted out to them at the border crossing by bigoted Anglo officials was shocking. Anglo authorities had clamped down on border crossings after Francisco "Pancho" Villa, the Mexican revolutionary, attacked Columbus, New Mexico, in 1917 and remained at large despite the military expeditions sent to hunt him down in Mexico. World War I interrupted that manhunt, and the American soldiers pursuing him, General "Black Jack" Pershing and Lt. Colonel Joséph Swing, left for Europe. The year 1917 was when the transnational border communities such as Matamoros-Brownsville, Laredo–Nuevo Laredo, Eagle Pass–Piedras Negras, Acuna–Del Rio, Juarez–El Paso became two separate communities. Prior to that time, border crossing simply entailed walking or driving across the river without documents or interrogation. The border after the Columbus Raid not only became militarized but also heavily policed by U.S. federal authorities demanding passports, visas, solvency, literacy, physical inspections, and work permits in order to cross. They also began implementing a delousing campaign for all Mexicans crossing the border into the United States.

> By January 1917 El Paso immigration officials begin bathing an average of 2,800 Mexicans a day at the Santa Fe Street international bridge ... every "second class" Juarez citizen was to strip completely, turn in all their clothes and baggage to be steam dried and fumigated with hydrocyanic acid and stand naked before a customs inspector who would check his or her "hairy parts"—the scalp, armpits, chest, pubic area and anus—for lice. These disinfection plants spread to Nogales, Arizona, Del Rio, Laredo, and Brownsville, Texas. The baths continued for another four decades. In 1958 Raul Delgado was fumigated at the Eagle Pass border before being allowed to work as a bracero in the United States.[17]

Peña Sr., the furniture salesman, dance promoter, and part-time law student, was powerless to do anything about the accounts provided by recent immigrants. But the immigration problem was growing and becoming a booming business for those who began to recruit Mexícano laborers into the United States. The Alamo City Employment Agency, a contracting service for *braceros*, owned by W. J. Lewis, opened its doors as early as 1924 in San Antonio. Serious study of the migrant phenomenon was just beginning in U.S. universities.[18]

Peña Sr. must have heard from others about the downtown law school that was holding classes at night in the Bedell Building at 923 Crockett Street.[19] Peña Sr. undoubtedly went to meet with Colonel Weber about the prospects of attending law school. Peña Sr. did enroll and graduated from the Weber School of Law, according to State Bar records. Peña must have attended night classes on a part-time basis, because the normal law school course of daytime study and full credit load took about three years, as it does now. Peña Sr. must have attended classes for about a decade from 1925 until 1934 or 1935. He was admitted to the Texas bar in 1935 when he was almost forty years of age.[20]

With a bar card in his wallet, Peña Sr.'s life changed dramatically for the better. The day of being sworn in as an attorney and receiving his bar card was one of jubilation. The eight-member family crammed into the car and drove early in the morning to Austin from San Antonio for the event. His entire family was present: wife Dolores; oldest son Albert Jr.; daughters Madeline, Belinda, and Irene; even the toddlers, Richard and little Anthony. Both older boys, Albert Jr. and Richard, were so proud of their father they decided then and there to also become attorneys and practice with their dad. The swearing-in ceremony in Austin for Peña Sr. was also one of exhilaration for his many, many furniture customers and dance patrons who for years had asked him for advice, or as they would say it, *consejos*.[21] They also frequently asked him for referrals to a good attorney who could help them with their legal predicaments. Peña Sr. was always not only obliging but also visionary. He always told his friends and customers to see him for legal services once he became a lawyer. So many years had gone by without Peña Sr. getting his law degree that his many contacts doubted he really was to become a lawyer. When he stopped selling furniture at the store, his presence was missed by many people. They were told that Peña was no longer selling furniture but was an attorney with an office down the street at 223½ Dolorosa Street on the corner with Main.

Peña Sr. developed a lucrative law practice within months. All the former customers and dance regulars went to Peña Sr. for a *consejo* on a legal problem. Regardless, the visit eventually turned into a legal service for a fee. Peña Sr. was one of the few practicing attorneys in the city that spoke Spanish and that the people knew from a prior situation of trust and reliability. In that era lawyers would hang around the halls of the courthouse looking for persons with legal problems. Lawyers also hired Spanish-speaking interlopers to seek out those in need at the courthouse and bring them to the lawyer. Peña Sr. met, and made important contacts among, the other lawyers working clients in the halls of the courthouse, including Maury Maverick Sr. and son Jr. Maverick Sr. had been mayor of the city and a member of the U.S. House of Representatives until Paul Kilday defeated him in 1938.

When Eleanor Roosevelt came to San Antonio, New Deal Democratic Congressman Maverick Sr. escorted her into the neighborhoods where poverty was rampant and housing extremely dilapidated. What she saw shocked her to the point that she committed herself to building the first federally subsidized housing units in the city. She kept her word, because by 1939 the Housing Authority of the City of San Antonio had received a $5.6 million grant to build five different housing projects, one in each neglected area on the East and West Sides and three more to alleviate poverty-stricken Anglos' housing needs.[22] The annual income of tenant families in San Antonio in 1939 was extremely low. Approximately 20,000 tenant families earned less than $950 a year, and of these 50 percent were "Latin American tenants" and 10 percent were "Negro American tenants."[23] The lowest median wage paid in the country among cities over 200,000 in population was in San Antonio in 1940, where "Latin-Americans" comprised 103,000 of the population or 40.7 percent of all people in the city.[24] By June 28, 1940, the first housing project built in San Antonio,[25] Alazan Courts, was inaugurated by then Mayor Maverick. Alazan Courts were a few blocks from the downtown area and in the West Side barrio.

Peña Sr. financially supported his son Albert Jr. while he was doing undergraduate work at St. Mary's University—living expenses, tuition, books, even daily bus fare. When Emma Tenayuca was arrested along with many other workers during the Pecan Shellers' Strike in 1938, Peña Sr. admonished Albert Jr. not to bring any more clients for free legal services. Albert Jr. knew Emma; she was only a year older, and he admired her courage. Albert Jr. also wanted to help the strikers, but was constrained by the dictates of his father and his financial help.

Peña Sr. also wanted to help Richard pursue a law degree, but this son wanted and did join the Navy right out of high school in August 1942. The youngest son, Anthony, also wanted to join the Navy, and entered the service on August 3, 1943. Peña Sr. dreamed of the day his sons would become lawyers and join him in the practice of law. Peña Sr. had his daughters, Madeline and Belinda, working in his law office. He wanted to involve all his children in the business and build a successful, high-caliber law firm, Peña, Peña, and Peña.

CHAPTER 2

Peña, the Sailor Man

ALBERT A. PEÑA JR. JOINED THE NAVY WITHIN MONTHS OF THE ATTACK ON Pearl Harbor in Hawaii in March 1942, as did thousands of other American young men. His two younger brothers, Richard and Anthony, were making plans to join the Navy before him. Albert Jr., however, had entanglements. He had fallen in love with Joséfina Herrera. He wanted to marry her, but he also wanted to serve his country. He felt shame that his younger brothers were talking about joining the Navy and he was working and just having fun with Josie, as he called her. It was more than fun; he and Josie were sexually involved and she was with child when Albert Jr. presented himself for enlistment at the San Antonio office at age twenty-five. He was tested for intelligence, aptitude, and administered a physical examination. He passed every requirement and was told he would be part of the Navy's Signal Corps as a radioman. Peña was puzzled about that assignment; he had never heard of the Morse code and did not know anything about the Navy's flag signaling from ship to ship. He did know how to listen to the radio, his second favorite pastime at home; reading was his first.

His military orders arrived by mail at the family home with instructions to board the local train to San Diego, California, and report for basic training.[1] The whole family went down to the Santa Fe railroad station near the Mercado in downtown San Antonio to see him off, including Josie. Having to say goodbye to his sweetheart was very difficult for him. They both knew Josie was pregnant; his mother suspected as much. They both knew he might not come back from the war. They had secretly married in civil ceremony just weeks before he shipped out but had kept it from his family. They had been lovers since he met her at one of the dances his dad promoted. Now, as he waved from the train, he was not sure when, if ever, he would see his loved ones again. He had concerns about the baby being born while he was away, but he had not been ecstatic about the pregnancy. He knew his income could not support a family. But Peña also felt compelled and obligated to serve his country in this time of peril.

His mother, Dolores, did not understand his value system that held patriotism over family. As a mother, she had argued with him against volunteering: "You were my firstborn. I had you when I was sixteen years old. I can't lose you." She tried other arguments: "How can you leave Josie and child at this time of need? She is due very soon." She tried being logical: "Why are you volunteering? You are too old for the military. They have not called you. They need you here at Kelly Air Force base, doing your job. Your father didn't volunteer to go to World War I when you were to be born. And he was only 20 then, 21 when I gave birth to you."[2]

The arguments did not get to Peña's conscience; he had made up his mind to join and that was that. At an early age, Peña had begun to demonstrate personality traits of decisiveness and discipline that masked his soft, compassionate side for the underdog and meek. Once he mulled over a situation and reached a decision, he stuck to it "come hell or high water," as he said to me on various occasions about other decisions he had made.

The train ride from San Antonio to Los Angeles, then San Diego, was long and boring, but not as boring as being on a ship, as he later found out. Upon arrival for basic training at San Diego's naval station, he was processed and issued his gear: sea bag (duffle bag), two "Cracker Jack" uniforms (sailor outfit), the famous Dixie cap, undergarments, pair of boondockers (ankle-high boots), toiletries and "douche" bag, and his bedding. At the barbershop, his curly hair was completely chopped off. At the medical facility, he was given nearly a dozen immunizations. Lastly, he was escorted by a sailor representing the master-at-arms to his barracks and turned over to the company commander (drill instructor). He met other sailors from all over the United States at the barracks. His bunk was the bottom one of three stacked. Each sailor had to position himself opposite the other bunkmates, sleeping head to toe. Later, he encountered the same sleeping arrangement on the ships he boarded.

The following morning consisted of early morning wake-up call by the drill instructor, a quick wash, classes on military duties and the Code of Conduct, and exercise with lots of running in between. The major part of the daily routine was running to the company formation, running to the galley (dining hall), running to the exercise field, running to the barracks, and running back to all those places several times a day. Peña, having been somewhat athletic since high school and not being much of a smoker, withstood the running part of the training well. And Peña was lean and hard, not overweight and out of shape like some of the enlisted personnel. Others were not so fortunate and threw up their breakfast, lunch, and dinner daily until they got themselves in shape by running everywhere. They ran in sailor uniform with full canteen, ammunition clips on a belt, plus steel pot helmet and M-1 rifle. The M-1 weighed about eight pounds and got heavier by the hour.

After basic training came the specialized training at the school for radio and signal corpsmen, also held at the naval training station in San Diego, California. The physical training took a backseat to radio classes—no more running here and there—and water safety. As sailors were expected to be on ships, each was taught the basics of swimming, floating, and lifesaving. Peña was amused at his incompetence and that of others trying to make a life preserver out of his Dixie cap by inverting it and trapping air above his head with the cap while in water.

Once in the regular training regimen, he had the run of the huge naval station, some 77.2 acres of land, and weekends in the city. The naval station was a very large complex with hundreds of ships coming and going with troops, supplies, equipment, and weaponry, although the main purpose was ship repair and upkeep of warships. The naval base was a bustle of activity day and night. San Diego also had its share of delights for Peña; it was small but had many entertainment areas and a delightful climate, always cool and breezy. Tijuana, Mexico, was but a short ride away and he visited the border city more than once.

Peña learned the rudiments of signaling, flag and Morse code, in a matter of weeks. The latter course bored Peña; he could not imagine a Navy career listening to and sending out beeps, short and long ones, for the next four years. He barely passed the test with the blinking spotlights, which was Morse code by light signals. The flag course consisted of two types: handheld flag signals and those hoisted above ships for communication with other ships. Radio school was a bit more complex in that he learned how to build a radio, the laying of line, walkie-talkie etiquette, use of various frequencies and bandwidths, and trouble-shooting on transmission and receiving signals. After an expedited training schedule of ten weeks, Peña was shipped off to the U.S. Naval Station at Guantanamo Bay, Cuba, rather than to the action theater in the Pacific. He was elated with that assignment. Peña's troop carrier went down the California coast to the Panama Canal. The locks that moved his carrier through the canal fascinated him. Then it was out into the Caribbean. The ship stopped in open sea soon after they processed through the canal for the sailors to swim—the Navy's way of affording some recreation and forced hygiene. He didn't attempt the swim; he just watched from the sun deck. "Water," according to Peña, "is for drinking and washing." Peña's affinity for the Navy was the Cracker Jack uniform, the warships, and the opportunity to travel to faraway places. It never occurred to him that all of these Navy attractions had to do with water.

After eight long days and nights aboard the ship with several hundred other sailors in cramped quarters, with not much to do on board except talk, play cards, smoke, walk on the sun deck, and smoke some more, the ship arrived at the mouth of Guantanamo Bay. Peña noticed that the ship had carefully maneuvered for hours as they approached, and even once inside the bay at the naval station the ship inched its way into the docking area. Once docked the men eagerly went ashore, but not before the "protocol," as Peña called it. The coming aboard each ship in the Navy required the sailor to go up the gangplank to the bow, sea bag in hand, salute the flag first, then salute the officer on deck, and ask, "Permission to come on board, sir." Of course the officer in charge of greeting oncoming sailors would then say, "Permission granted." After that ritual, the sailor was escorted to his sleeping area and, with others, given a mini-tour of the ship's layout. Getting off the ship was the same process but in reverse. The saluting and asking permission to go ashore seemed pointless to Peña. It was a slow, time-consuming process with so many sailors performing the ritual.

Peña was glad to be on land, even though he had not gotten seasick or terribly anxious like other sailors from being on the ship and inside its bowels for more than a week. The sleeping quarters were cramped and stacked three high just like in the San Diego barracks. Each bunk had only about two feet of headspace, and each sailor had only 8 inches of space beneath the thin mattress to store his personal gear. In the barracks they had had footlockers, deeper than eight inches. Peña learned to fold neatly and store his items tightly while onboard ships.

The Guantanamo Naval Station was huge, occupying about 116 square kilometers of Cuban land. And Peña quickly learned that the reason for the slow entry by the ship was due to the hundreds of underwater mines the Navy had placed to ward off intruders. The primary purpose of Guantanamo Bay's naval station was to protect the eastern flank of the Panama Canal and also to be on readiness alert for any hostile action directed toward Florida.

Peña did not stay long at Guantanamo Bay, for he was deployed for duty off the coast of Africa. Peña dreaded another period of cramped quarters and boring days and nights. Hundreds of sailors were boarded on a destroyer being sent to hunt down German U-boats or submarines. The fear was that the Germans would slip into the Mediterranean Sea by way of the Strait of Gibraltar and attack Europe from the rear. Again, Peña found himself on a crowded ship with too many sailors, but this time they were like sitting ducks in the open Atlantic sea. The destroyer that Peña was on did see action and took some hits from both German U-boat torpedoes and aircraft. He told his baby brother, Tony, that the boat "had been shot out from under him" with only minor casualties. Peña himself was not injured.

Fortunately, Peña had not spent three months on the Africa duty when he was transferred to a communication ship and returned to Guantanamo Bay. He was able to go home after eight months of service and see his family for Christmas. He celebrated his twenty-sixth birthday in San Antonio. A couple of weeks earlier, Josie had his firstborn baby boy, Albert Anthony Peña.[3] He met the baby at San Antonio's Kelly Field, where returning soldiers of all types arrived and made connections with other Air Force flights across the country. Baby Albert III had been born November 23, 1942. Josie was elated to see him, but concerned as to why Albert had not answered any of her many letters. Albert claimed he never got them, and when he did it was several at a time, and that he could not easily mail letters from sea or overseas. Josie knew that was not true. She grew more concerned about Albert's lack of affection for his firstborn male child. Albert claimed it was that he did not know what to do with a baby. Josie did not believe him. While home those few days, Albert spent more days and nights out playing with his former buddies and other relatives than with her and the baby.

The brief furlough was over before long, and Peña had to fly back to Guantanamo Bay on a cargo flight from Kelly Field. Albert Jr. tried over the Christmas holidays to dissuade his younger brother Anthony from joining the Navy. Baby brother Tony said he was joining right after graduation from high school. Richard had already joined the Navy eight months after Albert's induction during the end of summer 1942. And Tony did just what he said—joined the Navy and became a torpedo gunner's mate.[4] Mother Dolores "Lala" Peña was devastated by her three sons' decisions to enlist in the U.S. Navy. All of her three sons were now on active duty. What if something happened to them? This was her ever-ready statement and her most frequent question to all who would inquire about her boys. Contrarily, Albert Sr. would brag he had three sons in service to America in the U.S. Navy to all who came into the law office. Every time his boys came home on furlough, the first order of business was to take photographs of them in their Navy outfits. He placed those photographs of the boys in uniform on his desk for all to see.

Signal and radio corpsmen were not needed at Guantanamo Bay—they had plenty. The Navy needed construction workers and experts with explosives plus a small contingent of military police for the growing American presence on the island base. Peña volunteered for military police duty; he did not want to do construction in the hot sun or handle explosives. Shore Patrol school was a quick four-week course consisting of pistol firing, self-defense, handling and disarming detainees, and learning the rules and regulations of the Military Code of Conduct plus local Cuban city ordinances and customs. Most sailors at one time or another were ordered to put in Shore Patrol duty to pick up the slack or to give time off to the regulars assigned to the Shore Patrol. Peña would later joke about the "training" he received to be a shore patrolman: "Basically it was a piece of paper with about 4 Don'ts, things to prevent sailors from doing." He said they were "Don't fight; don't pee in public; don't cause trouble with the locals; and, don't embarrass the Navy."[5]

Peña enjoyed his newfound air of authority—with sidearm, handcuffs, walkie-talkie, and billy club—as a shore patrolman. He was part of an elite group of men charged with taking care of their own. Peña made many friends among the other shore patrolmen and Cuban military and police personnel who would come in handy when he was later assigned to Havana.

Guantanamo was the staging area for naval activity in the Gulf of Mexico, not the Atlantic Ocean. After duty hours, sailors had plenty of time on their hands and got themselves into mischief at every opportunity. Although Guantanamo Bay was located at the southernmost tip of the island nation of Cuba, the city Guantanamo was but twenty-one kilometers away from the northern edge of the naval station. Outside the north gate was a small city, Caimanera, but no real hot action was to be found there or in Guantanamo City—or Gitmo, as the natives called it. The real hot spot was Havana, with all the nightlife in dance clubs, hotels, bars, cabarets, and casinos. Prostitution, gambling, and other vices were not legal by any means, but much tolerated. Since the 1920s, Havana had been the playground of both United States underworld figures and corporate magnates. The Cuba of the 1940s was more so.

The nation's capital city was a six-hour bus ride from the naval station across Cuba. And the sailors flocked there in droves, to the point that the U.S. Navy had to establish an extension of the Guantanamo Bay military installation in Havana to house a small detachment of shore patrolmen and a detention facility for unruly sailors. Before long, Peña was stationed in Havana as a shore patrolman. The Signal Corps duties became a thing of the past. Peña now sported a holster pistol plus a wood baton-shaped club, wore sharp white webbing over regular combat boots, and had the distinctive "SP" white letters on a dark blue armband on his right side. Peña was the most unlikely military policeman on the island, certainly in Havana. Peña was more of a party animal than the sailors he attempted to subdue and make behave, which he seldom did; instead he would escort them away from danger and lecture the sailors about not misbehaving to avoid a court-martial. Peña missed the commissary at Guantanamo with its many U.S. goods; Havana's stores and shops did not carry those items and the black market goods were expensive. Peña would call his Shore Patrol buddies back at Guantanamo and place an order, which was brought to him by other sailors on shore leave who ventured to Havana. He had a steady supply of goodies and bundles of mail from Josie. In exchange the sailors bringing him the goodies got to meet a policeman that they might need in case of trouble. It was always good to be in with the shore patrolmen, especially in sinful Havana. Peña did not answer every letter from Josie, only an occasional one.

Good mentors always crossed Peña's path. His Cuban mentor, Ignacio "Nacho" Díaz Peña, a policeman with the local constabulary, made his nights and days in Havana more entertaining and exciting.[6] Nacho called Albert his "primo" because they shared an identical surname. The Cuban government has had a long relationship with the United States—sometimes good, sometimes bad, but never indifferent. In 1903, shortly after the Spanish-American War, the U.S. government imposed the Platt Amendment on Cuba as a condition of independence and took possession of Guantanamo Bay as well as all 116 square kilometers of land surrounding the inlet. Guantanamo Bay is the oldest U.S. military installation on foreign soil. It is still the largest minefield in the Western Hemisphere. During World War II the sailors at Guantanamo were mostly utilized for mining the harbor, mining the surrounding land, and constructing dependents' housing, hospitals, schools, infrastructure, theaters, a golf course, a yacht club, sporting facilities, and shopping facilities.[7] Peña was glad to have been given Shore Patrol duty in Havana and to avoid the hot, humid days doing construction work or the dangerous work of land and sea mining with explosives. The Cuban government did not allow U.S. military personnel to police their sailors or Cuban citizens on Cuban soil. U.S. Shore Patrol personnel could only work side by side with a Cuban policeman or military man in the performance of their duties. More importantly, Peña felt lucky to have been paired with Nacho Díaz Peña. Nacho was an imposing man over six feet three inches tall, very dark-skinned, muscular, and Spanish-speaking. He was the first Cubano Peña had ever met. For that matter, Nacho was the first Spanish-speaking black person Peña had ever met.

Blacks in San Antonio were segregated in the East Side of town when Peña was growing up. When he was older he frequented bars and clubs on the East Side because he liked jazz, rhythm and blues, and swing. But none of the black acquaintances he made in San Antonio spoke Spanish; English was their mother tongue. Peña, growing up in segregated Texas, had not really grasped the idea that African slaves were not only brought to the United States but also to Mexico, Central America, South America, and especially the Caribbean.

Nacho and Peña got along really well together, on and off the job. They both were married and enjoyed storytelling, especially jokes with sexual connotations. After hours they still spent time together carousing in clubs and cabarets, dressing up and dining. Both lived in Havana—Peña at the U.S. Embassy along with the other military personnel attached to the ambassador's residence and charge, and Nacho near the train station off Merced y Picota by the Parque de las Flores (now Parque de los Agrimensores). And they shared a passion for the many, many chocolate-colored Cuban *mulatas* with the voluptuous bodies they met daily.[8] Curbing their lust was a job hazard.

Peña worked mostly nights and weekends, sleeping during the day. Nacho and he patrolled mostly in two areas of Havana: Havana Vieja and Centro Havana. Peña particularly enjoyed working on foot the Avenida de Maceo, better known to Cubans as the "Malecon," the bayfront boulevard eight kilometers long with many fine hotels and women. Peña had occasional use of a jeep, but he preferred to walk and talk rather than ride and look. Working girls, mostly *mulatas*, met their sailor customers in the street and along many of the hotels along the bayfront. It seemed to Peña that Nacho knew every prostitute on the Malecon; they acknowledged him with *abrazos* (hugs) and kisses as he approached to greet them. Soon Peña, the American sailor man, *el marinero Americano*, was on the *mulatas*' hug and kiss list as well. And the *marinero Americano* also provided endless supplies, obtained from the commissary at Guantanamo, of lipstick, nail polish, mascara, hosiery, perfumes, and scented lotions for Nacho's and his favorites. The goodies dispensed generated tons of goodwill and other personal amenities for the U.S. sailor man and his Cuban buddy, including free meals, cigars, drinks, or cups of strong *café* at many establishments along the Malecon and other places. Tall, dark-skinned Nacho and short Peña made an odd pair, but Cubans and U.S. servicemen would rather meet them than other military personnel and policemen.

The Hotel Nacional with its Cabaret Parisien was home to the most spectacular of floorshows. It was situated on the Malecon. The eight-floor Nacional with 442 rooms was home away from home for the New York Mafia dons coming to party, as well as famous political and other public figures. It was said that Winston Churchill stayed there, as did Ava Gardner and Frank Sinatra in 1946.[9] Nacho introduced Peña to the Hotel Nacional staff and some of the showgirls they occasionally met on the street. On days off, Peña would take in the shows at the various other hotels, and tour the cigar factories and the barrios of Havana's fifteen different surrounding communities. Peña's favorite place, however, was the Capitolio Nacional, the capitol. The awesome building was an architectural wonder and it reminded Peña of Washington, DC's Capitol, which he had only seen in photographs. The Capitolio was very similar to the U.S. Capitol, only richer in detail. The endless marble floors and staircases amazed Peña. The many huge bronze doors captivated him each time he walked the halls. He liked the clicking his Boon Dockers made on the marble floors. He particularly liked to see the Statute of the Republic, a gigantic seventeen-meter-high woman, and the inlaid marble replica of a twenty-four-carat diamond directly underneath the capitol's dome. Nacho told him distances in Cuba from

Havana were measured from that very point. After touring the Capitolio, Peña and Nacho, or Peña by himself, would walk behind the capitol area between Barcelona and Dragones Streets to the Partagas cigar factory for a smoke and a listen to the lector. Peña occasionally liked to smoke a cigar or Cuban cigarette, but they were too strong for his lungs and throat, as was the coffee. He stuck to Lucky Strikes or Camel cigarettes brought from the United States and rationed to servicemen, rather than the Cuban Partagas or Upmann brands, and *café Americano* with milk. What Peña loved about the cigar factories were the atmosphere and smells, the aroma of freshly roasted and ground coffee (not the brew itself), and the people at the cafés.

Each cigar factory had a reader, *el lector*, whose job was to read the newspaper, a novel, poetry, song lyrics, and other literary works to the cigar rollers as they hand rolled cigar after cigar, all day long.[10] Peña had loved to read since childhood and thought this practice should be in every U.S. factory where work was also repetitive and boring.

There were many cigar factories in Havana and Cuba, but the Real Fabrica de Tabacos Partagas was Peña's favorite because the cigars made there were smoked by the rich and famous the world over. The huge cigar, almost a foot long, was named "Churchill" because it was Winston's favorite smoke—or chew, as he sometimes did not light the cigar, just chomped on it. Other shorter in length and fatter cigar types were like the ones Lucky Luciano and Meyer Lansky smoked, U.S. Mafiosi who hung out at the Hotel Capri in the Vedado district. Nacho had taken him over there on several occasions, but it was out of their patrolling area. Peña frequented the dance clubs and cabarets on his nights off. His lack of interest in dancing during high school changed during his stint in Havana. Together, he and Nacho would party into the night like there was no work tomorrow, dancing and drinking from place to place, La Bodegita del Medio (Ernest Hemingway's favorite), Bar la Marina, El Caseron del Tango (Peña didn't tango but liked to watch), Bar Dos Hermanos (for oyster cocktails), Cafe Paris (for mojitos made with rum), and jam sessions. Nacho introduced him to tiny "holes in the wall" with good food such as *lechon asado* (roast pork), Peña's favorite meal, and the many other places for fun and sin. Peña never took much of a liking to Cuban food, it was too bland, but he loved the ice cream, *helados, jimagua, tres gracias, bocaditos* (ice cream sandwiches), and the Popsicles, *paleticas*.

In November 1944, Peña was given another chance to go home, but not for Christmas, just Thanksgiving, and he hopped a plane for San Antonio. The family was happy to see him and learn that he was in Cuba and not in the dangerous Pacific. Josie was happy to see him as well, but raised her same concerns about no response to her letters and not asking about the baby, not even for a photograph. Albert just shrugged off the criticism and showed her how much he loved her by getting her pregnant again. And again, he spent most of his time while at home with friends and relatives, not with her and the baby.

Albert Sr. had a serious talk with Jr. about his future. Sr. insisted Albert make up his mind to return and finish college, then go on to be a lawyer. He promised to help the young couple with all he could so Albert would hurry up, finish schooling, and become a lawyer. Albert Jr. placated his father with verbal agreements to these plans, but the reality was he was happy in the Navy, in Cuba, away from responsibility, family obligations, and the war. He did not know what he really wanted in life at this point. He thought about it during the flight back to Guantanamo Bay. And he thought about it during his final months in the Navy. Before he knew it, his discharge from military service was upon him and it was time to go home. He still did not know what he was going to do in San Antonio. Go back to being labor at Kelly Air Force Base? Go to school? Buy a house? Josie had written that she was pregnant again from his last visit and due in July. The Navy had notified all returning service personnel about the opportunities available to them because of their service to the nation. President Franklin Delano Roosevelt had signed into law the Servicemen's Readjustment Act of 1944 (June), which provided education, unemployment compensation, and loans for home purchase to returning veterans in addition to medical care. Money was not to be an issue for Albert Jr. anymore if he availed himself of the G.I. Bill, as it was popularly called by the soldiers and public.

Albert Jr. was stationed in San Diego during the last months of his service. On the last day of July 1944, he learned that he had a daughter. He insisted she be named Belinda like his sister, and Josie acquiesced—it was a nice name. Peña Jr. now faced a larger family than when he had left, and he felt a stranger to them, including Josie. He really did not know them. He was discharged on September 29, 1945, and took the train home after a few days of frolicking in Los Angeles.

CHAPTER 3

Peña Jr., the Lawyer

When Albert Jr. arrived in San Antonio in the fall of 1945, he went home to the Peña house, not to Josie. She had moved in with her mother and spinster sister, Rosie. He chose not to live with her and the babies in that house. He also learned that Peña Sr. had bought a building near the Main Plaza and San Fernando Cathedral. He was the first Méxicano to own an office building in downtown San Antonio since the Anglos had taken political and economic control of Texas a century earlier.

Albert Sr. rented out offices on the top floor to other lawyers and had tenants on the bottom floor. His law office was upstairs. Downstairs was a barber shop, a restaurant, and a pawn shop. Joe's Café had a backyard that was the favorite spot of late-night revelers and the ever-expanding Peña clan for holiday festivities, particularly during Fiesta Days.[1] Many of Peña Sr.'s clients paid him with appliances or items and not cash. A pawn shop was the logical place to resell these items and recoup the legal fee.

Albert Sr. started on Jr. about his plans within days of arrival. During those talks, Jr. did not seem concerned about the welfare of Josie and the babies. Sr., however, knew how much it cost to raise a family and assured his son that he would take care of them provided that Jr. went back to school. He wanted Albert Jr. to finish school and become an attorney. Albert Jr. was not ready for such a commitment; he had enjoyed the Cuban party life in the Navy and wanted to continue that for a while. Instead he went back to work at Kelly Air Force Base. He continued to be estranged from Josie and the kids until 1947, when he divorced. Albert Sr. began to pay the child support for Jr. The amount was $42.80 per month. In later years, Jr.'s firstborn son, Albert III, would collect the modest sum from Grandfather Peña at the law office.

Albert Jr. had not finished college when he joined the Navy, but he did when he returned. He also began legal studies at the downtown law school of St. Mary's University.[2] Problems arose when he quit his studies at the law school over some incidents. He put it this way:

> Well, I had problems with St. Mary's Law School and I think they were about to throw me out, so I told them that I was going to go, that I was going to switch schools and the Dean says, "you will never graduate from law school." Oh, yes I will. I had problems because I was always raising hell there. About anything. I didn't really want to be a lawyer. My dad was a lawyer and he insisted I be a lawyer. I really wanted to be a politician. So, I figured the best way to get there was through law school.[3]

Neither Olga Ramos, wife-to-be, nor Julio Reyna, another law student at the time, could recall exactly what these incidents were about except to say, "there was discrimination at St. Mary's."[4]

In 1947, the political winds began to change in San Antonio. Both before the Navy service and after, Peña Jr. frequented black clubs located in the East Side, such as the Eastwood Club, and closer to downtown, the Key Hole Club and Avalon Grill. He was familiar with black faces from the days in Havana; he made some new friends among them. Sometimes they talked politics and about their respective problems as minorities. On occasion, he would pick up a copy of the *Snap News*, started in 1949 by Eugene Coleman. It contained information about blacks in the East Side primarily, and also about their continuing civil rights struggles.

Blacks in San Antonio faced the same conditions as Méxicanos did in all aspects of life. For a century and a decade, blacks and browns in San Antonio suffered the yoke of segregation. The local police enforced U.S. apartheid. Both Méxicanos and African Americans had their own parks, restrooms, drinking fountains, schools, and restaurants and businesses. Riding the bus and going to a movie were segregated ordeals. Like Méxicanos, the local black community was economically depressed, with 70 percent employed in domestic service jobs, and unskilled and semiskilled manual labor. The first institutions to integrate in the 1950s were the military and churches.[5]

About that time, Peña Jr. learned of two minority candidates for local office. Two eager young men were seeking public office to the school board: G. J. Sutton, an African American funeral director from San Antonio's East Side, and Gustavo García, a bright and emerging young attorney. Peña and his friends gravitated toward the campaigns of these two men and offered their help. Volunteers could not do much in that campaign because few minority persons were registered to vote, because of their failure to pay the $1.75 poll tax that was in effect in 1948. No minority person was deputized to register voters and collect the poll tax. A potential voter had to travel to the downtown courthouse during business hours, pay the tax, then register to vote. Few Mexicans and blacks were eager to do that until they heard of the García and Sutton campaigns. But there still was the matter of whether the exclusion of blacks and Mexicans in partisan races, the "White Primary" held by the Democratic Party in Texas until 1944, would be applied to this nonpartisan election for the school board. It was not.[6]

Albert Jr. discovered a passion for politics coming from within. He knew he already had a compassionate streak in him for animals and the downtrodden, but for politics? The sting of discrimination he had faced in earlier years and upon return from military service found a salve in this campaign. Peña Jr. felt that while he was not a candidate, he was doing something positive to end such injustices in the schools by helping these men. He learned firsthand by watching and listening to Gustavo García the power of the spoken word and argument. Gus, as he was called by friends, was a brilliant orator and gifted debater. He had been the champion of the University of Texas Law School debate team. This dynamic duo won election to the surprise of their opponents and many others. Peña Jr. realized the potential in registering voters and electing candidates from excluded groups. He also realized he liked politics, more so than law, and if he had to become a lawyer to become like Gus and his dad, so be it.

When Albert Jr. wanted to marry Olga Ramos, his father offered to turn over the pawn shop on the ground floor for the young couple to manage and make a living. Olga, however, did not want to operate a pawn shop, nor did she want Albert Jr. to busy himself with that. She wanted him to become a lawyer just like his father, and the sooner the better. He had interrupted his studies by enlisting in the military and getting married to Josie; those were delays enough.

Meeting Olga

Olga Ramos worked at the Pérez Manufacturing Company—which made exclusive women's dresses—located directly across from the local newspaper, the *San Antonio*

Express.[7] Olga was a green-eyed beauty and very talented. She had grown up dancing *folklorico*, typical Mexican dance routines, since grade school at the age of eight. She knew "over a hundred dances." Her jet-black hair, light skin, graceful walk, together with a dancer's body with firm, strong legs, made her a very attractive young woman. As a teenager, she became a "spot dancer." "That means that I didn't work in a place, a *cantina* [bar] or nothing like that, you know. I worked whenever there was [*sic*] conventions and they wanted entertainment and things like that," she explained to me during her oral history interview. "We would go to Laredo every Washington's Birthday and stuff like that when they celebrate there, to the school there, to dance at the school." Olga also danced for organizations that her father, Guadalupe Gutiérrez Ramos, belonged to, such as the Masons, a *mutualista* (mutual benefit society), and the social club Monte Carlo.[8] During the many festivities associated with Mexican *fiestas patrias*, Olga would be called upon to join as a dancer. During World War II, the many military bases that ring San Antonio hosted entertainment for the troops in training or returning from the war, and Olga frequently was a featured Mexican dancer. Her mother, Francisca Navarro Díaz, was the ubiquitous chaperone on these occasions. When Olga finished high school, she enrolled in the local business school, Draughn's, to learn secretarial skills and took a job at the Pérez dressmaking plant.

On one of her lunch breaks while working at Pérez Manufacturing, she took a stroll and met a friend. The friend told her he was marrying a girl she knew who had attended school with Olga. He asked Olga to be in their wedding. Readily and enthusiastically, Olga accepted: "Sure. I will be very happy to." "Well, come on upstairs. I want you to meet someone," said her friend. And it was Albert. "Well, I have a boyfriend," Olga said, "if I can stand with him." The problem that had emerged was that Albert A. Peña Jr. had already been asked by the groom-to-be to stand in the wedding, and he needed an escort. The future groom insisted Olga stand with Albert: "No, I want you to stand with him. Would you? Do you mind?" Olga accepted the arranged matchup. "I wasn't interested in him or anything like that," she explained.

The wedding transpired without any hint of what was to happen in the near future. Albert and Olga were part of the wedding party as one of the many couples. They were together but not romantically linked. Olga had a boyfriend. Albert, on the other hand, was separated from Josie but still married to her. Moreover, he had not even filed for a divorce and had two children from that relationship. Olga would not have anything to do with him because of that status. For the next six months after that wedding, Albert was relentless in his pursuit of Olga. Unrelenting, Olga set down the rules: get divorced, ask my parents for my hand in marriage, and then, maybe.

Albert Jr. did just what Olga wanted; he divorced Josie, formally asked Mr. Ramos for his daughter's hand in marriage, and proposed to Olga that they marry right away. They married in September 1947, but only after Olga made Albert Jr. promise to return to the study of law and finish becoming an attorney. Having quit the St. Mary's law program, there was no other option if he wanted a law degree but to move out of San Antonio to attend another law school. The options were limited to Austin or Houston; private law schools in Waco and Dallas were too expensive and distant. His brother Richard had also returned from the Navy and had finished his course of study to become an engineer. Now he had enrolled at the South Texas College of Law in Houston. His sister Belinda was recently married and also living in Houston. These two siblings encouraged Peña Jr. to attend law school there. While Albert and Olga spent time making arrangements to transfer to law school in Houston and relocate, and getting advice from the family members there, Olga gave birth to their first son, William "Bill" Albert Peña.

Albert and Olga joined Richard and Belinda in Houston; they moved to Pasadena, Texas, an emerging suburb of Houston. Because Albert Jr. was a war veteran and eligible for educational benefits under the G.I. Bill, the financial burden of attending school away from home while married with a baby son and another child on the way, and the costs of attending a private law school were lessened. Housing was a problem for the young couple in Houston; the rents were too high. Discrimination had been a problem for Albert Jr. at St. Mary's, but Pasadena in the late 1940s was a redneck haven. The rental housing available and affordable was denied to Mexicans, including public housing. Fortunately, Albert Jr. was befriended by two Anglos: Sam Hoover, the Anglo mayor of Pasadena and a pro-union man, and another law student, Eddie Ball, from the Rio Grande Valley. Ball lived next door to Albert and Olga when the Peñas finally got an apartment. Mayor Sam instilled in Albert a love for the working man and unionism. Eddie also became a union man with the Steelworkers, working as a lawyer.[9]

Olga recalled,

> We moved to Pasadena because he met this man who was a mayor then in, in Pasadena and he got us into the, the housing there and we lived in the housing projects there. We were the only Mexicans there and, as a matter of fact, they told Sam that, the mayor, they told him that they didn't want any Mexicans there. And Sam got us in anyway. And then, when, when we left, they cried because we were leaving. . . . they wanted to have Albert stay there. And they wanted him to stay out there. Sam and, and another, some other people that practiced law there and Albert asked me, "Well, what do you say?" And I said, "No. Let's stick with the issue you said; with our plan. You said you were

going to go back and help the people. So we are going to go back and help the people. I don't want to stay here."

Classes at the South Texas College of Law were challenging for Albert, but with help from his brother and his own abilities, he did well and in quick time completed his studies. Olga gave birth to Sandra Frances Peña, the first of many daughters, while waiting on Albert's bar examination results. Albert Jr. was licensed on August 20, 1951.[10]

Just as Olga had convinced Albert Jr. and made him keep the promise of finishing law school, she made him keep his promise to help the people. The couple moved back to San Antonio and lived in Albert Sr.'s duplex apartment on Palmetto Street in the Denver Heights area of the South Side of San Antonio. Albert Jr. and Richard, both having been admitted to the State Bar of Texas, began practicing law with their dad. The law office name was changed to Peña, Peña & Peña.

PART 2

The Making of a Political Leader

CHAPTER 4

First School Desegregation Cases

SEGREGATION OF MEXICAN CHILDREN DURING THE EARLY PART OF THE TWENTIeth century did not begin to end in the United States until local Méxicanos began to complain and form civil rights organizations such as LULAC in 1929 and the American G.I. Forum in 1948.[1] One of the first cases in Texas challenging school segregation was filed in Charlotte, Atascosa County, south of San Antonio, in 1928 by the parents of an adopted child. The adopting Mexícano parents of the child, Amada Vela, did not know if she was of Mexican ancestry, but the local school district classified her as such when they enrolled her in school. She was sent to the Mexícano school. The parents pressed their claim before the local school authorities, to no avail, and ultimately before the state superintendent of public education; they did not seek relief in district court. The official argument that was to be used for decades to follow by local school districts in segregating Mexican children was not based on race but on English language ability. The state of Texas began and finally did adopt an English-only language mandate for instruction in the public schools. Amada Vela could speak English well and was able to translate from both Spanish and English languages with ease. She was reassigned to the Anglo school. This was an individual case heard by the state superintendent and not binding on any other school district or even other Mexícano children in Atascosa County.

In 1929 the League of Latin American Citizens (LULAC), on behalf of Mexícano parents and their children, filed a class action lawsuit against the San Felipe Del Rio schools under the style *Del Rio Independent School District v. Salvatierra* (33 S.W. 2d 790, Tex. Civ. App.—San Antonio 1930). The plaintiffs complained of segregation. The trial court agreed they were segregated because the Mexican population were racially considered "other white" persons and therefore not being afforded equal educational opportunity. On appeal by the school district, the case was reversed because the segregation was not based on the "other white" racial designation, rather on the lack of English proficiency of Mexícano students. The United States Supreme Court denied the writ of certiorari for rehearing on the merits and therefore the state's appeal was upheld (284 U.S. 580, 1931).[2]

The state superintendent of public instruction in Texas during the 1920s was Annie Webb Blanton. She stated: "A State may, with safety, admit as residents only those capable of being assimilated—those who can adopt its standards of living, its language, and its ideals of citizenship and of government . . . honest emigrant who desires to become a genuine Texan . . . in fact as well as in name . . . born and reared in the Lone Star state. If you desire to be one with us, stay, and we welcome you; but if you wish to preserve, in our state, the language and customs of another land, you have no right to do this . . . you must go back to the country which you prize highly and rear your children there."[3]

"In the early 1900s, fewer than one out of five Mexican children attended any school. As late as 1944 nearly half the Mexican children in Texas still received no school education," according to James D. Cockcroft.[4] The lost battles in court led parents into the streets. These early Mexícano protests against the prevailing and prevalent attitude held by Anglos toward Mexicans and institutionalized by de jure segregation in San Antonio led Eluterio Escobar and Maria Hernandez to form La Liga de Defensa Pro Escolar in 1934. They protested, marched in the streets, held rallies, confronted local and state public school authorities utilizing the tools of the poor: direct action. Those able to raise funds to litigate turned to the courts.

Albert A. Peña Jr. grew into adulthood in the midst of these turbulent times. He participated in protests with other Mexícanos and blacks to integrate theaters, downtown restaurants, and businesses with little success before he left for law school in Houston. Peña Jr. returned from law school ready to begin the practice of law with his father and brother Richard. He was thirty-four years of age when he received his license to practice law from the state bar on August 20, 1951. The early legal practice was not much different for Albert Jr. as it had been when he assisted his father with his cases, except now he also had a license to practice from the state bar and could earn his own money and develop his own client base. Now he was earning real money, and most of it he got to keep. His father's legal business was good and so was the paycheck. In time, Albert Jr. and brother Richard developed their own clients and separate money.

Albert Jr.'s ex-wife, Joséfina, and children, Albert III and Belinda, increasingly needed more money for clothes, entertainment, and school, not to mention groceries and rent. Albert enjoyed making money but not handling cases or paying child support. He was most interested in politics. Besides, the clients, he found out, paid little if at all. He recalled how his father spent almost as much time collecting his fees as resolving cases. Mexícano lawyers of the time had Mexícano clients, and they were poor but hardworking people with little money to spare. Being Méxicanos, his clients often were the targets of the police and arrested for minor infractions of the law. Albert liked the money but not the practice.

As a practicing attorney, Albert was able to meet and make friends with important local Mexícano lawyers, pioneers in civil rights like Gus García, Carlos Cadena, Richard Casillas, John Herrera, and Pete Tijerina, formerly from Laredo, Texas. Tijerina had relocated to San Antonio in the early 1950s and had been involved with LULAC in Laredo. His interest in LULAC led him to seek office within the local San Antonio LULAC council. He led the "New Blood Ticket." Tijerina was successful in defeating George de la Garza. Also elected LULAC officers along with Tijerina on the same slate were Albert A. Peña Jr. and Eugene Ramirez. LULAC national president John Herrera from Houston was present at the election meeting held at the International Building on Houston Street. Herrera, Cadena, and Gus García were the attorneys in the *Hernandez v. Texas* case heard by the U.S. Supreme Court two weeks prior to *Brown v. Board of Education.* In the Hernandez case, a unanimous decision from the U.S. Supreme Court held that jury service discrimination against Mexican Americans in Texas was unconstitutional. Herrera and Cadena had prepared the case for appeal, and Gus García argued the matter before the court on January 11, 1954.[5] The significance of this case went largely unnoticed by Méxicanos nationally and was unreported by the mainstream media. The Spanish-language media made no mention of the case at all, as far as I could find. The significance, other than including Méxicanos in juries, was that in 1940 the U.S. Census Bureau had racially reclassified Méxicanos away from "other race" to "Caucasian" or white. As whites, Méxicanos had no constitutional protection as a minority. The Hernandez case, however, found discrimination against Méxicanos despite the new racial classification as "Caucasian" and ruled that this group needed and should be afforded "equal protection" under the Constitution. In other words, Méxicanos, while they were now white, were still treated as nonwhite. Therefore they were not really white and could avail themselves of civil rights laws and protections.

The local San Antonio LULAC council and American G.I. Forum chapter both raised funds with which to send the Mexícano legal team to Washington to present the *Hernandez* case. San Antonio LULAC had a *tamalada* at the Pearl Corral one December evening in 1953 to raise funds for the legal case. While those that bought tickets to the *tamalada*, a traditional Christmas event, watched spot dancer Irma Rodríguez and listened to Sylvia Acosta sing, the people danced to the music by Eugene Nolasco's orchestra. The *tamaleros*, those serving the tamales, were LULAC members, including Albert Peña Jr., Albert Fuentes, Alex García, Benny J. Cantu, John A. Esquivel, and Gene Ramirez, among others. Together, Texas Forum chapters and LULAC's *tamalada* raised over $1,236 for the legal team. Peña made that announcement to the press and credited Hector P. García for having raised the bulk of the money.[6]

Gus García was a genius and had been the first Mexícano elected to the local community college in 1948. García with the *Hernandez* case became the first Mexícano to present oral argument before the United States Supreme Court, with Chief Justice Earl Warren presiding. The *Texas Bar Journal* reported that García's oral argument had "awed the U.S. Supreme Court." García had been born in Laredo in 1916 but raised in San Antonio. He was a brilliant student in high school, college, and law school. He graduated from law school and was licensed to practice law in 1938 by the time he was twenty-two. García left San Antonio in the early 1950s, however, and relocated to McAllen in South Texas, and later Kingsville near Corpus Christi, only to return to San Antonio to die penniless and of alcoholism, perhaps violence, on a park bench at La Plaza del Zacate.[7]

In 1947 Gus García prepared to file a major case against the segregation of students in Texas. He felt the time was ripe for such a challenge. In January 1948 he filed on behalf of Minerva Delgado, a student in the Bastrop Independent School District, and twenty other parents. Bastrop is east of Austin, the state capital of Texas. Mexícanos in LULAC began raising funds for the litigation, as did the American G.I. Forum members once they organized themselves in March of that same year. Judge Ben H. Rice ruled on June 15, 1948, on behalf of Minerva Delgado and the others and enjoined the public schools from segregating Mexican children. Furthermore, the court also held that retaining children on the pretext of teaching them English could not be permitted beyond the first grade. Gus García had fought and won another great legal case that began to end segregation in Texas and the nation. New lawyers, such as Albert A. Peña Jr. and his brother Richard, could use these legal precedents to protect Mexícanos from discrimination of this sort in other Texas cities.[8] A year after the filing of the *Delgado* case, another young Mexícano, Cristobal Alderete, filed a complaint with the State Department of Education alleging segregation in the Del Rio, Texas, schools. His efforts led to the withdrawal of accreditation of the school district by the state agency because of their segregation of Mexican children. A newly installed commissioner of education, J. W. Edgar, reversed the decision. On May 8, 1950, Gus García, the legal champion, and Dr. George I. Sanchez—representing the American G.I. Forum and LULAC, respectively—appeared before the commissioner and the State Board. Again, García was brilliant. He presented evidence of segregation in no less than twenty cities. He reminded the board that segregation in Texas was unconstitutional and illegal. He had won that case already. The board issued a new policy that recognized segregation as being illegal but instituted a new grievance procedure. Those alleging segregation must address themselves to the local school district officials. It was a setback for Méxicanos that would last well into the early 1960s.[9]

Like most returning veterans interested in politics, Peña looked into the American G.I. Forum once he learned of it, and into LULAC. Both organizations were engaged in fighting discrimination and unequal opportunity for Méxicanos, especially veterans.[10] Albert joined the San Antonio chapter of the Forum and met Hector P. García, the organization's founder, from Corpus Christi, Texas.[11] He introduced the founder of the American G.I. Forum to his dad and sister Madeline and her husband, Manuel Davila. This membership and meeting with the founder led to Albert's early legal civil rights work on behalf of parents and their children affected by school segregation, a problem not experienced by the Peñas and other middle-class Méxicanos of the 1940s and '50s. The introduction of the Forum's founder also led to García becoming an investor in the radio station that his brother-in-law and sister Madeline started up in San Antonio. Albert, with the aid of García's contact with then congressman Lyndon B. Johnson, helped them obtain a license from the Federal Communications Commission.[12]

Hector P. García called Albert Jr. one day and asked him to help the Forum investigate a complaint made by Mexícano parents on behalf of their children in Hondo, Texas. They alleged school segregation of their children by the school district. García told Peña to contact the Max Orta family in Hondo. With Olga as his driving partner, Albert headed out Highway 90 toward Hondo, some forty miles west of San Antonio. When they reached Hondo and found the Orta home, they were surprised at the greeting. Albert knocked on the screen door and heard a voice inquiring what they wanted. Albert explained he was a lawyer and wanted to help them with the school problem. The voice answered, "We don't want to talk to any more lawyers. You are probably like the rest of them that come down here to investigate and never do anything. They only take our money and do nothing." Undaunted by the rebuff, Albert explained who had called him, how he was not charging them or being paid by the Forum, and that he could help if they would talk to him about the matter. He said, "First of all, I am not going to charge you anything and if there is segregation, I will follow through with it." Convinced finally that he wasn't going to charge them for attorney's fees, the Ortas provided him with the necessary information. Albert wrote:

> I investigated the case and learned there were two schools in town, called the Main Plant and the other the West Ward School. If you were Chicano, no matter how good your English was, you went to the West Ward School up until the seventh grade. I went and talked to the superintendent and I told him what I had found and said this is unconstitutional and he said, "Well, I can't do anything about it. You are going to have to talk to the school board." We didn't have any money . . . to go to federal court . . . so I asked for a hearing before the school board and they granted me a hearing. I had a hearing. I took my client, Max Orta and I sat him down. He was the only Méxicano there and they had brought in a law firm, big law firm in from Houston to represent the school board. They had about four or five lawyers there and I was there. I made my pitch and I said, "I have only one witness, I have only one witness." I had already told them what I had found. They had two schools. Clearly unconstitutional. And of course their excuse was that they were teaching them how to speak English. I said, "The person who made the complaint speaks fluent English, but I have one, only one witness," and they thought I was going to call Max Orta. I called the superintendent. The superintendent came and I said, "you remember when I visited your office and I gave you the statistics about what was happening in Hondo and you told me it was true? You had two schools. One for white and one for Mexicans." He said, "Yeah, that is correct." And I said, "Well, that is all. You may sit down. I have only one witness . . . that is it. I have proven my case." And so they say, "We will let you know and we will let you know what our decision is." The school board predictably held against my clients.[13]

Peña appealed the case to the State Board of Education. His clients had no money to file in federal or state court; besides, he had promised not only to follow through with the case but also to not charge them anything for his services. Peña had to follow the administrative route in order to avoid costly litigation that neither he nor the Forum, the Ortas, or other parents could afford. The State Board did nothing for a year. In this case no decision was a decision.

Schools were to start again in the fall, and segregation was still in effect. The Méxicano parents were disgusted and upset at Peña. He was doing nothing, just like previous lawyers. In a bold move, his first utilizing direct action and the print media, he called for a meeting of all Méxicano parents in Hondo at the local Guadalupe Church. The San Antonio news media was there to report on the plan of action Peña had alerted them about, and they did. It made the San Antonio paper the next morning of the protest.[14]

Peña told the parents assembled there in direct and frank words, "I am not like the rest of them. This is my first case and I am not the best lawyer in the country, but we are going to integrate these schools. And we are going to go and we are going to enroll our kids in the Main Plant and we are going to stay there if it takes all day or it takes a week or it takes a month. But we are going to stay there until they enroll our children in the school."

On registration day, the Mexicano parents and children lined up to register at the Anglo school. Albert and Olga were there with them, watching and encouraging the parents into the school building, one by one. Parent after parent would walk up at their turn and ask to enroll their child in the school. Upon giving the Mexican surname for their child, the clerk would say, "Well, you have to go to the West Ward School." Albert and Olga would send the next parent in and ask the rejected parent and child to go to the back of the line and try again. They kept this up all day. They sang, they talked, they laughed, but one by one the parents and children would walk in and ask for admission into West Ward. Albert said, "About one o'clock, they received a telegram from Austin, from the State Board saying, integrate. So, we had won our case. . . . Immediately I started getting letters, phone calls, and personal visits from Chicano parents from all over the state complaining of the school segregation in their area. I investigated. I wrote letters to the media, parents, educators, and school boards. I met with people telling them about the Hondo experience and exhorting them to resist in mass and force the school systems to change and open education to all students equally."[15]

It was not long before LULAC Council No. 2 in San Antonio contacted Albert Jr. about school segregation in another rural community just south of San Antonio: Lytle, Texas. He was asked to investigate the matter as an unpaid attorney. Albert recalled the event in an article he wrote:

> When I arrived, I asked a lady where the school was. She pointed to a typical school building and said, "That's the American school and on the other side is the Mexican school." The so called Mexican school was a one room shack with about 60 students from age 6 to 12 years old. The teacher could not speak Spanish and the student [sic] could not speak English. The 12-year-old served as an interpreter. A pet parrot was the closest thing to a bilingual creature. It cussed in English and Spanish. Satisfied that Chicano children were segregated, I crossed the street and talked to the Superintendent of the schools. He admitted that the children were separated because they couldn't speak English. He was vague about what was being done to teach them English. I told him that the practice of separating children was unconstitutional. He said he could do nothing about it. It was school board policy. At the hearing, I used the Superintendent as my star witness. He recalled our previous conversation and admitted that the children

were separated. I told the board that was my case. About that time someone in the audience, who claimed to be a minister got up and said "Mixing of white children and Mexican children is un-American [sic]." I answered, "Sir, I don't know who you are, but I remind you our armed forces are fighting communism in Korea. Unfortunately, some of our American soldiers are defecting to the Korean communists. Not one of them is a Rodríguez, Martinez or Estrada. You know why? I will tell you why. Because they are coming home with Congressional Medals of Honor, and silver stars for gallantry. And they are coming home in coffins." For what seemed an eternity the room was very quiet, and the crowded room, mostly young white teachers, stood up and applauded. Shortly thereafter, the Lytle School Board integrated the school.[16]

After these two desegregation cases, Albert A. Peña Jr. continued to file complaints and legal petitions against other segregated schools in the area, including Natalia, Batesville, and Devine.

Peña was beginning to dedicate his life to civil rights and politics, not the practice of law. He used the law to end abuses, but his growing passion was in helping his people get organized and standing up for their civil rights. Albert's earlier contacts with East Side leaders of the black community during the G. J. Sutton election campaign, such as John Inman, Eugene Coleman, and Claude Black, also brought to his attention more civil rights work in the legal arena. They began to recruit him for their civil rights work and referred legal cases to him.

"Sporty" Harvey was a black boxer and a very good one. He was so good that he thought he could become the undisputed boxing champion in his weight classification. The black community certainly thought so, and they wanted a San Antonio black champion. The problem was not his pugilistic abilities; the State of Texas had banned mixed boxing matches between members of different races. The ban had been implemented in 1933.

Sporty Harvey was referred by his East Side black friends to Albert A. Peña Jr. with the Peña, Peña & Peña law office downtown. Peña reviewed the facts and accepted the case. It appeared that Harvey, a black man, had obtained a match against a white boxer, but the state labor commissioner had refused a permit on the basis of Harvey being black. Peña had to travel to an Austin courtroom to take on the state labor commissioner. The case was heard by District Judge Jack Roberts. He ruled against Peña's legal arguments that the Harvey case was an unconstitutional denial of equal protection under the law. Judge ruled that boxing was not a right, but a privilege extended by the state. There was no fundamental right at stake and therefore no constitutional protection. Peña was faced with the necessity of taking the case up on appeal. Again, his client had no money; the black community was asked to see about raising some money for the appeals, which could go as far as the U.S. Supreme Court.

Peña called on Carlos Cadena, who in turn called on Maury Maverick Jr. for legal assistance with the case. They agreed to help and prepared the appellate brief stating their legal position in opposition to the trial court's ruling. They argued that the ban was arbitrary discrimination against Negro boxers because it meant that they had no chance to become undisputed champion in their weight class in Texas. The state policy promoted splinter championships. It was a fundamental right that black boxers be afforded the equal rights guaranteed by the U.S. Constitution. The state attorney general, John Ben Shepperd, through his assistant Horace Wimberly, filed their brief with the Third Court of Civil Appeals sitting in Austin. They asserted the ban was meant to maintain order. "Since boxing is a dangerous and trouble-making sport, it was felt for a long time in Texas that it should not be permitted at all. Later, in 1933, the legislature saw fit to legalize it, but only under the strictest controls. The statute and rule in question were drafted as one of those controls. The intent of the legislature was not to grant privileges to white boxers denied to negro boxers, but rather to prevent brawls and disorders which might well arise out of the aggravation of racial antipathies due to matches between men of different races. That this was especially likely between white and Negro had been demonstrated to them by such disorders in the past. Since there was thus a reasonable and rational basis for the classification by the state, it may not be claimed that this is an arbitrary one so as to be struck down by the Fourteenth Amendment."[17]

At the trial court level, Peña and Maverick had put a deputy boxing commissioner on the witness stand along with a state representative who once had been a boxer, Edgar Berlin; both testified that no such brawls and disorders had occurred. Appeals take time and money; Peña's heart was in politics, not appellate briefs and oral argument, even though he was an effective and persuasive public speaker. Peña left the Harvey case in the hands of Cadena and Maverick for resolution in 1953; he was going into politics full-time. He had wanted to be in the state legislature just like Maverick and Berlin, the trial court witnesses; they were legislators. At-large elections for state representatives, however, precluded him from the opportunity. His success in the political arena was years away. Peña was badly smitten by the political bug by 1953.

Peña's Black Friends, G. J. Sutton and Rev. Claude Black

Like Peña Jr., G. J. Sutton was born in San Antonio to a large middle-class family, one made up of fifteen children. He was the eighth child born to Samuel and Lillian Sutton, who were schoolteachers—his father being the first such black educator in Bexar County. All the Sutton children graduated from college. G. J. attended

Wiley College in Marshall, one of a few colleges for blacks in segregated Texas in the 1930s. He graduated from Wilberforce University in 1932 and later obtained a degree in mortuary science from Cincinnati College. He and a brother began a funeral business in San Antonio's East Side in 1938 and later founded a cemetery for blacks, Gates of Heaven Memorial Gardens, where he and his second wife, Nellie, are buried. He died in 1976 on June 22, his birthday. Another brother, Percy, moved to New York and at one time owned the famed Apollo Theater. Percy became a lawyer and successful politician in New York.

During his adult years as an independent businessman, G. J. became the leader of the black community, a coleader with Peña Jr. in many of the civil rights struggles, and cofounder of the Bexar County Democratic Coalition. In his own right, Sutton also became a successful politician in Bexar County like Peña. Sutton was elected to the community college board and later was selected along with Peña as the only two minority national delegates from Texas to the Democratic Convention in 1960. In 1972, the year Peña lost his seat on the Bexar County Commissioners Court, Sutton became the first black official elected state representative from San Antonio. Upon his death, his wife Lou Nelle "Nellie" succeeded him, also becoming the first black woman to represent Bexar County in Austin. Together, G. J. and Albert were a formidable team and best of friends.[18]

The Reverend Claude Black returned to Texas from Massachusetts, where he had been pastor in Haverhill, to report for duty as pastor of Corpus Christi's St. Matthew Baptist Church in 1946. Rather than continue his studies to become a doctor when he was attending Morehouse College in Atlanta, another black institution of higher education, Black turned to the ministry and was ordained by Andover Newton Theological School. Claude had been born in San Antonio, like Peña and Sutton. And like Peña he was born about the same time, on November 28, 1916. His father, Claude Black Sr., was instrumental in helping A. Philip Randolph organize the local Brotherhood of Sleeping Car Porters in San Antonio. Black Sr. rose to a leadership position in the Texas branch of the union.

Black Jr. came from Corpus Christi to San Antonio in 1949 as pastor of Mount Zion First Baptist Church. He served in that capacity until 1998. During those early years and until Peña's death, Rev. Black was another of his intimate political cohorts and friends. Sutton, Black, Eugene Coleman, Harry Bellinger, and Harry Burns would regularly lunch with Peña and discuss politics and strategy. This core group of black leaders together with Peña's Loyal American Democrats (LAD) helped organize and maintain the Bexar County Democratic Coalition for decades.

Reverend Black led and joined in many of the civil rights protests in the city and state throughout the 1950s and 1960s. He ran unsuccessfully for the San Antonio

City Council and later was elected to that body in 1973. He served on the city council until 1978 and was selected by the council members as mayor pro tempore, the first black person to hold such a position. Rev. Black founded the first black credit union in the city and organized other black pastors into the Baptist Ministers' Union of San Antonio. This ministerial alliance was for decades the vehicle to register blacks and get them out to vote in city, school, and county elections.

Rev. Black was the lone representative from San Antonio at the White House Conference on Civil Rights in 1966. He challenged Peña Jr. to find ways to bring Méxicanos into this important gathering that predominantly served to promote black issues and obtain political patronage at that high level. Peña took this advice to heart and did find ways to get White House access but via another route. On November 28, 2007, Rev. Black celebrated his ninety-first birthday with friends and family. While Peña was not present, one of his top coleaders, Arnold Flores, and other surviving members of what was the Bexar County Democratic Coalition were there.[19]

Peña and Labor

The early 1950s also brought Peña into close contact with labor leaders working in the area. The state required all labor organizers to register with the secretary of state—a move designed to keep track of who was working for whom and to what end. Emmanuel Coutalakos, of Greek origin, came to San Antonio en route to Yoakum to organize workers there for the Fur and Leather Workers Union. He had failed to register with the secretary of state and was summarily arrested and jailed. Other labor leaders affiliated with other unions, such as the Needle Workers, Plumbers, Teamsters, and the Amalgamated Workers Union, left over from the old Congress of Industrial Organizations (CIO), immediately called on San Antonio lawyers for help. The case was going to be tried in San Antonio, and Pat Maloney, assistant district attorney, was prosecutor. Gus García was recruited by Herschel Bernard to defend Coutalakos, and Albert Peña Jr. was given the task of finding a bail bondsman to get him out of jail.[20]

During his future travels across the state on behalf of AGIF and LULAC, then later organizing the Viva Kennedy clubs, Peña would meet other labor leaders, such as Pancho Medrano with the United Auto Workers in Dallas, Paul Montemayor with the steelworkers in Corpus Christi, and Franklin García in San Antonio. He had already become aware of local Anglo labor leaders, such as Hank Brown with the Plumbers Union and Ray Shafer of the Teamsters. The labor movement excited and attracted Peña; he was for the working men and women to earn better wages in order to get out of poverty, which he viewed as endemic to Méxicanos and blacks. Peña began to encourage young Méxicanos to join the labor unions of their trades, and to organize a union if one did not exist. But he was still more excited about politics and wanted to get elected to some position.

CHAPTER 5

Barrio Presidential Politics

IN 1948 HENRY WALLACE REACHED OUT TO MEXICAN AMERICAN VOTERS ACROSS the nation, but mainly in the Southwest and Midwest, in his quest for the presidency. Wallace attempted to mount a campaign in Bexar County, primarily San Antonio.[1] The county had an estimated population of 338,176 of which only 65,700 had paid their poll tax in 1946 and were registered to vote. The odious practice by the Democratic Party in Texas of holding a "White Primary," limited to voters who made a sworn statement that they were racially white as a prerequisite for voting in the election, had ended in Texas in 1944.[2] In 1940 the U.S. Census Bureau designated persons of Mexican ancestry as racially white. Prior to 1940 the racial classification for persons of Mexican ancestry by the U.S. Census Bureau was "other race." Black and Mexícano voters, somewhat more empowered by these changes, began to vote in the Democratic Party elections in larger numbers. The black voter realignment from the Republican Party to the Democratic Party had begun since the Depression. Franklin Delano Roosevelt's (FDR) campaign appeal built a grand coalition of labor, liberals, minorities, and the poor that had repeatedly elected and reelected him to the White House.

Henry Wallace, former vice president with FDR, had organized the Amigos de Wallace as the ethnic component to his presidential campaign, and was a pioneer in this regard. He obtained the nomination of the Independent Progressive Party, meeting in Philadelphia June 1948. The Progressive Party, however, was not yet on the ballot in Texas. Ralph Cuaron, the national organizer of Amigos de Wallace, insisted that the Texas chair of the Communist Party USA, Emma Tenayuca, who resided in San Antonio, seek ballot status for the Progressive Party.[3] The state electoral requirements and procedures were mostly insurmountable, but they worked at it and managed to get Wallace on the ballot. Tenayuca and her husband, Homer Brooks, both approached Albert Peña Jr. about his group's support for Wallace. Peña, however, did not get involved with trying to get Wallace or the Progressive Party on the Texas ballot. The previous year, he and his buddies had worked feverishly on the local campaigns for Gus García and G. J. Sutton; now they were looking at the Truman campaign.

In the Democratic Primary of 1948, Peña Jr.'s candidate was Harry Truman. Vice President Truman became president on April 12, 1945, when President Roosevelt died while in office. But Peña was oblivious to the power struggle between the Truman supporters and those who opposed his continued presidency, among them the supporters of the States Rights Party's nominee for president, Strom Thurmond. U.S. Senator Thurmond received 3,418 Bexar County votes in the General Election. Peña Jr. at this point was unaware of the workings of the governance structure of the Democratic Party—not for long, though.

Also on the local ballot for the Democratic Primary was Frank G. Cortez, who was running for U.S. senator. Cortez, a local man from San Antonio, had the support of most West Side Mexícano groups, including Peña's. Unfortunately for him, this was also the infamous election that Lyndon B. Johnson won in the Democratic Party runoff election of August 28, 1948, by the narrowest of margins, a mere 87 votes statewide. He earned the sarcastic nickname "Landslide Lyndon" from that election. Bexar County in the Democratic Primary election of July 24, 1948, went for Coke Stevenson rather than Lyndon Johnson, and Frank Cortez polled most of the Mexícano votes from the West Side, a respectable 3,891. In the runoff election, Lyndon B. Johnson got the Mexícano votes and those of others to pull off a narrow victory over Stevenson, 15,610 to 15,511, a margin of only 99 votes. From Peña's perspective and that of his cohorts, the West Side Mexícano had pulled it off for Lyndon Johnson. The problem was Peña's people, namely Rubén Munguía, who was unsuccessful in getting congratulatory messages to Johnson for lack of an address or even phone number. The Bexar County liberal faction was denying them any information and access to the newly elected U.S. senator. Instead, the Anglo liberals in Bexar County were claiming all the credit for the victory. West Side Mexícano voters remained ignored and taken for granted. Peña took notice.[4]

Peña Jr. was a novice at national politics, having just begun to immerse himself in local Bexar County politics in San Antonio's West Side, the Chicano barrio. As for Truman's campaign and his subsequent presidential nomination, Peña Jr. and his new wife, Olga, simply helped with promoting the payment of the poll tax, $0.50 at the time, to become registered voters among the Méxicanos in the West Side and blacks of the East Side where they lived on Palmetto, a duplex apartment owned by Peña Sr. Albert Peña Jr.'s group was elated when they learned that poll tax receipts issued in Bexar County had hit an all-time high with 86,672. During the presidential race of 1944 only 67,492 Bexar County persons had paid their poll tax, and that figure had dropped in the midyear elections of 1946 to 65,700. Payment of the poll tax was an annual duty; not many persons in the West Side were focused on paying their poll tax. They saw the elections only as contests among white men of the Democratic Party. Texas was a one-party state: Democrats since Reconstruction. Frank Cortez's candidacy tremendously helped generate interest in paying the poll tax among West Side Méxicanos and Méxicanos across the state. The budding young political activists like Peña and Olga, their *compadres*, their friends, and coworkers involved with voter registration had someone of their own to promote in the upcoming election. While they voted for Truman, Cortez, and other candidates in the first primary, they did not attend the Democratic Party's precinct convention, popularly called the Governor's Convention, where the party rules and platform were hammered out every two years; they knew nothing about it or its governance function. The other Democratic Party convention was the presidential nominating convention. Attending their precinct conventions and being selected as delegates to attend these two conventions at that time was not on the couple's radar screen as a way to involve themselves with party politics.

The county judge for Bexar County was Charles W. Anderson, and all of the Commissioners Court members and other county officials were Anglos. Similarly the Democratic Party's State Democratic Executive Committee (SDEC) was comprised completely of Anglo men and women. Bexar County had as their representatives on the SDEC from Senatorial District 26, the only such district in the county, Josh H. Groce and Mrs. Claude Hudspeth, both of San Antonio.

President Truman was reelected, and Texas contributed a resounding victory for the Democratic nominee. Truman carried Texas and obtained its 23 electoral votes because he received 750,700 votes to the Republican nominee Thomas Dewey's 282,240. Strom Thurmond, the staunch segregationist, received a healthy 106,909 votes, and Henry Wallace less than 4,000. In fact Wallace ran fourth in Texas and only received over 10,000 votes in thirteen states, with California providing him the largest bloc of votes: 190,381.

LAD and PAPA

Albert A. Peña Jr. and Rubén Munguía were *compadres*. Rubén and wife Marta had baptized one of Peña's children. Henry B. González was the Munguías' nephew. The Munguías and Peñas personally liked each other and complemented each other very well; both were staunch Democrats, nationalistic Méxicanos, witty and combative, articulate, and hard drinkers, especially Albert. Munguía was from an affluent family from Mexico and had a thriving printing business. Peña's father had a thriving law practice, though Albert was just starting and he was not very good at the practice of law. He did not care for it. The two couples had other things in common. The Munguías were frequent guests at the Peña home after their return from Pasadena. Olga and Marta got along really well. The men, typically at the time, would sit in the front room and the women in the kitchen. During the hot summer days, the men would go outside to drink and smoke in the warm, humid air while the women suffered in the house. Olga, however, was no typical woman; she often would sit with the men in the front room or outside. Albert gave up trying to get her to conform lest there be a public row in front of his friends. The *compadres* and other friends grew accustomed to Olga being one of the "guys." At one of these informal get-togethers, Munguía and Peña decided after some brainstorming that a new Mexicano organization was needed. Both the League of United Latin American Citizens (LULAC) and the American G.I. Forum (AGIF) were admittedly nonpartisan, and therefore ineffective in electoral politics. The ban on politics was incorporated in both of the organizations' principal founding documents. Neither LULAC nor AGIF even encouraged the payment of the poll tax. There was no local political group among Méxicanos in Bexar County.

Albert and Rubén knew that Henry B. González and some West Side businessmen had gotten together from time to time in years past and organized the Pan American Progressive Association (PAPA). They had not heard much about PAPA since 1948. The PAPA group was also not a partisan political group, and now it seemed defunct with Henry B. González having left the group for a job in government. The only political group was the Citizen's Committee, a forerunner of the Good Government League (GGL), but they were not a Mexicano group, rather they only had token Méxicanos as members. Among them were Rubén Lozano, Dr. José San Martin, and George de la Garza. Peña, G. J. Sutton, and Lalo Solis sought out Henry B. González about joining their group. He refused. Years later González would refuse Peña's invitation to join the Political Association of Spanish Speaking Organizations, claiming he could not serve two masters.[5]

Albert, Olga, Marta, and Rubén took turns suggesting names for their new group. From among all the various names proposed, one emerged as a combination of parts, Loyal American Democrats. The name stressed they were loyal Americans and specifically identified them as Democrats. Peña liked that a lot, as did Munguía and their wives.

The couples brainstormed some more over what LAD was to do, but stalled on the particulars. No one had thought out an agenda, much less a plan. But Albert had heard at the courthouse that Dwight D. Eisenhower, the Republican nominee for president in the 1952 election, was coming into town in early October. The rumor was that the local Republicans, with the help of many conservative Democrats, were going to host a rally at the Alamo for Ike, as he was called. Peña also knew that many a schoolchild in the West Side and South Side had come home from school wearing "I Like Ike" buttons given them by the local teachers. Some parents had called him about that activity, and Peña, in turn, had called some of the principals in the West Side and South Side to complain of this gross manipulation of students and politicking by teachers, maybe even with tacit approval of the school principals. Peña suggested that LAD's first foray into Bexar County politics be the hosting of a political rally for Adlai Stevenson, the Democratic Party presidential nominee, in the West Side. Munguía loved the idea, but threw cold water on the possibility of having a rally in the West Side attended by Stevenson. "He won't come, and even if he wanted to, Bond Davis won't let us go with this," Munguía said to Albert.[6] Bond Davis was the Bexar County Democratic Party chair and not particularly fond of Mexícano voters. Peña asked Munguía to talk it over among those they were trying to recruit into LAD; meanwhile he would talk it over with Jimmy Knight, the Bexar County clerk, the next time he ran into him at the courthouse. The guess was that the Democratic nominee would have to come into Texas to blunt the massive defection of prominent Democrats over to Ike.

Governor Allan Shivers already had been quoted as saying he would welcome Ike in Texas. The former governor, Coke Stevenson, was rumored to be organizing a "Democrats for Ike" campaign committee. Surely the Democrats would fight for votes in Texas.

With the idea of a political rally in the West Side, Albert Peña Jr. and Rubén Munguía began to merge the informal group of West Side Mexícano Democrats into the Loyal American Democrats (LAD). Peña brought most of the membership into the group: Richard Casillas, Hector Díaz, A. M. Ramirez, Joe A. Estrada, Fred M. Ramirez, Roger T. Saldana, Joe Tovares, and Bill Maldonado. Munguía had recruited Hilario "Lalo" Solis, Charles R. Knopick, and George de la Garza. Both George and Lalo had been involved with Henry B. González and the Pan American Progressive Association (PAPA). While LAD was unmistakably partisan in electoral politics, PAPA was a loosely defined and nonpartisan advocacy group comprised of West

Side businessmen looking for economic opportunities with the downtown Anglo elites and politicians. PAPA was apolitical as an organization.

Albert A. and Henry B.

The political careers of Albert A. Peña Jr. and Henry Barbosa González are very much intertwined. The two men, plus Rubén Munguía's brother Romulo Jr., "Chacho," knew each other from childhood; they lived in proximity to one another, but their lives were very different. Albert's father came from Laredo in 1901 when he was five, grew up in San Antonio with seven other siblings, and was raised by a single mother. Henry's father, Leonides González Cigarroa, came from Mexico to San Antonio through Laredo as an adult in February 1911, a refugee from the Mexican Revolution. After a brief stay in Laredo, the González family moved to San Antonio. Leonides had been an influential man in his home state of Durango, mayor of Mapimí and a successful operator of silver mines. The family had wealth, but in the turmoil of the revolution, Leonides fled to escape death by firing squad with just the clothes on his back and family in tow. Henry's older brothers, Leonides Jr. and Carlos, were born in Mexico. His mother, Genoveva Barbosa Prince, was of mixed Scotch-Irish and Mexican ancestry from a family of Spanish merchants in Saltillo, Mexico.[7]

The mothers of Henry and Albert also differed greatly. While both were stay-at-home mothers raising large families, their lifestyles were vastly different. Genoveva's husband quickly became influential in San Antonio as managing editor of *La Prensa*, a job he took in 1913 when Alberto Sr. was selling furniture and promoting dances. The González residence was an intellectual and political center for the growing Mexícano refugee community continuing to arrive in the city. The Peña Jr. household, on the other hand, seldom had the father leading any family conversation or activity. Leonides would include his children in political discussions and topics such as literature, religion, art, music, and life before and after dinner. Luz, the only sister Henry had, was a talented musician. The older brothers became an engineer and a doctor. Henry was the baby of the family. He got all the attention and benefit of the older siblings. Albert Jr. was the oldest child and surrogate father to his siblings. The González family had a library at home of books in Spanish. Albert's books were those brought from school and were in English. Consequently, Henry was retained in the first grade for his lack of fluency in English.

Albert hung out with the River Side Cats. Henry, a loner, was often the target of the gang's harassment. Had it not been for Henry's larger physical stature and athletic prowess, he would have been a victim. Henry and Albert briefly attended

Main Avenue High School until Henry transferred to Jefferson High School when it opened. Both graduated in 1935 from high school.[8] They knew each other throughout childhood and into adulthood. At one time or another both Albert and Henry attended St. Mary's University and then law school. Albert joined the Navy right after the bombing of Pearl Harbor, while Henry "was called into government service as a civilian cable and radio censor under military and naval intelligence."[9] Albert was a veteran while Henry was not.

Henry graduated from St. Mary's Law School but did not pass the bar examination after several attempts. Albert transferred from St. Mary's University to South Texas College of Law and graduated. He passed the bar on the third try and was licensed on August 20, 1951. Henry married Berta Cuellar in 1940 and Albert married Joséfina Herrera. Both began to have large families; Henry and Berta, his only wife, had eight children. Albert had several wives and ten children, one adopted.

In 1948 both actively supported the first successful bids for public office by Méxicanos, namely, Gustavo "Gus" García for the school board seat, and M. C. Gonzales, a Bexar County assistant district attorney seeking to become the first Mexícano state representative from San Antonio. Gustavo García was a brilliant attorney. M. C. Gonzales was a competent attorney as well, but better known for his work with LULAC and the Mexican Chamber of Commerce. Henry and Albert both supported G. J. Sutton, an African American seeking a community college seat. M. C. Gonzales lost his race, but G. J. Sutton and Gus García both won. Both Henry and Albert had their eyes glued on these first successful political races. Both of them also wanted political careers.

Albert began to organize his friends and coworkers into a group of political activists. He only sought out Méxicanos; he was not interested in creating a mixed group with others. His goal was to organize the West Side, where most Méxicanos resided. Peña also realized how the Anglo leaders, regardless of whether they were liberal or conservative, co-opted Méxicanos to do their bidding in the barrio. Peña imposed his rule of having no politicians or political workers for Anglo candidates allowed to join his fledgling Loyal American Democrats (LAD).

Henry B. helped organize a business group of West Side Mexícano men seeking to do business with Anglos and get banks to loan them money or extend short-term credit. He was more of an executive director for the group than leader. The Pan American Progressive Association was not involved in politics, just business. In seeking to open economic avenues of group ascendancy for Mexícano businessmen, Henry B. encountered discrimination and began getting an understanding of the root causes of endemic poverty in the West Side of San Antonio. Henry B. left PAPA when he became an adult probation officer. In that capacity, he became intimate with families of felons and miscreants in the barrio. These families looked to him for advocacy, intercession, and brokering their problems with the criminal justice system and other societal entities. His ability in Spanish and English paid off handsomely for him in terms of persuasion, argument, and charisma.

Henry B. ran for the state legislature in 1950 and made it into a runoff against Stanley Banks Jr. He lost. Also earning a runoff spot in the same election was Maury Maverick Jr., who defeated Frates Seeligson, an incumbent and conservative Democrat. In 1953 Henry B. ran again, this time for the city council as the token "Latin American candidate" on the anti–Citizens Committee slate, the San Antonians. The Citizens Committee (CC), the precursor to the Good Government League (GGL), was the political machine. The CC had its own token Méxicanos, incumbent Rubén Lozano and George de la Garza, an automobile salesman, on their slate. Henry B. ran against de la Garza, who had the task of heading the West Side campaign for the slate. De la Garza had access to Anglo money with which to conduct a massive media campaign in Spanish and English on television, radio, and in the newspapers. González nevertheless defeated de la Garza without a runoff. The seven other San Antonian Candidates, as the GGL slate was called, were in runoffs. Henry B. renewed his efforts and, with additional money, again turned to the media to get the vote out. His efforts in both elections paid off handsomely, with huge Méxicano voter turnouts in the West Side. He even managed to persuade Méxicanos in the West Side to vote against Rubén Lozano and for Mrs. E. M. Stevens. The San Antonian slate won all runoff seats at stake. Henry B. was grudgingly rewarded by his colleagues by being named mayor pro tempore, becoming the first Méxicano since Juan N. Seguin to serve as leader of the city council. A few months later the CC reorganized itself into the GGL, and they chose not to oppose González in his reelection bid to avoid energizing a large Méxicano voter turnout in the West Side. Moreover, there was a chance the GGL could entice Henry to their side, and they still needed his vote on the city council. Henry, however, was too independent a politician to join anybody's group.

1952 Presidential Campaign in the Barrio

The pursuit of the presidency in 1952 came down to two men: Dwight David Eisenhower and Adlai Stevenson. Eisenhower was the Republican nominee, a decorated military general without prior political experience. Stevenson, the Democratic nominee, on the other hand, came from a family of political figures. His grandfather had been a vice-presidential candidate in 1892 for the Democrats. His father was appointed secretary of state for Illinois and also considered for the vice-presidential slot in 1928 by Al Smith, the Democratic nominee.

On September 20, 1952, the Stevenson presidential campaign came to Richmond, Virginia. He spoke at the Mosque Auditorium to a large crowd about the New South:

> In the broad field of minority rights, the Democratic Party has stated its position in its platform; a position to which I adhere. I should justly earn your contempt if I talked one way in the South and another way elsewhere. . . . One thing that I have learned is that minority tensions are always strongest under conditions of hardship. It is always better to reason together than to hurl recriminations at one another. . . . On the right to vote, we must do right for right's sake alone.[10]

The Democratic Party had been deeply torn within itself between conservative and liberal wings since the days of Franklin Delano Roosevelt's administration. Under Harry Truman, another Democratic president, the party struggled to keep within its ranks the reactionary elements particularly prevalent in the South and Southwest that opposed the continued inclusion and participation of ethnic and racial minority groups such as Mexicans and blacks; religious groups such as Jews and Catholics; labor unions; and women. Peña's involvement in the 1948 presidential race taught him the tensions between the opposing factions within the Texas Democratic Party. The states below the Mason-Dixon Line had evolved since Reconstruction into one-party dictatorships controlled by Democrats. Minority voters in these states had only three options: not vote, vote for, or vote against the white male candidates sponsored by the Democratic Party. Southern Democrats historically insisted on major concessions by the national party either in candidate selection or planks in the party platform.

The office of Vice President was key because the occupant was the presiding officer of the United States Senate. The platform was important because liberals sought egalitarian propositions such as civil rights and minimum-wage scales, which threatened apartheid society and hegemonic white culture. Stevenson, a Northerner, was known as a liberal and friend to labor. His views on civil rights were being heard on the campaign trail, not only by white voters but also minority voters across the country.

In the months before the November election, Stevenson had agreed to speak in states with major cities across the southern sector of the country from California to Virginia. Texas was not on the list of campaign stops. The Stevenson campaign during the month of September 1952 began in San Francisco, moved down to Los Angeles, across to Denver and Phoenix, then Albuquerque, but skipped Texas and other Southern states. The staunch segregationists along with the conservative elements in charge of the Democratic Party machinery in Southern states had not only declined to invite him to their state but also let it be known he was not welcome or would not be welcomed if he chose to appear. The Stevenson campaign handlers decided against any visit lest there be an embarrassment or affront by Democrats to the nominee. Those headlines were not wanted.

Stevenson went to Richmond, Virginia, instead and returned to campaign on familiar ground in Detroit and New York. Stevenson was courting the voters that were attracted to his message. In San Francisco, for example, he spoke about world policy; in Los Angeles about political morality; the need for change in Denver; campaign issues in Phoenix; about Communism in Albuquerque; the New South in Richmond; labor policy in Detroit; and about labor issues to the AFL-CIO in New York.[11]

Among those interested in the Stevenson presidential campaign, in addition to the white conservatives and liberals within Texas Democrats were the Loyal American Democrats (LAD) in San Antonio, Texas.[12] They wanted Adlai Stevenson to come to San Antonio, county seat of Bexar County, and meet the Méxicanos who had paid their poll tax and were eligible voters. This posed a serious problem for all interested parties. No presidential nominee of any party had ever met with, addressed, campaigned among, or worked a Mexícano crowd in Texas. Republican candidates never did. The typical scenario in the state, particularly among the southernmost counties along the U.S.-Mexico border, was for the most prominent white Democrat to invite and tour a statewide candidate around the county and stop at outdoor rallies at which the politician would speak in English to the crowd. Invariably, an occasional Mexican American local officeholder and Mexícano voters would be in the crowd or at the fringes. If the candidate spoke some Spanish, he was encouraged to utter a word or two, shake a few hands, and say, "Vote Straight Ticket: Democrat, Adios."

Major statewide Democrats, including Texas Governor Allan Shivers and former Governor Coke R. Stevenson (no relation to the Democratic nominee), had not only broken ranks and endorsed Eisenhower, but also were recruiting other Democrats into the "Texas Democrats for Eisenhower" campaign organization. Ike was going to campaign in Texas. He had accepted the invitation to attend a political rally at the Alamo, the shrine for white people in the state, in San Antonio.

The Stevenson campaign had no choice but to come to Texas and attempt to stem the voter hemorrhage. After all, next to California with 32 electoral votes, Texas had 24. The national Democrats developed a strategy for the candidate to fly into the Dallas–Fort Worth area for a brief whirlwind campaign tour of the two cities, then be received by the most prominent Texas Democrat, John Nance Garner, a former vice president during Franklin Delano Roosevelt's first and second terms. Over the course of the next two days, Stevenson would hit the campaign trail in search of votes in San Antonio and Houston. The Stevenson strategists contacted John Nance Garner in Uvalde, Texas, some ninety miles west of San Antonio.[13] They prevailed on the frail eighty-four-year-old to greet and host the candidate at his home. The expectation was that the symbolic messages inherent in the visit and the meeting would go a long way toward mending the rift between conservatives and liberals in the state. The rift had developed during the primary election for governor in which Allan Shivers soundly defeated Ralph W. Yarborough, the liberal. And the rift was being made wider now because Shivers and his conservatives were openly backing the Republican presidential ticket.

The struggle among the local Democratic officeholders in Bexar County, Texas, over hosting the Stevenson campaign was also bitter. Locally in San Antonio, the conservative forces were being organized under the banner of the Good Government League (GGL).[14] The GGL did not want Stevenson to come to Bexar County. The liberal faction consisted of "Negroes" under the leadership of G. J. Sutton; whites under the leadership of Maury Maverick Jr. and Bexar County clerk Jimmy Knight; labor, led by John Rogers working for Jack Martin of the state AFL-CIO; and the new upstart faction of Méxicanos under the label of Loyal American Democrats (LAD) being led by Albert A. Peña Jr. and Rubén Munguía. LAD had been organized by young and aspiring, but disenchanted, Mexican American professionals. This was the post–World War II generation of returning Mexican veterans.

When LAD leaders learned that Stevenson was coming to town, then driving to Uvalde to see Garner, they approached the liberal whites of the Democratic Coalition through Maury Maverick Jr. They proposed a rally near the West Side barrio at Milam Square, a small park known to Méxicanos as La Plaza del Zacate, directly across from Santa Rosa Hospital and the Mercado.[15] The park geographically was situated at the barrio's edge. Maverick and Knight vetoed the idea. Peña recalled, "They said, 'No,' just like that." The liberal pair insisted every Democrat must rally at the Alamo to show a bigger crowd than that for Eisenhower, who was going to be there four days prior. Defiant, Peña conferred with his cohorts and reached consensus to hold their own rally at Milam Square as proposed and not join the other crowd at the Alamo.[16] They agreed to let the candidate know of their invitation and consequences. LAD wanted to flex their political muscle with a public display of their organizational ability within the Mexícano community and in obtaining voter support for the Democratic nominee. Such a demonstration would also send a tremendous message about the importance of LAD and the Mexícano vote.

If LAD succeeded in attracting a large crowd with or without Stevenson, they would show the Democrats, both liberal and conservative, that the Mexícano vote was an integral and vital part of any future candidacy in Bexar County. Peña relayed that message to Maverick, who in turn relayed it to the county chairman of the

Democrats, Bond Davis. Davis wasted no time in calling Lyndon Baines Johnson, one of the two U.S. senators from Texas, about the developing situation. Johnson seemed to be the one wresting control of the state party machinery from Shivers, particularly since the governor was helping the Republican Party's nominee. The national Democrats and the Texas Democrats had no alternative but to bend to Peña's demands because they wanted thousands at the Alamo. Peña promised that after the Milam Square rally with Stevenson, the Méxicanos would march down the street to the Alamo mission.

Once the deal was cut, LAD members got busy organizing the event. At first they could not agree on who would meet Stevenson at the train station, deliver him to the rally, introduce him, deliver a speech *en Español*, or be part of the speaker's platform. Peña averted early dissension by insisting on respectful protocol. The one to introduce Stevenson had to be the only elected Méxicano on the city council, José Olivares, even if he was not of their group but a member of PAPA. Reluctantly, the group saw the wisdom in that choice. Besides, if LAD was to be the powerhouse among Méxicano voters in the city, then they had to do the recruiting and co-opting of emerging barrio leadership away from the GGL. Gus García, a noted civil rights attorney and former San Antonio school board member first elected in 1948, now resided in McAllen in the Rio Grande Valley. Peña called him to be a speaker at the rally and presented that choice to LAD. García was an impressive orator and still fondly remembered by the local Mexican ancestry community. Gus García had fond memories of Peña for his tireless fundraising efforts and organizing abilities dating back to the 1948 race. Peña had been a volunteer in his campaign. From time to time when he practiced law in San Antonio, García would run into Peña and they would have a drink together. During their trip to Washington, DC, to argue the *Hernandez* case before the U.S. Supreme Court on January 11, 1954, Peña had raised funds for the legal team. Peña also attended the celebration banquet held in Corpus Christi, Texas, after García had lost his campaign for state representative. Lico López had given Peña the photo taken of the lawyers honoring Gus García, Carlos Cadena, and John Herrera that was published in an organizational newsletter.[17] Peña pressed Gus García to speak at the rally. He accepted.

To ensure thousands at the rally, Peña suggested a broader strategy. Under the name of LAD he would call on other Méxicano leaders from the Rio Grande Valley and surrounding communities to bring their supporters. With LAD support for that idea, Peña called Dr. Hector P. García, founder of the American G.I. Forum from Corpus Christi, Texas, to be another of the speakers. In turn, Dr. García wanted assurances that he would be able to bring folks and other politicos and allowed time to introduce them all from the speaker's platform. Peña agreed and made Dr. García the first of the warm-up speakers of the rally.

The day prior to the Stevenson rally at the barrio's edge, the local white Democrats pulled the plug on the idea. Jimmy Knight called Rubén Munguía by telephone and told him Stevenson was not going to their rally after all. He explained how the state Democratic leadership, the conservative faction, opposed that idea, and that the national campaign personnel had deferred to the state leadership. He advised Munguía to cancel their rally and bring their folks to the Alamo to help augment that crowd. The rally was to be televised, so they wanted a huge turnout. Munguía was livid with rage and yelled obscenities at Knight. In no uncertain terms, Munguía told Knight that if Stevenson did not show up at the Plaza del Zacate to address the Méxicanos as planned by LAD, his group would call everyone invited from out of town plus every Mexícano leader they knew across the Southwest and tell them of the backstabbing by the Texas Democrats and Stevenson campaign.

Stevenson came to San Antonio by train from Uvalde early Saturday morning, October 18, then was driven over to the Plaza del Zacate, where he was met by thousands of Méxicanos. Peña had Munguía print large posters with all the details of the Saturday 11 a.m. event, which had been pasted on walls, windows, and boards and posted inside hundreds of Mexícano businesses in the West Side and South Side of the city. The poster read in part:

> This meeting sponsored by the LOYAL AMERICAN DEMOCRATS, is a momentous occasion in the political life of our Mexican-American citizens—It is THE FIRST TIME IN HISTORY that we have been recognized by a candidate for the highest office in the land as potential, influential, and thoroughly Americanized citizens.
>
> This marks the end of the hyphenated Americans in our governmental affairs and it is only fitting that this great liberating stroke be the action of the DEMOCRATIC NOMINEE—candidate of the people—ADLAI STEVENSON. We feel that this meeting is not just a San Antonio or a Texas meeting, but a symbolic meeting with the millions of Americans of Mexican extraction in our vast Southwest. WE STRONGLY URGE YOU TO COME,—TO BRING YOUR NEIGHBORS—TO RECEIVE THIS MAN OF GOODWILL WITH OUR TRADITIONAL HOSPITALITY![18]

The rally was an enormous success. Every one of the LAD members had their extended family members present; Peña's family alone accounted for twenty-three in the audience of thousands. The posters had spread the word. Spanish radio had helped bring out the crowds; no Méxicano had ever seen a presidential candidate or president. The newspapers, both English and Spanish, helped maintain interest in the Stevenson and Eisenhower visits to San Antonio. The Peña strategy of inviting South Texas leaders and politicians also paid off handsomely because hundreds made the trek from the Rio Grande Valley and other border cities to Milam Square in front of San Antonio's Santa Rosa Hospital.

Immediately after the barrio rally ended and Stevenson was whisked off by motorcade by Lyndon B. Johnson and John Connally to the Alamo for the Anglo Democrats rally, Peña and the other leaders got caught up in the surge of people that began walking toward the Alamo. Within minutes, thousands of Méxicanos filled W. Houston Street, blocking all traffic and taking over the road as they walked to the Alamo. When they reached the Alamo, the Méxicanos made up the largest contingent in that mass of humanity assembled there to hear Adlai Stevenson in English. Stevenson had tried to say a few words in Spanish at the plaza in response to the many "Viva Stevenson" and "Viva Adlaido" shouts emanating from the crowd.

Peña and friends met for coffee and *barbacoa*, Mexican-style barbecue, at his home the next morning and gloated over the front-page photo in the *San Antonio Light* Sunday edition clearly showing thousands in the audience, mostly Méxicanos. The newspaper stated that more than twenty thousand persons had attended the Stevenson rally. The newspaper also reported that Stevenson had met with others, including a group of women, at the Menger and Gunter Hotels near the Alamo. Peña and his group, particularly Olga, were incensed at not being informed of this reception and not invited to any of these meetings and events.[19] Another side benefit to the Stevenson rally was in meeting face-to-face the younger son of Maury Maverick Sr., Maverick Jr., a state representative; Herschel Bernard, an attorney about Peña's age; and many young labor activists and leaders, such as Hank Brown with the Plumbers Union and Raleigh Mull. Maverick Jr. had lost his father two years earlier, in June 1954, and both Peñas, Sr. and Jr., had attended the services, but no personal contact between the young men had occurred. And during the bitter negotiations to have Stevenson appear at the plaza, Maverick Jr. had opposed their plans, but now all those at the plaza were being attracted and recruited to his fledgling campaign. These new contacts would become the bedrock of Peña's liberal coalition in the years to come.

Albert A. Peña Jr. had thought of seeking election as state representative in the Democratic Primary held earlier in May 1952, but bowed to others. Henry B. González had sought the same office and lost in 1950.[20] Their liberal white running mates, however, both won their elections. LAD members realized from analysis of election returns that the Méxicano votes from the barrio precincts supported the slate of liberal white candidates without reservation, but white voters had not. The so-called Democratic Coalition of labor, liberals, blacks, and Méxicanos in Bexar County meant that Méxicano votes elected white candidates. There was no reciprocity. By 1952, Peña Jr.'s involvement in the electoral arena had become more sophisticated. Not only were he and Olga registering voters by organizing poll-tax drives in San Antonio's barrios but they were also getting those registered to the polling places across the city and county. The Peñas' (Olga and Albert) experience with both Adlai Stevenson's presidential bids in 1952 and 1956 had broadened. They were now active participants in delegate selection at precinct conventions at the county and state levels. They had become players in party politics and governance, adding more bodies and votes to the emerging liberal faction in Bexar County and the state. Olga had joined the Bexar County Democratic Women's organization, the first Méxicana to do so.

The GGL realized and appreciated the growing political efficacy among West Side Méxicanos as well and began a candidate selection process whereby every fielded slate of candidates for municipal elections contained at least one but not more than two Latin American businessmen from the West Side barrio of San Antonio.[21]

Peña's Race for State Representative

Albert Peña ran for Place 7 in Bexar County for the state legislature in 1954, along with three others. Frates Seeligson, who had been defeated by Maury Maverick Jr. the previous election cycle, was seeking this post again and was the favorite to win. The other two opponents Peña would have to beat were Tom E. Hoecker and W. C. Brickley Jr. Running in Places 2 and 4 were Peña cronies and known liberals, incumbent Maury Maverick Jr. and Charles Lieck Jr., respectively. These were the young activists he had met back in the days of the Stevenson rally.

Peña had problems with Eddie Montez, the other candidate opposing Maverick. Peña had refused Montez's appeal to endorse him over Maverick. And Peña had made additional political enemies within the Mexícano community by also not endorsing Martin E. Trejo, who had asked for his support. Trejo was going to attempt to unseat Dan Traugott, the incumbent county commissioner in Precinct One, the area where most Méxicanos lived within Bexar County. The positive aspect of Peña's race was that the Anglo voters in Bexar County would be split among three candidates for Place 7. Moreover, statewide the liberal Democrats had a candidate for governor, Ralph W. Yarborough against Alan Shivers. The liberals and union folks were expected to rally around Yarborough and produce a massive voter turnout sufficient to finally take the statehouse.

In the Democratic Primary election for state representatives in Bexar County, the Anglo liberals and Peña fared well. Charles Leick Jr. and Maverick won outright without a runoff election. Eddie Montez, a challenger in that race, only received 4,263 votes. While the other challenger, James McKay, received 17,760 votes, that was not sufficient to get Maverick into a runoff. Peña had to face F. S. Seeligson in the subsequent runoff election slated for August 28, 1954, and Fred Semaan, another of the liberal Democrats, faced R. L. Strickland. Peña had obtained 15,060 votes to Seeligson's 18,538, but the other two candidates had nearly 10,000 more votes split among them to deny Seeligson an outright majority of the total vote.

Both Peña and Semaan went down to defeat in the runoff election despite the help from Maverick and Lieck Jr., as did Ralph Yarborough.[22] In the runoff election, Peña's vote totals were 26,898 to Seeligson's 32,254. What was interesting about the county vote totals, and caught Olga Peña's eye, was that Yarborough's total votes in Bexar County were 30,874, a significant drop of 4,000 votes by the time voters reached Peña's name on the ballot. Olga wondered out loud to Sturge Steinert, a Young Democrat volunteer helping Albert, if the liberals were only voting for the Anglo liberal candidates and not her husband. The voter-turnout analysis subsequent to the runoff also indicated that 67 percent of the vote for Albert had come from voters in County Commissioner Precinct One. The expected liberal vote surge did not materialize sufficiently in Bexar County, and Martin E. Trejo, who once said he was running against County Commissioner Traugott, did not make the race. He failed to pay the $960 filing fee for that position.

During the 1956 presidential bid by Adlai Stevenson, Peña Jr. had learned how fickle liberal Democrats could be, and how difficult it was to engage and negotiate with the conservative element within the party. Still, the systematic exclusion of Mexican American and African American voters by the Democratic Party conservative elite maintained its hegemonic stranglehold on party rules, platform planks, delegate selection, and leadership. The poll tax, unit rule, favorite-son candidacies, runoff and at-large elections were the structural devices relied upon by the conservative elite to control the Democratic Party in Texas and across the Southern states.

CHAPTER 6

El Comisionado,
Our Man Downtown

ALBERT A. PEÑA JR. MADE HIS MOVE FOR A SEAT ON THE BEXAR COUNTY COMmissioners Court in 1956, the same year of the Stevenson presidential campaign. Peña Jr.'s political group, as an organization, was grassroots-based and dedicated to selling poll taxes and subsequently getting out the vote during elections. The Peña group knew Albert could win in the area of Bexar County that made up Precinct One on the Commissioners Court. Olga had studied the election returns after each election involving candidates for the Commissioners Court. She studied the precinct maps and the figures of voter turnout by each precinct voting location. It was as clear as sunlight to Olga that the Commissioners Court Precinct One was the Méxicano-packed district. Albert could win that position. Concomitantly Olga had adamantly refused to allow Albert to run for the state legislature again. Her argument, in addition to the observation that the liberal votes were not there for him in a countywide election, was that the growing Peña family could not financially afford his win and absence while in Austin. The county position paid very well, more than twice the amount, compared to the state legislature, she argued.

The first strategy was to make more Méxicanos registered voters in that part of the county by pushing them to pay their poll taxes on time and before January 31,

1956. The Peña group had to be extra careful with the business of getting Mexícanos to pay their poll tax. A decade earlier, Maury Maverick Sr. had gotten indicted for allegedly passing out fifty-cent pieces to Mexícanos and blacks with which they could pay their poll tax. Having been mayor of the city and congressman, Maverick Sr. had not been able to keep the opposition at bay and faced trial for those charges, during which he was cleared of wrongdoing in 1941.[1] The Peña group did not have Maverick's stature or political clout or money for legal defense.

The second order of business was to gather the $960 necessary to pay the filing fee for county commissioner. The fundraising began, and Peña Sr. was the first to hand over a crisp $100 bill; second was Rubén Munguía. Peña asked Sturge Steinert, one of the labor activists he had met from the Stevenson rally, to help him once again as his campaign manager, much to Olga's chagrin. She worked well with the young man, and he was a hard worker, but this race was different in that few liberal Democrats lived in the West Side of San Antonio. She was indispensable when it came to the Mexícano vote, and Precinct One had a majority Mexícano population. Olga was at the center of the barrio network of contacts to get Mexícanos registered and then out to vote.

It was rumored that the incumbent would not run again. But Commissioner Traugott kept making all the right appearances and saying the right things to indicate he was in the race for reelection. Peña got his filing fee money and set up a committee to raise more campaign funds with which to have *compadre* Munguía print push cards, sample ballots, flyers, yard signs, and pay for radio announcements, maybe even television. As time went by, but before the filing deadline, Dan Traugott announced he would not seek reelection and was endorsing his road-crew man, Harold Mussey.[2] Tim Hart, a plumbing contractor, and Alfred Callaghan, former mayor of San Antonio, also announced their candidacies for the same position that Albert A. Peña Jr. was seeking.[3]

Peña's group did all the right things: held backyard mini-rallies and big rallies at Pablo's Grove, got on the radio seeking to debate opponents, printed literature, held press conferences, raised money, and recruited volunteers to get out the vote. Olga made sure she had all her *comadres* lined up to help with food for volunteers, phone-calling voters, and knocking on doors offering to take voters to the polls. She also was in charge of the volunteers pushing the vote cards at each voting location to prospective voters. The massive effort paid off. Albert received 6,225 votes on Election Day and led the four-man group of candidates. The anointed successor came in a poor third with 3,666 votes, and former Mayor Callaghan barely made a showing with 879 votes.

Peña's challenger in the runoff set for August 25, 1956, was Tim Hart, whom the local newspapers had endorsed as the "reform" candidate early on.[4] In this race,

Peña had help from the gubernatorial race of Ralph W. Yarborough once again, and that of another Méxicano, Albert Treviño, running for justice of the peace in almost the same geographic area. Treviño was a sitting Municipal Court judge who was well-liked by many voters and could increase voter turnout. Quickly after primary election results had been posted, Peña got on the telephone to Treviño and proposed they campaign together and share a headquarters, which they did. Peña also called on Mussey and Callaghan for their endorsement, which he obtained.

In 1956 Henry B. González resigned from the city council to run for state senator, a move many thought was political suicide, including Peña. Bexar County surely would not elect a Méxicano as their only senator in Austin. More importantly, Anglo voters constituted two-thirds of all voters in Bexar County. The combined strength of black and brown voters would not be sufficient to win any countywide at-large election, unless white voters were persuaded to vote for a Méxicano as their state senator. Henry B., as he began to be called, got lucky. He had support from white liberals, labor, blacks, and the Peña campaign organization.

Henry B. was all about just Henry B., with no organization since PAPA. Eugene Rodríguez Jr. wrote in his master's thesis this about the two men in this race:

> Voter interest on the West Side, where González was a solid favorite, was intensified by an extensive campaign by attorney Albert Peña, Jr., for county commissioner of precinct one. His campaign organization covered every section of the precinct in behalf of both Peña, Jr. and González. (González has never campaigned within the framework of a tightly-knit organization and has always run independently, accepting equally the assistance of individual voters and organizations alike. Peña, Jr. on the other hand, is strictly an organizational man who relies heavily and almost exclusively on one for assistance.)[5]

The Peña political group helped Henry B. González beat his opponent, O. E. "Ozzie" Lattimer, in the Democratic Primary for the State Senate seat, by a margin of only 282 votes. Henry's victory came from voters in the black precincts of the East Side and ballot boxes in the West Side, where the Peña group had recruited Méxicanos to pay their poll tax and register to vote. And vote they did. The Bexar County district clerk estimated that in 1956, of the 140,000 eligible voters in the county, there were only 29,000 Mexican Americans and 10,500 African Americans. The majority were Anglos, with 100,500 registered and eligible.[6]

Henry B. then faced a tough challenge by a last-minute Republican candidate, Jesse Oppenheimer, in November. Again, Peña Jr. came to Henry B.'s rescue in the General Election. Peña's win in the runoff guaranteed his election in November as there was no Republican opponent in his race. With his grassroots organization and the mighty get-out-the-vote drive organized by Olga and Lalo Solis on behalf of Adlai Stevenson and all other Democrats, Peña delivered for Henry B. and other Democrats reluctantly, even for Price Daniel, who became governor by defeating liberal Ralph W. Yarborough. Henry B. won with over 13,000 votes against the Republican; he received only 6,000 fewer votes than Eisenhower and more than 2,000 over the total for Stevenson.[7]

History repeated itself for Eisenhower and Stevenson in 1956, with Bexar County going for Ike as it did in 1952; but locally the voters elected Peña, and Henry B.'s margin of victory in the county exceeded the votes for Adlai Stevenson. Again, Peña Jr. and González made history by becoming the first Méxicanos elected to the Commissioners Court and State Senate, respectively. Henry B. was the first Méxicano elected state senator in Texas history.[8] Both Albert and Henry B. were around the same age. At Henry's victory celebration on election evening, the crowd kept chanting, "Peña, Peña, Peña," demanding he make a speech. Henry B. called for Peña to join him on the platform. Those nearest Peña standing in the back of the crowd hoisted him on their shoulders and physically carried him to the makeshift stage. The crowd's applause increased in intensity; Peña was their *Comisionado*, their man downtown. Henry B. was to be their man in Austin. Henry, always attuned to who could help him the most, graciously thanked Peña and lavished praise on his organization that had brought out the voters for him and other Democrats. Henry acknowledged that Peña's group had made it possible to get him elected.

Statewide, Méxicano voters in the Rio Grande Valley had defected from the Democratic Party ranks in large numbers and voted for Ike. The Peñas noticed this in the various newspaper accounts that began to surface days after the election. Governor Shiver's organization, Democrats for Eisenhower, had recruited such local leaders as Reynaldo Garza of Brownsville and J. M. Sanchez of Zapata County. Cameron County (Brownsville) and Hidalgo County both went for Republican Eisenhower, but in Zapata he narrowly lost the county. Peña expressed his disgust with such *"vendidos,"* as he called the sellouts from the Democratic Party who voted for the Republican candidate. He understood why Anglos would shift loyalties between candidates—after all, both parties had many Anglo candidates for voters to choose from—but Méxicanos? Peña and Olga believed, as did his fellow inner-circle supporters, that the Méxicano's best interests lay with the Democratic Party and none other. If Méxicanos would run for office as Democrats and vote for the issues they championed, Méxicanos would be elected and those issues would become solutions.

The race for Bexar County Commissioner Precinct One in 1956 was an uphill battle for Albert A. Peña Jr., age thirty-eight. He was reluctant to challenge the ten-year incumbent, Commissioner Dan Traugott. Peña had wanted to get elected to the state legislature and failed twice. Wife Olga, the real grassroots organizer, had repeatedly told him the votes were not there for him. She insisted the votes for him were in the Commissioner Precinct One position. Time and again she had showed him the results, election precinct by election precinct, within that commissioner precinct. He had won every one of the West Side boxes, many in the South Side as well. She also argued that the salary from the state as legislator was meager—certainly not enough to support a family; they had four children at that time plus his two others from Josie Herrera. Moreover she pointed out how long he would be gone from his law practice while serving in that capacity. On the other hand, the county commissioner position paid very well and he could still do his civil rights work and help the law office. Peña reluctantly agreed with Olga that she was a better analyst of election returns and had a keener sense of the possible and doable in terms of elective office than he. He would make the race.

Albert called on his buddy Lalo Solis to handle his precinct organization together with Olga. And he asked Sturge Steinert, active with the Young Democrats of Bexar County, to be his campaign manager. The campaign offices were to be located in the South Side, at 3622 S.W. Military Drive, and downtown at his father's law office, 226½ Dolorosa Street. His LAD friends and others began organizing an announcement banquet to be held at DeWinnie's Belgium Inn at 3119 West Commerce Street for April 12, 1956, at 7:30 p.m. Rubén Munguía, banquet coordinator, printed the $5 tickets at his print shop to sell and make the announcement event also a campaign fundraiser. More than one hundred persons paid for tickets, including councilman Henry B. González, who spoke in Peña's favor, and state representative Charles Lieck Jr. Black leaders from the East Side, G. J. Sutton and Claude Black, were present as were an assortment of candidates for other offices. Maury Maverick Jr., no longer seeking reelection as state representative, was also present, shaking hands and backslapping as if he were campaigning himself. He enthusiastically campaigned for Peña and raised money for the effort.

The next battle at the beginning of the race was about his commitments with LULAC Council No. 2 and the Catholic Council for the Spanish Speaking. He was president of both organizations and would have to resign, given that the internal rules of both prohibited partisan political activity. Peña offered to resign from both leadership positions. The Catholic Council readily accepted the written letter of resignation; LULAC did not. Some LULAC members wanted him to resign, while others did not and actually voted against accepting his resignation. The argument that won the day with LULAC members was that his primary election was not until July, and June was the month for regular election of officers. Peña stayed as president and led the fight to have Edgewood Independent School District annexed into the San Antonio Independent School District. The proposal was rejected by the voters of San Antonio ISD. Peña felt he had failed to lead the annexation fight effectively; he just had no time to mount an organized campaign for this issue. He chose to focus more on his commissioner's race, having just started his campaign in mid-April. The election was less than ninety days away.

Commissioner Traugott threw the race wide open with his announcement that he would not seek reelection. Peña was in the race and was joined by Tim Hart, a fifty-two-year-old plumbing contractor. Rumors circulated that Traugott was encouraging his Road and Bridge superintendent, Harold Mussey, to make the race. Ex-mayor Alfred Callaghan also signed up for the race before the May 7 filing deadline. The battle for County Commissioner Precinct One became a four-man race between Hart, Mussey, Callaghan, and Peña.

On the eve of the primary election, the *San Antonio Express* endorsed Tim Hart as the reformer.[9] The *San Antonio News* also endorsed Hart two days later.[10] Peña led the four-man pack of candidates with 6,225 votes, but not enough to prevent a runoff election set for August 25th. He did not obtain a majority of the votes cast. Hart was second with 4,331, and Mussey and Callaghan came in third and fourth, respectively. Fortunately for Albert A. Peña Jr., another Albert was on the ballot in a different race. Albert Treviño was running for Justice of the Peace, Precinct One, Place 1. Treviño also was the leader of his four-person race with 14,411 votes, but those votes were enough to keep him out of a runoff election.

Not wasting any time, Peña and Treviño agreed to campaign together and opened another campaign office at 210 Pleasanton Road. The Mexicano community in Bexar County was energized; they had two of their own to vote for in the next election. Peña challenged Hart to debate him on radio and television on the issues and campaign platform. Peña took the initiative at every confrontation and came up the winner each time. Peña called and asked Harold Mussey for his endorsement, which was not forthcoming, but the locations for Mussey's political signs were turned over to Peña. Johnny García, Peña's sign man, had no trouble putting up his candidate's signs within days. Olga and Lalo Solis signed up enough volunteers for the runoff election to staff each of the thirty-eight election precincts in the district. Olga and Lalo also began getting applications to elderly and ill voters for casting an absentee ballot. Given Peña's bilingual abilities, he hit the airwaves with radio spots and a few television commercials in both languages, and written columns in black-owned newspapers and *La Prensa*. *Compadre* Munguía and the LAD team began organizing a last-ditch effort with a giant barbecue at Pablo's Grove in deep West Side territory.

Peña trounced Hart by nearly a 2,000 vote margin: 9,242 to 7,368. Of the thirty-eight election precincts, Peña won in nineteen of them, or half the total number; the real victory was in the actual votes, however. Peña carried some election precincts by huge margins, such as in voting precincts 12 through 18, which he won with margins of 321 to 47; 339 to 31; 445 to 49; 491 to 40; 610 to 167; 431 to 35; and 562 to 82, respectively. Lalo and Olga's work with absentee ballots yielded great results as well: 727 for Peña to 145 for Hart. Olga also worked most of Election Day at their voting location at the Collier School, Box 119. Peña carried that polling place 233 to 69. Albert Treviño also won handily his race to become the first Chicano justice of the peace in the county.[11] There were many celebrations that night. Olga was most happy for her husband now that he could do what he loved and get paid $9,600 a year while doing it. The Peña children now numbered six: he had Albert III, thirteen, and Belinda Irene, nine, from his previous marriage, and with Olga he had William Albert, seven, Sandra, six, Mary Magdalene, four, and Olga, one. The house at 1131 Gerald could barely contain them all, especially when the older children came for their regular visit.

The Bexar County Commissioners Court now had two new members-elect, Peña and Sam Jorrie in Precinct Three. At one of the election victory parties, Peña stated his love for politics: "It is my favorite pastime. I live and breathe it. And I think good politics is the thing that makes good government."[12] After the round of victory celebrations, Peña began to seek out County Judge Charles W. Anderson to inquire about county finances, issues, and his office space. It had been no secret that the county judge in recent years had been marginalized by two other commissioners on the court, A. J. Ploch and R. L. Reader. Now with Peña and Jorrie coming on board, Anderson could forge a new governing coalition for the county. Commissioner Ploch could be the odd man out. Peña, as commissioner-elect, also realized full well that he was the first Méxicano on the governing board. As commissioner for Precinct One, Peña's budget was the largest amount of money he had ever handled. The county budget in 1956 was just over $6 million, and for 1957, Peña's first year on the court, it was increased to $7,471,151.

The number of employees he could hire to work in his district began to sink in, and he started mentally making lists of campaign volunteers in need of jobs. Peña met the secretary in the office of Commissioner Dan Traugott and assured her he had no plans to replace her unless she did not want to work with him. Olga, Lalo, Rubén, and Lico, all inner-circle advisers, had urged him to get rid of her and hire his own secretary, but Albert refused. He reasoned with them that he knew little of the workings of the Commissioners Court and the courthouse and that she was necessary to educate him on who was who and did what.

In the month before the November election, Senator John Fitzgerald Kennedy came to Texas for a 24-hour, whirlwind campaign to help the Democratic ticket. The Massachusetts native had been instructed by the Texas Democratic Party leadership to campaign along the border to help bring out the Méxicano vote; they would take care of the rest. The Texas Democrats were leery of Kennedy's sudden interest in

Texas. The conservative wing in charge of the Texas Democratic Party understood how ambitious Kennedy was because he narrowly lost the vice-presidential slot to Estes Kefauver at the nominating convention. And Kennedy was a liberal, just like Adlai Stevenson, but younger.

Kennedy's entourage planned on stops at El Paso, Fort Stockton, Laredo, and San Antonio. Peña learned of this Kennedy trip from Henry B. González, and they began to figure ways to include themselves in the welcoming committee and subsequent campaign events. The best Peña could manage was to have Kennedy visit the Adlai headquarters in the West Side at 2024 S. Flores. Earlier in the campaign season, Kennedy had made an appearance in Austin, and as state senator nominee, Henry B. made his acquaintance when they both shared the speaker's podium.

From successful events in El Paso and Fort Stockton, Kennedy flew to Laredo and on to San Antonio by private plane, accompanied by Senators Lyndon Johnson and Price Daniel. Waiting at the San Antonio airport were Speaker of the House Sam Rayburn, the U.S. senators' wives, along with Albert A. Peña Jr. and Henry B. González. After the introductions and handshakes, with plenty of opportunities for the press to take photos of the youthful senator with the reddish brown hair, the motorcade headed for the Alamo, where Kennedy laid a wreath commemorating the dead. Texas Speaker of the House Jim Lindsey conducted the ceremony and introduced the young senator. Hundreds were on hand to get a glimpse of the young man. Hundreds more were on hand, organized by Peña and his group at the old Adlai headquarters. Peña had to rush away from the Alamo ceremony in order to be at the headquarters with Henry B. to greet and welcome Kennedy. The entourage arrived in a cream-colored Cadillac on time at 5:30 p.m. Peña and Henry B. both spoke, but it was Peña who predicted the West Side would go for the Democratic ticket 8 or 9 to 1. Kennedy was pleased with the red-and-white bunting covering the building and even more pleased with the larger turnout than expected. Olga's Spanish dress outfit that the young women had worn when they had the Stevenson rally at Milam Square caught his eye. She explained the significance of the costume to Kennedy and pointed out that she was Mexican American, not Spanish. As quickly as they arrived, they left, but Peña felt he had met the man he would campaign for in the next presidential election. He had connected and bonded with Kennedy.[13]

CHAPTER 7

The Commissioner Years, 1957–1960

EVEN BEFORE HE TOOK THE OATH OF OFFICE, PEÑA BUSIED HIMSELF WITH learning what a county commissioner was supposed to do. He read the Texas Constitution and found little information in Article IX on "Counties" and just a bit more under Article XVI. He read the law books and found more information on duties and responsibilities of the office. Peña was surprised to learn that only two years before, in 1954, the legislature and voters had extended the term for commissioner from two years to four, beginning in January 1955. He found out that his pay as commissioner also included an additional amount for an auto allowance. Peña traveled the extent of his district with the sitting commissioner, Traugott, to inspect firsthand the roads, bridges, culverts, and parks. Bexar County had an area of 1,247 square miles.

He was surprised to learn how many people he would employ. The more he learned about the job, the more he was eager to start and propose his own ideas for the county. Peña enrolled himself in classes at City Hall on municipal administration so as to be somewhat informed on the administrative workings of county government, particularly budgeting, personnel management, and police powers of the county. What he liked most about the Commissioners Court was its work schedule: only two regular meetings a month on the first and third Mondays. He could continue politicking every day and making a dollar as a lawyer when he could.

Peña shared all his newfound information about county government and business with his inner circle, and they began making recommendations as to who to hire, particularly in the Road and Bridge Department, which had lots of money and employees. The Commissioners Court, however, had pooled all the Road and Bridge Fund money into one account and had ended the practice of each commissioner managing their own funds.[1] Sturge Steinert needed a job, as did Albert Fuentes Jr.; both had worked hard to get Peña elected. Peña agreed to propose the idea of an administrative assistant for each commissioner at a good rate of pay. Peña's inner circle also recommended he keep Harold Mussey on as the top man in the Road and Bridge Department, because after Peña defeated him in the primary election, he endorsed Peña and had been out of a job since filing for the office. Peña agreed, but insisted that Fuentes become the number-two man in that department at a good salary to keep an eye on things. Fuentes was an extraordinary man full of ideas and keen insight, and most assertive. Peña relied on both his own instincts about people and those of Fuentes, which were often shared.

During these months of preparation for the job, Fuentes was at Peña's side constantly. Along with Lico López, a real estate broker, and a new recruit, Arnold Flores, they became known as Team Peña. Peña had several parks in his district, so he asked Johnny García, another valuable campaign worker, to head up the parks section of his overall employment group. Johnny García was instructed to make Mission County Park a showcase.

Marie Swartz had been a loyal worker in his campaign office, not missing a day or weekend even though she had a baby girl, Mimi. According to Marie, the first words out of Mimi were "Viva Peña."[2] Herschel "Herky" Bernard, a lawyer, recommended to Peña that he hire Marie rather than keep Commissioner Traugott's secretary. Peña valued Herky's advice and counsel and went with the recommendation.[3] As it turned out, the secretary voluntarily vacated the position, but not after thanking Commissioner-elect Peña for offering to keep her. She was grateful and most helpful to Marie in finding documents, letters, contracts, budgets, personnel rosters, policies, procedures, and courthouse gossip, all of which were invaluable to Peña.

On January 1, 1957, a Tuesday and New Year's Day, County Judge Charles W. Anderson administered the oath of office to Albert A. Peña Jr. and Sam Jorrie, the two new members of the Bexar County Commissioners Court. Present were well-wishers of both men, but mostly family members—because the room could only accommodate seventy-five persons, including the media. The newly installed commissioners were given an opportunity to make remarks. Peña thanked voters and his opponents, and pledged to be his own man, saying that he would not be dictated to by anyone, "including the opposition newspaper." The flashbulbs popped around the room. Everyone knew he was referring to the editorial endorsement of his opponents and the negative coverage of his comments, proposals, and ideas for county government, including the proposal to ask for an administrative assistant.[4]

The new pair of commissioners did their best to pose for photographs.[5] After the congratulations and hugs, Peña stepped into his precinct office and opened desk drawers. He sat in his chair. He made mental notes of what he needed and was going to bring to his new office. County Judge Anderson made the rounds of the offices and passed out the agenda for the next Commissioners Court meeting.

The next day was the meeting, and Jorrie and Peña could not decide which chair around the table to take, since none were labeled or had name placards in front of them. As soon as all the commissioners were seated and the county clerk representative was ready to take minutes of any votes or resolutions passed, the meeting was called to order by Judge Anderson. The media in days prior had made mention of two items Judge Anderson was proposing: fingerprinting all employees and requiring physical examination of all potential employees before hiring.

Peña locked horns with the county judge on both issues immediately and began arguing like a lawyer that fingerprinting was "a violation of civil liberties" issue and "a fundamental invasion of privacy." He had written out his argument.[6] When he had scouted the workings of the Commissioners Court the weeks prior to taking office and during the months after the runoff victory, Peña had noticed that a most effective argument on any measure was the question raised by a commissioner or the judge, "What will this cost the county?" Because the county budget was fixed and adopted prior to expenditures, there was little wiggle room—only if you took from one department or program and transferred money to another. Moreover the county should not go into debt based on future tax collections or state allocations or fees for services that might be generated. Noticing that two commissioners seemed to be supportive of the proposal, plus the judge, Peña asked what were the costs involved with the dual undertaking of physical examinations by a doctor and fingerprinting by the sheriff.

Peña won his first round of debate as commissioner. The Commissioners Court voted to study those proposals more in depth and look into costs. An unexpected benefit to this first fight with the county judge was that Anderson began a practice of appointing committees to look into issues, proposals, programs, expenditures, resolutions, and the like. The judge was going to run the county business by committee, it seemed. Committee work with other commissioners opened doors to more close contact and dealmaking among them; it also opened the door to stop progress and kill initiatives if any one member of the committee opposed the matter, or just simply did not make time to attend the meeting, thereby breaking quorum. More importantly, some committees were composed of one or two commissioners.

Clearly, from Peña's listening to the sentiments expressed and body language around the table, there were no votes among them for the judge's proposals on physicals and fingerprinting. The next day the media blasted Peña immediately on his opposition to fingerprinting employees, posing the questions of what he had to hide or who he wanted to hide.[7] Peña realized life on the Commissioners Court was life in a fishbowl; everything he did, said, voted on, opposed or proposed, ignored, missed, and was not prepared to discuss would be in print and on the radio or television the next day. Only in the Spanish-language media did he have an outlet to present his views and opinions to the public without question. The main reason was low budgets among this type of media that prevented any reporter from attending Commissioners Court meetings or visiting him for interviews. He learned to go to them with written comment before actually proposing an item or taking a position on an issue.

The English-language media with reporters and photographers were always around and attended meetings. These news sources began to vilify him with regularity, and specific reporters and columnists made him their number-one target for a story. As time went on while on the Commissioners Court, Peña also made friends among some reporters, such as Jim McCrory and Peter Panfeld of the "Don Politico" column in the *San Antonio Light*. Peña relished the give-and-take with the media; publicity was publicity, good or bad. Peña made for good copy and had a ready quote that made headlines.

Peña's next fight during the January meetings of the Commissioners Court was over a bill being introduced for legislative action in Austin, requiring runoff elections to be held as special elections. As it stood then, the person with the most votes was declared the winner in any special election. Peña was taught the implications for Mexícano candidates by local state representative Charles Lieck Jr. and Albert Fuentes, who first brought this issue to his attention. In any special election held by the city, school district, junior college, county, or special district, a Mexícano candidate could win a plurality of the vote, but it would be very difficult and expensive to win a majority of the vote in a runoff election. Astutely, Peña once again argued costs to the county, approximately $20,000 for each such election. This fiscal argument brought over to his side Commissioners Bennett and Ploch; they were fiscal conservatives to the core and believed county government should be limited. Peña's final argument was that votes for president and any other office in the November General Election should be won by plurality not majority. His arguments were persuasive, and the Commissioners Court voted to oppose the measure; Peña personally sent their unanimous resolution to the Bexar County legislative delegation, to the attention of state representative R. L. Strickland. In quick response to the media, Representative Strickland took a bite at Peña by mentioning that this commissioner had wanted to spend money on administrative assistants and not on a "Democratic election."[8]

Peña learned from opposing this issue to frame his arguments in coded language and appealing rhetoric, such as money costs and Founding Fathers' constitutional intent. On the practical and personal side, he had trouble with how quickly his opponents on an issue would rather end up on the winning side than be the odd man dissenting. To Peña the essence of leadership was sticking and speaking to principle even if it meant leading alone. On another issue he did lead alone in dissent. Bexar County had a position of official courthouse notary public. When prospective bidders for the post were rejected by the Commissioners Court over the fee structure for such services, County Judge Anderson and Commissioner Jorrie clashed bitterly. Peña opposed the county judge in wanting to eliminate the practice of courthouse employees charging fees for such services by designating a person as the official notary. Commissioner Jorrie also wanted an open market for such services. He adamantly opposed designating one person as official notary. Peña pointed out that when he was a beginning attorney, he paid his rent bill from notary fees. The commissioners went ahead with plans to name an official courthouse notary by a vote of 3 to 1, Peña's dissent. Judge Anderson declined to vote.[9]

Peña was not the one dominating the first business meetings of the Commissioners Court the first months of his term; he felt like a rookie, bided his time, listened more than talked, made mental notes of group dynamics, and picked his fights. Commissioner Jorrie, the other rookie, seemed not as concerned about his junior status. He and Ploch typically would begin the fray against the county judge on issues. Jorrie, for example, wanted to fire an appointed county employee, Dr. G. D. Boyd, the health officer. Boyd had been on the job for the previous nine years. Jorrie, in the company of Commissioner Ploch, had visited Dr. Boyd to ask that he resign. This chain of events prompted a heated exchange at the meeting between Ploch and Anderson when the county judge questioned why they would take it upon themselves to interfere with an employment and appointment matter without Commissioners Court consent. Rather than respond logically or calmly, Ploch began using offensive, vulgar language. Ploch questioned the judge's leadership on the court with the remark that Anderson should learn to crack the whip more and take prompt action on items when requested by the commissioners. Jorrie previously had made remarks in open session about complaints he received about the health officer. At that time the county health officer not only received a salary from the county but also could charge and keep fees for private work done on county time.

The various justices of the peace did the same thing when performing marriage ceremonies for a fee they kept while on county time and salary.

Peña, acting like a lawyer once again, intervened in the heat of the verbal barrage between Ploch and the judge; he suggested a way out for all the members. Why not ask for a legal opinion on the matter? He argued that the justices of the peace were elected officials with a constitutional and statutorily defined job description, whereas appointees were under the direction of the Commissioners Court. If the county had a policy prohibiting Dr. Boyd from having a private practice on the side while on county time, the matter was clear. If not, they should get an opinion from the county's elected legal advisor on the issues of firing an appointed employee and fee generation for private service.

Judge Anderson liked the rationale; besides he was responsible for appointing Dr. Boyd and keeping him on all these years. He and Dr. Boyd were friends. Commissioner Bennett also was impressed with Peña's legal arguments that protected the county from scandal and possible litigation for an illegal act. Bennett began to look at Peña with a different eye and to Peña for solid analysis on issues. He began to listen and vote with Peña on many items he initially felt inclined to oppose just because it was Peña bringing it up. It seemed at the point of Peña's intervention on the Boyd controversy that Ploch and Jorrie were going to lose on the issue.

The firing of Dr. Boyd did not take place; instead, the Commissioners Court asked the district attorney, as Peña had suggested, to look into the method by which any employee, particularly an appointed official, could be terminated. Having Peña on the Commissioners Court saved the day on this point for the presiding officer. Further, Judge Anderson asked Ploch to refrain from using such profane language during their meetings: "And let's not have any more profanity in the court. It's not proper." Ploch responded, "My daddy knocked me cold trying to keep me from cussing. It didn't do any good and I doubt if the judge does."[10]

Peña began understanding clearly the dynamics on the court. He was sizing up his peers. Ploch was a bigot and racist. Peña now knew that Ploch's private remarks to him during which he revealed his bigotry and racism easily became public speech when Ploch was agitated. He had a quick temper and was reckless. The problem was that Ploch was the senior member of the court with lots of experience and networks among county employees and the business community. Ploch also, despite his personal views about Mexicans and other commissioners, had good political skills. Ploch, for example, never forgot Peña's birthday and for years invited him to lunch on that day.

Bennett was hot and cold, a weathervane, Peña assumed. Sometimes Bennett was with him or the judge and at other times with Ploch. Bennett was someone to always be in touch with, particularly just before meetings, to try to get a reading. It seemed that Bennett would go with what he last heard from another commissioner. County Judge Anderson seemed to Peña to be affable, courteous, and reasonable, but also secure in that he was the highest-ranking member of the court, the presiding officer, and the only one with hands-on daily information on budget matters. Now in his third term in office, Anderson at times gave the impression that he knew best what course to take, and that upset the other commissioners, particularly Ploch. Jorrie was another personality entirely, wealthy and well-connected with the Country Club Set, as Peña called the North Side Anglos. To Peña it seemed Jorrie had sought election just to have something more exciting to do than oversee the family business of selling furniture. Unbeknownst to Jorrie, he had offended Peña in a deep way with an off-the-cuff remark about Peña's dad. Jorrie inquired if Peña Sr., the one now practicing law, had once been an elevator boy and salesman at one of those furniture stores that had layaway plans for the Mexicans of the West Side.

In matters affecting Precinct One, Peña had complete authority; that was his bailiwick and his own budget to spend. On all other county business he had one vote out of five. In the first few meetings he was not made the lone wolf on the court; he was treated as one of them. Peña was expecting to be the "Mexican" on the Commissioners Court, but soon found out his vote counted more to the others than did his background. He was not the tie-breaker on the court as he had assumed he would often be, watching Ploch with Bennett in tow opposing the judge. Instead he was needed by at least two others on any given issue. He was the dealmaker between all of them if he joined two others occasionally and the other two also occasionally.

If Peña wanted something placed on the agenda of Commissioners Court, he had three paths: propose it in open meeting and force the hand of the other four; ask the county judge to place it on the agenda; or lobby two other votes knowing that his measure would likely pass. He did learn quickly, however, that lobbying two others also invited them to lobby him; trading favors was expected and relied upon by the other members. He joined the judge's proposal, for example, to rent out the county election machines and not loan them to local jurisdictions. He had joined Jorrie and Ploch in finding out how to terminate an employee or an appointed official. And he got nailed in an open court meeting by the other commissioners and in the media, both English and Spanish, when one of Peña's appointees, Pete Gutiérrez, the cemetery sexton, was arrested at a night club, La Cita, for allowing a minor girl to consume alcohol. He had to fire him, a loyal campaign worker, within two weeks of his appointment.[11]

Peña settled into a routine as commissioner; nothing much happened on the court that he was passionate about. The job did not call for much creativity, and there were constraints on what county government could do for people; it was mostly limited to fixing roads, bridges, and culverts for large landowners. They and the business people wanted their property values and taxes to be kept low. The hospital district always wanted more money and less interference and oversight by the Commissioners Court. And his constituents would call with complaints about government services that Peña most often was powerless to do anything about, such as police brutality, city services, school problems, taxes, crime, job discrimination in the city and the military bases, and low wages in the Bexar County area. Peña and his staff spent as much time explaining what county government could do for them as they did making referrals and explaining why they could not help with non-county matters. Peña's office became the unofficial courthouse information and referral center.

Marie Swartz began to field calls from Spanish speakers from the first days in January 1957, but by the end of the first year, Peña's office was handling dozens of calls from Méxicanos wanting to speak to their *comisionado*, their man downtown. Marie had limited Spanish-speaking ability. The commissioners had already vetoed Peña's request for administrative assistants for each commissioner early in the first year of his term. He had raised the issue of the practice of using any county employee who spoke Spanish to translate and interpret for persons bold enough to visit the courthouse in search of assistance or to complain. He stressed how inadequate that was and also unfair to employees to have to do that additional work without compensation, particularly maintenance men who had to leave their job to attend to the translation, then return to finish their regular job when everyone else was already leaving for the day.

The commissioners likewise had ignored Peña's plea for more bilingual, bicultural county employees in every office, particularly the courts and jail. When Peña had asked for a bilingual, bicultural assistant secretary to handle everyone's calls in their offices, Ploch contemptuously had suggested to Peña privately that he "fire Swartz, the Jew woman," and hire himself "a Mexican." Peña, of course, knew he could do that, but he wanted to have the county hire more Méxicanos in all departments and offices. His efforts toward that goal were not working; he was being thwarted at every turn.

Peña did take Ploch's admonishment to heart; he instructed the road supervisor, Mussey, and his assistant Fuentes to begin hiring more Spanish-speaking and black workers who were qualified for the job and resided in his district. Peña hired the first African American employees in Bexar County government. His East Side political allies, G. J. Sutton, Claude Black, Archie Johnson, Valmo Ballinger, Eugene Coleman, and various other black preachers, were surprised at his actions. They had not asked him to hire blacks. The commissioner whose district included the black community of the East Side was Ploch. They knew he held blacks in blatant disregard and disdain. With these first hires, Peña made headlines in the black newspapers read in the East Side and was the topic of complimentary conversation in many beauty and barber shops. For blacks, Peña was also to become their man downtown. Many black leaders and regular folks recalled from the late 1940s reading Peña's writings in the *Snap News*, Eugene Coleman's newspaper with circulation in San Antonio's East Side. Peña's writing in the *Snap News* expressed his views on their issues of concern dating back to 1948 when he was studying at St. Mary's University.[12] Coleman particularly made a point to call Commissioner Peña when he heard of the first black hires at the county and said, "Brother Peña, you are alright, my man. When do you want to start writing for me again?"[13] Coleman explained shortly after Peña passed away that Peña's integrity, character, and reputation among blacks of the East Side were such that you did not have to call him on an issue or for support; he knew what to do and did it without prodding. Peña could be counted on always as a man of his word and unwavering in commitment to the cause of civil rights for blacks and browns.

Peña had received praise and acknowledgment from black leaders and the community before for his work in desegregating downtown businesses. Peña had worked with G. J. Sutton, a funeral business owner and state representative, against segregated lunch counters in downtown San Antonio. Several of the major department stores and drugstores, not to mention restaurants, had lunch counters, and these maintained a segregated business open only to whites. Peña had heard of these "Whites Only" places, but he himself had not frequented them or been denied service at downtown restaurants. He had heard about "No Mexicans Allowed" signs posted in restaurants in other cities, such as New Braunfels to the immediate north of San Antonio and over in Uvalde to the west, but he had not been to such places either.

One day while at the courthouse, G. J. Sutton told Peña about Joske's department store in downtown San Antonio, just a few blocks from the courthouse and very near the Alamo Mission, maintaining a segregated restaurant inside the store. This was a jolt from the past because both men had assumed those fights had ended earlier; maybe Joske's as the expensive department store had escaped scrutiny. Peña invited Sutton to go with him to eat lunch at Joske's Camellia Room. They went to Joske's and sat down. They waited and waited but did not receive service. They were not told they were being denied service, they were just ignored. Peña finally called the waitress to take their order. She reluctantly did so, and after more waiting finally served their meal. They ate without further incident, paid their bill, and left. After that day, blacks and other Méxicanos began to go eat at Joske's Camellia Room without incident.[14]

Peña improvised on the employment issue around his colleagues on the Commissioners Court. Peña first relied on volunteers to sit in his office and help Marie with calls from constituents. Lico López would often come in early mornings to handle calls. At other times his wife Olga, when she came to visit or to get money for family expenditures, would answer calls or follow up on pending calls. His *compadre* Rubén Munguía and friend Perry Salinas, both of whom regularly dropped in for coffee, also answered the office phone. Munguía was a real bear on the telephone; Peña loved to hear him tear into other county supervisors and even elected officials about this or that type of discrimination and problem.

Later, when the volume of telephone calls increased and the trail of personal visitors seeking an appointment with Peña began to be another full-time job, Peña asked both Johnny García, his man at Mission County Park, and Albert Fuentes, his other man at the Road and Bridge Department, to come in on different days to the courthouse office to help with constituent services *en Español*. Both men, being seasoned campaign workers and part of the inner circle of advisors to Peña, went beyond the usual efforts on behalf of any caller. García and Fuentes would take the information; ferret out persons regardless of where they were located within government, county or otherwise, and who were able to solve the problem; and make direct contact by phone in person. Every caller's or visitor's personal data and nature of the request would be entered into an index file. When Peña handled the matter personally, he recorded the same type of information on tiny notepads he kept in his shirt pocket. Peña's handwriting was hard to decipher for Marie, Lico, Albert, Olga, and Johnny, but they kept weekly track of what he was entering on those little notepads. Albert did not like them asking him for his notepad. But he often forgot appointments he had granted, calls he promised to return, and money he had collected or was to collect as either a campaign contribution or legal fee.[15] Peña did practice law throughout his sixteen years on the Commissioners Court, but less so in the later years, mostly referring cases to other attorneys. Peña's favorite and personal attorney was Herschel "Herky" Bernard. Herky recalled that Peña "had no real understanding of money; doesn't know how to get it; doesn't know what to do with it other than spend it."[16]

Peña instructed García and Fuentes to dress in business attire, a suit with tie, when going in person representing his office. Other commissioners, when they came into their offices, began to notice these visits by county employees in suits. They were accustomed to seeing their employees in overalls, jeans, and khaki pants with work shirts, not wearing coats and ties with white shirts. The county judge who was in the office daily was more direct with Peña. He wanted to know the occasion for which these men were dressed in business attire. Peña was ever ready with answers. He would recite the litany of votes recorded at each Commissioners meeting and name the numerous times he had asked others for help to serve his constituents and provide county services. "Helping people is our job," he repeatedly said.

Peña's approach to problem-solving by sending his representatives personally to City Hall, school district offices, state agencies, other county offices, and even other elected officials—although as a matter of respect and courtesy to that person he often made those personal visits—began to have an unexpected result. Peña's representatives began noticing and reporting to him that increasingly more and more offices had Spanish-speaking employees. According to Romulo "Chacho" Munguía Jr., Rubén's younger brother, Peña relished this and smiled when he heard the news. He would ask of the person bringing the news of the new hire, "Did you get their name and direct phone number?"[17] Peña was always looking for new voters.

By the end of his first two years on the Commissioners Court and two budgets later, Peña realized that the other elected officials and department heads, while they were reluctant to let Anglo employees go in favor of hiring Spanish-speaking employees or blacks, were more concerned about not getting the budget allocation they sought from the Commissioners Court, and Peña was one of the essential three votes necessary for getting their money. Peña was not talking their language but was voting their interests.

Driver's license suspensions and driving-while-drunk cases involving arrests by county constables or the Sheriff's Office were brought to Peña's attention by those charged. These types of requests for help had a dual payoff for Peña. In a criminal matter, he could refer these court cases or handle them if the arresting officer was someone not associated with the county. With a county issue, he could inquire as to the Spanish-speaking ability of the persons being complained about, the police conduct during the arrest, whether this case was one of selective enforcement; he could also request a report on the larger set of statistics for budget purposes, for example.

The parks and the personnel he employed with Road and Bridge plus Lateral Road funds were the most attractive to Peña and where he learned to be creative. He began to use the parks for lawful activities: dances, gatherings, rallies, fiestas, special events, and meeting places with his employees. Poor people, mostly his constituents, did not have funds to rent a hall or a venue to host a reception, dance, fiesta, and the like, but he had three major parks and a few smaller locations available for their use, free of charge at his discretion. And if he was hosting an event as commissioner at one of these parks, it was free of charge to him. When the first evidently political events were held at his parks, the commissioners balked, but Peña showed them the reservation book indicating a first-come, first-served policy and a bipartisan allocation of use by all kinds of groups. It was not his fault that some groups asked while others did not; besides, in his view, these were the people's parks to use for whatever legal purpose they wanted. And, he controlled events at his parks in Precinct One just like the other commissioners controlled their parks as they saw fit.

It became clear to Peña and his group that he had to educate the public about the workings of county government and the myriad issues impacting people lives. He had to start writing again and getting back on the radio and television, and not just react, answer allegations, or provide counter-opinions. His advocacy had to take a constructive and instructive approach; he had to be proactive. Back when KCOR, the first Spanish-language radio station, started broadcasting and KWEX, the first Spanish-language television station, started on the air, Peña took advantage of both to make speeches and comments, state opinions, and get free airtime for events and meetings. He had acquired the habit of writing opinion editorials and commentary for both Spanish and English newspapers. His major outlets in English had been the labor union newsletters and black press. In Spanish, *La Prensa* carried his columns from time to time.

Shortly after he joined the Commissioners Court in 1957, Peña once again began an all-out media campaign that was to continue until months before his death in 2006. For the next half-century Peña wrote and spoke at every opportunity, issued press releases with frequency, gave interviews, and made headlines. He had published literally hundreds of opinion pieces and debated others on radio, television, and in newspapers on pressing issues or his activities and views. Peña was a pioneer among those seeking another tool and new technology for mass persuasion. He was the first in Bexar County, perhaps in Texas, to influence public opinion among Méxicanos via the mass media.

As a political activist he found outlets for his views and commentary where he could. As an elected official the task of finding outlets became easier. When he became a county commissioner he started two regular opinion articles made available to any media outlet: "As I See It" and "County Comments." Oftentimes he supplemented his regular opinion writings with letters to the editor.[18] The writing of articles and letters also began to take time from Peña's many other duties and responsibilities, not to mention his political organizing. The writing had a political payoff; both supporters and opponents would call him about the articles. Those that called in support or agreement would be entered into the now famous, among his inner circle, index file that Olga kept handy.

In 1957 several nonpartisan elections had been held by other jurisdictions within Bexar County. It was time now, as 1958 would bring the midterm election for the county. Ploch, Bennett, and the county judge would have to run for reelection, as well as many other officials and all members of both the state and federal House of Representatives. The Democrats of Texas (DOT), the liberal Democrats, had first organized in 1952 across the state and reached a measure of organizational success by 1956 with Ralph W. Yarborough as their titular head. Peña's LAD had been an integral part of this statewide coalition of the left-of-center Democrats. They were looking for candidates to field a full slate from top to bottom of the ballot. But Peña was faced with a tough decision involving his peers on the Commissioners Court; should he recruit and help candidates against them or not? Adela Navarro was asking for support should she file for commissioner in Precinct Two against Bennett. They could return the favor to him in the next election. What about other county officeholders? They could also return the favor in the next election. State representative Charlie Leick Jr. was rumored to be running for the district attorney slot. Herschel Bernard assured Peña that this developing race was more than rumor; Charlie was going to file very soon. What about positions subject to election within his own district, such as justice of the peace and constables? Would he create ill will among these elected officials if he endorsed or helped candidates in those races, and actually foster ambitions to run against him down the road? These are the questions a political boss grapples with constantly, and Peña was evolving into that type of politico. To be sure, there were many Peña detractors who already saw him in that role.

Peña decided after long discussions with Rubén Munguía, Herky Bernard, Olga, Lalo Solis, Albert Fuentes, Lico López, Kathleen Voigt (the DOT leader), Henry Muñoz, and Johnny García that it was best for him to stay out of recruiting, helping, and endorsing Bexar County candidates. Peña's group figured they were the grassroots organization and as such, when the time came, they would get the votes out for whomever they decided privately to support or oppose. In a speech to a DOT gathering, he urged that organization to endorse the real "Democrat in the race"—that it was imperative to endorse candidates in the primaries. He asked the group to start working toward an uninstructed delegation to the National Convention of the Democratic Party in 1960. In a most eloquent plea for party unity he said,

> We must remain unified to remain strong. We cannot go kiting off in several directions with notions about Westside Democrats, Eastside Democrats, Northside Democrats or Balcones Heights Democrats. We must not set up satellite organizations revolving around the Smith, Jones, Brown or Rodríguez Democrats. There should be no place in our party for jealousies, or personal power machines, but unless we are alert this is precisely what will happen.[19]

Peña's group set two priorities and began work to be selected as delegates at Democratic Party conventions and to increase Mexicano voter participation. The state Democratic Party convention was going to be held in San Antonio in 1958. Senate Majority Leader Lyndon Johnson, Senator Ralph Yarborough, Speaker of the House Sam Rayburn, and many other prominent elected officials representing Texas would be coming to town. Peña wanted to make sure he was on the welcoming committee as cohost with the city to greet and rub elbows with these important people.

The first order of business for Peña's group in 1958 was to beat the bushes in search of Méxicanos eligible to pay their poll tax. During off years, as some people called midterm elections, the number of people paying their poll tax dropped dramatically from the presidential year. This was an off year and neither Peña nor Henry B. González would be on the ballot. Méxicanos needed a reason to pay the poll tax, otherwise it was another primary election in which they would read an Anglo name after another Anglo name on the ballot and vote for or against them as instructed by the Peña group. The Peña group volunteers would inform the Méxicano voters which Anglos were their liberal friends and which were not. To Méxicano voters they still were all Anglos, but they did vote for Peña's choices.

Olga's index file was the second order of business. The Peña group made contact with all whom Peña had helped as commissioner with one thing or another, even use of the parks and places, and those he had consulted with as lawyer. These names were the first ones approached with a personal appeal from Peña via his representative that he needed their help with the upcoming election. Could Peña count on their vote? Usually at that point the person would confess to not being registered to vote for failure to pay the poll tax or otherwise being ineligible. Peña's campaign volunteers would press for permission to place a yard sign, ask for a contribution of food or money or use of their car, and willingness to host a backyard rally so Peña could come speak to the person's neighbors. Arnold Flores recalls that he began working with Peña more closely, passing out flyers, taking necessary things to backyard rallies, and helping to drive the commissioner around the streets of San Antonio.[20] The backyard gatherings proved immensely valuable to Peña's grassroots organization because the person was perceived as Peña's contact by the neighbors, with a third layer of volunteers created just below those working on the campaign.

Fundraising was always a problem for Peña; he hated asking for money. His father had criticized him for that shortcoming as a lawyer. Peña, the lawyer, had trouble collecting legal fees from clients; he would rather do it free or for a token payment than ask and hound the client for full payment. Peña found relief with help from those in his inner circle, like Herky, Henry "The Fox" Muñoz, and Albert Fuentes, who seemed to relish the idea of raising hundreds of dollars in a matter of hours on the telephone if they said the magic words "Commissioner Peña would like to know if you can contribute money for this upcoming election?" All Peña had to do was go collect the money in person and sometimes take a photograph with the donor. Peña liked to come home with pockets full of cash and checks for use in the various campaigns.

In 1957, Peña worked with Senator Lyndon B. Johnson's office asking for help in getting a radio broadcast license from the Federal Communications Commission for Manuel Leal. Toward the end of the year, Senator Johnson's office called Commissioner Peña to inform him that Mr. Leal would be receiving his license for a radio station at the beginning of the year. The news formally came to Mr. Leal as predicted and he immediately set out to start operations. Commissioner Peña was among the first to address listeners of Radio KEXX on February 8, 1958. Mr. Leal invited Commissioner Peña to deliver a weekly commentary on county government to educate the public as a public service. Peña gladly accepted the offer. Speaking on the air from written comments in both English and Spanish, he sprinkled his presentation with ad lib comments. He discussed the importance of appointments by the county commissioners to the Bexar County Hospital Board. Peña said in part, "The Commissioners Court appoints the Members of the Hospital board and therefore I think it is incumbent upon the Court to see to it that the board is representative of all the people of Bexar County—all sections of this community. The Hospital Board at present is only representative of one section of town." He promised in his broadcast to ask the Commissioners Court to add staff to the Children's Service Bureau, a private social agency, but under the supervision of the county's juvenile department. He also promoted an upcoming American G.I. Forum dance and dinner and gave a clue as to his next topic on the air the following week, "Status of the Democratic Party in Texas." He concluded with commentary in Spanish, and somewhat translated what he had said into English.[21]

In the following months Peña would take to the air in Spanish, and at times in English, and provide his own translation to explain the workings of county government and his office, plus commentary on issues. During the March 8, 1958, broadcast he congratulated the public for the rise in poll-tax payments among Mexicans. He made reference to a letter he had received that asked him if he wanted more Mexicans registered to vote to increase the numbers and try to control their vote. Peña argued that he did not see more Mexicano poll-tax payments as a bad result. He explained how difficult it was for any person to control votes with the use of voting machines in private booths. The ballot remained a secret and private matter. He concluded this broadcast with the statement "I sincerely believe we have eliminated the two-legged coyote's role in politics that would sell his vote and dignity for a couple of dollars."[22]

Recognizing the power of radio, Peña also heeded his sister's request for help in getting a broadcast license for her and her husband, Manuel Davila, which he later did. That AM station became known by the call letters KEDA and also "Radio Jalapeño," with his nephew Richard "Guero Polkas" Davila as the most popular disc jockey. Peña had yet another radio outlet for his announcements and commentaries almost at will at KEDA.[23]

The Kamikaze: Henry B. González's First Statewide Race

Henry B. González, since his election to the State Senate, had been making fewer and fewer ethnic appeals for Mexicano group solidarity and cohesion over the radio and television. When he did, it was only on the Spanish-language stations and sometimes in newspapers. Henry B. was working on a new image with cross-cultural appeal. He was also seen less and less by Peña's group at their meetings and gatherings the year before when they were making early plans for the spring primary election campaign season. The last time Henry B. invited Peña to an event was to attend the upcoming August 1958 American G.I. Forum convention in New Mexico, where González was to be keynote speaker. Peña declined because he had promised Olga and the children a vacation to the beach in Corpus Christi when they were out of school, which was right after the primary election.

Lalo Solis, a Peña insider, also began to be noticeably absent and missing during crucial times in 1957 as they began to prepare for the primary election in 1958. It was soon reported to Peña that Solis was now working full-time for pay building a grassroots organization of supporters for Henry B. and replicating for him what Olga had done for Albert. Solis was calling on many of Olga's contacts asking for their help on behalf of Henry B., not anyone else. The key question was why Henry was doing this when he was not running for office. Solis had either copied many of the entries on the index cards or had a very good memory and recall. The Peña group, however, did not lose many volunteers to Lalo Solis. Consequently the group thought it best not to make any mention of his defection or of the fact that he was calling on their volunteers. The Peña group just took notice and got ready for a grassroots showdown sometime in the years to come. Henry B. was now in competition with Peña over the building and maintaining of a grassroots organization in San Antonio's West Side.

The political bombshell hit the morning newspapers in early spring 1958 and made top story on all radio stations, English and Spanish. Henry B. González was running for governor of Texas, not reelection to the State Senate. Peña was furious. What was Henry B. thinking? Getting lucky in carrying Bexar County when he sought election as state senator was one thing, but running for governor? Running a campaign statewide? These were the types of comments and questions on everyone's lips, including Peña's. He could not confirm this directly with Henry B.; rather it was Lalo Solis who told him Henry was making the race. Supposedly, Henry B. had made up his mind when he learned that Price Daniel was going to run for reelection without serious opposition. Back in 1952, the Democrats had Allan

Shivers running for governor and the Republicans had also nominated him as their candidate for governor; cross-filing was permitted then.

Republicans had begun to contest statewide elections, particularly the governorship, in the 1950s.[24] In 1958 former governor "Pappy" W. Lee O'Daniel was trying to make a comeback and play on the surname; he was the most serious contender against the incumbent governor Price Daniel. After checking with informed sources, Peña learned that Henry B. had not confided to anyone his plan to run for governor. It was a spur-of-the-moment whim—a costly one to Méxicanos, blacks, and liberals in terms of a lost State Senate seat if he had to resign to run for governor. Now, Henry B.'s statewide campaign was going to drain money resources in San Antonio and Bexar County that under other circumstances would go to Peña's group. The Democrats of Texas (DOT), the liberals and labor, similarly were furious that Henry B. would make the race and force their hand. More importantly, DOT had spent their last dime on Ralph Yarborough's campaign for the U.S. Senate seat just months before in a special election. If Yarborough, a most popular candidate, had not been able to beat the conservative Democrats, including Price Daniel in 1956, how could Henry B. González be the winner in this race for governor?

Henry B. wasted no time in hitting the campaign trail; he was not to be bothered or deterred by those opposed to him being in the race. He drove around the state in his station wagon speaking before any group at any time asking for their votes. His campaign did attract Anglo liberals and labor groups in the larger cities; some volunteered to help. In Waco he met and recruited a young coed volunteer, Gail Beagle, who became dedicated to Henry B. her entire life. She eventually became his main staff person until the last four years of his political career in Washington, DC.[25] Despite the low numbers of registered Mexícano voters in the state, shortage of volunteers, and limited campaign budget of $17,000, Henry did manage to come in second to Price Daniel with a respectable 246,969 votes. Daniel, however, trounced all three challengers, Henry B., Joe E. Irwin, and W. Lee O'Daniel, with 799,107 votes of 1,317,492 total votes cast in the race—more than enough to win without a runoff election. And, Henry B. returned to the Texas Senate not having had to resign to run for governor.

The 1958 primary election cycle came and went, with some but not many changes among the politicians holding office, locally or statewide. Most Bexar County incumbents were reelected during the primary election, but not all. Commissioner Bennett had been defeated by Ollie Wurzbach. Adela Navarro had filed in that race but lost in the primary. She helped Wurzbach in the runoff election. Charlie J. Lieck Jr. was going to be the new district attorney, and Clinton Uhr was elected as treasurer for Bexar County. The November General Election was sure to be a formality. Peña's group began to work on the party machinery by attending the precinct conventions and other meetings culminating in the state convention, where Peña and Olga met many other statewide activists, particularly labor and liberal contacts and some Méxicanos from the border counties.

Olga again began another index file on these contacts, and she learned that in Houston there was a Democratic Women's Club. Upon investigation, she found out that Joyce Peters and Kathleen Voigt were organizing a similar group for Bexar County. Olga was among the first to join. Olga was clearly the organizer while Peña often talked about organizing. Herky Bernard said of Peña, "He was not a good organizer, too lazy. He was good to set the tempo; set the goal for other people. He was a good speaker and writer. His content was good. Peña was forceful, good voice, nervous at it but good, good presence."[26]

In Bexar County, as across the state, liberals were under siege by the conservative wing of the Democratic Party. It was time for liberals, blacks, Méxicanos, labor, and the few unaligned moderates to unite and take control, from the bottom all the way up to the Capitol. Ralph Yarborough was now in the U.S. Senate. Some other liberals had won seats in the legislature. And, of course, Peña had to begin to get ready for his reelection campaign.

Back at the regular meetings of the Commissioners Court it was business as usual. Not many issues were being presented—usually routine approval of payments for services and goods, and reports from agencies and the hospital district. The big events at Commissioners Court each year, Peña learned, were the budget, the setting of property valuations and tax rates, appointing administrators, and appointing election officials for the General Election; the political parties took care of the personnel for the primary election and runoffs, if necessary. The stream of calls and visitors had increased at Peña's office, both as commissioner and lawyer. He had moved out of his office with his father and opened his own office at the Tower Life Building with another group of lawyers, Johnny Alaniz and Matt García. But Peña seldom went to his law office; his love still was politics.

Peña's former opponent for county commissioner, and now his Road and Bridge man, Harold Mussey, had retired. Mussey had been the Road and Bridge man in charge for the previous commissioner for ten years. Rather than hire another person, Peña reorganized the entire department. Earlier the Commissioners Court had cut employees in the Road and Bridge Department to twenty-five per precinct, based on county road engineer Thomas Coghill's recommendation. Peña had lost seventeen men.[27] Peña made Fuentes the head with Johnny García as his assistant and added Henry Muñoz; all were his main political operatives. The department could and did run very well without the heads. Now with Harold Mussey gone, the entire department could work on projects for the people or for politics without regard to what their immediate "boss" would say. And Fuentes, García, and Muñoz could devote more time to the building of a West Side grassroots organization and spread into the South and East Sides of the county. Few complaints were ever heard from constituents about the state of the parks and public places. Peña ensured that all parks were clean, had running water, operating flush toilets, lights, and security. The people loved their parks. Peña often would tour these parks with Olga and the kids and see them overflowing with people at play and picnicking.

At one time Peña was approached by the San Antonio Charro Association about the building of a bullring and stock pens at a corner of Mission County Park off White Avenue and connecting it by a cobblestone pathway with the San José Mission directly behind on Mission Drive. Peña's support for this idea was short-lived; he did not have the votes. The other commissioners and county judge were leaning the other way to slash park funds and merge all park operations into one department. Commissioner Jorrie had cut his park operations and costs to a bare minimum of $1,720 a month. Peña, fortunately, was not the highest spender on parks, with a monthly expense of $2,080; Commissioner Bennett was the top spender, at $2,608 a month, and he wanted more money.[28]

A *Señorita* for a Lake and the People

On some evenings Peña and his drinking associates, newly elected state representative Jake Johnson, Rubén Munguía, and G. J. Sutton, at times, would tour the same parks, places, and rural county roads. The music, dancing, parties, and family outings were a joy to Peña and his friends. People had not had this kind of access or attention to detail of services, now including flush toilets and fresh water, from prior commissioners. Peña was the man who made this possible, and they loved him for it.

On one drinking night occasion, Peña and Jake Johnson came across an erected barricade on the county road about fifteen miles from downtown San Antonio leading to East Lake. They both knew this was a public road still in Bexar County, and they also knew Victor Braunig was the head of the Metropolitan Water Board that supplied that area of Peña's district with water as well as the city of San Antonio.[29] Yet, when they got out of the car to inspect the lock and gate, they heard music and saw lights coming from a rather large cabin at the water's edge in the distance. Someone was having a party by the lake and they had not been invited. Peña was incensed by the fact that he did not know anything about this lake or cabin or locked gate on a county road. He planned to get Fuentes on this first thing the next morning. And he did. Fuentes reported it was a county road and that no permission had ever been granted to barricade it. Furthermore, he told Peña it seemed it was Braunig's doing to deny public access to this lake or use of the cabin, but he could not get any straight answers from staff or employees of the Metro Water Board. Upon further investigation, Peña's folks found out that old man Braunig used the cabin and lake as his private property for parties and poker games during the time the manmade reservoir was being constructed and scheduled to be finished by 1962. It was public property owned by the Metropolitan Water Board, not Braunig. The only aspect of the property belonging to him was that the board had named the manmade lake after Braunig, the board chairman.

Johnson and Peña, on another drinking night, decided to break the lock and go see the lakeside cabin and its amenities up close. Herschel Bernard recalls Peña telling him the same story, but that they had gained access by cutting the fence. Shortly after that night, Peña received a call from old man Braunig wanting the commissioner to go see him. Peña called Johnson to find out if he knew what the summons was about. Johnson did not. Peña asked Fuentes if he had been so obvious in his questioning of staff and employees and searching for records that Braunig learned he was behind the investigation. He assured Peña that he had been most discreet and relied on third parties to gather information; nothing was direct. Not knowing what it was exactly about, but that it was highly coincidental with their break-in, Peña made the call for an appointment but was told to come right over. He did and was admitted to an inner lobby leading to the chairman's office. He was nervous about the meeting. When Peña got nervous his hands would sweat, and he developed the habit of rubbing both his palms simultaneously on his coat at waist level as if he were smoothing out fabric wrinkles.

Old man Braunig welcomed Peña into his office with a firm handshake and told him what a fine job he was doing as commissioner. Without looking in Peña's direction, he offered him a drink, which Peña declined, but accepted the compliment without saying much; he wanted to get to the real purpose of the meeting. He tried to keep direct eye contact with Braunig. Peña felt that while the old man was talking, he was really sizing up Peña with occasional glances in his direction. Braunig was inspecting Peña's suit, his shined shoes, his tie, his hands, and studying his face when he did focus on him straight on. Braunig also complimented Peña on his interest in, and the allocation of money and personnel for, fixing the parks and places in Precinct One. Again Peña accepted the compliment without saying much; Braunig was getting closer to the lake in his district. Braunig eventually got to the point as Peña listened intently and sat as relaxed as he could fake it under the circumstances. Braunig told Peña that he was not going to press charges against him and his accomplice for trespassing on private property, his. The old man was staring down Peña, eye to eye. Additionally, he said without breaking eye contact or blinking that he was shocked that two public officials would do such a thing when a simple telephone call to him would have gotten them an invitation. "What were you thinking?" Peña recalled Braunig asking him. Peña was flabbergasted that Braunig knew it was Jake and him out there that night. How could he know?

Before Peña could answer Braunig's question, much less rebut the assertion that Braunig Lake was private property and not public, Braunig disarmed Peña. Braunig asked, as he broke into his first smile, if the commissioner knew this very good-looking "*señorita*" working in some department in the courthouse. Peña was puzzled and dumbfounded. Braunig continued nonstop: "If Peña would arrange a meeting with the '*señorita*' Braunig would open the gate and allow public access to the lake and Peña's crews could help with maintaining the grounds." The cabin use would be for later discussion.[30] Peña heard the offer loud and clear and stood straight up as if reporting for duty while still in the Navy. "Yes sir, Mr. Braunig, that is something I can do for you. The people will love you for that. We will work out the details. You know her name?" Peña asked. Braunig did not, but described where she worked by floor of the courthouse and her general looks and physical attributes. As both men smiled at each other, they shook hands on the deal and then walked toward the door. Peña wanted to leave immediately and go tell Jake the story. But Braunig had one last comment: "You know, times are changing and people will say you made me do this Commissioner, but we both know different. And about that *señorita*, call me as soon as you can, tomorrow or later today. I sure want to meet her." Peña did find the beautiful *señorita* as described, told her about Mr. Braunig's interest in meeting her, and begged her to do it. She agreed.[31] Peña had another feather in his cap; the public could use the East Lake, later to be known as Braunig Lake.

Having been on the Commissioners Court for nearly two years, Peña now had more information about the business of appointments to various county-dependent entities such as the pauper's cemetery, juvenile home, hospital district, historical commission, health officer, and welfare assistance. He had seen the nominations pass his desk, and he voted on them without much discussion. The appointments seemed to be a done deal even before the meetings. When he asked about specific ones, such as the hospital district, Peña was told the appointments were on a rotating schedule and his turn for that one would come in due time. On other occasions, he was told by the county judge or another commissioner that Peña had gotten this one and that one, and they had this other one and that one, suggesting that some commissioners and maybe even the judge had held a prior meeting to work out the division of appointments. Peña did not broach the subject directly; he just took notes and bided his time. And when the time came, he pulled out the records now maintained by Janice McClure, his new secretary. McClure was married to an activist plumber in the union local, Hank Brown. Before Peña offered his own nomination on any given appointment coming up, Janice McClure would research records and provide him with copies of the official minutes of the Commissioners Court that noted who had made which appointment and when. By this intelligence-gathering maneuver, Peña would be knowledgeable as to when his turn for making appointments came up.

Working the Media

Over the air every Saturday morning at 11:30 a.m. on his radio broadcast, Peña would inform the public in both languages on his choice of issues and accomplishments. His weekly program on KEXX, 1250 AM on the dial, was called *The Commissioner in a Glass House*. He encouraged listeners to write in with questions and comments, which he often used to discuss an issue such as distribution of food commodities for the needy. He invited listeners to come see him and attend the public meetings held at the courthouse. The Commissioners Court had begun to meet three times a week—Monday, Wednesday, and Friday at 9:30 a.m.—to manage county business. Because of his efforts, the city and county began to offer distribution of foodstuffs from one location on Alamo Street just south of the courthouse; he informed the public because of a letter he had received about this service.[32] He spoke in favor of voting for passage of the bond issue to build better jail facilities and renovate other county buildings. With regular frequency, he encouraged voters to attend precinct conventions and become delegates during Primary Election Day, and gave details of political party governance as the September 9, 1958, state Democratic convention neared. "The decisions made at this convention will have great impact in 1960, a presidential year. Texas, I believe, is in a keystone position to decide the Democratic Presidential nominees and the complexion of the party platform in 1960. *Quien sabe?* We will see," he read over the air.[33] Proudly on one occasion he claimed credit for the establishment of an information booth on the first floor of the courthouse with Mrs. Mary Batista, a bilingual person. She would direct people to the right office to handle their problem or concern. During that broadcast he also read a statement from newly elected District Attorney Lieck thanking the voters for their support. Peña had invited Lieck to the program, but he was unable to make the Saturday time slot. Peña promised that he and Lieck as district attorney would rid the courthouse of "coyotes," those who approached persons in search of assistance for one thing or another at the courthouse with offers to help for a fee. Some of these "coyotes" were courthouse employees preying on the poor and illiterate persons desperate for help. Peña asked listeners to report such incidents to his office.[34]

In addition to his columns in newspapers and radio broadcasts, Peña was approached by the *Weekly Shopper*, a consumer-oriented newspaper with circulation citywide and in surrounding communities in Bexar County to publish yet another column in that paper. In his first efforts, Peña tried to be original in each written piece for each different newspaper and for the radio broadcast—not write or say the same thing in each venue. He soon learned that he could not keep writing original articles for each source. He also adamantly refused help from ghostwriters. He wanted to write his own commentaries in his own handwriting to express his views. He did accept help in typing his many scribbles, a habit he developed to write down ideas regardless of where he was or what he was doing, and format it into readable text. And, while each column and broadcast had original material, Peña learned to cross-fertilize his writings with reference to his radio program, and use the radio to refer to his written columns. He did at times repeat information in both venues, either deliberately to stress its importance or because of the incredible demand for production for the media on top of all other commitments and deadlines he had to observe.

In the *Weekly Shopper* column, "Com. Peña's Weekly Report," Peña was patently partisan, as he was in his other written columns and on the radio. The debut column in the *Weekly Shopper* on September 7 was basically a repeat of his radio broadcast of August 29 explaining the purpose of his column: the workings of the Commissioners Court, results of the runoff elections, and a new item, a call for citizens' awareness of a possible upcoming city charter review and election. In the subsequent column for this newspaper, he acknowledged not being able to make deadline and keep his promise to report on the outcomes from the State Democratic Party Convention; instead he attacked "coyotes."

He classified coyotes into two categories: political and courthouse ones, and wrote:

> The "political coyote" is the political hack who for the proverbial thirty silver pieces will support any candidate, regardless of the principle involved. If he is a speaker of sorts, he is paid to vilify and to destroy with deliberate falsifications. I resent them. And the court house coyote, worst of the breed because he preys for the most part on the innocent and/or illiterate is a self-styled know-it-all, who for a small fee will supply you with information, a "good" lawyer or notary public. He's a "Fixer" with lots of "pull" in the right places. Beware of these Leeches. For your convenience, the Commissioner's Court provides all citizens with an information booth, a legal aid clinic for the indigent, and a

directory of lawyers if you are seeking competent legal aid. Help me rid the courthouse of this scourge by reporting these people to me.[35]

In subsequent columns to finish out the year, Peña began to push for persons to pay their poll tax early. He wrote in the *San Antonio Weekly Times* his "As I See It" column of October 9, 1958: "On October 1, I joined with other LULACS and paid my poll tax on the very first day of poll tax paying time. As I said, you can pay your poll tax until January 31, but I urge you not to wait until the last minute and have to stand in line for hours and hours." And in the "As I See It" column of October 30, on the eve of the November 4th General Election of 1958, he railed against Richard Nixon because "he classified all Democrats as radicals and a threat to the nation." Peña also used this column to invite all to Mission County Park the following "Sunday, November 2, when the Bexar County Democrats will sponsor a get-out-the-vote picnic and rally . . . beginning at 1 p.m. . . . Henry B. González will be the main speaker. All Democrats and their families are invited."

The columns he wrote after the election were on the need for more low-income housing. He blamed the City Council and Housing Authority for not meeting this need: "In other words, the deplorable fact is that half of the low-income families in San Antonio desire decent housing [and] are doing without." By late 1958 San Antonio was operating "4,699 dwelling units in 12 projects. We have under construction 455 dwelling units, or a total on completion of 5,154 units. Compare this figure with 41,000 substandard dwelling units in our city according to the 1950 census plus the fact that *34% of our CITIZENS had incomes under $2,000 per year, again according to the 1950 census.*"[36]

Peña had been able to push for and obtain Commissioners Court approval for an indigent defender program, and in cooperation with the county affiliate of the State Bar of Texas, the professional and self-policing organization for lawyers, a referral program of attorneys. With the aid of his many information outlets in the media, he was the unofficial courthouse public relations man, and also becoming the political drum major for the liberal wing of the Democratic Party in Bexar County politics.

The Reelection Campaign

Beginning on October 1, 1959, the Peña reelection team went into full swing. October 1 was the first day in the period allowed for voter registration in Texas, which ended on January 3 of the following year.[37] In order to excite potential voters, Peña let it be known early that he was seeking reelection. The campaign goal was to have

Méxicanos pay their poll tax; the radio spots on Spanish-language radio began to be aired. Peña himself accepted and even solicited invitations to radio and television programs so he could make voter-registration appeals. Henry B. was also going to have to announce his intentions for reelection, and also get on the air to whip up the Méxicanos into an enthusiastic frenzy for the primary election.

Toward the end of 1959, Robert F. Kennedy came to Austin "feeling out" who would be supportive of his brother's presidential aspirations. Most of the people he met with discouraged him, including state senator Henry B. González. Henry B. flatly told him that Lyndon Baines Johnson's name as favorite son was going to be placed in nomination, but that if Kennedy got the nomination, he would campaign for him vigorously. Moreover, the state Democrats employed the unit rule, which meant that any votes in opposition to Lyndon's nomination would be added to the winning side and voted as one unit of votes. The Southerners had used this tactic for years to repress minority votes and used the bloc vote of a unit rule to increase the actual number of votes the favorite-son nominee actually had.

Peña learned of Robert Kennedy's visit, but not from Henry B.; he was told about the early foray into Texas by Kathleen Voigt, leader of the Democrats of Texas (DOT), and Herschel Bernard, his almost daily lunch partner. Bernard was at the courthouse daily and would drop into Peña's office for coffee. If Peña was in and available, they would chat, trade gossip, including rumors, and decide if they could eat together. When Peña was not available, Herky would visit with Marie Swartz, and later with Janice McClure, and also trade gossip, rumors, and issues coming up on the Commissioners Court.

During the 1959 regular session, the Texas legislature tinkered with election laws. The legislature moved the primary date up from July to the first Saturday in May. It also changed requirements for filing for certain offices: the LBJ law. The legislature permitted a candidate, Lyndon Baines Johnson, to file for the U.S. Senate and run simultaneously for the presidency.[38] While this change did not affect the commissioner's race, it did mean all candidates for partisan office had to gear up and begin campaigning earlier. And Peña did just that. Olga got to work early on the voter lists of who had paid their poll tax and registered. She bought the lists; they were public information. She began to make index cards for new names and recruited volunteer *comadres* to help with the get-out-the-vote drive. The early voting period for absentee voting began weeks prior to the actual primary date, and it was paper-intensive work filling out applications and waiting for the ballot to arrive, then providing assistance to the voter and mailing the ballot back to the county clerk. Olga had a trained crew that knew exactly what and how to do things. More importantly, they knew when to do it, because ballots had to be requested with sufficient time to receive the mailed ballot, complete it, and mail it back in time to be received and counted by the absentee election judge. The rule was that the ballot had to be in the county clerk's office by noon on Election Day.

Peña's group was a well-oiled reelection machine. He won the primary election without a worry and by a good margin. He was the commissioner-elect for another term, beginning in January 1961. The Peña group turned their attention to becoming delegates to the national nominating convention to be held in Los Angeles, California. The process to become a national delegate began with voting in the primary election, followed by attendance at the precinct conventions held that night after the polls closed. In the precinct conventions within County Commissioner Precinct One, Peña's people attended their respective conventions and were selected as delegates to the county convention to be held later. The DOT group, firmly in control of Bexar County party politics, had a substantial number of delegates from the other precincts at the county convention. A most important DOT leader, Kathleen Voigt had not been elected as delegate at her precinct convention and had to watch from the balcony of the Municipal Auditorium. Nevertheless, the DOT delegates were the majority and they voted her as leader of the Bexar County eighty-one-person delegation. The contentious issues at the county convention, besides the Shivercrats in attendance, were the unit rule and Johnson's favorite-son nomination for president. These votes forced Peña and his delegates, and G. J. Sutton and his East Side delegates to bite their tongues and vote reluctantly for both items. The unit rule repressed minority votes and Johnson was not their favorite candidate, which was Kennedy. The county convention voted 778 to 196 for the Johnson candidacy. The convention also voted to be bound by the unit rule.[39]

The next step in the process of becoming a national delegate was the most difficult and final one, the state convention at which the national delegates are chosen and the party platform is hashed out. The state convention in 1960 was set to begin May 22 in Austin. Peña was asked to give a speech to the statewide group of DOT members attending the convention. In his speech, he carefully but in detail outlined the concept of liberalism. It was delivered with much passion and forcefully. In part, Peña said, "There is no such thing as a moderate view or a middle of the road policy. You are either a liberal or you are a conservative or as somebody has stated, mediocre. There cannot be a moderate view on the rights of labor because some people will not like it. There cannot be a 'do not attitude' on civil rights because we might lose some of our East Texas friends. I have no fear of losing my political friends, all my political friends are liberal." And he tackled head-on the contentious issue of the favorite son, or as he labeled it, "the Johnson dilemma," in this same speech. "Personally I believe that debate on favorite sons is premature. For I believe first we must decide what we stand for; . . . and then we must fit our selection of favorite son to our strong statement of principles; and not conform our statement of principles to the wishes and dictates of our favorite son."[40]

In mid-1959 Peña began taking a position on the proposal before the Commissioners Court of establishing a medical school and the possible relocation of the Robert B. Green Hospital, a county agency, out of the downtown area by the West Side barrio to an outlying area in the Northeast quadrant of the county. His interest in diversity among the board of directors for the hospital was awakened. He began writing his views in his "As I See It" columns.[41] This issue would be a long-term affair.

PART 3

Chicano Nation-Building

CHAPTER 8

Viva Kennedy Clubs

IN THE SUMMER OF 1960, TWO CONVENTIONS TOOK PLACE IN SAN ANTONIO THAT for the first time placed Peña Jr. in a strategic role to challenge and crack open the conservative stranglehold on Democratic Party politics in the state and nation. First, the Texas Democratic Party held its primary election in May and selected delegates from the precinct to the county convention, and ultimately the state convention to be held in Austin. At the Bexar County convention, the liberal coalition of DOTs managed to control various important committees: Resolutions, Nominations, Rules, and the convention chair and parliamentarian. While his coalition group of labor, minorities, Anglo liberals, and independents had prevailed in most battles, particularly about a strong civil rights plank in the party platform, the delegates had accepted the odious unit rule and agreed to nominate LBJ as their favorite son. Albert A. Peña Jr. and G. J. Sutton became the lone minority delegates elected at the state convention to attend the national convention held in Los Angeles, California. Secondly, LULAC held its national convention in San Antonio at the Hilton Hotel from June 30 through July 3, 1960. Peña Jr., as member of LULAC Council No. 2 in San Antonio, was part of the host committee. As Bexar County commissioner, he was one of the few Mexican American public officials in the entire state at the time.

He and San Antonio's only Mexican American city councilman, José Olivares, were at the podium welcoming the LULAC delegates on opening day.[1] Many distinguished Mexican American leaders attended the convention, such as the LULAC national president, Felix Tijerina, who previously had been an "Eisenhower Democrat," and the incoming national LULAC president, Hector Godinez of California. Also present and featured as luminaries during the convention were distinguished academicians such as Dr. Américo Paredes from the University of Texas at Austin and Dr. Arthur L. Campa from the University of Denver. LULAC members were treated to a one-day workshop on the brainchild program, the Little School of 400, developed by LULAC at the insistence of Tijerina during his tenure as national president. The program brochure, "LULAC in Action—Human Values, Unlimited: A Report on the 'Little School of the 400,' A Heart-Warming Project of the League of United Latin American Citizens," became a collector's item among the LULAC delegates and dignitaries. The Little School of 400 was conceptualized and implemented in collaboration with the Texas Education Agency. The program basically taught Mexican American children 400 basic words in English as an early childhood, preschool intervention process to aid English-limited students with the language. Inability to speak and recognize words in English plagued Mexican American students in the public schools. The Spanish-language dominance among Mexican American children was used against them to maintain segregation and tracking in classrooms. Successful students who mastered the use of these 400 basic words demonstrated remarkable progress with the English curriculum.

Peña Jr. and other members of LULAC Council No. 2 arranged for convention delegates to witness firsthand the implementation of the Little School of the 400 program in San Antonio's public school classrooms. Peña Jr. was proud of his record of litigating desegregation school cases in Bexar County, but this new LULAC program was evidence that Mexican American children could excel in an Only English curriculum provided they had a bilingual introduction from Spanish into English, even if limited to 400 basic words.[2]

Peña Jr. busied himself at the convention welcoming and encouraging attendees from thirteen states to participate in the Little School of the 400 workshop and tour the schools to witness the program in action. He used this opportunity to make new acquaintances among the delegates, particularly those from California and other Southwestern states. He did not miss an opportunity to mention that he was seeking to become a delegate from Texas attending the Los Angeles Democratic National Convention later in July 1960. When an out-of-state LULAC delegate made mention that he also was seeking to become a national Democratic delegate, Peña Jr. noted that name in his notepad just in case he met him at the Los Angeles convention. He was already conjuring the beginning of a national group of Mexican American political operatives. And as LULAC member and delegate at this convention, he helped push through resolutions during the various business meetings of the organization that would buttress his work on the civil rights plank for consideration at the Democratic National Convention.

Peña Jr.'s LULAC Council No. 2 and Hector P. García's Corpus Christi chapter successfully engineered the passage of strongly worded resolutions aimed at the Eisenhower administration. More importantly, given that President Eisenhower was at the end of his second term with half a year to go, and therefore a lame duck, the resolutions could also be used as the platform for a Mexican American presidential campaign agenda in the remainder of 1960. According to Thomas H. Kreneck, this LULAC convention passed resolutions that called for increased federal funding for public education, including higher education; assistance for the elderly; a minimum wage for agricultural workers; establishment of an institution to train foreign service workers; and at Peña Jr.'s LULAC Council No. 2's insistence, a resolution to create a new commission to investigate job discrimination against Mexican Americans at all levels, local, state, and national. The focus of the existing Fair Employment Practice Committee, and a very limited one at that, was on discrimination against Negroes. LULAC and Peña Jr. felt that it was failing Mexican Americans.[3] Felix Tijerina, the lame duck national president of LULAC, grudgingly signed these resolutions.

Peña Jr. had a hectic schedule in July 1960. Olga was frequently complaining about how little time he spent with the family and her. He promised to make time for those important relationships but found it most difficult. The Bexar County Commissioners Court had regular meetings set for the first and third Mondays of each month, and now were meeting three days per week. His role in the LULAC convention's planning had taken up a lot of his time, but county business was his first priority. His legal practice was practically nonexistent. He also had to ready himself for the national convention of Democrats beginning on July 11 in Los Angeles. Olga was reminding him of birthday schedules and other family obligations requiring his presence in San Antonio that month. He promised to find a way to take her and their older children to Los Angeles and see the sights of Hollywood and Disneyland.

Telephone calls made by Peña Jr. across the country, and follow-up with LULAC delegates on strategy for pushing a civil rights plank at the Democrats' convention had not produced many results. Peña Jr. felt the LULAC resolutions would help his cause to push for a civil rights plank in the Democratic Party platform, regardless of who became the nominee. He was committed to support Johnson, but he wanted Kennedy to become the nominee. Peña carried copies of those resolutions with him to Los Angeles. His elected-delegate status (if selected) at the national convention of Democrats would provide a forum at business meetings of committees to push for the Democrats' adoption of LULAC's single-shot resolutions. Taken together these would form a beginning civil rights agenda for both Mexican and African Americans. But he was going to become the only Mexican American delegate from Texas, an army of one.

Texas Democrats at their state convention voted to nominate Lyndon B. Johnson, their U.S. senator, for president as a favorite son. In essence this strategy would force Lyndon into the presidential sweepstakes and hold the delegate votes from Texas away from the other contenders, namely, Adlai Stevenson and John F. Kennedy; all three had sought the nomination in 1956. The same three were among the main front-runners contending for the presidency again in 1960. As early as 1959, at various meetings of the Bexar County Democrats Coalition and with state party regulars, Peña Jr. had opposed the nomination of Lyndon B. Johnson as favorite son. The word was out that Peña Jr. and the Bexar County delegation was a problem for Johnson's aims.

In Austin, Peña Jr. astutely maneuvered at the Texas state convention in 1960, with the support and backing of other minority delegates, for adoption of a civil rights plank at that stage of the nominating process. His group at the county convention in early May had managed to place Hank Brown with the Plumbers Union as chair of delegate selection, G. J. Sutton as chair of resolutions, Maury Maverick Jr. as parliamentarian, and Peña as convention chairman. With a total vote of 81 among 162 delegates with a half vote each, the Bexar County delegation was a bloc at the Austin state convention.

During this time, a tactic used by the conservative wing of the Democratic Party was to hold a second state convention in order to maintain solidarity with Southern states and oppose the liberal ideas that found their way into the national Democratic Party platform. More importantly, it was the tool used by the governor to control the state party apparatus and oppose the presidential nominee if he was a liberal, as they had done throughout the decade of the 1950s. This second statewide meeting held and dominated by conservative Democrats was known as the "Governor's Convention." It was slated to be held in September after the national convention in Los Angeles.[4]

The minority delegates had also demanded representation at the regular state convention held in June. They wanted to be included in the state delegation to the national convention; they opposed yet another lily-white Texas delegation. The conservative delegates and their leaders would have no part of such an agenda or minority delegates; they balked and loudly proclaimed their opposition. Peña Jr. allowed a rumor to circulate that the minority delegates would walk out of the convention if the state's Democrats did not adopt a civil rights agenda and select some of them as delegates. In furtherance of their opposition to Johnson's nomination, the minority delegates led by Peña Jr. voted to withhold their support for Johnson as favorite son. The state Democratic leadership and Senator Lyndon B. Johnson were extremely concerned that the media might get wind of this intrafamily squabble and cripple their leverage at the national convention.

Since the 1950 U.S. Census population estimates were released, Peña Jr. had been expounding to all who would listen about the growing Mexican American population in the Southwest. He estimated the percentage of Mexican Americans in the Southwest at 12 percent. Mexican Americans, he argued, were growing dramatically in numbers across the nation, particularly the Southwest; they demanded political representation and protection as a minority group suffering repeated discrimination and civil rights transgressions. Moreover, Texas Mexican Americans were all American; at least 81.8 percent of them were native-born. In Arizona 81.9 percent were native-born. In New Mexico and Colorado, the figures for native-born Mexican Americans were higher, at 95 percent and 95.8 percent respectively. California had the lowest figure of native-born Mexican Americans at 78 percent, but Peña Jr. stressed that 50 percent of all native-born Mexican Americans had parents who themselves were native-born. Peña Jr. also stressed that Mexican Americans were significant percentages of each state's population, with double-digit presence in Texas, New Mexico, and Arizona to be sure. He was right with his estimates that in California and Colorado they were just below 10 percent of the respective state's population in 1960.

Fearing a minority walkout at the state convention, even if it was a rumor, forced the state leadership to meet with Peña Jr. and negotiate a settlement of the issue. House Speaker Sam Rayburn and Senator Johnson, both Texans, sought a meeting with Peña Jr. He had no qualms about meeting in Speaker Rayburn's hotel suite to discuss issues. Once in the door, Peña Jr. was impressed by the Speaker and his demeanor. He surveyed the room and noticed the remnants of prior meetings: ashtrays full, half-empty glasses with dark liquid and coffee cups, newspapers strewn on the floor, and sat-in bed covers. Rayburn offered him a seat and a drink as a formality while the Speaker made a telephone call, but Peña Jr. declined the offer. Mentally he recalled the content of the LULAC resolutions he had in his inner coat pocket. It seemed Rayburn was talking to Lyndon Johnson. Peña Jr. took a chair by the window. The Speaker half-heartedly attempted to tidy the room after he hung up the telephone and waited without a word exchanged. As the silence grew conspicuous and before any more pleasantries were exchanged between Peña Jr. and Rayburn, the room door trembled with pounding by Senator Johnson. Peña Jr. was taken aback at the physical size of the senator. He towered over him as he half-jogged over to shake his hand. Peña Jr. felt Johnson's hand on his shoulder and realized it reached to his shoulder blade and completely enveloped him from the neck edge to his right shoulder. Lyndon got down to business without a pause in his monologue as he instructed Peña Jr. to sit, and he scooted a chair really close to Peña Jr. When the very tall Lyndon leaned over toward him, his face was inches from Albert's. He told Peña Jr. he understood the frustration Mexican Americans felt with the party's conservative leadership, but that with time it would change. He stressed how much a friend he had been to Mexican Americans from his early teaching days in Cotulla to aiding Hector P. García with the hateful Felix Longoria incident. He asked Peña Jr. point-blank for his support for his favorite-son candidacy. The Democrats must be united to have any say at the national convention, he emphasized. Peña Jr. in his characteristic stoic posture and poker face looked the senator in the eye and repeated his litany of demands to Lyndon's face, still but inches from his own. He pulled a copy of the LULAC resolutions and thrust them into Lyndon's hand, only to see the senator hand them over to Rayburn while maintaining eye contact. The paper shuffling did cause the senator to move back a bit into his chair and listen to Peña Jr.'s comments. The meeting did not take long. It was clear that Peña Jr. meant serious business. All three knew that Peña Jr. as leader of the Bexar County delegation had their complete backing. Peña Jr. laid it out in a few terse sentences: it would be all or nothing because his delegation had nothing to lose. Peña Jr. wanted minorities as part of the delegation to Los Angeles and for the Texas Democrats to vote for a civil rights plank in the party platform. Johnson looked at Rayburn, and Rayburn looked back as intently toward Johnson. Peña Jr. seized the opportunity and asked of the senator, "Do I have your word on this?" In this era, a man's word was the full and total measure of his integrity. Lyndon Baines Johnson, majority leader and senior U.S. senator from Texas, and now the favorite-son candidate, nodded assent as he said "Yes" to the civil rights plank. He also promised to see to it that Peña Jr. would become a national delegate. They shook hands. Peña Jr. had gotten both concessions; the one-man army had won the battle at this stage of the process.

As soon as he got back to his room, he hugged Olga with such gusto and fervor that she asked him, "What's wrong?" He simply replied, "I got it all. We are going to Los Angeles; pack the bags and get babysitters." Immediately he began making calls to various rooms: G. J. Sutton, leader of the African Americans, was first, then his fellow delegates from the Loyal American Democrats before he called his Anglo liberal and labor friends with the news of the deal. If Johnson and Rayburn would keep their word, this was a major victory.

Days before leaving San Antonio for Los Angeles, Peña managed to write his "County Scene" column, berating the city council for hiring at $4,000 a consultant from Montgomery, Alabama, as press agent for sixty days, and protesting the imposition of a fee for service he termed "Sewerola" as a new tax on water. He also suggested the city council "forget about the Northside expressway" and "resubmit the other three bond issues."[5]

Leaving the younger children behind in care of relatives and friends, Olga and Albert with Bill and Sandra hit the road to Los Angeles and arrived late afternoon on July 10. The Peña family went straight to the convention hotel. The children had been in awe during the long drive through the wonderful landscapes of the Southwest. The other big cities on the way—El Paso, Phoenix, and now Los Angeles—were huge places full of people and buildings just like San Antonio, it seemed to them. But foremost on the kids' minds was when they were going to Disneyland. Albert and Olga had barely unpacked and were discussing dinner plans when the telephone rang. It was Herschel Bernard alerting them to a caucus of the Texas delegation concerning the civil rights plank. The conservative Democrats did not like the deal struck by their favorite son and Speaker during the state convention. They continued to oppose such a program and had prepared a minority report, even though the state convention had adopted the civil rights resolutions as their recommendation to the national party platform committee. Both Peña and Olga begged Bill to care for Sandra and stay in the room, and hurriedly found the caucus location and entered the room to find scores of red-faced Anglo delegates arguing with one another and shouting down the caucus chair. For many of the delegates at the caucus, it was the first time they had learned of the civil rights recommendations adopted by their party at the state convention. Most convention delegates do not attend the multiple committee business meetings; they are too busy socializing and visiting the numerous hospitality suites with free drinks, food, and the ever-present party hostesses. The only real business for many convention-goers was the floor where the action took place. They were unaware that the real business deals had already been done in committee meetings; floor action was basically a formality for ratification and for broadcast of the news to the television viewers across the country.

It became apparent to Peña that the order of business before the caucus was to adopt the conservative minority report, not the state platform, as the Texas recommendations on civil rights to the national party platform committee. Both Olga and Albert were taken aback at how quickly the conservative Anglo Democrats had felt the stigma of being on the losing end of a fight, being in the minority. Peña attempted to be recognized by the caucus chair, Governor Price Daniel, without immediate success. The caucus chair had spotted him waving his hand in the air and finally motioned for him to approach.

The caucus chair knew Peña Jr. was the leader of the Bexar County Democratic Coalition that had been involved in the making of the deal on civil rights. He shouted at Peña as he approached, "Is this true? We gonna adopt your civil rights plank as our party platform?" "Yes," Peña said while nodding incessantly. At that very moment, the Speaker of the House of Representatives Samuel Taliaferro

Rayburn—"Mister Sam," as he affectionately was called by the closest of friends and enemies alike—made his way through the noisy delegates and other Democrats in the room, heading toward Peña Jr. and the caucus chairman. "Are you sure?" the chairman hollered above the din. "Ask him," Peña Jr. said, motioning with his thumb toward Mister Sam. Rayburn had the question repeated, and nodded. He simply said, "Yep that is what we are doing." With that affirmation, the caucus chair got busy quieting the crowd.[6]

The Texas delegation adopted the state party's recommendations on civil rights and a shift of how national delegates would be selected, away from the nominating Delegates Committee to caucuses by congressional district. As a compromise, it also adopted the minority report that no one on the platform committee had bothered to read.

Peña Jr. and Olga were all smiles and beaming with pride. Rayburn had sealed the deal and delivered. Johnson had kept his word. Albert A. Peña Jr. and G. J. Sutton were selected as national delegates to the Los Angeles convention. The one-man army was on a roll.

By the time of the national convention, John F. Kennedy had lined up a huge delegate lead over his opponents by winning many of the Democratic Party primaries across the country. Kennedy flew into Los Angeles on Saturday, July 9, and was greeted at the airport by thousands of well-wishers organized by his campaign staff. Bobby Kennedy, the campaign strategist, and the rest of the campaign crew occupied many floors of the downtown Biltmore Hotel. Texas was still in Johnson's column because of his favorite-son candidacy. John Connally was handling the gathering of uncommitted convention delegates for Johnson. Connally had been Johnson's campaign manager during the successful 1948 Senate race and became Johnson's administrative assistant during the first six months of the term. Now he was Johnson's presidential campaign manager, but had no experience in this arena.[7] Besides, the Kennedy delegate lead seemed insurmountable, with 577 solid votes already committed to him and 761 needed to win the nomination on the first ballot.

U.S. Senator Dennis Chávez, Democrat from New Mexico, was for Johnson while Kennedy had U.S. representatives Edward Roybal of Los Angeles and Henry B. González from San Antonio backing his candidacy. The three of them had heard of Peña Jr.'s efforts over the civil rights plank and of his opposition to Johnson, and sought him out. The three wanted to meet and discuss strategy with Peña Jr., but meanwhile the trio managed a hurried visit during which Roybal and González persuaded Senator Chávez to meet with Robert Kennedy, campaign manager for his brother. Once they met with Robert Kennedy to discuss their role in the presidential campaign if his brother were nominated with their help, Senator Chávez switched his preference to Kennedy.

Robert Kennedy thanked them for their support and asked them how to form the Kennedy campaign across the Southwest among Mexican Americans. He mentioned that he had had success by organizing Kennedy for President clubs in each of the states whose primary elections they won. The clubs, grassroots networks, had been the key to victory, he stressed, but conceded that Mexícano legislators knew best how to reach the Mexican American voter.[8]

On Wednesday, July 13, the names of Kennedy, Johnson, and Stevenson were placed in nomination. Kennedy took the nomination on the first ballot. The roll call began alphabetically by state. The delegate votes began piling up. Texas cast its votes for the favorite son, Lyndon Baines Johnson. But when Wyoming's fifteen votes were cast for Kennedy, they were three more than necessary for a majority. John Fitzgerald Kennedy—JFK, as he was referred to in the press—became the Democratic nominee for president. The jockeying and posturing for the second man on the ticket began in earnest. Lyndon was upset that he was not the nominee. Kennedy realized he needed the votes from the Southern states for the General Election.

Lyndon Baines Johnson became the vice-presidential choice and accepted the acronym of LBJ to shorten his name. Peña had no love for LBJ from past skirmishes with him as congressman and senator, but he had also helped Peña on occasion. Now Peña had two points of access to the presidential campaign about to begin: LBJ and a young JFK staffer he had met while at the convention.

Peña Jr. met with John Kennedy's staff member Carlos McCormick at the convention. Carlos was born in Tucson, Arizona, to Mexican American parents, and now was a resident of Santa Barbara, California. McCormick had been part of the Kennedy campaign since the West Virginia primary. He had been working Spanish-language public relations and Latin American affairs for the senator's campaign. McCormick was a senior law student at George Washington University in Washington, DC.[9] Peña Jr. and McCormick discussed the need for Mexican American involvement with the Kennedy campaign, as had the only three national Mexican American political figures with Robert Kennedy. Neither group, however, had agreed on specifics; nor was any detail offered as to a division of labor among themselves on behalf of the presidential campaign after the convention.

Once Kennedy locked up the nomination by selecting Lyndon B. Johnson as his running mate, the jubilation among the Democrats subsided, and everyone went home. The Peñas returned to San Antonio happy and ecstatic. He and Olga made time during the convention to tour Hollywood and spent a day at Disneyland with the older kids they had in tow.[10] The Peñas, like most delegates, left Los Angeles without any real commitment from the Kennedy brothers on a plan to work for JFK, only that they would continue their regular effort of registering more voters and getting them to the polls come November. There was not much time for a campaign and even less money in Texas for such a mobilization. Peña's LAD group and the DOT coalition had organization. Henry B. did not, but he had broad appeal and vote-getting ability. Peña knew it was up to him to take the organizing lead of what was to become the Kennedy Clubs.

McCormick met with Robert Kennedy before they left Los Angeles to map out a role for Mexican Americans in the campaign. Robert Kennedy instructed McCormick to call his contacts within the Mexican American communities in the various states and see if they could come together in some fashion to support his brother's presidential campaign. Ignacio García claims that the idea for an ethnic component, Mexican Americans specifically, in a national presidential campaign originated with the Richard M. Nixon camp. Reportedly, Nixon rejected the idea and name "Viva Nixon" as smacking of too overt an ethnic appeal.[11] The Kennedys took up this idea.

McCormick first called Commissioner Peña Jr. in San Antonio and asked if he would support a Viva Kennedy movement for JFK. Would Peña accept the statewide leadership mantle? Albert Peña Jr. agreed, but only with certain conditions, and he wanted to discuss those personally with Kennedy. Peña had grown accustomed to Texas's rough-and-tumble face-to-face confrontations to extract promises and commitments. He wanted the same from John Kennedy. Time being short, that was not likely except possibly by telephone. From his office in San Antonio, Peña Jr. instead was able to talk directly with Robert Kennedy about his concerns. McCormick had gotten Bobby on the line with him, and made it known to Peña that the younger Kennedy was to be in charge of the campaign, not the nominee.

Peña Jr. knew from experience that prominent Democrats, particularly the conservative Texas leadership, had sold him down the river on prior occasions. He insisted that the Mexican American Viva Kennedy Clubs, which he would organize, would be an independent and distinct group from the Texas Democrats. Peña Jr. wanted to have direct contact with the Kennedy campaign and not work under the Texas Democrats. Moreover, he wanted John Kennedy, as presidential candidate, to speak out against the poll tax as a prerequisite for registering to vote. The poll tax had to be eliminated. And he wanted a commitment on civil rights legislation. Lastly, he complained that too few Mexican Americans were employed by the national government. He wanted assurances that qualified Mexican Americans would have high-level appointments in the Kennedy administration and in government agencies, including the military bases around the country. Robert Kennedy accepted Peña Jr.'s conditions.[12] The one-man army was rolling again.

Before Peña could get into full swing, he had to divert attention to the upcoming Governor's Convention held in Dallas on September 23, 1960. The conservative Democrats led by the governor were going to repudiate the national ticket and platform over the liberal civil rights issues, federal aid to education and the aged, revision of the anti–closed shop legislation, and for Connally's reservation of limiting the powers of the World Court. And they did so by not even seconding Peña's motion to approve the national platform, and the state platform was gaveled through. Peña cast the lone dissenting vote for the Bexar County delegation.[13] With this last battle within the Democratic Party of the state, Peña got down to the business of getting out the vote for the national ticket.

Even though Henry B. González and Dr. Hector P. García had been named as national co-chairs for Texas of the Viva Kennedy Clubs, it was Peña who was to travel the breadth of the state calling on LULAC and American G.I. Forum (AGIF) members in other cities to form a Viva Kennedy Club in their area. Since both LULAC and AGIF were nonpartisan organizations, members of these groups could only find room for partisan political participation in the Viva Kennedy Club campaign component. Peña felt confident his group would see to it that his reelection campaign would be successful, and devoted much time on behalf of John Kennedy's campaign for president. Dr. García was too busy with his medical practice and AGIF activities to be out organizing Viva Kennedy Clubs. He was glad Peña was on the road. Peña traveled incessantly; called contacts; wrote and delivered countless speeches in public, on the air, and in print; and built a statewide network of political operatives for JFK and LBJ. By the narrowest of margins, mainly coming from election boxes in Chicago, the Democratic ticket won the presidency. Peña won reelection.

Henry B., although he was named national co-chair of the Viva Kennedy Clubs, in addition to the Texas title, faced opposition from several candidates in the primary; he did go on to defeat R. L. Strickland in the runoff election. Henry B. also had a Republican opponent, Ike Kampmann, a local attorney. Only after assurances from Lalo Solis that the Peña organization was working on his behalf, as well getting assurances from the local DOT group, did Henry B. make time to go campaign in eleven states for the national ticket. Henry B. won reelection and polled more votes than the national ticket in Bexar County. The national Democratic ticket prevailed over the Republicans in the county by more than 12,000 votes. The coalition under DOT, of which Peña now was the leader, was firmly in control of the county.

Finally, after years of waiting, the Democrats, under a liberal leader, were back in the White House to run the country. That wishful thinking was short on analysis. As the newspapers and weekly news magazines began to report later in November, the Democrats had lost over twenty seats in the House of Representatives. The president-elect was not going to be able to pass legislation in Congress. And, LBJ's positions as majority leader and senator were going to be vacated. In the political arena, vacuums seldom occur, do not last when they do, and are rapidly filled.

Upset at Democrats

Peña was growing impatient with the lack of progress within the Democratic Party to cause change in leadership of the state party. He had taken the opportunity to convey his view when he was asked to speak to the Minorities Division of the National Democratic Party Executive Committee, headed then by Michigan Governor Mennen Williams. He shared the platform with all three presidential contenders: Stevenson, Johnson, and Kennedy. Peña talked about the Latin American in Texas.

> He told them Latin-Americans had throughout the years voted 98 percent for the Democratic Party. But I had been in Washington the year before and visited the Pentagon and the Federal Buildings. Nowhere had I seen a Latin-American holding a job or position of consequence. And this is true in the Texas State Government. And this was true at the City Public Service Board in San Antonio. And as a consequence, the Latin-American was tired of being considered in the pocket of the "Democratic Party."[14]

Peña felt that because of those remarks, he had been sought out by Carlos McCormick at the convention and asked to head up the Viva Kennedy Clubs organization for the campaign in Texas. "I accepted on two conditions. First, that we would work directly with the Kennedys; because the state leadership had sold us 'down the river' before. Second, that we would get recognition and representation."[15]

The Kamikaze Strikes Again: HBG's Run for the U.S. Senate

No sooner had LBJ become JFK's selection for the VP position than the political wheels of the main factions within the Democratic Party in Texas began to roll. Peña called on his friends in labor circles and Anglo liberals, inquiring about potential aspirants for the soon-to-be-vacant senator's position. He wanted to be in the know about who might run. A major problem arose that disturbed Peña a great deal. His friend and collaborator Henry B. González was going to make the race, according to rumors from the courthouse and from Austin. To Peña, González making this race was as crazy an idea as the last one he had when he ran for governor. Henry B. was just too independent to suit Peña. He never let his political friends in on what was going to be his next move. González's friends and enemies had to read it in the newspaper. Peña also heard that Henry B. had been offered an ambassadorship by the Kennedy transition team, but he had declined.[16]

Peña heard the next bit of disturbing news: Maury Maverick Jr., his liberal friend and co-counsel on some legal cases, had announced for the soon-to-be-vacant seat. Henry followed suit. The liberals across the state, however, did not caucus as a group. Individual liberal groups within major cities began to ask themselves who they should support for the U.S. Senate seat. In Texas, as in most states, the vacancy of a U.S. Senate seat is filled by gubernatorial appointment, and William Blakley was appointed by Governor Price Daniel in 1961. Blakley's appointment was too much for Texas liberals to stomach. Blakley, a multimillionaire from Dallas, was a "Shivercrat," a member of those within the conservative wing of the Democratic Party led by Governor Allan Shivers that openly supported Republican candidates for president and opposed all liberal Democrats in the state and nation.

In 1952 and 1956, Blakley had been part of the "Eisenhower Democrats" that opposed Adlai Stevenson's presidential bid. As a reward for his campaign contributions to conservative candidates and his efforts in support of conservative statewide officials—namely, the governor—he was first appointed by Governor Price Daniel to fill a temporary vacancy from January 15 to April 28, 1957, as U.S. senator. He ran against Ralph Yarborough in that special election for the U.S. Senate in 1957 and lost. Yarborough won by a plurality of votes—680,000 to Blakley's 486,000—because he and two other conservative candidates split the vote, allowing the liberal faction to prevail. Texas legislators under mandate from Governor Daniel immediately changed the Texas Election Code to require a majority vote, thus creating a new control mechanism to ensure conservative candidates won in special elections.

Again in 1961 Blakley was tapped for the vacant U.S. Senate seat and served a few months. He sought the seat in a special election and faced seventy-one other candidates. While a governor can fill a vacancy by appointment, if more than half of the six-year term for U.S. senator is pending, a special election must be held. A fee of $50 was set to file for a ballot slot in the open special election. Those who paid the nominal fee were listed by name as drawn by lot on the ballot, without any political party designation. Among the seventy-two total candidates, two San Antonians filed, Maury Maverick Jr. and Henry B. González. Republican John Tower from Wichita Falls, Texas, was another name on the ballot list of candidates.

Peña was pressured by both Maverick and González to persuade the other to drop out of the race so as to not split the liberal vote in San Antonio and across the state. The names of both candidates had statewide recognition and appeal—Maverick Jr. because of the family name and legacy of Sr., and González because of his most recent statewide campaign for governor in 1958. Peña was torn between his ideological leanings toward Maverick's views and proven record while in office and efforts on Peña's behalf, and his ethnic solidarity with González. The two of them, González and Peña, had begun to energize and coalesce the Mexícano vote into a powerhouse on the West and South Sides of the city. If Peña was after group cohesion, he had to support González and reluctantly did so. Peña was trying to put together a statewide organization of Mexícanos from among those he recruited into the Viva Kennedy Clubs. Now the González campaign was taking attention and resources away from that. González's campaign seemed to Peña to be splitting the DOT coalition of Anglo liberals, blacks, labor, and Mexícanos in two. Maverick was going to draw support from Anglo liberals and labor. Maverick was also going to split Mexícanos from blacks who respected Maverick's civil rights work on their behalf.

González likewise had his share of support among blacks for his valiant filibuster in the Texas Senate against race-based segregationist bills in San Antonio and statewide. The only group solidly behind González was the Mexícanos, but without a grassroots organization in the city or across the state, he had to rely on Peña to get them out to vote on his behalf.

Peña's group began to work the precincts in Bexar County searching for Mexícano votes. Peña himself got Spanish-language radio urging voter support for Henry B. He wrote in the "County Comment" of March 24, 1961, about Henry's candidacy and implored people to help with volunteer work, money, and votes. And in this same column, he alerted his readership that effective at the end of the month, on March 27, he was going to be broadcasting daily at 11:30 a.m. in both languages on Radio KUKA. Peña's crew helped put together a voter rally at Mission County Park for Henry B. on April 3, the day before the election, and he publicized it via his various media outlets, including "County Comment."[17]

Lalo Solis had earlier moved into the González camp, but now rejoined the Peña efforts. During this election it seemed to Peña that all Mexícano groups were working together to elect one of their own to the U.S. Senate. It was not to be. When the returns came in the night of the special election, Tower led the pack with 30.9 percent of the vote or 327,308 votes, followed by Blakley with 18 percent, and Jim Wright from Fort Worth with 16 percent of the vote. Maverick came in fourth with 10 percent of the vote, and González came in sixth with just over 9 percent of the vote or 97,659 votes. Maverick was hot about his loss. He figured that if González had not been in the race, those votes would have been his and he would have been second behind Tower and not Blakley. The two men did not speak to one another for the next twenty years.

Peña Makes the Kamikaze into a Congressman

Peña got sidetracked when he learned in 1961 that the local congressman, Paul Kilday, was being considered for appointment to the U.S. Military Court. Immediately, Peña called his group members asking what they thought of the idea of supporting Henry B. González for Congress. Almost everyone was in agreement, but with reservations about Henry B.'s track record of being independent and not a team player. Albert Fuentes did not agree. He thought little of Henry B. despite his civil rights record and voter appeal. Fuentes was abrasive at times, Herschel Bernard recalled.[18] Peña knew better than many about that streak in Henry B.'s ego and his reckless behavior at the most inopportune times and usually at his political organization's expense. His closest advisors and political supporters asked Peña why he wasn't going for the position. He could call LBJ, now the vice president, and get his endorsement and help in winning the nomination. Peña explained he was not interested in going to Washington; his job was in Bexar County, in Texas. He was committed to the local Democratic Coalition and building PASO. Peña called his friends in the East Side and with labor. The East Side leaders loved Henry B. for his work to desegregate public facilities in the city. Labor did not trust him. Henry B. had not endeared himself to labor the way Peña had. Peña got a tepid endorsement from his Bexar County coalition to promote Henry's endorsement. His most trusted allies, Alaniz and Jake Johnson, wanted Peña to make the race, not Henry B. With support growing for Henry B., Peña called on a potential candidate from Bexar County, Franklin Spears, a state senator. He flat-out told Senator Spears not to run, and that if he did, the Democratic Coalition would not support him. Another potential candidate was Maury Maverick Jr., who recalled the last time he ran against Henry B. for the U.S. Senate seat and topped Henry's votes. Peña stood solidly with Henry B. and informed Maury Maverick Jr. of this; Peña made it clear to Maverick that he should not run. Maverick was angered and disappointed. He told Albert Peña, "You wait and see. I will prove to be a better Mexican than Henry B." They didn't talk to each other for years; Herky Bernard eventually brought them back together.[19] Maverick's words would prove to be right on target.

Peña called LBJ's office, which confirmed the impending Kilday appointment to the federal judgeship. The staffer on the telephone further advised him that the vice president would be in San Antonio in a matter of days; they could talk then.

Peña had courted some of the local newspaper reporters for years and gained their confidence for being truthful and honest with them in his sharing of information and answering their questions. Jim McCrory was one of those reporters with whom Peña had a very good working relationship. On the other hand, Paul

Thompson, another columnist, was Peña's nemesis. Peña read the Thompson column attacking his politics and proposals at every turn. With regard to Peña's organizing of PASO, Thompson had begun to characterize that effort as "segregation in reverse."

When LBJ came to town, Peña and he met. The vice president asked Peña if he really wanted Henry B. in Congress. Peña said yes. He asked for LBJ's commitment to endorse Henry in the special election to be held very soon. LBJ was reluctant and argued that this special election was not between a Republican and a Democrat, as it was in the General Election; he couldn't do that. Peña educated the vice president on who was the Republican in the race, John Goode. He said, "Henry is a Democrat and the other man is a Republican. I don't care what they call that, but it is still a Republican against a Democrat." Johnson said, "OK" and he committed not just to endorse Henry B. but to return and campaign for him.[20] Peña ran into reporter McCrory back at the courthouse and informed him of the deal cut to help Henry B. McCrory immediately knew he had a front-page story and that Peña was a straight shooter with information; but he wanted corroboration. Somehow, McCrory was able to corner the vice president at another event and asked LBJ if what Peña had said was true. It was confirmed and the story broke.[21]

Henry B. was most appreciative of Peña's securing this level of support for his aspiration. Peña's invaluable gift to Henry B. was that by securing the LBJ endorsement and commitment, he had in effect cleared the field of important and powerful Democratic competitor candidates. The vice president used his influence to direct money and attention to Henry's campaign; he also came to San Antonio and campaigned for Henry B. The Republicans in response had former President Eisenhower come to San Antonio and campaign for their candidate, John Goode. Peña took his four-week vacation due as time off from the county job. He became Henry's officially designated campaign manager. Peña asked his precinct workers, Fuentes, García, Muñoz, and Raleigh Mull, to join him in hitting the streets in search of votes for Henry B. He also called Hank Brown to bring in his plumbers to put up signs and walk the precincts in search of votes. Peña reached beyond Bexar County to Dallas to recruit Pancho Medrano to bring UAW resources to the campaign. He called Paul Montemayor in Corpus Christi for help and got more than he expected. Montemayor, with the Steelworkers Union, brought men and money. Peña got on the radio and television programs, wrote his columns, and started one of the most impressive get-out-the-vote campaigns in the district. The congressional district was basically all of Bexar County. Johnny Alaniz and Jake Johnson had both run at-large elections in the county and won. González had carried the district when he ran for both the State and U.S. Senates. He had done well in the same area when he ran for governor in 1958. This was a winnable race. The Peña forces went all-out in the barrio, and in conjunction with liberals, labor, and blacks, got the vote out for Henry B. Peña made converts to the González campaign of labor leaders who were not enthusiastic about Henry B. Labor unions came across for Peña and joined in the massive get-out-the-vote campaign. Labor also contributed the manpower to put up the hundreds of "González for Congress" political signs in the district.

On Election Day, Peña had his operatives and volunteers organize a motorcade parade through the barrios of San Antonio in the West and South Sides of town, including the near downtown area. It would be a parade of cars with "González for Congress" signs taped on the automobiles; hand placards of the same sign were given out to spectators along the route. The idea was to create excitement among Méxicanos and get the voters among them to the polls that day before 7 p.m. The motorcade parade was the last-ditch effort reminding Mexícano voters to go vote for Henry B. The motorcade began at the International Building on W. Houston Street. Riding in one of the cars was the vice president, waving his Stetson hat and smiling at the spectators. The Peña forces had made sure everyone knew who was going to be in the parade and in support of Henry B. González. On radio and television appearances, Peña had made repeated references to a special guest coming to town to campaign for Henry B. It was going to be a surprise. The surprise was not the vice president; he had been in town campaigning for two days already. The surprise was Cantinflas, the popular comic movie star from Mexico. Vice President Johnson had called Peña asking if Cantinflas coming to town would be a help for Henry B. Peña enthusiastically said, "That would be great!"[22]

Throngs lined the streets to get a glimpse of Cantinflas as he drove by in another of the motorcade cars. Peña was in another car and also waving to the crowds. At stops, Peña, Vice President Johnson, Cantinflas, and Henry B. would talk to the people. The big rally was held at Eloy Centeno's parking lot by his grocery store on W. Commerce. The Centeno family had the largest chain of grocery stores in the Mexícano barrios of San Antonio. Eloy and Peña had reconciled some previous differences, and this venue at his store brought them back together. Centeno had been upset with Peña since he had obtained a radio license for his sister and brother-in-law, Manuel Davila. Centeno was the other applicant for the available frequency in San Antonio, but Peña had gotten LBJ to get the Davilas the license and not Centeno. LBJ, as U.S. senator, was a member of the Senate committee with oversight of operations of the Federal Communications Commission (FCC).[23]

That night after the parade and rally, Johnson called Peña to inquire about his thoughts on the likely final results. Peña told him Henry B. would win by 10,000 votes. As it turned out, Henry B. won by 100,100 votes; Peña's math was off a bit. González won the election with that healthy vote coming from all precincts. He lost by narrow margins in the Anglo precincts deep into the North Side of San

Antonio.[24] The celebration that night was a rerun of the victory parties when Peña's group had helped Henry B. win the State Senate seat. At this victory party, the crowd demanded and chanted for Peña to share the stage with Henry B. And the crowd carried Peña to the podium. Henry B. would remain in Congress for nearly the next four decades.

Not much later, Henry B. González would turn on Peña. González in later years also disclaimed that any help or assistance from Peña had been necessary in securing the LBJ endorsement in that race or getting votes out for his election.

CHAPTER 9

PASO and Cristal's Los Cinco Candidatos

Toward the latter half of 1961, Peña focused as best he could on local events and on organizing the first statewide PASO meeting on August 20th. He received reports that the military bases in San Antonio were permitting the John Birch Society, an extremist group, to hold Americanism seminars sponsored by the Jaycees, Chamber of Commerce, Southwest Research Administration, and Fourth Army Headquarters. Peña protested this political intrusion by the military into civic life and culture by permitting the views of this right-wing group to be passed off as "Americanism." In his weekly newspaper opinion editorials, radio programs, and in speeches Peña pressed loudly for these seminars to cease. He wrote letters to Washington, DC. He called the commanding officers at the various bases inquiring as to their support and participation in these seminars. Peña got their attention and the seminars stopped in early 1962.[1]

Also late in 1961 he began to challenge the leadership of some newly appointed board members of the county hospital. The district had been formed and the board appointed the year before he was elected, in 1955. Some board vacancies were filled while he was on vacation the previous year. Peña wanted to secure reappointment of those members he supported and was being shut out of the process by his lack of votes. He had been outmaneuvered on appointments by the county judge, and commissioners Jorrie and Wurzbach; they had met in private session.[2] He would wait for another time.

PASO, the Political Association of Spanish Speaking Organizations, emerged from the Viva Kennedy Club movement as the successor organization.[3] Peña had been involved with the Henry Wallace for President campaign in 1948 as a law student in Houston, and with Adlai Stevenson's two presidential pursuits in the 1950s. He had made contacts and traveled the length and breadth of the state urging Méxicanos to pay the poll tax and donate a dollar to join the Viva Kennedy Clubs for John F. Kennedy's presidential bid in 1960. He had made many more contacts and political friends. During his travels he saw the emerging majorities of Méxicanos in the rural communities, but they were not registered to vote for failure to pay the poll tax. Once the Viva Kennedy Clubs had outlived their campaign usefulness with Kennedy's victory, Peña simply called on these new political friends and collaborators and urged them to regroup and rename themselves as the Political Association of Spanish Speaking Organizations (PASO). He envisioned a national Méxicano political organization.

In earlier years, Peña and Gus García, the prominent civil rights attorney who argued the *Hernandez v. State of Texas* case, had long discussed the need for such a national organization.[4] García had traveled to New York immediately after his judicial victory in the *Hernandez* case before the U.S. Supreme Court, braving seven degree weather, and sought out influential organizations for discussion of the needs of Méxicanos. García contacted and met with persons at the American Civil Liberties Union, the National Association for the Advancement of Colored People, the Anti-Defamation League of B'nai B'rith, the Japanese-American Citizens League, the Rockefeller Foundation, the Marshall Trust Foundation, the American Federation of Labor, and the Congress of Industrial Organizations. He pressed these institutions to help establish a national organization to advocate for the Mexican American. As García saw it, "What we need is a powerful, rich national organization to fight our battles, with a lobbyist in Washington and each state capital where we constitute a substantial portion of the population."[5] Unfortunately, García was way ahead of his Méxicano people, and even Peña, in this type of thinking. The Eastern liberal establishment did not have a perception of the 4 million Mexican Americans in the United States, predominantly in the Southwest, by 1960.[6] The closest group to Mexican Americans these Easterners had in mind were Puerto Ricans who lived in New York. Since Gunnar Myrdal had published *An American Dilemma* in 1944, most of white America knew only of the tribulations of Negroes. Liberals, as did most other Americans, lived with an incomplete, national, binary view of the people of the United States; they were either white or black. The establishment of a national advocacy group for Mexican Americans was a ways into the future.

The First National Organizational Efforts

Peña sought out others across the nation that he had met while working with the national Viva Kennedy Club network. Peña made telephone calls to as many as he could find and pushed for a national organizational meeting in Las Vegas, Nevada. The group met but did not come to agreement on forming a national organization under the PASO name.[7] Instead, two groups emerged intact from that meeting—PASO and the California-based Mexican American Political Association (MAPA)—each group unwilling to accommodate a name change to the other. The other various participants not from California or Texas at the Las Vegas meeting could not agree on a name or a national agenda either. Regrettably, the group also continued to ignore the work of the JFK transition team seeking names with résumés for political appointments in the new administration. The Mexican American leadership was too inexperienced about post–presidential campaign activities, such as the work of the transition team headed by Sargent Shriver, the president's brother-in-law. Most political leaders in the Southwest only wanted to be invited to the inauguration ceremonies.[8] Some settled for a thank-you note signed by President-Elect Kennedy as their reward for political work done on his behalf. A handful, Hank Quevedo Sr., Bert Corona, Ernesto Galarza, Herman Gallegos, and César E. Chávez from California (then leading the Community Services Organization), and the one-man army from Texas, Albert A. Peña Jr., realized the need for a national organization, agenda, goals, and leadership team. None of them had worked side by side with other Mexican American leaders in the Southwest. They not only did not know each other; they did not conceptualize that they needed each other. Regional concerns prevailed over national interests at the Las Vegas meeting. Peña returned home dejected but convinced that he had to organize PASO in Texas, then spread the organization to the Southwestern states of Arizona, New Mexico, Colorado, Nevada, and perhaps Illinois. Peña knew the migrant streams heading out from Texas branched out west and southeast, but the largest trail led into the Midwest. Peña's hope was that in time, the California counterpart, MAPA's leadership, might see the wisdom in combining groups into a national powerhouse for Mexicano political action.

Organizing PASO

With his friend and political lieutenant Johnny Alaniz now a state representative, the first Méxicano elected from Bexar County to the legislature, Peña felt comfortable that the stereotype that Méxicanos had been labeled with as "The Sleeping Giant" was no longer applicable. The Méxicanos had their eyes opened with the Viva Kennedy Clubs, and now with PASO the giant would walk and talk. After Peña and Herschel Bernard had long discussions about what a disaster the Las Vegas meeting had been, they began brainstorming on the aims and purposes of PASO. They agreed as a first organizational step to invite local and area leaders to a meeting. Bernard made the arrangements and secured some money to host the group at the Gunter Hotel in downtown San Antonio. Labor leaders in San Antonio, Hank Brown with the Plumbers Union, and Ray Shafer of the Teamsters Union were invited. Liberals who had stayed the course during the many battles with conservatives were also invited to attend. But Peña was most clear in the reason for their invitation; they were being asked to become supporters of the effort to organize Méxicanos statewide. PASO was going to be a Méxicano-led organization. He argued that an organized Mexícano group across the state would augment the growing power of the Democrats of Texas; all would benefit from that—labor, Negroes, liberals, and, of course, the larger Mexícano community.

Peña got busy with his own political operatives, Munguía, Fuentes, state representative Johnny Alaniz, Pete Tijerina, and Olga and her women's network. He engaged them in the same discussions of aims and purposes for PASO. In 1961 he began calling contacts in South Texas to attend the first meeting of PASO. The response in San Antonio and the South Texas area was positive; they would make every effort to attend, and they did. The group discussed their political posture vis-à-vis the existing political parties. Peña was recommending that PASO be nonpartisan, but not in the LULAC or AGIF fashion of not being involved in politics; rather they would be very involved with politics but independent of the Democratic and Republican Parties. Peña's view was that PASO, as an organization, should be open to listen to, meet with, and scrutinize candidates from either party so as not to be taken for granted. Those candidates willing to sit down with PASO leaders and support PASO goals deserved to be endorsed by PASO in a process to be developed. The various persons in attendance at this first meeting volunteered or were recruited to work on specific matters such as fundraising, developing a constitution and bylaws, a program of action, poll-tax drives and voter registration, organizing, and preparation of a leadership slate of first officers for PASO. They agreed to report back to Peña in the near future while he busied himself with preparing and mailing a statewide invitation to as many contacts as he could find addresses for to join in founding PASO at the earliest possible opportunity. As a practical matter PASO was underway and Peña was its leader.

Peña's group began formalizing the rules and regulations for the founding meeting of PASO. Peña traveled to the Rio Grande Valley and Laredo in the weeks prior to the meeting to ensure attendance and to discuss the PASO role in the unfolding political campaigns in Texas. A major point of divergence and conflict among Mexican American leaders across the state was their individual political capital and the notion that PASO would now endorse or oppose candidates, not them. Would they not be able to cut deals with individual candidates as they had done for years? Would a local leader be able to get patronage from successful candidates? Who would take advantage of those appointments and salaries? Who would be able to vote at the PASO convention if no one was a member yet and no one had paid dues? What were the dues to be? Peña did the best he could in answering these questions in person or by telephone.

Between out-of-town trips, Peña kept up with events and made Commissioners Court meetings. He found time to help draft his mother's will and prepare his written editorials and radio talks. On March 17, in "County Comment," he pointed out the job discrimination at the City Public Service Board. "Out of 2,066 employees, 688 are of Mexican descent."[9] He demanded more be hired, and not just as common laborers, and that they be paid better.

Back to Work on PASO

PASO held the first annual convention in San Antonio at the Granada Hotel on February 9–11, 1962. A constitution and bylaws were adopted and Peña was elected its first state chairman. The other officers were Roberto M. Benavides, first vice-chairman; Chris Aldrete, second vice-chairman; James De Anda, secretary; Nick Pérez Jr., treasurer; Franklin García, state organizer; Manuel Velasco, legal advisor; Rev. Peter Parra, chaplain; Hector P. García, national president; and Gilbert C. García (no title).[10] The office or the duties of Gilbert C. García are not found in the first PASO constitution. Perhaps the election of Dr. García to this nonexistent post was deferential and honorific. While PASO adopted a constitution with a provision that membership was limited to U.S. citizens and residents of the county with a PASO chapter, Article 2 allowed persons over the age of eighteen to join. Article 5 permitted college students and faculty to organize a subchapter with approval from a preexisting county chapter, but no such group was organized and accepted into membership until 1966.[11] I organized the first group at Texas A&I College, now under the name of Texas A&M University Kingsville (TAMUK).[12] Women also could join PASO, but clearly it was a male-led organization, with Chicanas in secondary supporting roles as political workers.

PASO groups formed across the state in many locations. The word on PASO reached most of the remote locations in the state, such as Midland. Rogelio Robles wrote to Peña in early February 1962 asking when they would get PASO membership cards. He sent $10 in a check to cover the dues for ten men: Donato Barela, Adan González, Jesse Aguilar, José Martinez, Ciro Sanchez, Raymond Brito, Paz Brito, Jesse Martinez, G. R. Navarette, and Sam Martinez. Mr. Robles and his wife had already paid dues, but they were members of the nearby Odessa PASO chapter. The group forming in Dallas sent in $20, Port Arthur $13, and Odessa $25.[13]

PASO held a subsequent convention in Austin on August 25 and 26, 1962. The organization and Peña, its leader, were constantly being called upon to defend themselves against the charge that as an organization of "Spanish-speaking groups" they were in fact segregating themselves and promoting segregation in reverse. At this Austin conference, Peña addressed the issue head-on: "Critics of PASO have called the movement segregation-in-reverse—some because they would like to see us disunited; some because they fail to understand the reasons that motivate us; and some who sincerely believe they have valid reasons." And he continued systematically making his case:

> First of all our membership is open to all American citizens regardless of their race, color or creed. Second, we are organized to correct problems peculiar to our ethnic group. This is not a new concept. Many social and economic groups have the same or similar political action groups—such as COPE the AFL-CIO political arm. Doctor's groups, lawyer's groups, Negro groups, and many others have organized politically—all for reasons peculiar to their group. Third, and I believe most important, we urge our groups to form alliances with groups who have been our friends in the past.[14]

In the Democratic Party elections of 1962 another Yarborough, Don, contested the Texas gubernatorial position, as did the incumbent, Price Daniel. The winner that emerged from the runoff was John Connally, the political ally of Vice President Johnson. Connally narrowly beat Don Yarborough—the liberals' choice—565,174 to 538,924 votes. Peña and the statewide DOTs were disheartened at yet another loss, this time to the moderate wing of the Democrats. Connally, however, soon proved to be as conservative as Daniel had been. After the November General Election, Peña turned to a pressing issue that was close to his view of how county government should be organized. The Citizens' Committee for County Home Rule had petitioned for home rule—the mechanism whereby a county, like a city operating under a home rule charter approved by the voters, could govern itself. Peña was for the initiative. He had written and spoken about the need for such a measure; he had proposed the creation of a metropolitan government for the county, a merger of city and county governments. He mailed letters with his opinion on the issue to several groups in the county, such as the Chamber of Commerce, League of Women Voters, Taxpayers League, and the Mexican Chamber of Commerce.[15]

The local chairman of the Democratic Party for the county, John Daniels, had been employed by the San Antonio Housing Authority, a delegate agency of the city council. The mayor and council members had supported the Americanism seminars Peña had fought against; Daniels openly criticized the New Frontier, President Kennedy's national agenda and program; and they were not loyal Democrats. Peña took them on, especially Daniels, in his radio programs and opinion editorials. He wrote:

> Mr. Daniels cannot serve two masters. He cannot shake hands with the Democratic Party, have his other hand in the G.G.L. pocket [name for the business group that controlled City Hall], and carry the Republican Mayor's brass ring through his nose. Having learned the value of 50 pieces of silver, and by his singular devotion to the G.G.L., Daniels has done more damage to the Democratic party than all the Republicans combined could ever do.[16]

Representative Johnny Alaniz had alerted Peña to a bill working its way through the legislative session seeking to prevent closed-door sessions, pre-meeting sessions, and what Peña dubbed "Bat-Roost" sessions of officials holding local government elected positions. Peña wanted transparency in public deliberations and votes. He wanted to end pre-meeting sessions for he had been the victim of this practice when the other commissioners and county judge worked their deals without him. He editorialized on this bill in his "County Comment."[17]

The city elections in San Antonio were coming up, and his friend Reverend Claude Black from the East Side was seeking a council seat. Peña's larger group, the Bexar County Democratic Coalition (BCDC) had met and endorsed Black. Peña's LAD was no more; he had helped organize a larger county group that mirrored the statewide coalition of DOT—labor, liberals, blacks, and Mexicans. Peña endorsed Rev. Black in his columns and radio addresses. But Black lost the election. Had he won, Black would have been the first Negro to win a San Antonio city council seat.[18]

While Black did not win despite Peña's endorsement, albeit PASO, other Mexican Americans won all the seats in Crystal City's council. Peña had had a hand in that election victory since the day Moises Falcon, a PASO member of a chapter in that city, had walked into his commissioner's office months before in 1962 and asked him for help. Peña learned from Falcon that the Teamsters had a local union in that city; that Méxicanos had organized a PASO chapter in the hopes that they could get representation on their city council and school board; that they were helpless and hopeless without outside help; and that they looked to him as their leader.

After that visit, Peña called Ray Shafer of the local Teamsters to verify the existence of a local in Crystal City. He asked if Shafer knew of the stirrings in that city by Mexican Americans, and if he would help with getting his members there to sponsor and conduct a voter registration drive to get Mexican Americans elected to local governments. Shafer told him two of his union representatives and a disgruntled Anglo businessman had visited him with complaints about this exclusion from public office. But Shafer also told Peña he was not eager to put his union on the line; he had seen and heard Mexican Americans complaining about local matters before, and seen them cave in when the going got rough. Peña countered Shafer with the idea that a Mexican American project of this type could help the Teamsters organize labor in more cities in South Texas. Before committing to any grand plan, Shafer and Peña agreed to go visit Crystal City together and assess the situation.

Crystal City, aka Cristal

Albert A. Peña Jr. had helped Henry B. González campaign for the governorship of Texas in 1958.[19] During one of the many campaign forays, Peña accompanied González to Crystal City, Texas, and held a political rally adjacent to the Rodríguez Food Store on W. Zavala, a major shopping location for Méxicanos in town. Candidate González and other speakers stood above the crowd on a flatbed truck. Peña was one of these speakers, but he also worked the crowd, shaking hands, passing out palm cards with González's name, and introducing himself as well. Both González and Peña were dressed in business suits with white shirts and ties. The payment of the poll tax was a prerequisite to vote. Peña's remarks, when it came time for him to speak to the crowd, zeroed in on the need for Méxicanos to have a political voice and that they therefore must pay their poll tax in a timely manner. Peña's favorite political topic was twofold: organize and register to vote. He astutely gauged the *Cristalenos* interest in electoral politics by the large numbers of those in attendance at the González for Governor rally.

Peña knew of school segregation issues in nearby Batesville, in Zavala County, and in the adjacent counties to the south and north of Cristal: Carrizo Springs in Dimmit County and Uvalde in the county by the same name. While he did not directly participate in the desegregation of schools in those cities, he was involved in the planning and legal strategies used by the San Antonio lawyers who traveled to those communities in the late 1950s.

Peña, as Texas state president of PASO, returned to Cristal in the fall of 1962, as the period for payment of the poll tax began, to support the local chapter. He promised that if Méxicanos in sufficient numbers paid the poll tax, he would bring resources to help elect five Méxicanos to the city council. A year earlier, several people from that city, including some members of the Teamsters local, had visited with him and obtained certification as a PASO chapter for their group in Cristal. They reminded him of that visit and its purpose. Peña knew the PASO chapter had organized and members were trying to register people to vote by paying the poll tax. He also learned firsthand that they were meeting with difficulties from the county officials and the presence of Texas Rangers intimidating those who went to the courthouse to register to vote. During the course of those two years, 1962–1963, Peña became acquainted with many of the local leaders from Cristal and the neighboring communities.

I had first seen Peña during the González campaign for governor, but did not know who or what he was; like most young men my age, we were just about to enter high school. The men with González were Mexicans in suits, arrived in big cars, spoke eloquently, and were as articulate in English as in Spanish. My friends and I had never seen such a sight: Mexicans in suits and one of them running for governor—whatever that meant. For that matter, most Cristal Mexicans had not seen such a sight or met a candidate for governor in the company of men who looked and spoke like them either. The only ones in suits were Anglos at the courthouse, bank, city hall, and schools. Cristal Mexicans for the most part were seasonal agricultural workers who migrated to northern states every year during March–April and September–October; they did not wear suits. I recall that the only Mexicans in suits I saw were working in banks and offices in the Mexican border town Piedras Negras, across from Eagle Pass, Texas, forty-four miles away. On occasion my father would wear a suit when we traveled to Piedras Negras or San Antonio and sometimes to church services.

When Peña came to discuss with the local PASO leaders the question of helping get Méxicanos to pay their poll tax, the larger, looming question was toward what end. He was assured that the local Mexícano community was tired of second-class status and the dictatorial nature of city government. They wanted change. Mayor Bruce Holsomback had been in office for thirty-seven years. The police, city and county, regularly arrested, beat, and held in jail scores of Mexicans, working men, every weekend for some alcohol-related incident, usually walking while drunk. Mexican men would gather on Fridays and over the weekend to drink beer in the local cantinas. Those without cars, pickup trucks, or rides home would walk and be arrested. Those with vehicles would also be arrested for driving while intoxicated. The local police would sit and wait for dances to end and for cantinas to close so they could stop and arrest Méxicanos going home. The school board, county government, and city council had no Méxicanos in public office. They had no voice or representative. Salvador Galvan, on the city council, had a Spanish surname but was not perceived as being a Méxicano. He did not mix or mingle with the Mexícano community; he lived across the tracks in the Anglo side of town. In Cristal, few Mexícano children made it past the middle grades and into high school. The streets in the Mexican barrios of Cristal were unpaved and without sidewalks. The local public swimming pool was segregated, as were the Boy Scout troops and Catholic Mass services. The 9 a.m. Mass was in English and for Anglos. The local newspaper, the *Zavala County Sentinel*, seldom carried any news about Méxicanos other than arrests and convictions and an occasional photo of a wedding or *quinceañera*. And, of course, it was written in English for and about Anglos. Peña was shocked at what he heard. The situation in Cristal to him was like stepping back in time. How could a Mexícano majority of the population allow this to happen? Why did they not organize and take control of local government? He knew that poverty, illiteracy, fear, dependence, unemployment, lack of leadership, no resources, and no contacts outside of Cristal kept the Méxicanos oppressed.

I had graduated from high school in May 1962 and was attending the local community college in Uvalde in 1963, commuting daily by bus. Beginning in fall 1962, my friends and I had volunteered to raise funds with which to pay the poll tax, which by then was $1.75. There was talk that Méxicanos were going to run for public office on the city council and school board. The women members of the local PASO chapter and other volunteers began to hold raffles, cake walks, bingos, tamale sales, and dances to raise money. We would help them with volunteer labor. The PASO men did not take young men or any woman seriously. In our case we were under the age of twenty-one and therefore ineligible to register to vote. Politics was a male thing, not for women or young men.

Peña and Shafer had discussed what they learned about conditions in Crystal City with their respective coleaders in San Antonio. Together they had discussed the potential in that city for PASO's aims and purposes and labor's interests with other members of the BCDC. Other labor leaders in the BCDC agreed the city was ripe for change. Once Peña and Shafer reached an accord on the plan of action, they began allocating resources to Cristal's PASO chapter. The strategy was simple. First, Méxicanos needed to pay their poll tax and register in sufficient numbers by January 31st. Without a majority of voters, the Méxicanos would not be able to outvote the Anglos. Second, they needed to form a slate of candidates to oppose the local Anglo officeholders on the city council and school board. Third, they must get out the Mexícano vote for their candidates and win. The voter registration drive was most successful. At the end of the period for voter registration on January 31,

1963, the local PASO leadership was instructed and provided with money to go buy the list of registered voters. Juan Cornejo, the Teamsters local job steward and now candidate-to-be, attempted to buy it and was rebuffed by the county tax assessor-collector. Juan Cornejo, in the company of Carlos Moore, a Teamsters representative from San Antonio, again went to purchase the list and was successful. The tax assessor-collector explained to Moore that he had not refused Cornejo; he had just informed him it was not ready for sale to the public. But, now it was.

In a matter of hours, Cornejo's sidekick Natividad Granados counted the Mexícano names and Anglo names on the voter list. He shouted with glee that Mexícanos had many more voters than Anglos. Moore, not as familiar with Spanish surnames as Granados, checked the count by only counting the Anglo names. His numbers for Anglos matched Granados's numbers. If the number of Mexícano voters was correct, the Mexícanos could win if they voted for their candidates. The number of registered voters was 1,681 and a whopping 1,139 were Mexícanos. The Anglo maximum vote potential was only 542.

The two pending items of the plan proved to be most troublesome. Other than Juan Cornejo, who was encouraged to run by Ray Shafer himself, and was a single man without dependents, no other Mexícano wanted to run. Virginia Múzquiz, a PASO member, was mentioned as a possible candidate but never even asked to consider making the race. Many of the male PASO members refused the nomination in meeting after meeting called for that purpose. Moises Falcon, one of the architects of the plan, declined to run, citing family and economic obligations. Natividad Granados declined, claiming he was not qualified. Jesus Maldonado, a warehouseman at Del Monte and not covered by the Teamsters Union contract, declined to run for the city council but ultimately accepted to run for the school board. Eusebio C. Muñoz, an insurance salesman, declined. He had run three years before and had been defeated for lack of Mexícano support.

The main concern among the PASO men and others not affiliated with PASO was fear of reprisals from Anglo employers. There were not enough full-time jobs in Cristal; those with a job wanted to keep it at all costs. Most of the jobs were at the Teamster-unionized Del Monte Plant. And even though the Teamsters promised legal assistance to anyone in case any of their union members, particularly Juan Cornejo, was threatened with reprisal by the Del Monte plant Anglo supervisors, no one stepped up to the challenge. With the filing deadline for the city council and school board rapidly approaching, the plan seemed to fall apart simply because no one wanted to run. Peña and Shafer both recommended local PASO recruit candidates not working at the Del Monte plant. Finally, Manuel Maldonado, a ranch foreman, stepped up to run. He had asked his employer and was given permission to run. Antonio Cardenas, a labor contractor who ferried migrant workers to and from Cristal, also became a candidate. A photographer, Reynaldo Mendoza, whose clientele were Méxicanos, had little to lose and stepped forward. Finally, a used car salesman, Mario Hernandez, was recruited and completed the slate of five, Los Cinco Candidatos. PASO suggested they run under the banner of "Citizens Committee for Better Government" (CCBG), with Moises Falcon as its head. Two other candidates were found for the school board, Jesus Maldonado and Lorenzo Olivarez, a barbershop operator. Like Mendoza the photographer, Olivarez's clientele was Mexícano; he did not depend on Anglo business to make a living year round. Among all the Mexícano candidates, only Jesus Maldonado had a high school education. Immediately, the allegations and accusations that the Teamsters Union were going to run a bunch of unqualified and ignorant Mexícano rabble for local government offices were heard throughout the Anglo community and among the Mexican employees who worked at those businesses and homes. These Mexican employees were the Anglos' conduit to information on what barrio residents were planning.

As had been the case in trying to buy the poll list of voters, the Mexícano candidates were stymied by June Broadhurst, the city secretary, and the school board secretary when attempting to formally file their candidacies. They were told no forms existed, and on another occasion that they were out of the new forms. With the help of Carlos Moore, Martin García, and Natividad Granados's typewriter, the candidates were able to generate correct forms that complied with Texas Election Code requirements. Carlos Moore was an expert on the election code; it seemed that way to Anglos who accepted the forms and placed the names of all seven Méxicanos into nomination. Peña frequently made the pilgrimage to Cristal. He was driven there by Arnold Flores, a thirty-five-year-old military veteran who had become fascinated by politics during the Henry B. González campaign for U.S. Senate. He had met Peña during that campaign, and Peña had encouraged him to volunteer and help in this campaign. Among those attorneys present from time to time and supportive of Los Cinco Candidatos, as the all-Mexícano slate began to be known, were Johnny Alaniz, Arthur Gochman, Herschel Bernard, and non-attorneys Carlos Moore and Henry Muñoz. The local Anglos in Crystal City assumed Moore was an attorney, and he did nothing to disabuse them. Moore played attorney to the hilt and successfully; initially they thought he was an oil man searching for land to lease for such exploration. Anglos confided in him their opinions of the stirrings in the city and their plans to subvert the Méxicanos' plans. Moore was Shafer's union employee who regularly reported his information-gathering to him, Peña, and locally to Cornejo. The team that PASO and the Teamsters recruited and supported as paid staff included a St. Mary's law student, Martin García, who stayed in Cristal to coordinate day-to-day activities, and Albert Fuentes Jr. Fuentes, who was now Peña's top lieutenant in PASO, was no longer on the Bexar County payroll and made frequent trips to Cristal. He and Peña, and on occasion state representatives Johnny Alaniz, Jake Johnson, and Rudy Esquivel, would make the trek and be guest speakers at PASO rallies held by Los Cinco Candidatos. The San Antonio Teamsters paid for printing of posters and flyers. Local PASO and the CCBG paid for the sound truck rented from the Luna Theatre owner to announce the rallies and meetings to be held by Los Cinco Candidatos. The focus and primary effort was on the PASO-Teamster sponsored campaign for the city council and not the school board candidates. The school board election was to be held several days later than the city election. If they won the city, it was assumed they would win the school board; besides, the potential for control of the city council was greater in that all five seats were being contested, while at the school board only two of seven.

The short campaign between candidate announcement and election was grueling and getting dangerous. Local Anglos called on Captain Alfred Y. Allee, head of Company D of the Texas Rangers, to help contain the Mexicans. The Texas Rangers were enormously feared by Méxicanos since their atrocities dating back to the period 1910–1930. Captain Allee resided in Carrizo Springs, only twelve miles south of Crystal City. Ranger Company D had its headquarters on the outskirts of that city on the road to Eagle Pass. Local police, city and county, now augmented by Captain Allee and his Texas Rangers would regularly patrol by circling the Mexícano crowds that gathered to see and hear the speeches of Los Cinco, other supporters, and the men in suits from San Antonio. The menacing stares of these law enforcement types did intimidate the people. The practice of remaining in their cars and honking approval rather than clapping became the norm. Few people dared to be seen standing under the lights of the dilapidated structure from where the speakers held the microphone at the Mexico Chico barrio park known as La Placita, the only park available to Méxicanos in Crystal City at that time. Supporters feared recognition by the police and Rangers; they suspected that their Anglo employers, upon such reports of their presence at the rallies and meetings, would fire them the following work day.

Economic reprisals did occur during the campaign; Teamsters-paid attorneys immediately would jump on the cases and usually got employees reinstated. Nevertheless, the firings, threats, and intimidation had a chilling effect on supporters of Los Cinco. But the Mexícano voters did not withhold support; they just kept their opinions and activities more private. One of the most effective economic weapons controlled by Anglos was raising wages. The Del Monte plant, as did many growers, the employers of farm workers, increased the price for piecework and hourly rates as soon as the period for absentee voting began and through

Election Day. The Del Monte plant increased the hourly wage to $2.00 an hour, but workers had to stay on the job without a dinner break or any break until 10 p.m. Albert Fuentes insisted Carlos Moore call the Teamsters national president, Jimmy Hoffa, because Shafer's calls to local plant officials were being ignored. Hoffa did call the local plant officials; he called the company headquarters in San Francisco, California. Hoffa threatened the company with immediate litigation if they did not allow workers time off to go vote before 7 p.m. when the polls closed. Del Monte plant officials did allow time to go vote if an employee asked permission. Many did and hurriedly went to vote.

Los Cinco and their supporters called on the labor contractors, who picked up and drove the field hands to work and back, not to keep the workers away from voting at the hours and days indicated. The labor contractors complied and, to the dismay and protest of growers, would drive back with dozens of workers in time for rallies, meetings, and voting. Mexícano workers themselves left work and went to vote at the only polling location, City Hall, by car and on foot, especially on Election Day. The lines were long throughout the day at key times, such as before 8 a.m., at noon, and between 5 p.m. and 7 p.m. The Texas Rangers and all local police attempted to intimidate Mexícano voters by staring them down when eye contact was made; walking close to voters with their guns swinging; often yelling at voters to stay on the sidewalk and off the street; and yelling at them to not block the sidewalk for others. The city officials in charge of the election process refused to allow Los Cinco's poll watchers into City Hall before the poll opened at 7 a.m. Carlos Moore again confronted the authorities with references to the provision in the election code that allowed for poll watchers designated by candidates. Moore got some of the poll watchers admitted; it was going to be hard for the election officials to cheat in sight of them. The various Anglo tactics of intimidation, harassment, and illegal obstruction of the election process did not work. The Mexícanos voted in record numbers and they voted for Los Cinco. Manuel Maldonado was the highest vote getter with 864, and Reynaldo Mendoza obtained the lowest total of 795 among the five Mexícano candidates. The top vote getter for the Anglo candidates was Ed Ritchie with 754 votes, just 41 votes less than Mendoza. Salvador Galvan was the lowest vote getter for the Anglo ticket with 664 votes. During the campaign it was said that both Ritchie and Galvan were of Mexican ancestry. The presence of two Independent candidates, Henry Daly and Arnold López, on the ballot complicated matters for both sides, and these candidates received 164 and 146 votes, respectively. Had they not been on the ballot, the election could have gone the other way against Los Cinco or the Anglo slate. Daly was the only optometrist in town, with many clients, Anglo and Mexican; his mother, it was rumored, was Mexican and he did speak fluent Spanish. He was well liked. López was a Baptist minister who had been approached to run so he could split the Mexícano vote. He filed and stayed in the race as an Independent.

Peña got word of the victory immediately that night from Martin García. Moore in turn informed Ray Shafer that the Mexícanos had won. Besides news of the victory, both men reported to Peña and Shafer that violence on the part of Anglos and especially the Texas Rangers was imminent. They urged Peña to get help, even if it meant calling Governor Connally to order Captain A. Y. Allee to stop his and his men's actions directed at councilman-elect Juan Cornejo. Allee was furious at the Mexícano jubilation and informed Cornejo at one of the victory celebrations that he was declaring martial law and imposing an immediate curfew. Particularly aggravating to Anglos and the police were the spontaneous car caravans that sprouted everywhere with horns blaring in the air.

The press widely reported the unprecedented victory the next day. The news of Los Cinco winning all seats of the city council in Crystal City was a political shot heard around the world.[20] Anglos had controlled City Hall since the founding of the city in 1907; now they were out of office. Across the state the eyes of Texas focused on the Mexícano "takeover" in Crystal City, as it was headlined. John Shockley, in his book *Chicano Revolt in a Texas Town*, wrote, "Crystal City was the only community in Texas, and perhaps the Southwest, where Anglos had been ousted from decades of rule."[21] Shockley also reported that the Crystal City election story that year was voted "the second most newsworthy event occurring in Texas during the year. It was second only to the assassination of President Kennedy."[22]

Three days later, the Mexícano school board candidates lost their election bids by nearly a 100 vote margin. The school district boundaries were larger and included more Anglos than Méxicanos.

Los Cinco Candidatos were victorious in their election challenge against the Anglo establishment in Cristal in 1963. Now they needed more help from the Teamsters and PASO in governing. Peña was not directly involved with the Mexican American city councilmen after the election, but he was most instrumental in making suggestions, offering advice, and finding resourceful people to help manage the city's affairs. Peña's calls to state legislators and the governor's office complaining of Captain A. Y. Allee and the Texas Rangers did get attention. Governor Connally called Allee and made him turn over the keys to City Hall to Juan Cornejo, who became mayor. Manuel Maldonado, the highest vote getter, was fired from his job and declined to be mayor. Martin García was installed as the interim city manager with Ed Shapiro as his assistant. Later Peña would recommend George Ozuna as city manager—the first Mexican American in Texas to hold this appointed position. Ozuna was from San Antonio. Peña also recommended Emmett Tuggle as an architect and Arthur Gochman as the city attorney. Gochman (now owner-operator of Academy Stores in Texas), Shapiro, and Tuggle were friends of Herky Bernard, Peña's closest legal advisor. All these men went to Crystal City to help implement reforms in the city and improve its facilities and services.

The Aftermath of PASO's Victory in Cristal

After the victory in Cristal, Peña received countless congratulatory letters, telegrams, telephone calls, and personal comments from across the state and country. Other letters from Killeen, Wharton County, Pearsall, Devine, Beeville, Mathis, and Martindale asked Peña to bring PASO to their communities and repeat the Cristal model. Lionel Castillo, much later to become U.S. commissioner of immigration and naturalization during the Jimmy Carter presidential administration, sent a congratulatory letter from "Cebu City, Philippines." Edward Frazer from Cusco, Peru, and Emilio Garza from Bogota, Colombia, both wrote letters of praise and enclosed a copy of an article on the Crystal City story that appeared in *Life* magazine.[23] There were many angry letters as well addressed to Peña. Cameron County Judge Oscar Dancy wrote a lengthy three-page letter disclaiming any discrimination against "Latins" in his South Texas county. He expressed outrage with Jimmy Hoffa's leadership of the Teamsters and warned Peña not to allow them to take over PASO. Dancy suggested to Peña that he follow the leadership of Dr. Hector P. García of the American G.I. Forum. Dr. García and William and Tony Bonilla, LULAC leaders from Corpus Christi, openly criticized Peña and PASO in the media for allowing the Teamsters a role in the Crystal City elections. They began an orchestrated campaign to run a slate of officers at the June 1967 PASO convention. The *Corpus Christi Caller* ran a story on June 7, 1963, containing many rumors about what was to happen at the PASO convention, none of them laudatory of Peña or the Teamsters or Fuentes. The rumors were that Peña was stepping down as PASO chair and asking that his executive secretary, Fuentes, be elected chair; that Peña was organizing a "draft Peña" movement to show his popularity and support among the membership after the Crystal City election; that the Teamsters were financing Fuentes to take over PASO; and finally, that the Bonilla brothers and Dr. García were bringing hundreds of delegates to the convention to take PASO away from Peña, Fuentes, and the Teamsters.[24]

At the Commissioners Court, his colleagues voted to censure Peña for his role in the Crystal City elections. Peña fought back. He denounced them. Commissioner A. J. Ploch and he had a verbal war during that meeting that made headlines in the local papers.[25] William Bonilla had gone to Crystal City and formed a LULAC chapter in opposition to the PASO group. Bonilla had called for Texas Ranger protection as he feared for his life, he claimed, as he responded to the cries for help from his contacts in Crystal City. His friends in LULAC and the American G.I. Forum in many cities were having to take sides for or against Peña, according to the media quotes attributed to Dr. García and the Bonilla brothers. Astute Anglo politicians began to frame the growing Mexícano voter activity as a bad omen and referred to any such stirrings in other localities as creating "another Crystal City" as if that were a bad result, not democracy in action. That phrase became the euphemism for hiding the racist white backlash to growing potential electoral power among Méxicanos. Nevertheless, in his writings in "County Comment" for May and June 1963, Peña continued his advocacy of Crystal City–style direct electoral action, labor rights against the Taft-Hartley "right to work law" provision, and the elimination of the poll tax.

At the PASO convention, Peña ran for reelection as chair and won handily against all opponents. In his speech to the PASO delegates, he refuted many of the baseless allegations and rumors circulating during the days of the convention, which had been fueled by the media and Dr. García and the Bonilla brothers of LULAC. In the first twenty-five words of his speech, Peña stated loudly and clearly, "I have no apologies to make." The response was an immediate ovation of thunderous applause. He continued,

> The most effective answer to these charges is that these Mexican-American voters in Crystal City are native born, having lived and worked there all their lives. Contrary to some reports there were no unusual disturbances. The Sleeping Giant simply woke up and realized that the people who were in public office had long neglected and forgotten them. That it is the duty of all civil government officials to seek the common good of all its people, and in its police power to defend the rights of all the people, and it also has a duty to assist the weak and the needy. So the Mexican-American voters organized politically and made the necessary changes—not by bullets, but by ballots.

He included in his remarks that 95 percent of all eligible voters in the city had voted—a remarkable turnout in and of itself, unmatched anywhere in the country. He went on to say that

> as long as 95% of the citizens vote anywhere in the United States or everywhere in the United States our democracy will survive no matter what the obstacles. . . . We are Americans. We are proud to be called Americans. And we insist on being treated like Americans. . . . We have lifted the Cactus Curtain.

Again more thunderous applause from the audience interrupted his speech; U.S. Senator Ralph Yarborough was among those in attendance and on his feet showering

Peña with applause. Peña closed with future work for PASO: civil rights, voting to eliminate the poll tax, farm workers and labor, more political organizing, and to continue being a "PASO servant." The Peña speech was reduced in part and reprinted in "County Comments," and some parts were read over the air in his radio program on KUKA and KEXX.[26]

The remainder of 1963 was as tumultuous as the spring following the Crystal City elections. Similar efforts to spark a Crystal City–like movement among PASO members in Beeville and Mathis did not get off the ground. Labor was not in Peña's corner for more Crystal City–style elections. There were noticeable fault lines developing in Peña's liberal statewide coalition, DOT, and the local counterpart, BCDC. Peña was beginning to question if what was good for labor necessarily was good for Mexican Americans. The Anglo liberals did not seem too happy with the emerging Chicano nationalism Peña called "lifting the Cactus Curtain." The Sleeping Giant stereotype was shattered and the giant was now walking in South Texas, or so it seemed to Anglos in those communities.

Then, President Kennedy was assassinated in Dallas and Lyndon Johnson became president. Peña had his new administrative assistant Henry Muñoz send an immediate letter from both of them to President Lyndon B. Johnson expressing sorrow for the death of President Kennedy. President Johnson acknowledged Commissioner Peña's letter.[27] The end of Camelot also meant Peña's access to the Kennedys was short-lived. Now Dr. Hector P. García, ally of LBJ since the Felix Longoria incident in the late 1940s, had the greater access to the White House.[28] Toward the end of the year, Peña had to pull back on PASO travel to install chapters and organize new ones, and tend to county business. His last effort that year was to revise the PASO constitution at the behest of Carlos Truan; a convention was called in Brownsville, Texas, on December 8 for that purpose. His speech at that gathering was a eulogy for JFK that extended sympathy to the widow. Peña also called on the delegates to stand behind the new president and pray for the full recovery of Governor Connally. Peña conferred with other officers and delegates about a PASO meeting in Waco for February 1964 to screen candidates running for office. Olga and he returned to San Antonio ready to file for reelection as commissioner in 1964.

The drive back to San Antonio for the Peñas was a four-hour opportunity for Olga to discuss family issues and priorities; Albert attempted to reason and negotiate with her that he had important political work to continue as PASO's state chair, and plans for the Bexar County Coalition, which was still shaky from the Crystal City election. It seemed the two were not looking at or reading from the same page. Olga must have realized that she had a part in getting him to "help his people" and must find ways now to juggle family obligations and needs with the upcoming reelection campaign. She must learn to make do without Albert at home when he was on the road.

Little did either of them realize how much more demanding of Peña's time the next four years would be. PASO executive secretary Albert Fuentes Jr. tendered his resignation at the Waco, Texas, PASO Executive Meeting. He also announced he would be seeking the lieutenant governor position in the 1964 elections.[29] State representative Johnny Alaniz had earlier in 1963 announced at a press conference that the Bexar County Coalition would file candidates, a full slate, against the GGL-sponsored candidates for the city council in the next election. These moves had Peña's fingerprints all over it, for he still was the head of the coalition and probably would be most involved with candidate recruitment, selection, fundraising, and campaigning as well as his own.

Right after the New Year celebrations and resolutions, Congressman Henry B. González arrived back in the home district with representatives of the U.S. Department of Agriculture to discuss the wage rates for beet workers. The congressman had invited Commissioner Peña to address the group. Peña wrote out his remarks to the group and printed these words in "County Comment" for January 10, 1964: "Our Chamber of Commerce brochure . . . points with pride to the blending of two cultures—one Spanish, and one Anglo-Saxon. But the brochure doesn't mention our third culture—the culture of poverty, disease and illiteracy." He was talking about his constituents in the edges of his precinct, particularly the *colonia* by Mission Espada on the South Side. He quoted the family income for migrant families at "less than $1,000 a year." And he told them about a pair of old sisters who had lived in a chicken coop for the last thirty years. He pled with them to "begin . . . by raising the minimum wage for beet workers . . . and then, and I can't emphasize this too much . . . and then ENFORCE that minimum wage" (emphasis in text). Clearly, Peña could see that a person earning a minimum wage could take care of themselves and not depend on government for support and assistance.[30]

The 1964 reelection campaign from primary to General Election was not difficult for Peña to win. His efforts in 1963 on behalf of the city police force, firefighters, and other city workers seeking better working conditions and pay had won him their support. The problem was that many of them did not vote in his precinct; they lived elsewhere.[31] The only surprise from the November election was that the Bexar County Commissioners Court now had a new county judge, Charles Grace; all others who had voted to censure him in 1963 would remain on the Commissioners Court for at least two more years. Peña wishfully hoped that in 1966 he could pick up another commissioner seat and therefore a majority. His trusted coleader in PASO as executive secretary and former county employee, Albert Fuentes Jr., had left Peña's side and filed to run for lieutenant governor as a

Democrat. Peña did all he could in Bexar County for Fuentes, but could not help him across the state as he once had done for Henry B.

Fuentes was running against a racist theater owner, Preston Smith, from West Texas who was among the last to integrate his theaters. Smith was in the state legislature and had more resources than Fuentes and was most conservative. Peña's problems statewide were compounded by the fact that he had refused President Johnson's personal plea to endorse John Connally's reelection bid. Johnson and Peña had come to a crossroads, even though his Democratic Coalition had within days of Kennedy's assassination pledged their support to see him elected as president.[32] Fuentes lost. He did not even carry Bexar County. Peña's forces could only get 26,559 votes for Fuentes compared to 40,927 for Smith. The statewide results were even more lopsided. Fuentes was able to get more votes than when Henry B. ran for governor, but not enough to make a credible showing. He lost to Smith: 304,350 to 1,160,218.[33] Peña also noticed that there had been a 100,000 vote drop-off between Fuentes's vote total and that of the liberal candidate for governor. Could it be that the Anglos and labor in his liberal coalition were not able or willing to get their constituencies to vote for the Mexícano candidate Fuentes?

Worse yet for Peña, John Connally became governor of the state. Peña still recoiled every time he recalled a memory or heard the Connally name. Moreover, Governor-elect Connally had beaten the state liberal coalition's candidate, Don Yarborough, by nearly a four to one vote margin: 1,877,793 to 471,411 in the primary. PASO had launched a Viva Johnson campaign to help the president win a full term and they did. Peña did gain some political capital for that victory, and perhaps that is why John Connally received such a high vote number riding on President Johnson's coattails. After the General Election confirmed both Connally and Johnson as governor and president, Peña was invited by President-Elect Johnson to a barbecue at the LBJ Ranch near Stonewall, Texas, in the Hill Country. President Johnson had invited Mexican president Gustavo Díaz Ordaz as his special guest and one hundred others, with Peña included among the thirty Mexican Americans. But the occasion was not the time or the place to get into many details about LBJ's plans for his administration. Peña spent most of his time with the other Mexican American officeholders, including Congressman González, who had flown with the president to Texas, and with Anglo labor leaders.

The payment of poll taxes for voting in 1964 in Texas had reached a historic high of 2,411,679, and with the exemptions for the elderly who did not have to pay the tax to vote, the total figure of those eligible to vote was 3,014,597.[34] Apparently those who had paid their poll tax voted for the more conservative candidate among the Democratic field. Clearly, the focus for the state and local liberal coalition and other similarly minded groups in the state and nation was on seeking a registration period shorter and closer to the election, plus the elimination of the poll tax. Perhaps the latter idea was most important, as without the tax more people would register and vote liberal.

State PASO had recruited and endorsed candidates in counties and cities with chapters, and many of these had won. The PASO scorecard in 1964 was good at the local level. Peña congratulated these various chapters by letter, telephone calls, and personal visits between commitments in Bexar County. He had traveled to McAllen at summer's end that year to kick off a PASO membership and voter registration drive. His speech was typical of the Peña style of presenting his views. First, he lauded the local PASO chapter for electing two PASO-endorsed candidates and a third moderate out of four possible. "Three out of four is a good batting average in any league," he stated. He used that opening salvo to defend the PASO record and viability and then said,

> "And what happened to the leader, organizer and president of the Anti-PASO group here in Hidalgo County? Who said PASO is dead? There may be some dead politicians here and there, but it isn't PASO." Then, he invoked the legacy of John Kennedy and even Pope John Paul, the "two Johns." And he closed in the remaining half of his talk with a list of "to-do's" for PASO: "The number one problem is illiteracy;" "Two other problems facing the Mexican-American minority is job and wage discrimination;" "and the plight of the migrant;" and then added, "We must organize, we must mobilize the strongest and most effective campaign yet to defeat these ghosts from the 18th century who have come to haunt our mid-20th century America. We must do this not for the sake of PASO, not for the sake of the poor Mejicano, but for our country.... This was the legacy left to all of us by the two Johns. This is PASO."[35]

With the elections behind them, PASO chair Peña and Olga once again reviewed the same issues of their marriage. With more children now, Olga needed him to travel less and stay closer to home. She made the case for retirement from PASO by going over the many hits he had taken as PASO chair that had not helped him in Bexar County. Even his labor and liberal friends had gotten shaky, and things were not going any better with Connally as governor and Congressman Henry B. González now working actively to displace hundreds of Mexicano families just blocks from the courthouse with plans for an international fair to put San Antonio on the map as a world-class city. The War on Poverty program was organizing in Bexar County and he needed to study and learn about this program. He had had previous conversations with many about the War on Poverty, but he remained clueless as to the details of implementation. The Commissioners Court had been briefed, but he had not read any of the material. Major George S. Sprague asked for an appointment with him to discuss just that, but he had failed to keep it. He called the major and promised to reset the appointment and make time to hear him out. Meanwhile, Commissioner Peña wrote to a congressman who was asking for help in getting President Johnson to meet "for no more than ten or fifteen minutes" with one of his constituents, Major George S. Sprague, on his trip to San Antonio on the 29th or in Austin on the 30th of August, 1962. Peña sent the letter to Congressman González rather than the White House because he learned from González that he now often hitched rides back to Texas with the president on Air Force One. González forwarded the Peña letter with a handwritten note to Jack Valenti, who in turn forwarded it to Bill Moyer, the press secretary for the president: "I'll appreciate whatever can be done in order to answer the Commissioner. Henry."[36] Peña and Major Sprague had managed to discuss the evolving details of Johnson's War on Poverty by telephone. Peña found that the major had "some interesting ideas on the War on Poverty." Peña was beginning to get a grip on the implications of this massive program.

Olga flat out asked him to quit PASO, at least for a while. To her utter amazement he agreed. And Peña did just that at the Fifth Annual PASO Convention held in San Antonio on July 10, 1965. Of course, he had informed key PASO members and supporters of his desire after five years at the PASO helm to let another person take over. In the first line of his speech at the convention he said, "Ladies and Gentlemen: It is with a feeling of nostalgia that I report to you today, for it is my last report as your State Chairman. You have honored me with this position since the Viva Kennedy movement, five years ago." He pledged to continue being active in PASO and to cooperate with the next state leader. And again, in typical vintage Peña fashion at the podium or at the campaign stop, he went on to list the political priorities for PASO: to eliminate the poll tax; promote redistricting of legislative seats top to bottom; organize the barrios; oppose Governor Connally's attempt to subvert the mandated War on Poverty program wage of $1.25 an hour for participants; bolster PASO's image and encourage Méxicanos to be proud of their heritage, and to not endorse as their candidate one who is not in support of the anti–poll tax amendment, the Civil Rights Act of 1964, or the Voting Rights Act of 1965.[37]

Governor Connally had refused to accept various programs within the War on Poverty, the centerpiece of Johnson's administration. Peña, after some study, found a favorite one for children—Head Start—in the mix of programs under the War on Poverty. Governor Connally rejected that program. In May 1965, Governor Connally vetoed a second program for youth, the Neighborhood Youth Corps. Connally did not want youth earning a dollar an hour, more than their parents earned.

Johnson had initiated the War on Poverty, and its effects were being felt locally with the implementation of programs for youth, women, and children, plus the housing, labor, and economic development initiatives. Governor Connally opposed them all. The Community Action Agency, a grassroots component of the War on Poverty, was being organized in every community and neighborhood in the country, including San Antonio. The residents of the entire country felt connected to this major assault on poverty and deprivation—some because it directly benefited them and others because they opposed such "creeping socialism." Peña, as commissioner, began to turn his attention to how he could get around the governor and his colleagues on the Commissioners Court to bring those programs to Bexar County and South Texas. Peña was frequently asked by others why the president could not get the governor in line on this major domestic agenda. Peña knew the delicate balance between conservative Democrats in Texas and other Southern states and the White House. President Johnson could not crack the whip on Governor Connally any more than he could on any other governor in the South. Nothing much had changed in bringing change to Texas from Peña's perspective.

Early in 1964, Albert Fuentes Jr. made plans to run for the soon-to-be-vacated state position of PASO chair and won. Meanwhile Peña, despite promises to Olga to stay closer to and longer at home, continued to travel. He spoke at the LULAC convention and was asked to be the person to introduce the Republican U.S. senator from Texas, John Tower. Peña astutely answered in his first words the most important question everyone in attendance had on their minds: "A lot of people have asked me why I, a liberal Democrat, would want to introduce tonight's speaker, one of the most conservative of Republicans. I asked myself why, too." He then went on to explain to Senator Tower that LULAC and all Latin Americans felt as he did being a minority from Texas in the Senate.

> His philosophy of government represents a minority of the Congress of the United States. The same might be said for my own philosophy within the boundaries of Texas. Therefore, our speaker's minority position gives us something in common, I believe, and we should be able to understand each other's problems, at least, to some degree.

He concluded his introduction of Tower with,

> I truly believe in a two-party state—a real two-party state, with one party representing one viewpoint and the other party representing the other. The give-and-take between them has made this country's government democratically strong; the lack of two parties in our state had made democracy border on a sham, I think. A strong two party state would militate in favor of our ethnic group, for under a one party state, one party takes us for granted, and the other party has given up on us.[38]

Peña had never so clearly revealed his break with the state conservative Democratic Party in words and actions by standing and welcoming Senator Tower to the speaker's podium.

During that summer's state party convention, the Peña group and the Democrats of Texas coalition took a beating from the Connally forces. The coalition delegates were excluded from selection and Peña wanted redress from the national party. He called around to see if he had support for opening a national fight over the issue. Increasingly Peña was getting fed up with the lack of support and downright opposition to President Johnson's national programs, as were most of the state Democratic Coalition members. They were opposed by conservative Democrats at every turn, as were the president's initiatives, particularly the War on Poverty. Peña's coalition had met with failure in their attempts to get selected as delegates from Texas to the Democratic National Convention. Peña had written to the National Democratic Party chairman, John Bailey, asking how to protest these actions taken by conservative Texas Democrats to the National Democratic Credentials Committee. The state Democratic Party had refused to recognize or select minorities as delegates to the national gathering. Peña wanted to get his group's credentials recognized as an alternative slate to that of the conservative Democrats. If he could not persuade the national committee, they would not get to the convention floor; for now he just wanted to know the process to make a protest. But he got no answer. Peña called Maury Maverick Jr., state Democratic committeeman, for help. Maverick wrote Chairman Bailey in mid-June and received no reply. Maverick wrote again to Bailey with a copy to Jack Valenti at the White House asking for a response "as to the manner of making a protest to the Credentials Committee." Valenti prepared a note to President Johnson and attached Maverick's letter to Bailey.[39] Nothing changed.

The Commissioners Court meetings were becoming contentious. Despite winning reelection for a new term, Commissioner Peña was still being denied by his colleagues on the Commissioners Court an appointment to the Bexar County Hospital District Board of Directors. He raised the issue at a Monday public meeting of the Commissioners Court. He pledged to withhold his vote to set the tax rate for the hospital district until his precinct was represented on the board of directors. He accused the Good Government League and backers of the Oak Hills site for the proposed medical school of pressuring his colleagues not to allow him an appointment. He said, "I've reconciled myself to the Oak Hills site. I was one of the few public officials to lobby for the medical school appropriations." He asked out loud, "How does the district propose to finance two hospitals? Why haven't they raised the minimum wage to at least $1 per hour? Why do people still have to wait for long periods of time before being treated?" He pointed out that he had asked those questions to the hospital district directors and not received a satisfactory answer.

The report they did produce was evasive and never addressed these questions directly. He stated that "the hospital district will receive no cooperation from me until certain questions are answered to the satisfaction of taxpayers."[40]

The next PASO state constitutional convention was set for October 22–24, 1965, in El Paso. The program PASO State Chairman Fuentes had printed for that meeting contained a paid "Welcome" advertisement on each bottom corner of the booklet from both political parties, Democrats on the left corner and Republicans on the right.[41]

Now free of the PASO leadership mantle, Peña regained his focus on local concerns that now had the support of the new county judge Charles Grace. Peña convinced him to sponsor public meetings at the courthouse and around the county for the citizenry to attend and learn about their civil rights. Judge Grace named him to head such a project. Peña announced the upcoming meetings in a series of radio and print venues. The focus was to learn about civil rights and listen to complaints from citizens on this topic, and of course their opinions. He continued during 1965 with more radio and print commentary on the rights of citizens on wages, discrimination, housing, and educational opportunity, and gave information about components of opportunity developing under the aegis of the War on Poverty. By late summer Peña was attacking the Chamber of Commerce and large employers for low wages and job discrimination. He assailed them for the reputation San Antonio had acquired as a result of these practices. He admonished them, particularly the Chamber of Commerce, that they should not brag that San Antonio is a "cheap labor town." For private smaller employers, he repeated complaints he had received: "I will give you only one example; a famous restaurant on Broadway street hires Anglo waitresses, Mexican American girls pick up dirty dishes, and Negroes sweep the floors."[42] The next week he left to attend a White House Conference on Fair Employment Practices. Peña was also intent on waging war against the president and Congress for not ending the Bracero Program, as had previously been announced. Congress had voted to end the program that had been in existence since 1947, started as an emergency war measure during World War II. It was now 1964 and agribusiness, among others, had become addicted to cheap Mexican labor being imported from across the border in the millions of men. President Johnson's undersecretary of state, Thomas R. Mann, had been quoted as saying the White House was asking for a three-year extension of the Bracero Program. Peña wrote the president protesting and received a vaguely worded reply that assured the commissioner there was no proposal to extend the program.[43]

An opportunity arose in early 1966 to have three new federal judges from Texas nominated, for sure at least two locally. On April 24, 1966, a Sunday at home with the family, Commissioner Peña faced a personal dilemma and possible family tragedy. A tornado alert had been issued for Bexar County. Yet he had committed to attending an important meeting at the home of Henry X. Carrillo, a local attorney who lived in Castle Hills in north San Antonio. Peña would have to leave the family and travel across town from the South Side braving the wind, rain, some hail, and the specter of a tornado dropping down at any time anywhere. He decided to go anyway, imploring Olga to be careful and stay indoors with the kids. Olga was livid.

Peña felt he had to go to this meeting because two federal judgeships had opened for the Federal Western District that ran from San Antonio to Del Rio and into West Texas. Another important position on the United States Fifth Circuit Court of Appeals for Texas was also open. Peña had been down this road before when he, the American G.I. Forum, and Senator R. W. Yarborough had sought a federal judgeship in the Southern District of Texas for state judge E. D. Salinas from Laredo and lost. President Kennedy, on the advice of Lyndon Johnson and the Rio Grande Valley Anglo politicians, had gone with the nomination of Reynaldo Garza of Brownsville. The various Mexicano groups and attorneys had not gotten together to caucus and promote one name. This would not happen again; Peña had promised himself.

Peña was centrally involved with creating an ad hoc committee to place in nomination several Chicanos for these positions.[44] He had organized a group of lawyers to meet and reach agreement on which among them to nominate for these judgeships. The ad hoc committee had met several times before at Peña's urging, and the final meeting was on that Sunday. He must be there.

Although eighty-two attorneys were invited to this final meeting, only forty-two braved the weather and attended. Others called in with excuses of prior commitments. Only thirty pledged to support the actions taken on nominees by the group. Some who failed to answer the call to attend sent word with others also expressing support and approval for whatever the group decided to do about these vacancies. The leadership of the ad hoc committee was comprised of five persons: County Commissioner Albert Peña Jr., County Court at Law Judge Hipolito "Hippo" F. García, Henry X. Carrillo, Joe L. Hernandez, and Gregory Peña. A sixth member was added at the Sunday meeting, Judge Carlos Cadena of the Fourth Court of Civil Appeals for the state. Judge Cadena and Joe L. Hernandez were selected as the co-chairs of the permanent committee at the meeting. An action taken was to write a letter to the president, who ultimately would make the nomination to the Senate Judiciary Committee for screening and a vote. Senator Yarborough would also have to be contacted for support of the committee's recommendations. The committee also discussed which of them were interested and willing to be nominated to these three positions. And, they also discussed who else to contact in the large geographic expanse of the Western District. There were important political players just like them in other cities and counties to the west. Undoubtedly, other groups would also seek to make their own nominations. They would have to be contacted if not consulted over the list of potential names of nominees. Some among them would have to be very involved with contacting these competitors to seek support for the Chicano nominees. Someone had to negotiate for all three or at least some of the positions.

At the meeting Peña insisted that a letter to President Johnson be written and sent immediately. Saying and doing are two different things, as Peña had long ago learned, and the committee membership was too large; other competing groups were lobbying them to support their nominees. Too many names were being suggested for these positions, and not all those mentioned were clearly committing to entering the protracted, difficult nomination process; and Peña had other fires, as usual, to attend to. He focused on the content of the letter and collaborated with Joe Hernandez in the drafting.

The letter sent to the White House said in part,

> The concerns of the committee that Latin Americans be given recognition in the federal judiciary prompted the call. The allegations and conclusions were that: 1. There has never been a Latin American in the judiciary of the Federal Western District. 2. The Latin American attorney is not considered in the selection of the federal judiciary in the Western District of Texas. 3. There are numerous Latin American attorneys well qualified in the district. 4. The large number of Americans of Latin American descent in the district are being deprived of proportionate ethnic representation in this judiciary. 5. That the same conditions prevail in our state District Courts in Bexar County. 6. That we, as attorneys, owe a duty to our ethnic brethren to speak to this disparity. 7. And that we, individually and collectively, ask to be considered not as supplicants but as a matter of right.[45]

The letter was finally approved, signed by Joe L. Hernandez, and sent on June 21, 1966. To the chagrin of all involved in this process, their requests for an opportunity to make recommendations fell on deaf ears. They were not consulted on the nominations by the president. No person of Mexican ancestry was considered. It would not be until 1980 that President Carter would appoint the first Mexican American judge for the Western District, Hipolito "Hippo" F. García, of San Antonio. García and Peña had attended St. Mary's University in the 1950s. García had been elected to a county court-at-law bench in Bexar County in 1964 with Peña's help, and was later elected as a state district judge, also for Bexar County.

The new state leader of PASO, Albert Fuentes Jr., decided on a strategy to ensure the organization was perceived as independent of the Democratic Party, particularly by Republicans. This move could be a way to obtain leverage and concessions from the conservative Democrats and even the president. U.S. Senator John Tower, a Republican, would be up for reelection soon, and this independent stance could be of benefit to PASO and Republicans themselves—a reversal for Mexicano voters of the "lesser of two evils" strategy always played on them by conservative Democrats against Republican candidates. Albert Fuentes on two occasions early in 1966 attended Republican functions as the top PASO official, clearly giving the impression he was on PASO business approved by the leadership and Peña. He attended a Republican State Executive Committee meeting in Austin and another in Alice, Texas, during which he shared the microphone and podium with Senator Tower. The vehement criticism against PASO poured forth as it had during the Crystal City elections—partisan, not racist. Some PASO members resigned immediately upon reading the news; others defended the action, including Fuentes and Peña. Peña issued a statement: "It was the first time in the history of PASO that the group had been asked to attend any executive meeting of either of the major parties."[46] Within a month Peña had received many inquiries about his new stance and "personal friend," as he had referred to Tower in a previous introduction, but one distressing call alarmed him. Earlier in the month, Crystal City PASO leaders had called to inform him that Jesus Maldonado, the PASO candidate in the 1963 school board election, had been severely beaten by the sheriff and a justice of the peace. Then in early September, Peña received another hysterical call about the new mayor of Crystal City, an anti-PASO member, Carlos Avila, who had suffered a great tragedy.

Violence in Crystal City

Mayor Avila's brother, Luis Avila, a PASO member, had been brutally beaten by local unidentified Anglos and was in danger of losing his life. He had been taken by emergency vehicle to San Antonio, and could Peña help investigate this gross civil rights violation. When Peña did investigate, the man was out of the hospital and back in Crystal City but was not much help with details; having blacked out, he had no memory of the events and was of little assistance with the investigation. Peña was able to have Avila retain him as his attorney. Peña also queried the local police but not the sheriff; no one, it seemed, had a clue as to who had committed these assaults. The local PASO folks were sure the beatings were warnings to Maldonado and Mayor Avila to stay in line with the Anglos or else they or their family members would answer with their lives. After the school board defeat, Maldonado had been appointed to two important positions on the Urban Renewal Agency and the Board of Equalization for the city. Local PASO leaders turned to

U.S. Senator Ralph Yarborough and congressmen Eligio "Kika" de la Garza and Henry B. González for help. In a long letter addressed to the three, they outlined the case as best they knew it by then:

> On August 1st, 1965, about 9:00 o'clock p.m. in the County Courthouse, in the office of the Justice of the Peace Harold Davis, Mr. Jesus Maldonado was brutally beaten by the County Sheriff C. L. Sweeten and Justice of the Peace Harold Davis. Mr. Jesus Maldonado is a respectable citizen of our community, and he and his wife are held in very high esteem and regard in our community. Mr. Maldonado is a member of the City of Crystal City Board of Equalization, is a former member of the City Board of Urban Renewal Agency, and holds a high position with the local plant of the California Packing Corporation; he is also a veteran holding an honorable military discharge. On September 3, 1965, about 10:00 o'clock P.M. on John F. Kennedy Street, at a Sinclair service station, within the city limits of Crystal City, Texas, A. Cox, a federal employee with the U.S. Department of Agriculture (local office), without warning and with absolutely no provocation severely and brutally beat up Mr. Luis Avila. Mr. A. Cox lured with deceit the said Mr. Luis Avila from the company of his brother, Mr. Carlos Avila, the Mayor of the City of Crystal City. The intended victim of this brutal assault was the Mayor, Mr. Carlos Avila, who refused to accompany Cox to observe certain things that Cox wanted, and insisted to show Mr. Carlos Avila. Mr. Luis Avila was the victim of countless kicks on the part of Mr. A. Cox, who was wearing pointed cowboy boots. Mr. Luis Avila suffered a dislocated elbow. His doctors have advised that he is in danger of losing one eye as a result of this criminal assault.[47]

They sent a copy of the letter to Peña and asked him to aid them in making sure an investigation was conducted by federal authorities. And Peña also received another handwritten document detailing more violence on the part of the sheriff. At a press conference, Peña pledged to prosecute this case and demanded the U.S. Department of Justice investigate all these incidents.

School Segregation Again

In San Antonio, the local PASO chapter investigated the public schools in the San Antonio Independent School District, particularly in the Kenwood Addition, and found segregation. When the PASO chapter leaders confronted school officials, they denied the allegations and went on the offensive. PASO leaders, including Peña, guest district attorney James Barlow, and members including state representative Johnny Alaniz, Charles Albidress Sr., and others, called for a rally. Peña was the master of ceremonies for those in attendance. School district officials were accused by PASO speakers of having launched a "mental terrorism" campaign against PASO for investigating the district, of supporting a slate of candidates for the school board, and of segregating children by race and ethnicity. PASO alleged that in the Kenwood area there were three schools within a six-block radius: one for Negroes, one for Anglos, and one for Latin Americans. The PASO group asked D.A. Barlow to investigate their charges.[48]

The 1966 Election

In 1966 Peña did see a change in the makeup of the Commissioners Court. His friend state representative Johnny Alaniz had filed and run a good race against commissioner Sam Jorrie but lost. County judge C. W. Anderson, who had sworn him in back in 1956, had lost the primary to Charles Grace, a member of the Bexar County Coalition. Peña finally had a bona fide ally on the court—the presiding officer, no less. His wish for a three-person majority on the Commissioners Court had been dashed. Commissioners Jorrie and Ploch handily won reelection.

Peña still was most preoccupied with local issues, and the demands from PASO were still on his table despite his not holding a leadership position. The War on Poverty had erupted into a local war. The conservative forces, headed by Mayor McAllister, had gotten more than a foothold in the membership of the superagency with oversight of the entire local War on Poverty. Ed Lucero had been hired as the executive director of the Bexar County Economic Opportunity Development Corporation (EODC) and contracts were being given out left and right to other groups favorable to the conservative element. The conservatives locally and in the state had given up the fight to oppose implementation and concentrated on taking control of the national patronage coming down into their communities and neighborhoods. Much in keeping with the adage "if you can't beat them, join them," they took early control, and the minorities and the poor then had to fight to get on the board or form their own delegate agencies.

Peña tried to get some appointments for the EODC Board; eventually he was able to place Juan Patlan of the Mexican American Youth Organization (MAYO) on the board. Delegate agencies had gotten contracts, such as the San Antonio Neighborhood Youth Organization (SANYO) headed by Catholic priest John Yanta. The Catholic Church through their parish councils quickly organized and took virtually all the seats allocated to the poor. A young Catholic priest, Henry Casso, had organized seventeen church-based groups into the nucleus of the poor, a category of representation on the governing board of War on Poverty programs at the local level. Rev. Casso had visited with Commissioner Peña, who urged Casso to continue his organizing efforts but took no further interest. He and Casso had collaborated in years past when the priest had asked him for use of county heavy equipment to fill and level dirt at a recreational facility he was constructing. Casso also had dealt with Peña on the multiple incidents of job discrimination at Kelly Air Force Base (KAFB) faced by Mexican Americans. Kelly AFB had a civilian workforce of 23,000 employees and few were Mexican Americans.

Rev. Casso then called on Mayor McAllister, who listened intently to the young native San Antonio priest outline the components of the War on Poverty. Philosophically, McAllister disagreed with Johnson's Great Society and now more particularly with the War on Poverty. McAllister, a staunch Republican, saw this program as a mechanism to redistribute wealth and hand it to the poor. More importantly, the poor were to be placed on boards as equals to businessmen and local political leaders. Unlike Peña, McAllister quickly summoned his circle of influential men running the city from among the ranks of his political machine, the GGL, and instructed them to go out and get on a local board. The most unimaginable coalition formed of GGL stalwarts and blacks from the East Side in competition with Mexican Americans from the West Side and the Catholic Church.[49]

Basically, the local boards had to have board seats divided into three groups: no less than one-third poor, no more than one-third others, and one-third elected officials or their designees. The Catholic Church in San Antonio, building on Rev. Casso's groups, obtained the votes to get on the board. The Catholic Church took all the money for Neighborhood Youth Corps (NYC) projects that Governor Connally had once blocked. Father Yanta, designated by Archbishop Robert Lucey, put together a Rainbow Coalition–type administration for the San Antonio Neighborhood Youth Organization (SANYO) with Romeo Vela, John Edwards, Belvin Stewart, and Lee Venzor just below him and running the various components of the NYC. Rev. Yanta controlled the money and jobs for youth in Bexar County. He and Peña feuded over Yanta's iron rule of those monies and opportunities, but the commissioner could not make changes.

Peña's group had to organize their own delegate agencies that could also contract with the county board for grants. Peña had organized Action for Community Development (ACD) and obtained a preliminary grant, but the Economic Opportunity Development Corporation (EODC) cut off their funding quickly. Early in 1967 Commissioner Peña called a press conference to release copies of the telegrams he had sent to the two Texas U.S. senators, Yarborough and Tower, asking for an investigation into actions taken by the EODC Board of Directors for Bexar County. This local War on Poverty agency, with oversight of all such programs in the area cities and county, had eliminated the Action for Community Development of which Peña was the leader. The ACD program had as its focus assisting migrants residing in the cities and rural Bexar County. Commissioner Peña's district covered a large rural area of Bexar County and a quadrant of San Antonio. The EOCD previously explained to ACD members that the reason for the termination of the program was an adverse government evaluation of the migrant program. Yet, when Peña and others involved with ACD had requested a copy of the evaluation, they were denied. Peña said at the press conference that he was demanding an investigation into this action because "We believe ACD was eliminated because it was doing the job it was designed to do, i.e. to organize people in the poverty areas to help themselves. This was a threat to the local power structure that controls EODC." And reading from the telegram, he urged the U.S. senators to "Please investigate and give the ACD board an opportunity to be heard in other than a sham chamber atmosphere."

Congressman González read a copy of the news clip reporting the Peña press conference and forwarded a copy to the White House. González added in his handwriting a personal note to the legislative counsel to the president, Jake Jacobsen: "Dear Jake: Thought you would like to see this. At least the SOB is considerate enough not to bother me. Henry."[50] No less than six years before, González was thanking Peña for making him the congressman representing Bexar County, and now he was not only backstabbing Peña to staff in the Johnson White House but also referring to Peña as a son of a bitch. Peña never knew of this intrigue and political treason at the time; he was to tangle with González in an open media brawl the following year. Those fights would be over HemisFair and the various labor and Ford Foundation–funded programs Peña was instrumental in bringing to San Antonio. The latter programs were the beginning of Peña's efforts at building Chicano institutions for the state, Southwest region, and ultimately the nation. These were his first steps in the direction of Chicano nation-building.

Vicente Ximenes: Second Chicano in the White House

When word reached Commissioner Peña about an invitation to the White House,[51] he quickly called Olga with the news. Did she want to go? Olga had to plan with relatives and friends to care for the kids and look after the house while she and Albert would be in Washington, DC. They had to leave Thursday and would not return until late Sunday afternoon. This was a trip she did not want to miss; she had never been inside the White House. The occasion was the swearing in of Vicente Ximenes as commissioner of the Equal Employment Opportunity Commission, and they had to be at the outside gate of the White House by 12:45 p.m. in order to make the 1:00 p.m. installation ceremony. He had told her about it upon his return from

Albuquerque. She was quite proud of Albert for leading the Albuquerque Walkout and demanding a Mexican American commissioner be appointed. Vicente Ximenes was formerly from Floresville, just south of San Antonio, but he was loyal to John Connally, who also was from Floresville, Texas. Connally was the one to suggest his name to President Johnson.[52] Ximenes had been the director of the Viva Johnson-Humphrey campaign for the Democratic National Committee (DNC) and moved over to help as inspector general at the beginning of the War on Poverty under Sargent Shriver. In that capacity, Ximenes could no longer oversee the developments of a White House Conference on Mexican American Affairs he had proposed early in 1966. This task was handed over to Louis Martin, vice president of the DNC.[53]

Olga had seen how busy he was after his return when she dropped in to see him at the courthouse. It seemed to her he was always making calls, writing letters, sending telegrams, and traveling to face-to-face meetings across the Southwest, on top of all his other duties. Olga knew how tenacious her man could be once he got into a fight. There was no backing down by Albert. He always told her he lost more fights than he won but those losses were what taught him how to stand up again. Peña and other Chicanos across the Southwest had organized as one unit with one goal and prevailed upon the President of the United States. This important lesson learned was not lost on Peña. Organizing across the Southwest into a major advocacy group had to become a first priority.

At the White House, Olga and Albert were congratulated by everyone including the president, who towered over them as he expressed gratitude for bringing this entire EEOC matter to his attention and even joked that at times it was overkill by Peña. At the White House were Mexican American elected officials, mostly from Texas, such as state representatives Tati Santiesteban and Paul Moreno (El Paso), Honore Legarde and E. D. Salinas (Laredo), Raul Longoria (Hidalgo County), and Chicano leaders from across the country, such as Eduardo Quevedo and his son from California, Henry Lacayo with labor, and Alex Mercure from New Mexico. Ignacio Lozano and his spouse, the founders of *La Opinion* in San Antonio (but now headquartered in Los Angeles), were also there. Professors Julian Samora, Miguel Montes, and George I. Sanchez were there. Everyone was dressed so nice, Olga noticed. She mentioned to Albert how glad she was that wives were invited to this important meeting; many were there. Olga met some important women such as Graciela Olivarez, Mrs. E. C. Toscano, Mrs. Raul Morin, and two young ladies, Aurita Othon and Sandra Padilla. The mayor of Laredo, J. C. Martin, was there. The president of the United Auto Workers Union, Walter Reuther, was also there, and Albert made a beeline to him for conversation. Albert managed to work the room, shaking hands with almost everyone, passing out his business card, and introducing himself to those he did not know.[54]

The president spoke briefly about pledging to end job discrimination and said that he was confident Commissioner Ximenes would see to it that it would be done. Vicente was then sworn in as commissioner and he also commented briefly, thanking the president for selecting him from among many other qualified candidates and promising to do the best job he could because he realized that with this appointment he was the highest-ranking Mexican American in the Johnson administration.[55] With the ceremony concluded and the speeches made, the photographers and media were escorted out and the president strong-armed some women and their spouses for an impromptu tour of the immediate rooms adjacent to the meeting area. Olga was thrilled at the personal attention they received and genuine affection she felt the president had for her husband.

Later that summer of 1967, the president committed to holding a White House Conference on Mexican American Affairs in El Paso in the fall, with Ximenes once again in charge of this gathering. Ximenes was named the head of a newly created sub-Cabinet-level agency, the Inter-Agency Committee for Mexican American Affairs. This agency would be headed by Ximenes with David North as the executive assistant in charge of the actual conference, which would consist of hearings at which selected participants would make written or oral presentations in the form of testimony about the pressing issues and concerns of Mexican Americans in the Southwest.

The president was scheduled to meet with the Mexican president to ratify a treaty over an El Paso border dispute, "El Chamizal," that had lingered unsettled since the infamous 1846 invasion of Mexico by the United States. With El Paso centrally located in the Southwest, Ximenes traveled to that city to make arrangements for the conference. He invited heads of five major Mexican American organizations to meet in El Paso and discuss their involvement as monitors of the hearings and to review a list of invitees. The U.S. senators and representatives from the Southwest had been asked by the president to submit names of their constituents who should be invited to present testimony at the hearings. Commissioner Peña was on the list of names submitted by Senator Ralph Yarborough of Texas. Peña, however, was preoccupied with a local area problem: Mexican American and other employees of the U.S. Gypsum Company plant in New Braunfels, just north of San Antonio, had gone on strike. They were affiliated with the International Association of Machinists Union; they were demanding an end to job discrimination against Mexican Americans and fair labor practices by the company. U.S. Gypsum had many plants with federal contracts. Peña wanted the EEOC and the Office of Contract Compliance to investigate the union complaints filed with these agencies. He had requested that, but had not received a response. Peña resorted to his usual opening salvo on any given issue of importance and called a press conference. At this meeting with media, Peña informed the press of the reasons for the strike and allegations of discrimination. He reported on a telephone conversation he had had with David North, who was organizing the El Paso hearings. He told reporters he had informed North he was not attending the hearings unless the strike was resolved. He raised other issues with North, such as discrimination practices at Kelly Air Force Base in San Antonio and that "it didn't seem right to be invited to a conference sponsored by the federal government when it's one of the worst offenders." He further stated that he was also going to call and meet all the people invited to the El Paso hearings to discuss "whether to go or not." According to Peña there were other outstanding issues surrounding the White House conference, such as a lack of an agenda and the lack of funding for travel and lodging of some invitees. David North promptly obtained a copy of the newspaper article and forwarded it with a note to the White House.[56] Pena did attend and made a presentation that later became known as the Marshall Plan for the Southwest.

Another competing event of importance to Peña was the U.S. Senate Subcommittee on Migratory Labor that took place in the Rio Grande Valley on June 29, 1967. Senators William Harrison (New Jersey), Paul Fannin (Arizona), Ralph W. Yarborough (Texas), and Edward Kennedy (Massachusetts) flew into the South Texas area at Senator Yarborough's insistence. Commissioner Peña and state representative Johnny Alaniz made time to drive down to greet Senators Yarborough and Kennedy particularly. The issue of farm workers' right to strike and the lack of minimum wage protection was boiling into a fight. The Texas Rangers were roughing up farm-worker strikers. La Casita Farms in Rio Grande City in Starr County was the target of the strike. The farm workers did not want to harvest the melon crop. Agricultural employers with more than seven full-time employees had to pay the state minimum wage, but migratory farm workers were not full-time, they were seasonal workers.[57]

Peña attended the hearings, but prior to that he also led a Teamsters-driven caravan of cars and two big trucks loaded with food for the striking workers on June 11th.[58] Later that next month, just after the 4th of July, the farm workers began a four-hundred-mile march from Starr County, Texas, to Austin to talk to the governor about their plight. On August 27, when the marchers reached San Antonio, Peña was there in the company of Archbishop Lucey, who offered Mass and a candlelight vigil. As the fifty marchers moved north and reached New Braunfels on August 31, Governor Connally, House Speaker Ben Barnes, and Attorney General Waggoner Carr with aide Mario Obledo arrived in a large black limousine. The marchers were glad to see the big car pull off the road and recognized the public figures. When Connally was face to face with the ministers Antonio González and James Navarro and the marchers, the dialogue turned nasty. The governor told them flat out that there would be no legislation filed for a minimum wage of $1.25 for farm workers, nor would he receive them at the capitol building when they arrived. He would not dignify the march with his presence in Austin. The photo of the governor and Rev. Navarro almost nose to nose, and the news of what was said were beamed around the country on radio, television, and in newsprint.[59] Chicanos from Brownsville to San Francisco to Chicago were incensed at the arrogance of these Democratic Party officeholders. Thousands congregated at the capitol steps to greet the marchers. Major liberal Democratic politicians such as Senator Ralph Yarborough and state senator Barbara Jordan spoke along with national AFL-CIO head William Kircher, and Hank Brown of the Texas AFL-CIO, and Commissioner Peña. Congressman Henry B. González was also present and spoke in support of the strikers and their demand for minimum wage. César Chávez flew in from California and also delivered a speech in support of the striking marchers and their efforts to unionize. Chávez had just won contract concessions from major wine producers in California after a long, protracted strike and product boycott. He pledged to return with them to the Rio Grande Valley and help organize their union.

The march and marchers took on a new dimension; the *huelgistas* (strikers on the march) and the march became *La Causa*—The Cause. The unionizing effort in Starr County flared into violence on the part of the Texas Rangers and led to many arrests. Leaders from the Mexican American Youth Organization (MAYO) traveled to Rio Grande City in Starr County to confront the Texas Rangers, led by Captain Alfred Young Allee of Company D from Carrizo Springs, who were beating farm workers, such as Magdalene Dimas and Benito Rodríguez. Other labor leaders, such as Francisco "Pancho" Medrano of the United Auto Workers and Benito Rodríguez's wife, Kathy, were beaten by Texas Rangers.[60]

A local state court had issued an injunction against farm-worker picketing. More arrests followed. Among the many arrested and beaten were Rev. Ed Krueger and the UAW's Pancho Medrano, who filed a police brutality action against Captain Allee. The case would take nearly seven years to be finalized at the U.S. Supreme Court in 1974.[61] The injunction had earlier been ruled unconstitutional and appealed by the state. This case also found Allee and the Rangers to have violated the civil rights of farm workers and supporters with their violence. Allee was retired by the Ranger force in September 1970 shortly after his attempts to contain the 1969 Crystal City school walkout by Chicano students.

Peña was appalled by the violence, particularly when he listened to firsthand accounts related to him by state senator Joe Bernal, who had gone to Rio Grande City and had dangerous confrontations with Captain Allee in the Starr County Courthouse. Joe Bernal, a former West Side GGL recruit, had beaten Rudy Esquivel for a legislative seat earlier but had gravitated toward Peña and the Democratic

Coalition. As state senator he was most productive with legislation and accompanied Peña into many political forays.[62] Peña was ecstatic about developments of the litigation against the Rangers. Captain Allee had previously been sued for violence against mayor-elect Juan Cornejo in Crystal City. Key witnesses for Cornejo did not want to testify, and Allee had walked out of the courtroom smiling. Peña had also been unable to pin responsibility for the violence on the persons who had attacked Luis Avila, the subsequent Crystal City mayor's brother. He had lost that case.

Peña was jubilant that the real Mexican American grassroots were joining *La Causa*. The Albuquerque Walkout had jelled the nascent Chicano senior leadership into a networking group, but they had no real grassroots members. Now, Reies López Tijerina was organizing the land recovery movement in New Mexico; Rodolfo "Corky" Gonzáles had founded the Crusade for Justice and was speaking for urban youth; Chávez was bursting onto the national scene with his successful organizing of farm workers in California; and the Rio Grande Valley was exploding with activity—there was a grassroots movement. Locally in the San Antonio area, MAYO leaders calling themselves Chicanos were fomenting school walkouts and these were erupting across the state. At the Labor Day 1966 Austin rally for the farm-worker marchers and supporters, Peña could see that youth, farm workers, and women would from that day forward challenge the leadership of elders heading major Mexican American organizations and compete for the leadership mantle. The rally was the public manifestation of the first major Chicano Movement activity of that scale in Texas.

Arnold Flores: Peña's First Real Organizer and Union Man

Arnold Flores had returned from military service in Germany after three and a half years away from San Antonio. He was twenty-three years of age. Arnold took jobs where he could find them and longed to return to college, but had no money. The G.I. Bill was available for educational purposes, but he was not familiar with the workings of that program. Later he would figure it out. Flores had volunteered to help in the local races in which Méxicanos such as Henry B., Johnny Alaniz, and Peña were running. He was drawn to Peña more than to the others because he found him focused on issues of social justice and the working people. In his childhood, Arnold often was taken to the home of Alonso Perales, the principal LULAC founder, near his parents' home. The Peraleses were childless and loved having "*el prietito*" (the little dark one) come over. It was there Arnold first met Peña, who came to visit, and kept seeing him at events the Peraleses would take their "adopted son" to so he could participate as a spectator. It was at these events that he first heard Peña speak, and he recalls being moved by his passion and the forcefulness of the message he delivered. Flores took jobs as a concrete mixer, sales clerk, and even as organizer for the Teamsters Union. Eventually he began working at Kelly Air Force Base and encountered rampant job discrimination. He and Peña would discuss that situation on many occasions since Flores had begun to shadow Peña and Lico López, his sidekick. Flores became the off-and-on driver for Peña, when he could.

By the time the 1964 election came around, Flores was deeply involved with helping Peña win reelection. He had Al Garza, Mr. Potato King in San Antonio, as an opponent. Garza was the largest distributor of potatoes in the area and had money. Flores became the key person for Olga and Albert's voter registration drives to get people to pay their poll tax. Because of the Kelly experience with discrimination, Flores sued the military base and fought for ten years before settlement. Peña helped him get Matt García as his attorney. During these years, Flores became a committed union man, a real labor organizer with a keen instinct for political opportunities and organization. Peña was an idea man, but seldom could implement his ideas into action; Arnold fit the bill to a T.

Arnold Flores began to organize maintenance workers in the various school districts in the metropolitan area. His first target was Edgewood Independent School District, where Dr. José Angel Cardenas was superintendent. Cardenas at the time was one of five Chicano school superintendents in the state. Flores succeeded and took control of his first local union of the Service Employees Industrial Union (SEIU). He moved on to successfully organize two more: San Antonio Independent School District and Harlandale Independent School District, all with Peña's help. This help consisted of lending Flores his political influence with other non-labor constituencies, such as the blacks on the East Side and their leadership, and giving speeches to Flores's union men. Flores liked the working group Peña had around him of Anglo liberals, Anglo labor, blacks, and Méxicanos. Flores wanted to keep that coalition growing and added his own union men and women to the fold.

Beyond the school districts he organized, Flores began working forming a union at Brooks Air Force Base and the Catholic cemeteries. From representatives of these five groups, Flores organized a labor council; as his union recruits matured, he later organized the San Antonio Chicano Organizers (SACO), an organization of organizers. An example of Peña's invaluable help to Flores, and the reciprocal help to Peña from Flores was with the intransigent issue of black-brown relations. Blacks did not want to work with Méxicanos, and Méxicanos did not want to work with blacks. A local union divided from within could not face organized management opposition that could use the race issue to divide and conquer. Flores asked Peña for help with this matter and Peña recruited G. J. Sutton and Reverend Claude Black,

East Side leaders and part of Peña's coalition of liberal Democrats. The essence of the speeches Peña, Sutton, and Black would give to mixed groups of men and women, white, black, and brown, was that management was taking advantage of them, "screwing them," as workers. Flores knew from past experience and readings that if workers continued their ways of ethnic, gender, and racial divisions, the union would not succeed; jobs would not be obtained, better conditions would not result—in effect, they would be screwing themselves.

Flores became an indispensable part of the Peña group, accompanying them everywhere once Flores had an independent source of income, and collaborating in forming the many organizations Peña and others founded outside of San Antonio. Flores became the next best friend Peña had in the 1968 and 1972 elections, second only to Olga.[63]

CHAPTER 10

The Commissioner Years, 1965–1972

ALBERT A. PEÑA JR., AS PASO'S REPRESENTATIVE, ATTENDED THE REGIONAL meeting of the Equal Employment Opportunity Commission held in Albuquerque, New Mexico, the summer of 1965. He had been supportive of the president's speeches and pronouncements about labor, civil rights, poverty, and education, but he did not see those promises translate into action in Texas. He wrote and stated his support locally in speeches, press conferences, radio, television, and his opinion editorials. He wrote letters and sent telegrams to the president saying as much.[1] He had grown disgusted over the years with trying to get the White House to address in a major way the concerns of the Mexican Americans in Texas and the nation. His list of grievances had evolved and now was long: the White House ignored Mexican American needs and focused solely on the African American community;[2] Mexican Americans were discriminated against by private employers and government, the federal government being the biggest villain; federal programs intended to reach local communities were practically nonexistent in the Southwest, or under the control of unsympathetic politicians; the median income, educational attainment, health, housing, medical services and health care, and life expectancy of Mexican Americans were deplorable; and few Mexican Americans held policy positions in the federal government. Mexican Americans had no voice or presence in the White House.

When EEOC chairman Franklin D. Roosevelt Jr. traveled to Corpus Christi on December 14, 1965, Peña attended the American G.I. Forum–sponsored event. He was encouraged by what he heard Roosevelt say about the condition of the Mexican American. Roosevelt said,

> The Spanish-speaking population comprises the largest stricken group in the Southwest. We are aware of over 800 national companies in the Southwest who have over 600,000 employees who do not have one Mexican American employee. We are going to change that. I will personally be in touch with these national companies within the next few days. We will change patterns of discrimination through the use of Commissioner Complaint. Commissioner-initiated complaints will be primarily directed at large corporations in a major industry.

He specifically made mention of companies in Corpus Christi, Houston, El Paso, and

> other cities throughout the Southwest. How can there be equality for the Mexican American in the state of Texas . . . when . . . in June 1965 there are no Mexican Americans employed in the federal postal service above the level of a PFS 11 although there are 196 total employees serving in that capacity; when there are only 132 Mexican American employees serving the federal GS levels 12–18 although there are 8,717 total employees serving in these capacities?"[3]

There were no "commissioner-initiated" complaints made by Roosevelt against any major companies in the Southwest, however. It was just talk, as Peña saw it. Rowland Evans and Robert Novak, two nationally syndicated journalists, reported that long-serving EEOC commissioner Dr. Luther Holcomb, from Dallas, had not been happy with Roosevelt's remarks made in Corpus Christi. They opined that not only had there not been any complaints filed, but also no other such speeches since.

The EEOC was concerned about the continuing stream of stinging criticism coming from major organizational leaders of Mexican American groups in the Southwest. The EEOC decided to call and invite fifty leaders of these organizations to a regional hearing in Albuquerque at the University of New Mexico. Peña and other representatives from Texas attended: Father Sherrill Smith, Henry Muñoz (Texas AFL-CIO staff), Dr. Joaquin González, and LULAC national president Alfred Hernandez. From California came other prominent figures, such as Bert Corona representing MAPA and Augustin Flores of the American G.I. Forum, for example.

There were about fifty Mexican American leaders who filled the room for the meeting. Peña, Flores, and Corona were among the morning speakers. Every one of them made public mention of their disappointment with the absence of Chairman Roosevelt. They were also incensed that only one EEOC commissioner, Richard A. Graham of Wisconsin, out of the five was in attendance. What kind of hearing was this going to be if they were to be talking to themselves? They already knew their problems with EEOC and employers across the country. Other speakers complained that Mexican Americans, as the second largest minority in the country, had no EEOC commissioner; that even the EEOC regional offices were geographically in the wrong place for concentrations of Mexican Americans to reach. For example, the Dallas office was hundreds of miles away from the Rio Grande Valley, home to thousands of Mexican Americans, and similarly, California's EEOC office was located in San Francisco instead of Los Angeles, home to thousands of Mexican Americans.

Peña's turn to speak came and he got quickly to the point. The reason for the lack of complaints filed against major companies for discrimination against Mexican Americans in hiring was that "the power structure put the pressure on" supervisors to let employees know not to file complaints or they would face termination. He articulated a list of eight demands of EEOC, which included that the president call a White House Conference on Mexican American Affairs and meet with them in the White House to plan such a conference. They wanted many more high-level federal appointments and staff positions, beginning with EEOC and across all federal agencies and in state government. The Chicano group seemed to believe the president could prevail upon state officials to emulate federal appointments. The Chicano group wanted an increase in the federal minimum wage; elimination of the 14(b) section of the Taft-Hartley law that prohibited closed union shops; better and higher paying jobs in the defense industries and military bases; inclusion among the protected group, such as African Americans, under President Kennedy's Executive Order 10925, which mandated private contractors of the federal government to be fair employers; and to have EEOC staff in offices near them in the Southwest to investigate and follow up on Mexican American complaints and grievances. This was the essence of Peña's hard-hitting, point-by-point speech.

After he finished making a record of the demands on the conference recording device, he walked up to the secretarial staff and plopped the list of these written demands on the table. As he turned to the audience, he announced it was time for an immediate walkout from the hearing. He gave the signal and the room emptied of Chicanos. Programmed to be an all-day session, within an hour the White House–heralded meeting of March 28, 1966, was over. Despite the pleading of EEOC staff members and other speakers for the leaders to stay, they filed out of the room and straight to their hotel rooms to recaucus and plan their next moves. The group sent a telegram to President Johnson with the eight resolutions from the demands they had formulated. The Albuquerque Walkout against the EEOC was on.[4]

Unbeknownst to the EEOC staff and lone commissioner, the Chicano leaders had caucused the previous night. Peña had led the discussion and they adopted the walkout strategy, prepared their press release in the predawn hours, and selected Peña as the spokesman for the group. He also was chosen as the one to give the signal for the walkout and to hold a press conference. Peña did just that and the major dailies carried the story. Peña had not yet reached San Antonio when the governor's office in Austin was already talking with the White House office about the Albuquerque Walkout and its participants. They wanted to know if Commissioner Peña of Bexar County had officially been invited by the EEOC to this meeting. Special assistant W. Marvin Watson confirmed to Larry Temple, executive assistant to Governor Connally, that "your friend from San Antonio was invited to the Conference on Equal Employment Opportunity. Those in charge were Franklin Roosevelt, Jr. and Dr. Luther Holcomb. Any rate, it's been done; good, bad and otherwise, and we'll just have to grit our teeth and live with the 'bragging' that has followed."[5] That White House presidential assistant did not think much of Peña's press conference and list of demands contained in the telegram until the following Easter Sunday. A group of Chicanos from the D.C. area, mostly affiliated with the American G.I. Forum and led by Rudy Ramos, picketed the White House. Surprisingly EEOC Commissioner Graham and family joined the demonstrators for a while, expressing solidarity and support for their actions.[6]

Peña was not done "bragging." He wrote to President Johnson asking that he appoint Dr. George I. Sanchez as chairman of the EEOC; wrote to Congressman González to intercede and get the vice president to visit San Antonio and also appoint Richard A. Flores to a White House staff position; and called Senator Ralph Yarborough to press the president for a White House Conference on Mexican American Affairs. Peña had A. A. Flores send the White House names of persons to call when the president was ready to meet. The nine names submitted to the White House after the Albuquerque Walkout of EEOC by A. A. Flores, the immediate past national chair of the American G.I. Forum, were Albert Peña (San Antonio), Alfred J. Hernandez (Houston), and Roy Elizondo (Houston) from Texas; Augustin Flores (Riverside) and Bert Corona (Oakland) from California; Rudy L. Ramos (Washington, DC); Louis P. Tellez (Albuquerque); Rudolph Gonzales (Denver); and Maclovio R. Barraza (Tucson).[7]

Congressman Henry B. González was not too eager to help Commissioner Peña. He did as requested and wrote his own letter. He also enclosed press clippings of Peña's press comments on the matter to further poison the White House well against the commissioner.⁸

Vicente Ximenes: Brown Man at the White House

Vicente had resettled in New Mexico upon military discharge to pursue his higher-education goals. During those years, he aided the organizational efforts of the American G.I. Forum by organizing chapters in that state and in Arizona, Colorado, and even some in California. He and Hector P. García became close collaborators with the American G.I. Forum. García's access to U.S. Senator Lyndon Johnson got Ximenes his appointments to federal jobs located in South America. When the time came for an organizational man from the Southwest to help LBJ with his presidential ambitions, Ximenes was there.

Vicente Ximenes was born in Floresville on December 19, 1919, to a family most involved in politics during the late 1920s and into the 1930s. His father, who Vicente described as a *patron*, helped people, registered Mexícano voters by getting the money for poll taxes, and sought public office—one of the first Mexícanos to do so. He won as district clerk, serving two terms in the 1930s; the Connally family were his political overseers. Ethnic politics prevailed in Floresville and in Wilson County because Mexican Americans had to coalesce with other groups in the county such as Poles, Germans, and some blacks in addition to the Anglo landowners and businessmen.⁹

Ximenes saw LBJ once again to be told about the Inter-Agency Committee on Mexican American Affairs. In his oral history interview with me in 2010, he stated:

> The President said he was going to create it by Executive Order, and he put his Cabinet on the committee and me as chair. Two jobs. One paid not the other; two offices, EEOC below, Cabinet Committee above. Our people, the Mexícano did not know the system of complaining. We did not understand. We ... Our people do not complain. The EEOC requires you to complain. I had to find a way to help the Mexícanos to complain. You are graded, effectiveness, on the number of complaints, women did, blacks did, Mexícanos did not. I was criticized for not having complaints; of not doing my job. The Cabinet Committee helped me. I could not reach the President at will, the Cabinet members could. Affirmative Action [AA] was the solution, I found. With such a directive I could send letters to every corporation in the nation. Each company had to formulate a plan to hire minorities. I was as responsible for the development of AA as anyone. I got more people involved in government because of AA than anyone ever. Ximenes had the

backing of the president and he ran with the directive. Of all the Cabinet members on the Inter-Agency Committee, the best one was John Gardner, a Republican, who called his underlings to hire Mexican Americans and get the job done.[10]

Ximenes figured the White House conference was not the vehicle to fix what needed fixing in the country for Mexican Americans.

> At these conferences, usually folks come to get on TV and pass resolutions. I thought hearings would be a better forum. I scouted Los Angeles and met with the mayor, San Antonio, Albuquerque also, never went to El Paso. I told LBJ about the three, he said, "Vicente let's go to El Paso and get two presidents. I'll bring Díaz Ordaz. Pick up the phone and get the Chamber of Commerce and tell them." I did. Mayor Williams said, "Hell No! The Mexicans will tear up my town." The Chamber of Commerce representative who initially took the call was flabbergasted but said, "Come on, we'll build a hotel if we have to."

Ximenes told LBJ, "The mayor does not want us there nor does the State Department." "Tell them to go to hell, we are going there," Johnson retorted:[11]

> I never could get Henry [González] to go speak anywhere to help other Mexican Americans, he would not do that.[12] He took care only of his constituency. Peña would if I invited him. He would come. I invited Peña to the first conference, about 100 folks to meet with the Vice President and Cabinet members, and DNC in June 1965. Peña participated over the 2-day conference. Peña came and made his pitch. He always gave a tremendous presentation, good facts, tough issues. He laid it out to the Cabinet members. I like that. It is very helpful for someone other than me to say that to my superiors. Second, he did it again at Cabinet Committee hearings. Others found reasons not to come in October 1967; El Paso. But Peña did. I invited everyone to come. George Sanchez did not attend. Chávez did not want to come. He wanted the Bracero Program to end then he would attend. I called and urged Willard Wirtz, Secretary of Labor, but he did not stop it until after. Peña came. Galarza did and was with MAYO kids in organizing the rump conference. He had a paper which he delivered at the hearings, then went out with the protestors, Julian Samora, Corky, Tijerina all were invited. Come talk to the Cabinet officers. I made sure each part of the hearings were headed by someone from LULAC, AGIF, PASO, MAPA. Peña did the best of all with his Marshall Plan for the Southwest. This is what you have to do if you want to help the Méxicano. I also invited the politicians but they came later, not to speak to Cabinet officers. Being close to the President, head of the Cabinet Committee, that is what I needed to have and others to hear.[13]

And for Mexican Americans attending, Ximenes was the brown man in the White House. LBJ was escorted by Ximenes from the airport to the hearings and the attendant events. MAYO leaders, Velásquez and Compean for the state office, Gregory Salazar from Houston, all were there. Ximenes had met some of them in Houston at EEOC hearings. "The best presentation in Houston, better than anyone was those in Houston from MAYO. We borrowed their phrase for the title of our report: 'They have the power! We have the people!' I had heard of MAYO's plans to protest the hearings and found them, met with five of them. We discussed their reasons for protesting. Heard them out." Ximenes promised to put them on the agenda Friday or the next day, Saturday. And he did. Ximenes was then invited by MAYO to be a speaker at Sacred Heart Church Sunday morning, the location of the rump conference billed as La Raza Unida Conference. The rump conference group prepared and issued a statement, El Plan de La Raza Unida. The Preamble read:

> On this historic day, October 28, 1967, la Raza Unida organized in El Paso, Texas, proclaims the time of subjugation, exploitation and abuse of human rights of la Raza in the United States is hereby ended forever. La Raza Unida affirms the magnificence of La Raza, the greatness of our heritage, our history, our language, our traditions, our contributions to humanity and our culture. We have demonstrated and proven and again affirm our loyalty to the Constitutional democracy of the United States of America and to the religious and cultural traditions we all share. We accept the framework of constitutional democracy and freedom within which to reestablish our own independent organizations among our own people in pursuit of justice and equality and redress of grievances. La Raza Unida pledges to join with all our courageous people organizing in the fields and in the barrios. We commit ourselves to la Raza, at whatever cost.[14]

To avoid any adverse publicity and direct confrontation with potential protesters, Ximenes rearranged LBJ's schedule from first arrival at El Paso. It was changed to avoid any visible view of protests where the president and the Mexican president would visit. LBJ was taken to the Hilton Hotel escorted by Governor John Connally and Congressman Henry B. González. Ximenes suggest to the president that Ximenes introduce him and he then would introduce his guests, including the Mexicans. "When Connally was introduced by LBJ the governor was loudly booed. The Mexican Americans were still full of resentment and harbored ill will toward the governor for his insult to farm workers in New Braunfels. The Vice President did good." No more speeches were allowed by Ximenes after those two. "Let's go to work; we have to start the hearings. Go hear from the people who have come to talk to you about their problems." The hearings proceeded with minimal interruptions, as did the rump conference. Both interested parties got the results they sought by attending and/or protesting the hearings in El Paso.

The third time Ximenes recalls Peña being discussed was with the president, who was worried about the commissioner from Bexar County. "LBJ . . . Johnson was looking forward to the '68 campaign. He asked me about Peña. I said he's OK; he's raising hell but that is what he ought to be doing. Albert has enough constituency to be asked to attend and he has to deliver for his constituency which he cannot do unless he advocates." He chided the president not to worry about Peña: "A deputy below a Cabinet member has more power than a governor. We have never focused on that level for appointments. We did what we felt in our heart. Peña will be for us."

When speaking in public, Peña "never raised his voice; rather mild but serious, notes on a piece of paper, occasionally a script. He had great capacity to deliver a message, most persuasive." Peña, according to Catholic priest Henry Casso, when in opposition to an agenda item or discussion at a meeting would roll up his notes or script and hold it in one of his hands up into the air to make a point, or tap the table for emphasis.

Now in retirement in Albuquerque, Ximenes recollects those days and is working to gather material for his autobiography: "I was with LBJ from the days he was an aide to Rep. Kleberg then as congressman and to the White House. I was with him a week before he died at a symposium at UT-Austin."[15]

The EEOC ended in 1972 and "the Cabinet Committee [Inter-Agency Committee on Mexican American Affairs] ended in the middle of 1979 because Nixon . . . Castillo first, then Ramirez who killed it. . . . had found his own men. Last thing I did was to go before Congress at end of his term; LBJ had put it in the budget with instructions to me to go 'see if you can make it permanent.' Ximenes did but Congressmen Henry B. González, Eligio "Kika" de la Garza, began to lobby colleagues to stop the funding, and Congress did."[16]

Albert A. Peña Jr.'s last day as county commissioner. Olga Ramos Peña and Albert A. Peña Jr.

At White House Conference on Mexican American Affairs, El Paso, Texas. Standing is Dr. Fermin Calderon, Del Rio, Texas, and front with glasses is County Commissioner Albert A. Peña Jr., San Antonio, Texas.

Johnny Alaniz, U.S. Senator Ted Kennedy, and County Commissioner Albert A. Peña Jr. chatting about a presidential run by Ted Kennedy.

Leo Alvarado, Lionel Castillo, Arnold Flores, and Albert A. Peña Jr. on the occasion of Castillo being named the director of the Immigration Naturalization Service by President Carter and asking Flores to be his chief of staff.

Farmer's Market, San Antonio. Arnold Flores, Willie Velásquez, and County Commissioner Albert A. Peña Jr. during a cookout at the marketplace.

The young man clapping is Juan Flores; in the center with glasses and white coat is County Commissioner Albert A. Peña Jr. Embracing him is Ruben Sandoval, attorney who bailed him out of San Antonio jail during the San Antonio Savings and Loan Association Boycott.

During Walter Mondale's presidential campaign event at Mario's Restaurant in San Antonio. U.S. Representative Joe Kennedy was the featured speaker. Walter Martinez, Arnold Flores, Joe Kennedy, Albert A. Peña Jr.

Arnold Flores, Herschel "Herky" Bernard, Rev. Claude Black, Presiding Judge of the Municipal Court Albert A. Peña Jr., and Bexar County Judge Charles Grace at their monthly luncheon get-together.

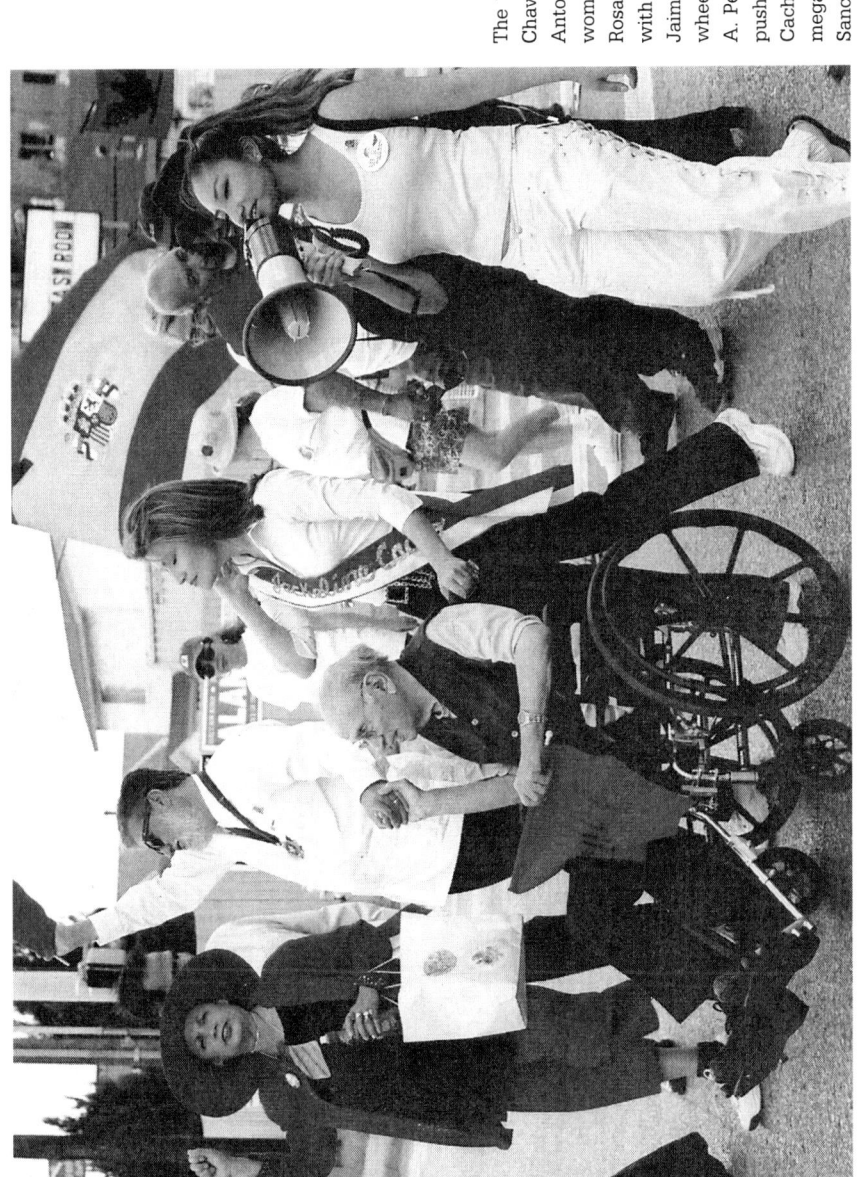

The 1992 Cesar Chavez March, San Antonio, Texas: woman in hat, Rosa Rosales; man with fist in air, Jaime Martinez; in wheelchair, Albert A. Peña Jr.; woman pushing, Jackiline Cacho; woman with megaphone, Claudia Sanchez.

Tino Duran and Albert A. Peña Jr. at a reception held at *La Prensa*, San Antonio's only Spanish-language newspaper.

CHAPTER 11

MALDEF: Peña's or Tijerina's?

A SUCCESSFUL ENTERPRISE HAS MANY FATHERS AND MOTHERS; FAILED CAUSES seldom do. So it is with the birth of the Mexican American Legal Defense and Education Fund (MALDEF). In recent news reports, annual banquet programs, fundraising mailings, and press releases issued by MALDEF, Peña's name is infrequently mentioned, if at all. Pete Tijerina is portrayed, and credited with the founding of MALDEF.[1]

MALDEF, the organization and institution itself, has not seen the need to document their full history and make it available to the interested public in book form. The records of the organization are at the California headquarters, and many documents from the early years are on archival deposit with Stanford University.[2] Few founders living recall the events that led to its establishment in San Antonio, Texas. Some founders, such as Peña, Joe Bernal, Greg Luna, and Rev. Henry Casso, have provided interviews on the subject.[3]

Mexican American Youth Organization (MAYO) members sought funding from the Lutheran Church with which to host a meeting with lawyers to discuss civil rights litigation. MAYO members were being arrested and jailed for protesting and demonstrating, particularly on education issues and police brutality. Umhau

Wolfe from Seguin, Texas, and a Lutheran Church leader, agreed to fund such a gathering, which he also attended. Meetings were held in the spring of 1967 at Hill Country cabins near Wimberley, Texas, with lawyers and MAYO members to discuss the formation of a legal defense group. These lawyers—Mike Gonsález (Uvalde), Warren Burnet (Odessa), J. B. Ochoa (El Paso), and Albert Peña Jr., for example—had been involved in the defense of militants of the Mexican American Youth Organization and farm workers from South Texas who had been arrested for their civil rights work. These lawyers had worked on these cases pro bono, on their own time and expense. Neither MAYO nor the farm workers had money to hire lawyers. More importantly, local Mexican American lawyers in communities where MAYO was organizing and protesting were reluctant to defend the MAYO militants.

Money had to be found and an organization had to be established to defend and promote civil rights litigation across the Southwest. There were no federal legal-aid programs in existence in 1967. Some of the initial money from New York foundations, Field and Ford, was used to host other meetings to discuss the formation of a civil-rights litigation unit such as the one in Bandera, Texas, also in 1967.

Peña's Role in the Founding of MALDEF

Peña recalls that in 1966 he had an employment discrimination case involving a Méxicano that he had filed in federal court. When the day approached for a preliminary court appearance, Peña realized he was involved with issues, federal statutes, regulations, and procedure in this case that he was not prepared for. A lawyer friend told him he was going to lose the case at this first hearing because he clearly was ignorant of employment law and had failed to file certain procedural papers. Peña did not sleep that night, realizing he had failed his client. He had met lawyers from the National Association for the Advancement of Colored People's Legal Defense Fund—the "Inc. Fund" as it was popularly called then. While he attempted to make contact with the Inc. Fund lawyers, Peña asked the federal judge for an extension of time on the case and was granted his motion. He was candid with the judge. He said in open court,

> Your Honor, because this is my first Federal case and because of my ignorance, I have failed to file the necessary papers in this case. I understand this case is subject to being dismissed. I implore your honor give us more time to prepare in this case, and not take it out on my client I believe has a good case of wage and job discrimination.[4]

Peña found Jack Greenburg, executive director of the Inc. Fund, after calling folks associated with Robert Kennedy's staff and Jack Conway with the Center for Community Change (CCC) in Washington, DC. Peña claims Greenburg mailed him documents and copies of cases relevant to his case pending in federal court. He also sent an able young black attorney to assist Peña in preparing his case. The case was settled prior to trial.⁵

Greenburg also invited Peña to New York to discuss the general legal problems associated with Mexican Americans in the Southwest. Greenburg promised to contact persons at the Ford Foundation willing to listen to a presentation on the Chicanos' need for funding to fight discrimination abuses. Peña accepted the generous offer of plane tickets and hotel expenses for Peña's group to visit the NAACP's Inc. Fund and staff and the Ford Foundation.

The Peña meeting with Ford Foundation program officers and Greenburg's staff went well. Both the foundation personnel and that of the Inc. Fund were surprised to learn that Méxicanos "had the same problems that Blacks had." Peña writes about the meeting:

> These are some of the issues I discussed with them: I told them about the school segregation case I had worked on and unequal education of Hispanics throughout South Texas. I told them of the job and wage discrimination, and that the Federal government was the number one culprit. I told them about restrictive clauses in housing, and how I was denied housing in certain sections of town after I graduated from law school. I told them and emphasized the lack of funding to pursue these problems.

He continued the MALDEF story:

> After several discussions with groups of Chicanos, the Ford Foundation funded MALDEF, and the National office was situated in San Antonio. I was a founding member of the board . . . I do not write this column to take any credit for the excellent job that MALDEF has accomplished in the field of civil rights for Hispanics. My only purpose is to place the founding of MALDEF in the proper historic perspective.⁶

There is another version of the MALDEF story—the institutional one—in a publication prepared for the tenth anniversary of MALDEF, in a section entitled "The Founding of MALDEF." In this booklet, Pete Tijerina wrote a lengthy article on his version of events.

Pete Tijerina

Pete Tijerina was a contemporary of Albert A. Peña Jr.'s in professional adulthood. Like Peña, he attended St. Mary's Law School, but unlike him he did graduate from that school in 1951. Both were licensed to practice law by the state bar that same year. Peña returned home from the Houston area to practice with his father and brother. Tijerina also returned home to practice in Laredo briefly, but relocated from Laredo to San Antonio and promptly joined the local LULAC Council No. 2. He liked the politics and social life of the organization; he was a bachelor with money in his pocket. Tijerina as lawyer frequently found himself elected or appointed to a leadership position within the LULAC local, state, or national structure. He served as president of LULAC Council No. 2. Peña was his vice president during that term. Tijerina also served as the State Civil Rights chair for LULAC in 1966. It was in this capacity that Tijerina met Jack Greenburg of the National Association for the Advancement of Colored People's (NAACP) Legal Defense Fund, the "Inc. Fund."

In a lengthy article Tijerina penned on the birth of MALDEF, he does not elaborate on the circumstances that led to his meeting Jack Greenburg, nor does he discuss who made the introduction or sought the meeting. He simply writes, "I developed a working relationship with Mr. Jack Greenburg, Executive Director of the NAACP Legal Defense Fund via telephone conversations and correspondence." And he continues,

> As a result of their great victory in *Brown vs. State Board of Education* they were recipients of grants from various foundations to continue their litigation of civil rights violation cases. Mr. Greenburg offered to make his staff available to litigate civil rights cases for our Mexican American community. My response was that we needed to have our own legal defense fund staffed by Mexican American attorneys. Because of a lack of funds, I never attended any Civil Rights Conferences until March 1967 when we started discussing the possibilities of starting a Mexican American Legal Defense Fund in Texas. In April of 1967, Jack Greenburg wired $500.00 to cover travel costs to New York City to meet with the Ford Foundation representative. I invited Roy Padilla representing the conservative faction of the Mexican American community and Albert Peña who represented the liberal faction, to attend the meeting.

At the meeting with Bill Pincus of the Ford Foundation and Jack Greenburg, the three Chicanos from San Antonio spent hours at a New York restaurant discussing the pressing and growing legal problems facing them in Texas. They asked Ford for

$6,000 seed money to start MALDEF, but Pincus denied the verbal request because they had no available cash for new programs. According to Tijerina's account, Jack Greenburg left the table and went to a public telephone. Tijerina writes of the dramatic announcement made upon his return:

> Within three minutes he came back and announced that we would receive a grant of $6,000. We then discussed who would write the proposal. I suggested Joe Bernal or José Cardenas from San Antonio. Jack suggested Mike Finklestein from Columbia University write it. He was the person who had done the statistical study for the case of Brown vs. State Board of Education and was available. Since Jack had been so helpful I agreed with his recommendation. Mike Finklestein was selected as the person to write the proposal for MALDEF.[7]

With the seed grant funneled via the Inc. Fund, and Prof. Finklestein doing the writing, the Chicano trio took the necessary steps to incorporate a nonprofit organization in Texas, then sought federal tax exempt status for MALDEF from the Internal Revenue Service under Section 501(c)(3) of the Federal Tax Code. The incorporators of MALDEF were Albert Peña, Roy Padilla, and Tijerina. The initial board of directors were Joe Bernal, Albert Armendariz (El Paso), Rev. Henry Casso, Gregory Luna, and Carlos Cadena. Only Bernal and Casso were not attorneys and they pressed for a programmatic inclusion of the "E" in MALDEF; they wanted scholarship money for education, for Chicano students to be trained as lawyers.

By May 1967 the Ford Foundation decided to consider funding MALDEF, but only if the Texas operation was expanded to include the entire Southwest and there were not any other competing groups for the available funds. Tijerina recalls in his article that once he confirmed that possible expansion of territory, he and his wife, Grace González, got in their car with the children and drove from Texas to California and back, meeting with groups of attorneys and leaders, organizational, political, and programmatic, serving the Chicano community. Tijerina met with as many such men as he could find in Arizona, New Mexico, Colorado, and California. He writes in his "The Birth of MALDEF" article:

> In Los Angeles, I was again assisted by LULAC and we met with other attorneys at Herman Silla's [sic] office. In Los Angeles I was introduced to Bert Corona who at the time was working on a legal services proposal to be submitted to the Ford Foundation. When I approached him he was quite indignant and stated, "We in California do not need Texas lawyers to handle our legal problems." But we talked for hours and hours and he finally graciously agreed to let us proceed with *the MALDEF proposal upon an agreement that there would be a completely staffed office in Los Angeles.*[8]

At a press conference held at the Gunter Hotel in downtown San Antonio in May 1968, Pincus, Greenburg, Peña, Tijerina, and the rest of the MALDEF board of directors announced the Ford Foundation funding of the organization with $2.5 million dollars, which included $250,000 for law school scholarships. MALDEF opened its offices in the International Building on Houston Street on August 1, 1968, with Mario Obledo acting as general counsel and Pete Tijerina as executive director. They hired the first MALDEF lawyers, Alvaro Garza, Juan Rocha, and Jerry López. With federal funding for VISTA, they were able to recruit five VISTA volunteer attorneys, among them Alan Exelrod and Mike Mendelson. MALDEF was operational and running with their legal team to fight in courtrooms across the country for protection of Chicanos and advancement of civil rights.[9]

Congressman Henry B. González did not like these unfolding events, among many others like him in San Antonio, the state, and the nation. He had been watching with alarm the growing number of Chicano political actors on the local scene: the militants from MAYO, councilman Pete Tones, archrival county commissioner Albert A. Peña Jr., state senator Joe Bernal, and Johnny Alaniz, former state representative. These political enemies had one thing in common: they could become potential opponents for his seat. In 1968, they had formed organizations with funding to carry out their plans, whatever they were. González did not like these developments and began a war to remove them all from "his" congressional district. González made protected speeches on the floor of Congress, where he enjoyed immunity from libel or slander by those he vilified. He turned on the Ford Foundation and used his position on the House Sub-Committee on Banking and Finance to join conservative House members to pass the 1969 Tax Reform Act that curbed many foundation funding practices, namely, voter registration, political activism, and voter education. By the early 1970s the Ford Foundation, most concerned with the continued attacks by Congressman González, demanded as a condition of continued financial support to MALDEF the relocation of the national offices away from San Antonio, Texas, to San Francisco, California; the complete defunding of the Mexican American Unity Council (MAUC) and its delegate agency MAYO; and the location of the Southwest Council of La Raza, precursor to the National Council of La Raza, from San Antonio to Phoenix, Arizona. The congressman did not share the Chicano view of building organizations with an eye toward making them institutions in the long run.

Poor People's Campaign

Commissioner Peña could not attend the organizational meeting called by Dr. Martin Luther King Jr. in Atlanta, Georgia, on March 14, 1968, of the Minority Group Conference to plan the incorporation of other minorities into the Poor People's Campaign.[10] Dr. King was committed to making this campaign truly representative of poor people across the country and not just another black civil rights effort. Peña called around and found Pete Tijerina willing to attend. Tijerina informed him that others in the city had also been invited: Catholic priest Miguel Barragan, working at the Bishop's Committee for the Spanish Speaking, and the local MAYO leaders. Peña inquired and found that Mario Compean, state MAYO chairman, was attending and being accompanied by other MAYO members, including this author. Father Barragan in turn had gotten an invitation for Rubén R. Alfaro, his Bishop's Committee counterpart in Michigan. Peña learned that Leo D. Nieto with the Texas Council of Churches based in Austin was also attending. The MAYO leaders informed Peña that Chicano leaders from the Southwest—Reies López Tijerina, Rodolfo "Corky" Gonzales, and Bert Corona—were attending, but not César E. Chávez. An Ohio Farm Labor Organizing Committee leader, Baldemar Velásquez, was going in his stead. Peña felt his presence would not be needed; these Chicanos could represent all Mexican Americans.[11]

An unintended consequence of these meetings in Atlanta with Dr. King Jr. was the contacts and networks established between Reies Lopez Tijerina and MAYO leaders and the leadership of the Student Nonviolent Coordinating Committee (SNCC), at that time led by Stokely Carmichael and locally by John Lewis, currently a member of the U.S. House of Representatives. SNCC members later would attend conferences held by Tijerina on behalf of his organization, La Alianza de Pueblos Libres. Texas-based SNCC leaders, particularly from the Houston area, had collaborated with MAYO in the protests against Governor Preston Smith and other cases involving police brutality. Later some SNCC members became candidates for local office under the Raza Unida Party banner—Mario Salas in San Antonio, for example.

The Del Rio, Texas, Palm Sunday March[12]

MAYO members from the local group in San Felipe del Rio, Texas (aka Del Rio), in Val Verde County gathered to discuss their tactics and strategy regarding the beating of a couple from nearby Uvalde, Texas, by a Texas Department of Public

Safety (DPS) patrolman in late 1968.[13] They had been called by attorney Mike Gonsález from Uvalde asking if they would attend the grand jury proceedings to be held at the federal courthouse in Del Rio investigating this incident.[14] Reportedly, the couple were Chicanos—Natividad Fuentes and his wife—and were traveling from Uvalde to Ciudad Acuña, Mexico, across the border from Del Rio, to make some purchases of Mexican products when stopped for a traffic infraction by the DPS policeman. The patrolman had been short on patience and quick on temper and began manhandling Mr. Fuentes. When the wife appealed to him to stop the physical confrontation, the DPS man also got physical with her, beating both persons with his fists and boots before handcuffing them both and transporting them to jail. Attorney Gonsález had filed a civil rights complaint against the DPS trooper and demanded a federal grand-jury investigation into this incident of police brutality.

The federal-court grand jury looked into the case presented by the U.S. attorney and issued a No Bill decision essentially exonerating the policeman of any wrongdoing. MAYO members had begun a silent protest during the deliberations and were incensed when Mike González came out of the courthouse with the news of the No Bill. In San Antonio, MAYO members were rallying around Commissioner Peña's efforts to get police investigated for the murder of Eloy Vidal by local city policeman Albert Teal. Vidal had been apprehended during a robbery and made a run for it. Policeman Teal shot him in the back twice, mortally wounding him. Peña, with MAYO members among his entourage, held a press conference January 6, 1969, to denounce this senseless killing of another Chicano by police. Peña had also taken to the radio, deploring police tactics in this case and demanding an investigation. The San Antonio Police Department, however, defended the shooting as self-defense. Peña at the press conference clearly stated his support of the local police and their need for better pay and training, and raised the issue of the lack of Mexican Americans among the ranks of local police officers. He also cited a recent Federal Bureau of Investigation report calling San Antonio a "crime capital." On the radio, Peña had outlined the procedure to be used by police when faced with the use of deadly force. Like a lawyer arguing his case before a jury, Peña cited the *Handbook for Texas Law Enforcement Officers* on the use of a deadly weapon against a suspect. Peña did not find the circumstances surrounding the killing of an unarmed Mexican American by shooting him in the back as constituting "self-defense." Regardless, Peña and MAYO's calls for investigation did not result in any sanction against Officer Teal, much less any redress for the Vidal family.

It was against this backdrop of mounting Chicano–police tensions over brutality and use of excessive force in South Texas that the Del Rio, Val Verde County Commissioners Court fight with MAYO and a War on Poverty program began to develop. In 1968, the Val Verde Commissioners Court had approved a new program for the city-county sponsored by the local Community Action Agency (CAP), a delegate agency of the War on Poverty. The new program was called Volunteers in Service to America (VISTA), a domestic Peace Corps. VISTA volunteers from across the nation were placed in impoverished communities to assist locals with accessing programs and information, and to promote self-help initiatives. MAYO members across the state questioned the wisdom of sending insensitive and uninformed Anglo volunteers into South Texas without a clue as to the Chicano community and culture. MAYO statewide leaders began to demand of the Office of Economic Opportunity, state and national, that a new program be instituted that would recruit Chicanos into VISTA to work in their own communities. This program was created and called VISTA-Minority Mobilization.[15] Quickly MAYO members were encouraged to apply and be paid for community work they already were doing. Other MAYO members were hired as trainers of VISTA-MM recruits, supervisors, and field directors, such as José Uriegas, formerly from Uvalde; Aurelio "Hershey" Montemayor from Del Rio; and others.[16]

As the VISTA-MM program in Del Rio got underway, a local attorney, Arturo González—no relation to Mike Gonsález—began to question in February 1969 why taxpayer money was being spent on such a program. He began to voice his opposition to the activities of these volunteers and charged that VISTA-MM workers were carrying on partisan political activity by attending MAYO meetings and causing dissension in the community. González specifically accused the VISTA-MM supervisor Aurelio Montemayor of allowing use of his office, equipment, supplies, and utilities not for legitimate ends but to further the political work of MAYO. To be sure, the division of labor and loyalties between VISTA-MM and MAYO members was overlapping and similar, but not illegal or partisan political in nature. Among one of the issues VISTA-MM workers had raised was the severe gerrymandering of existing county commissioner precinct lines. The Chicano community was segregated and packed into one precinct, thus able to elect only one commissioner of the four. The VISTA-MM research into this matter had uncovered that 94 percent of the county's population and 95.8 percent of those eligible to vote were packed into this one commissioner precinct, allowing the other three commissioners, all Anglos, to be elected by less than 5 percent of the population, all Anglo as well. Both MAYO and VISTA-MM volunteers had shared their findings with the Mexican American Legal Defense and Education Fund and Uvalde attorney Mike Gonsález. A preliminary lawsuit had been filed on this imbalance of representation, blatant gerrymandering.

Arturo González's allegations against VISTA-MM meanwhile were sufficient for the county commissioners to ask the district attorney, John Pettit, to travel to

Austin and confer with state OEO officials as to the duties of VISTA-MM volunteers. The county commissioners were also concerned that the chairman of the local CAP agency, Dr. Fermin Calderon, was also seen attending MAYO meetings in Uvalde. The meeting of concern was the one in which attorney Mike González and MAYO members were discussing the beating of the Uvalde couple by the DPS patrolman. Dr. Calderon and Mike González were old-time acquaintances and friends since the early organizing days of the American G.I. Forum in West Texas.

At the first regular meeting of the Val Verde County Commissioners Court, they voted to ask the local CAP agency to end participation in and sponsorship of the VISTA and VISTA-MM programs immediately. The local radio and newspapers carried the story. The commissioners sent copies of their official action to Donato Rodríguez, executive director of the CAP agency, and Dr. Fermin Calderon. The local CAP board, at a meeting with more than seven hundred in attendance, refused the commissioners' request. The Commissioners Court upped the ante by sending a letter with a copy of their official action taken against the VISTA and VISTA-MM program to Governor Preston Smith, asking him to direct state OEO to remove these programs from Val Verde County. The governor in turn asked the Washington-based OEO to end these programs immediately.

MAYO members in Del Rio called on their statewide leaders for help with this fight against the local commissioners and now the governor. They insisted the governor listen to their side of the growing accusations of partisan political activity by the county commissioners, all members of the local Democratic Party. MAYO members continued to hold weekend protests and demonstrations, leading to scores of their members and local supporters being arrested for such lame infractions as parading without a permit, disturbing the peace, and being loud and noisy. San Antonio–based MAYO leaders sought out and met with Commissioner Peña to brief him on the situation and ask his advice on dealing with the commissioners in Val Verde County and the governor. The governor refused initially to meet with MAYO members, and even admitted to a delegation of Chicano state legislators that he had not met with any of the concerned parties in Val Verde County. The governor insisted he had the power to side with the county commissioners and end the VISTA-MM program. The Chicano legislators insisted that while he had the power to terminate the program, he also had the discretion to investigate and hear all sides of the controversy. The governor refused. In an effort to appease the county commissioners and governor, the local CAP agency fired three persons affiliated with the controversial program—Aurelio Montemayor, supervisor, and two others: Raul Sanchez, a local volunteer, and Carmen Benavidez from El Paso—all VISTA-MM volunteers.

On March 20, the first of three arrested protestors appeared in municipal court to face the judge with their team of lawyers. Mike Gonsález was front and center of the lawyers; he had been a MAYO supporter since its founding. Warren Burnet from Odessa had traveled on his dime because he agreed with MAYO, despised Preston Smith, and was a friend of Mike Gonsález. Gerald López and Greg Luna were there representing MALDEF, and as proxies for Peña. J. B. Ochoa from El Paso also drove in for the hearing. Ultimately all MAYO members and locals charged with these types of cases had the cases dismissed because of the legal efforts of these attorneys. This vindication added fuel to the fire and culminated in a gigantic protest march on Palm Sunday in Del Rio, Texas.

The MAYO Militants

First tier MAYO militants were Patlan, Pérez, Compean, Velásquez, and this author. Second tier were Guerra, Luera, Fernandez, and Cortes Jr. Juan Patlan and I were from the Winter Garden area of southwest Texas, not locals from San Antonio as were Willie Velásquez, Mario Compean, Ignacio Pérez, and Ernie Cortes Jr.[17] Patlan had attended the Southwest Texas Junior College in Uvalde after graduation from high school and attempted completion for a degree at the University of Texas. However, Patlan had married his childhood sweetheart, Elena, at an early age, and the couple found it hard to earn a living, start a family, and attend school. Patlan left Austin and moved to San Antonio in 1967. He became a cofounder of MAYO. Later, he would succeed Willie Velásquez as executive director of MAUC until October 1983, when he resigned. Patlan was the principal architect in the development of MAUC, somewhat less so for the establishment and success of the Southwest Council of La Raza, and later the National Council of La Raza. Patlan was very competent, having acquired great social skills and possessing a ready smile and great sense of humor. He could not be ruffled and was a consummate negotiator and diplomat. Often Peña would turn to Patlan for service as his appointee to important boards and projects, and later when Peña needed help he would turn to Patlan. For years Peña served on boards with Patlan as well as on Patlan's MAUC board; Peña was a founder.

Willie Velásquez is profiled later under the section about the Southwest Voter Registration and Education Project. Carlos Guerra came to San Antonio from Robstown as a graduate of Texas A&I University to head up MAYO's other entity, the Texas Institute for Educational Development (TIED), and would later figure prominently in the statewide campaigns of La Raza Unida Party, particularly as manager of the Ramsey Muñiz campaign for governor in 1974. He later was a columnist with the *San Antonio Express*.

Ernesto Cortes Jr. was a bright Catholic student, a graduate of Central Catholic High School.[18] Unlike some of his peers, he enjoyed reading and studying. He was as voracious a reader of anything that came across his eyes and caught his attention as Peña was in his youth and into later life. The two came together when Ernie returned to San Antonio after college and affiliated with other bright young men and women in MAYO. But Ernie was cut from a different cloth than other MAYO members in that he was independent and did not like being in a subordinate role to other, more experienced MAYO leaders.

While attending Texas A&M University as an undergraduate, he studied and majored in economics and English, graduating at age nineteen. For a master's degree he attended the University of Texas in Austin and became further enamored with economics and theory. During those years he joined the campus Chicano group Mexican American Students Organization (MASO) and got involved with the University YMCA, where he boarded. His studies were interrupted by two major events, the death of his father and the plight of striking Texas farm workers at La Casita Farms in the Rio Grande Valley during 1966 and 1967. He did not finish his graduate studies. Along with fellow students in MASO and at the YMCA who were less militant than the MAYO members picketing and demonstrating in the Valley in support of the farm workers, Ernie instead organized among the students and at other campuses in the state a food drive and caravan to take canned goods and some clothes to La Casita strikers. This was his first real encounter with MAYO militants at various campuses, but primarily the St. Mary's University group in San Antonio, which had the founders of the organization.

MAYO was not a mass-membership organization; rather it was a group of active youth seeking social justice and engaged in direct action. Ernie seldom attended MAYO meetings, but regularly sought out the MAYO leaders. He engaged with them in protracted political discussions of issues and analyses of the statewide Mexican American organizations. MAYO members were highly critical of the leadership of LULAC, PASO, and the American G.I. Forum. Chicano youth, male and female, bristled at the age requirement of twenty-one for joining such organizations. PASO had been the first group to lower the age of membership to eighteen. Youth interested in those organizations were organized into youth groups. Women were relegated to auxiliary organizations and precluded from full membership regardless of age. MAYO was youth-led, and both Chicanos and Chicanas were decision-makers. MAYO would hold statewide meetings of their affiliates twice a year. At one meeting, MAYO representatives, two per group, would develop and commit to a statewide effort. At the subsequent meeting, usually midyear, MAYO members would review progress made on the agenda, tweak the goals and objectives, and also select a statewide leadership team.

By 1968 MAYO members across the state had organized issues conferences and scores of school walkouts, and participated in hundreds of demonstrations and protests.[19] MAYO activities regularly made headlines, and their press conferences were covered by print and electronic media. Ernie attended one statewide meeting held in San Antonio in January 1969, where MAYO voted to initiate a multicounty organizing project, the Winter Garden Project in Zavala, Dimmit, and La Salle Counties located in the southwestern part of Texas, some one hundred miles from San Antonio. By then MAYO had two federally tax-exempt entities, the Mexican American Unity Council (MAUC) and the Texas Institute for Educational Development (TIED). Peña was instrumental in obtaining the federal tax exemptions for both organizations by recruiting Herschel Bernard to do the legal work of incorporation for the two entities.

Juan Patlan and Willie Velásquez, two of the five cofounders of MAYO, headed MAUC, and Carlos Guerra, former PASO student leader at Kingsville's Texas A&I College and secondary-level MAYO leader, headed TIED. Ernie began to work with both organizations on economic development projects. His daily work brought him in close contact with Peña, other MAUC board members, MAYO leaders, and the Chicano community.

Ernie was instrumental in the writing of various proposals for MAUC and TIED, including the funding request document for the Committee for Rural Democracy (CRD), the tax-exempt organization to be the funding mechanism for the Winter Garden Project. At a meeting held in Carrizo Springs, Texas, at the home of Juan Patlan's parents, MAYO leaders committed to relocating and financially supporting two lead organizers for the Winter Garden Project. Ultimately, the Winter Garden Project was left under my direction while Juan Patlan, Ernie Cortes, and others returned to San Antonio and continued working at MAUC and TIED. In midyear 1969 Ernie became the deputy director of economic development and housing at MAUC, with Juan Patlan its executive director, replacing Willie Velásquez.

Peña as county commissioner had the opportunity in 1969 to name a representative to sit on the board of directors of the Bexar County Hospital District. He appointed Ernesto Cortes Jr. to the board. It was a good selection in that Ernie dove into the morass of statistics found in reports, budgets, personnel staffing patterns, and myriad services of the hospital district. Peña learned more from Ernie about the hospital district than he had in the last decade as overseer within the Commissioners Court. Cortes was such an incisive questioner during hospital board meetings that Peña's office began to get abundant telephone calls asking for his removal. Complaints from hospital administrators against Ernie were also being received by other commissioners, who in turn complained to Peña. Instead of being upset with Ernie, Peña relished the idea of his appointee being a burr in the hospital district's management team. Peña had long been critical of the district administration's lack of sensitivity and care for indigent patients, particularly the black and brown persons and their children who sought medical care and services from the county hospital.

CHAPTER 12

Loss of Power

FARAWAY EVENTS IMPACTED THE LIVES OF ALBERT AND OLGA PEÑA IN A WAY unbeknownst to them when friends from the East Side of San Antonio called on them for support. A well-known black activist, Angela Yvonne Davis, was being sought by the Federal Bureau of Investigation (FBI) for her role with the Jackson brothers, George and Jonathan, both in prison and known as the Soledad Brothers.[1] George was killed by guards at Soledad and brother Jonathan took hostages in a prison breakout in August 1970. Four persons were killed, including a judge, and subsequent allegations of murder were filed against him as well as Angela Y. Davis; the weapons used by Jonathan Jackson belonged to Davis. The FBI issued a "WANTED by the FBI" poster for her, charging her with conspiracy, kidnapping, and murder. Davis went underground and eluded capture until she was caught in a motel room in New York by the end of the year. Almost immediately "Free Angela" rallies were held around the world and in many U.S. cities and college campuses. Supporters organized the National United Committee to Free Angela Davis and All Political Prisoners (NUCFAD).

Angela was being held without bail pending trial. Advocates and champions of civil liberties denounced her detention without bail. Petitions were circulated for signatures urging bail be set and that she be given full protection of the law; besides she had to be found guilty of the murder charges at trial, not in the press. Angela was a firebrand. She had been associated with the Black Panther Party and had joined the Communist Party USA in 1968. She was a glamorous woman, tall, articulate, sporting a huge Afro hairdo, and a scholar.

Angela Y. Davis was born in 1944 to a middle-class family and raised in the Dynamite Hill section of Birmingham, Alabama. The name Dynamite Hill was due to the number of bombings white racist members of the Ku Klux Klan subjected the local black population to in their attempts at maintaining segregation. Davis was friends with the four girls killed in the bombing of the 16th Street Baptist Church in 1963. During the early sixties, as a student at Brandeis University, she excelled in academics and graduated with honors, magna cum laude. In her junior year she studied in Paris and met Algerian revolutionaries who exposed her to ideas about colonialism and imperialism. While in graduate school, she became involved with the Student Non-Violent Coordinating Committee (SNCC) and moved to Los Angeles, California, after studying abroad at the Goethe Institute in Frankfurt, Germany.

It was in California that she espoused the cause of the imprisoned Soledad Brothers and Fleeta Drumgo and John Clutchette. She had studied under Herbert Marcuse, renowned German sociologist and critical theorist. In 1969, the Board of Regents of the University of California system, of which Governor Ronald Reagan was ex-officio member, fired her from her teaching position at the University of California at San Diego. She was successful in her defense and reinstated to the academic position. Later, she relocated to the Bay Area and affiliated with San Francisco State University. Angela Davis also was a vice-presidential candidate in 1980 and 1984 for the Communist Party USA.

The Soledad Brothers were accused of murdering a prison guard. At a hearing for James McClain, a San Quentin inmate, on August 7, 1970, Jonathan Jackson, little brother to George, took control of the courtroom with a carbine and took the presiding judge, Harold Haley, hostage along with the prosecutor and several jurors. The police attempted to prevent their escape with the hostages and fired on the van being used for the getaway. When the smoke cleared, several inmates, the judge, and Jonathan Jackson were dead; many others were wounded. A .380 caliber automatic gun registered to Angela Y. Davis was used in the incident. She was quickly charged with murder, kidnapping, and conspiracy. Davis fled California for Chicago and ultimately New York, where she was apprehended October 13, 1970, and spent the next sixteen months in jail, first in New York, then California after extradition. She was held without bail until February 23, 1972. Her cause came to the attention of black activists in San Antonio. G. J. Sutton, Rev. Claude Black,

Valmo Ballinger, Eugene Coleman, and Mario Salas, a member of SNCC and the Raza Unida Party, called on Peña to sign the Davis petition demanding bail be set in her case. Albert gladly did and was vocal about his support for bail for Davis. Albert, as a lawyer, knew that bail is a fundamental right protected under the U.S. Constitution, and a trial is also guaranteed as a fundamental right in Texas. Yet, the voting public did not agree with him. As a lawyer, Peña's perspective and stance on this issue was in keeping with his heartfelt support for civil liberties. The voting public in Bexar County's Precinct One saw this issue in a different light. Red-baiting was still a weapon often used by Republicans and conservative Democrats in Texas to taint liberals and assassinate the character of opponents.

Angela Y. Davis was a communist and a national officer of the Communist Party USA. At her trial, *People of California v. Angela Y. Davis* (Case no. 52613, 1972), she was found not guilty by a jury of all charges on June 2, 1972, and freed.

How Did Peña Lose the Election of 1972?

One person in particular, Albert Bustamante, used Peña's support for Angela Davis's right to bail against him when the 1972 county commissioner campaign rolled around in Bexar County.[2] Bustamante had decided to run against Peña, not at the insistence of Congressman Henry B. González, as some of Peña's supporters suspected, but rather because he thought he could win.[3] Bustamante took to the airwaves with heavy red-baiting political messages. He framed the issue as Peña being a communist sympathizer and a leftist. To everyone's amazement, Peña did not respond to or rebut these allegations in any format—print, radio, television, press conference, or speeches. It was as if he didn't care or didn't think he should respond. Somehow he thought his supporters would figure out that he was neither a communist sympathizer nor a leftist, just a defender of the First Amendment right of free speech and association and the Eighth Amendment right to bail. Apparently they didn't.

Felix Treviño also opposed Peña in the 1972 race.[4] He had opposed Peña in 1964 and lost in the runoff.[5] Treviño's campaign possibly cut into Peña's support more so than Bustamante's because both of them had been supportive of one another as early as 1956. Treviño not only supported Peña in that race but also kept others from opposing Peña in 1960, he claimed in an interview with Rudy Rosales. In that interview Treviño described his own political growth and accomplishments from being a small businessman, printer, to serving on the city council from 1965 to 1971. He was part of the West Side group of Méxicanos supportive of the GGL machine. Treviño had been a member of LULAC Council No. 16 along with Peña, and both men were regular patrons of the Catholic Church, particularly the Holy Name Society. Both served Archbishop Lucey as officers of the Bishop's Committee for the Spanish-Speaking.[6] Peña was the chair and Treviño was the vice-chair at one time, for example.

Albert Bustamante, on the other hand, had his own new base of support among younger voters given his extensive work with youth groups in the city. For example, a twenty-five-year-old voter in the 1972 race was only nine years old when Peña first got elected. Younger Mexícano voters identified more readily with Bustamante than with either Peña or Treviño. When he worked for Congressman González, he had developed his own network of contacts among those supporters. Conservative or even moderate Anglo voters were more likely to support Bustamante than Peña. Bustamante curried favor with Dolph Briscoe, Democratic candidate for governor in that same election, while Peña supported Sissy Farenthold's bid for governor as th liberal candidate. Bustamante made it into a runoff with Peña and also obtained support from the former Treviño voters. Peña had no new base of support; he had to rely on getting out his voters in sufficient numbers to beat back the Bustamante challenge. And Bustamante was a relentless campaigner; he had learned from Lalo Solis and Henry B. how to seek votes and get people out to vote for him. Peña in 1972 was headed for a divorce from Olga. They both found it hard to live under the same roof because of Peña's comings and goings to so-called "out of state meetings" during the campaign. When he was in town, he would not campaign as he had loved to do in years past. He would disappear to be with Kay Duarte, and would often be found drinking too much. All his close friends called on him to hit the streets and campaign: Juan Patlan, Herky Bernard, Arnold Flores, Johnny Alaniz, and Ernie Cortes, his campaign manager. Peña would agree with their assessment of how poorly the campaign was going and promise to campaign, make radio appeals, hold a press conference, and the like. He seldom did.[7]

Ernie Cortes headed the Peña campaign out of one office while Olga headed her own campaign for Albert out of another location. It was confusing to voters and volunteers. Who was in charge? Ernie had some resources for the campaign; Olga did not. Olga had the ear of the Peña supporters; Ernie did not. Olga had run Peña's campaigns successfully in years past; Ernie had not ever managed an election campaign.

Ultimately, these factors all came together to close the political career of Albert A. Peña Jr. Treviño came in third in this race. Peña and Bustamante squared off in the June 3rd runoff election. Peña not only had personal problems with his marriage, the expenses of courting Kay Duarte, and drinking too much when he should have been hitting the streets and airwaves, but also political problems. Raleigh Mull, a close collaborator for years and an eleven-year county employee of

Peña's, opposed him in the 1972 race. Peña had asked for Mull's resignation from the county in 1969 and he had not forgotten that fight. Mull, now working for the local Teamsters Union, prevented that endorsement for Peña along with that of the Building Trades Union. These were two of Peña's former staunch supporters, campaign workers, and voters. Faraway endorsements and money from U.S. Senator Edward Kennedy and the Americans for Democratic Action did not help Peña enough to fight off Bustamante's relentless campaign and red-baiting.[8] He lost the runoff election to Bustamante. For the remaining months of the election cycle and term, Peña continued making the Commissioners Court meetings and not attending to repairing his marriage. Olga agreed to attend his last meeting as commissioner; then they parted ways and divorced shortly thereafter.

The Blonde Caught His Roving Eye

Kay Duarte was a journalist, outgoing, bright, very married, and fun. She was a blue-eyed, blonde beauty with five kids, originally from Kerrville, Texas, where she graduated from high school. Peña met her once when he ventured into the offices of the *Alamo Messenger*, the local Catholic newspaper. It was love at first sight. Peña had a roving eye and he seldom met a woman he did not attempt to romance. Kay's husband, also a journalist with the same newspaper, was a most devout Catholic, as she was. His name was E. B. Duarte. The couple had a lovely family, five children, and were regular churchgoers. On the surface they seemed content and settled in their relationship and work.

Peña helped her get a job with Project STAY after she worked at St. Mary's University and with the national *Journal of Speech and Hearing Disorders* in San Antonio. Peña ignored all that he knew about Kay and E. B., and he began his pursuit of Kay. As in politics, Peña focused on her and began finding excuses to talk to her on the telephone, invited her to activities along with her husband and kids, and went to visit her at work. In conversations with the couple, he learned they were looking for other work and better compensation. The church newspaper, like the organized Church, was niggardly with salaries for their employees; her other jobs did not pay much more either, and she kept having children. The Duartes could not make ends meet with their combined salaries. Peña again offered to help and made mention of how much the National Council of La Raza (NCLR) needed people like them at the national office in Washington, DC. He made calls and got them an offer from Raul Yzaguirre, head of NCLR; Peña was on the board of directors. As all directors did, Peña helped Raul with referrals of competent people for staff positions. NCLR was growing and always in need of talent. NCLR, like other organizations and programs in the nation's capital, found it hard to recruit and retain good help; employee turnover was a constant problem.

Chicanos and others who supported NCLR's mission, while they jumped at the chance to work for *La Causa* via NCLR, found it most difficult to stay, live, work in, and afford Washington, DC, while cut off from their cultural roots back home in the Southwest. Invariably, these employees would opt for going back home. The federal government had the same problem; underrepresentation of Chicanos and other Latinos generally in the ranks of government employment was a serious problem and would remain so into the twenty-first century, despite stalwarts like Raul who thrived in that environment and made careers in Washington.

Kay, E. B., and children relocated to Washington and settled into new surroundings. Peña placed his strategy to win Kay on the top of his list. She was in D.C. and sometimes in Phoenix at that branch office; he could attend meetings of NCLR and the Center for Community Change (another entity for which he was a board member), and go on "county business"—seeing Kay without worry that Olga would know or find out. First, he had to find ways to get E. B. out of the city on the days he was to be in town. Arriving at the airport, National or Dulles, he would be met by Kay at times; Raul had sent her. She never suspected Peña had specifically asked Raul to send her. He also asked Raul to send E. B. out of town on assignments. At other times they would meet in Phoenix. Raul knew what was going on. Peña was most transparent when he was chasing a woman. Not that he talked or gossiped about his conquests to male friends; he just disappeared from meetings, stopped conversations, arrived late, or declined invitations for dinner or a drink. Peña came to life, much like an anxious little boy on a first date, when the targeted woman came into the room or place where he was. Peña was plain obvious about his interest in Kay; besides, he had a reputation for being a womanizer. When Peña was on the prowl and he began pursuit, few women could resist the charm and attention. He was relentless, with a ready compliment, humor, and gentle caresses that seemed innocent, he disguised them so well. For example, a simple handshake would become a double-handed maneuver as if he were rubbing someone with cream and massaging each finger just enough; an embrace or cheek kiss as greeting would linger but not so long as to cause discomfort. At times, Peña would step back from such a ritual greeting and comment on how good she smelled: "What is that delicious perfume you have on?" He commented in complimentary fashion on shoes, hair, and jewelry, anything to show genuine attention to the person. He was not much on sending flowers or cards; he would call and invite the woman to dinner or early breakfast, sometimes dancing.

Peña was unabashed at saying he needed company and how the person he was calling was one of the few with whom he enjoyed talking. And he was a very good listener as well as a conversationalist with lots of stories. Both males and females found Peña to be a trusted confidant with their innermost thoughts, fears, dreams, and secrets. Peña was always a serious person in public, but most engaging and humorous in private. Slowly, Peña seduced Kay into a relationship with talk, dinners, and an occasional dance.[9]

Raul Yzaguirre grew increasingly concerned about Peña's increasing number of requests to send E. B. away, and about Peña's growing travel expenses to visit Washington or Phoenix. But Peña was on his board and was one of his most staunch supporters, a consistent vote for Raul's agenda items. Either E. B. found out or Kay told him; regardless, the couple split up sometime in the early 1970s, and Kay returned to San Antonio to Peña in late 1972. However, he was still married to Olga and had been in a most difficult losing campaign. The Democratic Party was in disarray after the assassination of Robert Kennedy; President Nixon was seeking reelection, and back home Peña's formidable opponent Albert Bustamante, who had been a former aide to Congressman Henry B. González, had won the primary election.

Peña lost his focus during that campaign for several reasons: Kay was a major reason and preoccupation. He preferred to be with her in Phoenix or Washington, DC, than on the campaign trail. Bills for his long-distance calls to her were huge. Courting her in San Antonio when she returned was risky business, as everyone recognized him anywhere. Olga confronted him with the rumors and he denied them all. They began to fight regularly when he got home from yet another "meeting." She was doing the best she could to help him win reelection, yet he made fewer and fewer campaign appearances. And he was not with the other campaign people—she checked. Where was he and who was he with? Peña never admitted his adultery. The final straw for Olga came when she found out Peña owed the county in excess of $2,000 for personal long-distance calls.[10] After the first days of January 1973, he moved out to an apartment that Arnold Flores obtained for him.

He had told Kay he was going to leave Olga and would divorce her as soon as he won the election. He asked her to marry him. Kay may have strayed from her marriage and faith, but she would not commit to what sounded like iffy conditions. When he was divorced, she would consider the proposal; until then, just more talks, dinners, and an occasional dance.

Peña lost Olga and the election in 1972. Olga stayed by his side until the end of his term, but their marriage was over. Peña moved in with Kay and the kids. He married her one afternoon the next summer in the backyard of the house on Pyron Street, across from the home of Wanda and O'Neil Ford. He had no marriage license or prenuptial agreement, just his words to friends at their private ceremony that he and Kay were going to live as husband and wife; her children were going to be raised as his children. Willie Velásquez was there, as well as Pete Torres, Joe Bernal, Tino Guerra, and others. The informal marriage lasted a few years and then they divorced.

During their brief marriage, Kay, as the new girlfriend then wife, tried to help him as he began to practice law. She was a journalist, not an office administrator, and tried to manage his law practice, but Albert was beyond help. Besides, she had a full-time paying job to support her kids, and little time to give him. He would leave the office on Saturday, her most frequent day to help, without saying where he was going or when he would come back, if at all. He would miss appointments with clients or opposing attorneys she had noted on his pocket calendar. He would not return telephone messages she left for him; clients did not want to talk to her—she was not the attorney. Peña was drinking too much, as if he could find some solution in the alcohol. Drinking too much instead of campaigning was another reason he lost the 1972 election. People would come looking for him; others would send him cases, but he didn't know what to do with them. He had no law books. He did not know how to split a fee with another attorney when he referred the matter to someone else. Kay was most frustrated with Albert, the lawyer. She had fallen in love with Peña, the county commissioner and national figure; somewhere along the way, that Albert Peña Jr. had disappeared. Tino Guerra worked out the details of the separation and divorced them. Kay moved to Estancia, New Mexico, and died later in a car accident on February 16, 1998; she was fifty-eight years of age.[11]

CHAPTER 13

Politics of the Palace

AFTER THE 1972 DEFEAT PEÑA WAS VERY DEPRESSED. HE HAD SELDOM PRACTICED law in his sixteen years as county commissioner; he counseled people, but never really practiced law. He practiced politics. As a lawyer trying to earn a living in 1973, he did not know what to do. He always hooked up with other lawyers to get the case resolved; lacking in legal scholarship, he was the hell-raiser, firebrand, idea guy, dealmaker, problem solver, but not a trial lawyer. He was starving to death. And he was fifty-six years of age now. He even asked his son Albert III—who had relocated to Corpus Christi, Texas—for a job. He and his son had one last big quarrel after Peña lost the primary election to Bustamante and before the General Election. The Raza Unida Party had formed and had acquired ballot status in 1972; their candidates were on the November ballot, not the primary. Albert III was running for state representative against one of his friends, Joe L. Hernandez. His lawyer from the SASA boycott, Rubén Sandoval, was also running for state representative under the Raza Unida Party. Peña had been supportive of the idea of a Chicano political party and held fundraisers at his home with Olga for the Raza Unida Party, but now it was politicking with relationships very close to him. He had been defeated along with state senator Joe Bernal in the primary election. Now the Raza Unida Party candidates in Bexar County were challenging his close personal friends, and these candidates were also very close to his heart.

Albert III, however, had prevailed on his uncles and aunt running KEDA radio to let him make public appeals for votes over the air. When Peña heard this, he and Herky Bernard raced over to stop Albert III from saying to voters listening, "This is Albert Peña speaking to you, asking for your vote . . ." or whatever they imagined he was going to say using the Peña name, which he was entitled to use. Bernard had to physically restrain Peña Jr. from attacking Albert III.

After the November General Election, which all candidates of the Raza Unida Party lost, Albert III left town to practice in Corpus Christi, Texas. They did not speak to one another for years, until they reconciled around Thanksgiving 2003.[1]

Single-Member Districts

During the 1972 Democratic Primary election, Peña read in the local newspapers about annexation plans by the city. The GGL-controlled city council of San Antonio had made an overt move to annex large areas with Anglo residents on the far north side of the metropolitan area in an obvious attempt to increase the pool of potential Anglo voters. If successful, this racially motivated ploy would dilute the growing voting strength of Mexícano voters in the city, particularly the West and South Sides. Peña immediately called Mario Obledo, MALDEF's general counsel, to fight the annexation plan. He suggested the legal strategy of invoking protections against vote dilution inherent in the Voting Rights Act of 1965 (VRA) and to sue the city in federal court if necessary. The state of Texas was not a covered jurisdiction under the VRA; only four counties in the eastern side of the state were. Peña, however, knew from information provided by his contacts in New York and Washington, DC, that political maneuvers in the U.S. Congress were underway to extend coverage to the entire state of Texas. Mexican Americans would soon find legal shelter under the VRA if extension became a reality. As it turned out, Peña's advice and prognosis of things to come was right on target. Texas was brought in, as were other states, when the VRA was extended, including protections for language minorities, Asians, Native Americans, Pacific Islanders, Eskimos, and Latinos in particular.[2]

The city went ahead with annexation, but also opted to negotiate with the Department of Justice in an attempt to postpone litigation over the annexation. The city began to test the resolve of the Department of Justice in pushing for de-annexation. The negotiations became protracted and involved, with neither side giving much ground. In 1975 the U.S. Congress voted not only to extend the

VRA for additional years but also to include many more states, including Texas. The champion from the Texas delegation that obtained extension and coverage was Barbara Jordan, the representative from Houston. Those in opposition were representatives Henry B. González and Robert Krueger. Peña knew long before that Henry B. could not be counted on to support an expanded Chicano electorate; his constituency was an Anglo one. Krueger's district, encompassing the areas with a history of anti-Mexican attitudes and behavior such as Fredericksburg, Kerrville, New Braunfels, and San Marcos, made it imperative he vote against extension of the VRA. Both Krueger and Henry B. decried the need for such federal intrusion into Texas politics and argued that voter intimidation, dilution, gerrymandering, and disenfranchisement were relics of the Deep South, not Texas, certainly not San Antonio. Fortunately for those like-minded folks as Peña, the U.S. Congress passed the VRA extension in 1975 over the objections of Henry B., Krueger, and other Texas delegation members.[3]

The previous year, in 1974, the San Antonio voters had approved a new method of electing the mayor: direct election by the voters. No longer could the GGL solely focus on electing a majority of council members who, in turn, would select one of their own as mayor. The GGL had to spend more money, recruit more supporters, and turn out sympathetic voters in all quarters of the city, not only for the various council-seat races but also for the coveted mayoral position. MALDEF filed suit, *Martinez et al. v. Charles L. Becker and the City of San Antonio*. One of the plaintiffs in that lawsuit, Cecilio "Snuffy" Martinez, would later become a council candidate for District 5 in the 1977 city elections. Part of the evidence in the MALDEF lawsuit against "at-large" elections was a city map that showed that over the history of past city elections the overwhelming majority of past council members elected resided in the far northeastern quadrant of the city. Thus, the huge areas of the city where minorities resided were underrepresented City Hall. MALDEF did win the lawsuit; Snuffy Martinez, however, was not successful as a candidate. His son, Walter Martinez, won a seat on the city council in 1985 and served until 1989, when he moved on to become a state representative.

In 1975 the GGL failed to win a majority of the city council seats up for election. In fact, only one GGL candidate won a seat, Henry Cisneros, and their mayoral candidate was headed for a runoff election. The GGL had not suffered such a humiliating loss since its inception on the municipal political scene in 1955. Moreover, with the VRA extension to cover all of Texas, the new city council was facing a direct challenge by the Department of Justice to either de-annex the North Side area or create single-member districts for the election of council members. The city moved to create ten single-member districts, and the voters narrowly approved the change in the city charter in a special election held in 1977.

The City Election of 1977

The GGL was increasingly finding their political machine breaking down. The carefully courted, recruited, and groomed Mexican American members from their West Side GGL were threatening to run one of their own for mayor of the city. These conservative Mexícano professionals and business owners thought it was time to step out from under the protective wing of the Anglo-led and dominated GGL and exert their leadership. They no longer needed political sponsors, *padrinos* or *madrinas*. One of their own, former mayor pro tem José San Martin, was their choice for mayor and was in fact nominated by the Candidate Selection Committee of the Westside Coalition for Mayor, their adopted name for the group, in this municipal election. Mrs. Alma Esparza chaired that committee for the group, which included Felix Treviño as chairman of the board and Val Mora as president. José San Martin, an optometrist by profession, had been supportive of the GGL; he was also in and out of public office after that year. He was appointed then by the GGL to finish out the term vacated by Henry B. González. San Martin was reelected in 1957 and 1959. He left politics for thirteen years and was reelected to the city council in 1973.[4]

The GGL ignored the West Side GGL's pleas for support of San Martin; they had plans of their own. The GGL again nominated Mayor Lila Cockrell for reelection instead. It was not time for a Mexican American, even a GGL one; their choice was not one of the most loyal and trusted members to lead San Antonio. At a morning breakfast, two former GGL-sponsored mayors of the city, John Gatti and Walter McAllister, opened the event-turned-fundraiser by announcing their selection of Lila Cockrell over John Steen, a former chairman of the GGL. McAllister, the old-time and venerable political boss of the GGL, praised Mrs. Cockrell and implored those in attendance to each pledge to raise $500 for her campaign. She had served on the city council with both Gatti and McAllister. The GGL membership was out in full force that morning, including former council members Jack Kaufman, Mike Passur, and Dr. Robert Hilliard from the black East Side GGL contingent.

With the Mexican Americans in defection and open opposition, Mrs. Cockrell once again faced a strong competitor in Falstaff beer distributor John Monfrey. He was not a political neophyte or without a political base; every business that sold, and every drinker that consumed, Falstaff beer knew who he was. The overwhelming majority of his beer-truck drivers were Mexican Americans who loved him for the kind of boss he was: generous, jovial, caring, and there when they needed him for a quick money loan or days off for family matters; he had a soft heart when the men were charged with minor infractions of the law, and provided free beer for celebrations. Moreover, Monfrey had personal money for his campaign; backing from scores of political operatives and disgruntled officeholders like John Steen, who had assumed he would succeed Mayor Cockrell; and a prior campaign against Lila Cockrell in 1975. Taken together, the Monfrey supporters in the 1977 election may not have been solidly in his camp, but they were solidly in opposition to the GGL and its slate of candidates. To make matters worse for the GGL and Cockrell's candidacy, the San Antonio Police Political Action Committee's president, Alfonso Peeler, announced the group's endorsement of Monfrey the night before the Cockrell breakfast. The police group also had endorsed a mixed slate of candidates for the various city council positions. The police group endorsed Dario Chapa, previously with the Committee for Barrio Betterment, a pre–Raza Unida Party, affiliated with the West Side Chicano group; Henry Cisneros, Bob Thompson, John Steen, and Frank Wing, all GGLers; D. Ford Nielsen, an incumbent and Independent; Jim Dement, a developer; plus Bob Billa, Charles Williams, and Richard Teniente, an incumbent and former school board trustee. An Independent Chicano and former Harlandale football star, Johnny Mata, was also running against Frank Wing, aligned with the Frank Tejeda and Frank Madla South Side political machine, for District 4. To be sure, the city voters had plenty of candidates to choose from if they were not disposed to vote a straight ticket for any slate.[5]

The Sunday late-morning edition of the *San Antonio Light* headline read: "Four Council Seats Won," and in bold print, "It's Lila vs. Monfrey." The Saturday, April 2nd, election for the city council indicated voter indecisiveness in many races—a majority of the council seats and the mayoral race. Mayor Lila Cockrell polled nearly 44,000 votes, while formidable challengers Monfrey and San Martin polled just under 35,000 and almost 30,000, respectively. The other six candidates in that race split the remaining 3,500 votes cast for the position. A total of 112,244 votes were cast in 188 precincts of the city. Henry Cisneros won handily against Roberto Rodríguez and Victor González. He had the GGL backing. So did other GGL-backed candidates, John Steen, Glen Hartman, and Phil Pyndus, who defeated the incumbent D. Ford Nielsen, an Independent. Others, Frank Wing, Helen Dutmer, and Richard Teniente, made it into runoffs. In District 2 in the black East Side, Joe Webb was the highest vote getter of the nine persons seeking that seat, but was forced into a runoff with Charles Williams, who edged out Alfredo Coy by 1,000 or so votes to earn the spot. Bernardo Ureste and Dario Chapa in the District 5 race got into a runoff. Rudy Ortiz and Bob Thompson were into a runoff having eliminated the incumbent Al Rhode, who had a mere 1,068 votes to their 2,172 and 1,524, respectively. In District 9, Glen Hartman faced Van Archer in a runoff; both eliminated developer Jim Dement.[6]

Within days of the April 3rd election, Henry Cisneros was first to endorse Lila Cockrell and was followed in suit by Dr. José San Martin. Monfrey accused them both of endorsing Cockrell because she promised each one her support for mayor in the next election. Monfrey received unexpected support from Frank Sepulveda, owner of West Coast Produce Company and a major contributor to San Martin's campaign. Sepulveda had cosigned a $10,000 loan for San Martin's campaign and sold $2,500 in fundraising tickets to one of his events. Sepulveda alleged that San Martin had assured him he would not endorse Cockrell and then went back on his word. Sepulveda was convinced that had San Martin not made the race, Monfrey would already be mayor of the city. Another San Martin supporter who switched to Monfrey in the runoff election was Henry "The Fox" Muñoz. Albert Peña Jr. had helped The Fox early in his career with a county job in his commissioner precinct, but Muñoz defected and even ran against Peña Jr. Albert was pleased to read that Muñoz acknowledged being at Rubén Munguía's print shop on Buena Vista when the group first supported the idea of San Martin for mayor. At least these two political defectors from his camp were supporting a Chicano—a conservative GGLer, but nevertheless of Mexican ancestry. His *compadre* Rubén Munguía had also run against Peña Jr., but they had reconciled somewhat.[7] Now, these former bosom allies were in a quandary. Their candidate San Martin was not going to get help from the GGL. What a golden opportunity Peña had; the GGL had tried for years to kill him politically and failed. He now could kill the GGL by helping the GGL's chosen candidate and breaking off the conservative Mexican component. And, if he could convince G. J. Sutton and Rev. Black that this was also in their best interests in the long run, he just might accomplish slaying both the Chicano miscreants and the GGL.

With prodding from Arnold Flores and Juan Patlan, Peña had agreed to meet with Lila Cockrell at the Patlan home, 137 Placid Street, to discuss mutual political interests before the election was in full swing. These two men knew Peña's thinking and agreed with the outlines of his strategy. One of them, as well as Herky Bernard, visited with Peña almost daily, or he would call them asking for help for someone or himself. Foremost in Peña's mind as well as that of his closest political operatives was a job. He had been starving to death without clients, cases, money, or the prospect of any for years. His closest friends, like Flores and Patlan and Herschel Bernard, were most weary of helping Peña, which was often, and of Peña not helping himself. Peña's years of helping others had one adverse effect: he was incapable of supporting himself and his multiple children and families. And, when Peña did manage to land a fee-generating case, he would send it without thinking to other attorneys, not necessarily his longstanding friends. It was inexplicable behavior. Peña was sixty-one years of age, in good health and capable, but helpless. Deep in economic despair, Peña needed a regular paycheck from some payroll doing what he loved, helping people.

Juan Patlan had helped get Olga's son Bill a promising job as management trainee at the first McDonalds that MAUC had opened on the South Side. Olga herself was employed at MAUC and given released time to finally get her college education. And Patlan once even dipped into personal funds and handed Peña a thousand dollars. Peña went through those funds in a couple of days. When approached with feelers from the GGL camp about visiting to discuss the municipal election, Patlan contacted Flores, who in turn contacted Albert. Patlan offered his home for the meeting. Lila, on the other hand, needed to siphon votes away from Monfrey. The only Méxicano who could do that was Peña, not The Fox or Munguía or San Martin, if he only would give the word and give his folks his blessing to work for her. Even out of office, Peña was still the man who could deliver votes if he called his operatives at the various barrio precincts. They were still there. His word was still trusted in the barrios of San Antonio; Peña enjoyed the perception and image that he always had their best interests at heart, because he had earned it over the years and battles.

The meeting at the Patlan home that Sunday afternoon did not last too long; the words exchanged were not specific, but everyone there knew what was the real agenda. Peña's folks would help Lila win the election. As mayor of San Antonio, Lila Cockrell would help them in return when they asked—strange bedfellows, indeed. Peña said nothing at the meeting other than pleasantries and greetings; his presence said it all. Patlan, immediately that evening, got busy contacting his employees, encouraging them to take time off and get involved with the elections. It was Sunday, not a working day; he could be a responsible, civic-minded person like any other, and he was not on the MAUC payroll at that moment. When asked, he would not say who he was supporting, only those he was not. Everyone knew Patlan was Peña's favorite person to appoint to important boards or head projects. Patlan had Peña on his MAUC board; Peña was a founder. Patlan was on the NCLR board, as was Peña. Both had been part of the forces behind the creation of these entities.[8] Patlan, Flores, and Peña were on the same page at the same time all the time. This had been so for years.

Arnold Flores was more important for Lila's campaign than Patlan because he could be partisan and openly for Lila. He had already begun to arrange a meeting with his union contacts for Lila, but first Peña had to agree this was what should be done. Flores not only had his union men, but he was also in charge of what was left of Peña's political soldiers. For years Flores had worked in the streets for Peña's elections, operating out of the Pleasanton Road storefront. Flores had taken over from Olga's network members Manuel and Mamie López, who owned that property. The Lópezes still were linchpins in voter registration and get-out-the-vote drives in every election. Olga still loved Albert Peña Jr., but he no longer was her husband. She stopped working on elections Peña was interested in; instead she worked on elections she was interested in—which usually were the same. The public appearance was that the Peña troops were still out there; neither Peña nor Olga had divorced the people of the barrios. Flores was most effective because not only did he have scores of union contacts that supplied free labor for the campaigns, he also had contacts with young people who would come out and do the legwork and door-knocking. Since Flores had joined the Peña forces as a foot soldier back in the early sixties, he had matured into a seasoned veteran and coleader within many of Peña's initiatives, now institutions, such as MAUC, the National Council of La Raza, and the Southwest Voter Registration and Education Project (SWVREP). Often he and Peña would serve on the boards of these entities at the same time. And just as often, when Peña could not serve on these boards in order to avoid any appearance of nepotism with his children and ex-wife as employees of same, or his own need for a little grant or travel or consulting contract, Flores would serve again. The Patlan-Flores team, with Peña's blessing, went to work for Lila Cockrell.[9]

Albert Peña Jr. stayed out of the limelight as much as he could. But as election day approached, he stepped out in his usual role of saying what he felt and taking a position regardless of what the consequences might be. Flores drove Peña around to visit key political operatives who had been with Peña over the years. Peña wrote, spoke, interviewed, commented, and made speeches in backyards or at rallies in support of voter participation. He never mentioned Lila Cockrell. He did opine on others. Peña, however, was livid at the news accounts of remarks made by Dario Chapa against Bernardo Ureste in District 5, where both were running for the council seat. Ureste, an academic with Our Lady of the Lake University, was not as well-known to Peña as was Dario. Chapa had been involved with the young people in the Committee for Barrio Betterment as a candidate for the city council. Peña had been supportive of them since 1967 when they challenged the GGL and he was a county commissioner. Peña had also been supportive of them when this same group had formed the Raza Unida Party. Now, Dario Chapa was attacking Bernardo Ureste as "one of the most radical, active members of the Raza Unida Party . . . that is trying to gain a foothold in San Antonio through whatever guile and deception they can muster."

Chapa was also using the example of Irma Mireles, who won election to the all-male, all-white San Antonio River Authority Board of Directors in 1974, as someone who did not say she was Raza Unida until after winning. "Eureste will try to do likewise if the citizens give him a chance."[10] Lost in Chapa's memory was his involvement with these same people in 1967 and 1969, and the fact that both the city council races and the San Antonio River Authority were nonpartisan races; no candidate was required to state a partisan political affiliation. Others from the

Peña group were equally incensed at Chapa. Persons at the Mexican American Unity Council, for example, had given Dario Chapa employment for years, and now many felt Chapa was a crass opportunist. He had to be beaten and punished. Henry Muñoz, The Fox, also had to be beaten and denied further opportunity to gain any semblance of electoral power over Chicano precincts. Going after just these two men was enough to hurt Monfrey's chances and at the same time help Cockrell. She was the top vote getter, but not with enough votes to win outright; she had to square off head-to-head with Monfrey. The Patlan-Flores-Peña team got busier on this second go-around.

Mayor Lila Cockrell, for the second time in her political career, was in a campaign battle with John Monfrey. A runoff election was necessary because neither candidate had obtained a majority of the votes in the city election of April 1977. The Cockrell campaign was in chaos over the defection of former GGLers such as John Steen, Dr. José San Martin, and others to the Monfrey camp. Both Dr. San Martin and Steen had felt slighted by the honchos in the GGL when they chose Cockrell to run for mayor on their slate over them. Both men had been loyal and staunch members of the GGL; they thought of themselves as important insiders.

Unfolding events with the Lila Cockrell mayoral campaign in 1977 gave Peña hope that he just might once again rise to public prominence. His trusted friend Arnold Flores told Peña that Cockrell had sent feelers out to him about getting support from his union members and also from Juan Patlan. Flores asked Peña for advice on this possible relationship. "Politics makes for strange bedfellows," Peña quickly commented and suggested that this possible alliance would surely further break the GGL structure. He also added that union support in the runoff would result in access to Cockrell as mayor. Peña had good feelings and appreciation for John Monfrey, but believed that his lack of experience in public affairs would not make for a good administration. More importantly, Peña felt that Monfrey as Falstaff beer distributor already had his own contacts among the many Mexícano bar owners and beer drinkers in the city. Intuitively, Peña felt that a more fruitful relationship could be developed with Cockrell than with Monfrey. He encouraged both Flores and Patlan to proceed with courting Cockrell. Peña knew that Arnold Flores was a seasoned and astute labor organizer and as such was not going to obtain the short end of the stick in negotiations over union support for Lila Cockrell. And he knew Patlan would facilitate but not negotiate; MAUC could be jeopardized if the nonprofit status of the organization was called into play for engaging in electoral politics—nonpartisan elections, but politics nonetheless.

Indeed, Cockrell desperately needed labor's votes and their grassroots work on her behalf. The union men always provided the legwork to put up political signs in campaigns and ably got out the vote for the candidates they endorsed and supported. Union men also had families and an extended network of friends and coworkers who were not necessarily union members but who followed their lead in political campaigns. She agreed not only to meet with the labor group represented by Flores, but also would go to the West Side and have a face-to-face with the union men. The local media provided coverage of her meeting with the Mexicano workers. The image of the proper Anglo woman walking, smiling, talking, and engaging with the Mexicano union men was a powerful message. The other affiliates Flores had organized also released information to the media that their group was endorsing Mayor Cockrell for reelection. To Mexicano voters, the message was clear; they were now being courted openly and enthusiastically by a mayoral candidate sponsored by the GGL. Among the GGL elite and their supporters, this move was repugnant. Unions were their political enemies. But Cockrell's future and any hope of keeping the mayoral seat in GGL hands lay with making inroads into these types of groups. It was an expedient and necessary tactical move on her part; the GGL didn't like it but understood why she was doing it.

During the meeting at the union office in the West Side with the Flores group, Cockrell was careful to not make promises she could not keep or that were illegal. The making of an offer or promise in exchange for their votes would be an illegal act tantamount to a bribe. Flores kept asking what she was going to do for labor specifically and the Mexicano community in general. The two veterans of political campaigns, Flores and Cockrell, both knew their words used in the exchange were general and vague; the substance was in the meeting and getting acquainted. The meeting went well, with the labor group feeling good about Lila Cockrell and she feeling comfortable with the union men. Everyone was pleased that she came to them, and she felt she had won over their support. Nothing specific was promised, yet the new relationship was being forged, with access to her guaranteed. As Peña had mentioned to Flores, access was better than a promise, because access is a longer-term process while the officeholder remains in power, whereas a promise is a one-time commitment either kept or forgotten.

Once Flores felt his men and the other union representatives would support Cockrell's bid for mayor over Monfrey's, he made his move. Flores sought a meeting with Mayor Cockrell before the runoff election to ask for a particular favor. He asked her to nominate and support Albert A. Peña Jr. for a municipal judge position. He stressed to her that as the sitting mayor she could make such a nomination and demonstrate her support for their hero. She understood the quid pro quo being placed on the table. If she nominated Peña, she would get labor and Mexicano support. If not, she might lose her reelection bid. Mayor Cockrell peered intently behind her massive glasses at Flores. Softly, almost inaudibly, she said that such a move would be very difficult for her. Peña had been the GGL's number one nemesis.

She asked for time to consider it. Flores left it at that. He departed, telling her he appreciated her candor and directness.

In the runoff election, Lila Cockrell beat John Monfrey easily, 62,477 to 43,039, a margin of victory of nearly 19,000 votes. Peña was pleased with the other results; he could claim them as products of his political work in the election. Rudy Ortiz won over Bob Thompson; Joe Alderete Jr. beat Richard Teniente; and Bernardo Ureste soundly trounced Dario Chapa. The new city council would now have five Mexican Americans as opposed to only two the previous term. San Antonio voters under threat of legal action by the Department of Justice for failure to redistrict its city council seats had earlier in the year amended the city charter to provide for ten seats from districts and to have the mayor elected at large.[11]

The city elections that year produced the first generation of council members chosen from local districts, and all except Henry Cisneros were new to municipal politics: Joe Webb, the first black council member; Bernardo Ureste from the West Side; Rudy Ortiz from the Edgewood area; Frank Wing, of mixed Mexican and Chinese parentage, from the South Side; and Joe Alderete from the Northwest Side, an emerging Chicano voter stronghold. Cisneros was the odd man out, and he faced having to break ranks with his GGL sponsors in order to curry favor with these new colleagues. Wing enjoyed GGL support, but he was more aligned with the Tejeda clan of the South Side.

A few months earlier, lawyer Leo Alvarado had heard from another attorney, Tino Guerra, that his hero, Albert A. Peña Jr., was having a hard time making a living.[12] For no apparent reason, one morning he decided to look for Albert in the South Side, where it was reported he had a law office. He called the listed number in the phone book, only to get a recording that the number was temporarily disconnected. Leo recalled he had seen a sign on S.W. Military Drive indicating the Peña law office was in some strip mall. Leo found the office without any trouble. He parked his car and entered a long hall between two other businesses that led to Albert Peña Jr.'s office toward the rear of this portion of the strip mall. He knocked on the door with Peña's name on it and heard a gravelly voice say, "Come in." Peña was sitting at his desk, a newspaper laid out as if he had just read it from cover to cover. Some boxes were in a corner, and the general impression Leo took from the scene was that Peña had just moved in or was packing and moving out. Peña recognized and greeted Leo. They exchanged pleasantries. Leo then stated his intentions. He told Peña that he had been thinking about him and wanted to know if Peña would join him in his own law practice. Peña was elated. He told Leo candidly that he was three months behind in rent and was being asked to vacate. He confirmed his phone had been disconnected. Kay, his wife, had left him and they had divorced. He very much needed a job.

Leo Alvarado moved Peña into his complex of offices in the Milam Building. Business at the Alvarado firm was good. Alvarado, like Guerra, had been friends with organized labor. Most union men and women brought their cases, particularly worker's compensation cases, to Leo and Guerra. Additionally, the law firm was handling divorces, criminal matters, personal injury cases, and the like. Peña still had many contacts all over town and was good for business. People came to visit him constantly once they knew he was in the Milam Building.

Money was coming into the Alvarado law firm before Peña arrived; now some of this money would save Peña from financial disaster. He began his legal practice anew. But he wasn't a good lawyer. The years of legal inactivity had taken their toll. Peña really did not know how to handle himself in court or process a case. He accepted reality and simply got his clients signed up on a contract and handed off the case to Leo, Tino, or any of the other attorneys. Peña didn't even keep track of which cases he referred to the Alvarado firm; he trusted they would keep a list. Most of the time he was talking politics to someone on the phone rather than to clients.

Peña's morning ritual consisted of having coffee and reading the newspapers. He would go into the office, newspapers under his arm, pour himself a cup of coffee, and go to his desk. He would spread out the newspapers and sip on the coffee as he read the news. One morning, several months into the new professional relationship with Leo Alvarado, Peña read with great interest that the city council was to fill vacancies on the municipal courts. Albert knew this was his opportunity. He walked into Leo's office, newspaper in hand, and said, "Leo look at this. I want to be a judge." Alvarado was taken aback by the sudden burst of interest in such a position by Peña. He asked him if he was serious about seeking the position. Peña replied, "Absolutely. I can really do this job well." And Leo knew that was a true and sincere statement. Albert Peña Jr. was still passionate about the public's welfare. When visitors came to see him, Albert would receive them all, with or without an appointment, with or without a potential case, and listened to all. Albert was available for advice, *un consejo*, to anyone who asked him for it.

Leo recalled that he said, "OK, Albert, let me see what I can do." Alvarado literally walked out of the office building and went over to City Hall, where he ran into Henry Cisneros. He told Henry about Peña's interest in becoming a municipal judge. Cisneros was cautious and suggested that both of them see Lila Cockrell about the nomination. The duo promptly walked into her office and Cisneros explained Peña's interest in the current municipal court vacancies. Cockrell was flabbergasted that Peña, the GGL's archrival for decades, was interested. She peered at her two visitors through her thick and very large glasses for a few seconds. Alvarado recalls she just said, "I will think about that one. That's a good one, Henry." And Lila said nothing else. She knew she was indebted to the Patlan-Flores-Peña team—not to Cisneros, much less Alvarado. But she was intrigued at how Peña, if he was interested in a position, was orchestrating the approach from multiple fronts and with support from unlikely sources: Henry Cisneros, a GGL member from her team, and Leo Alvarado, a prominent attorney with aspirations to be in the state legislature.

The Players in the Peña Strategy

Tino Guerra attended law school at the University of Texas and took the bar exam while lacking a credit to graduate. He received favorable results from the state bar in November 1976 and began his law practice from an office within the larger law firm headed by Leo Alvarado. The Alvarado office housed other attorneys. The group consisted of Alvarado, Aaron Valenzuela, John Smith, and Albert Peña as an attorney of sorts, and now Guerra.

Albert A. Peña Jr. had a small law office at the McCreeless Shopping Center off Southcross Street when he was offered a job by Leo Alvarado. Peña, given his connections and friendship with Arnold Flores, had an inside track to the countless cases of injured workers that the union would refer to him. Peña brought in the cases to Leo Alvarado, who handled them to resolution. Peña and Alvarado split the attorney fees. Guerra had been the one who recommended that Alvarado bring Peña into the firm and out of the suburban shopping center. That relocation proved fruitful economically for Peña. Alvarado and Guerra were making money; Peña was also now making money for the first time in a long, long time. Guerra had an affinity for Peña going back to his high school days. Tino Guerra had frequently heard of Albert Peña Jr., having been born in San Antonio in 1948 and met him when Guerra worked in the Peter Torres city council campaign.

Guerra attended Central Catholic High School with Willie Velásquez and Henry Cisneros. Willie introduced Peña to Guerra while both were still in high school. Guerra also attended several of Peña's rallies and worked on his campaigns. It hurt Guerra to see Peña down and out, and with few friends. To Guerra, the circumstances that befell Peña were simply not fair. How could a man who made life so much better for all Méxicanos now be treated like a disposable rag and cast aside? Guerra pledged to himself that he would find some way to get Peña, his hero, a job he could handle and regain prestige and standing in the community. To his surprise, Leo went and offered Peña a job. Guerra had not belabored the point with Leo, he had just mentioned it. Now that Peña was in the firm, he did generate business, but not that much. Leo knew and Guerra suspected that somehow Peña had to be retrained into an efficient and competent attorney in some practice area. They could not indefinitely keep him on the payroll. Neither of them knew that Peña also knew he could not keep making a living just from referrals, or that he was making plans to seek a municipal judgeship with Arnold and Juan Patlan. Leo thought he was the first to know of Peña's intentions. Guerra also made the unsolicited request to Mayor Cockrell as a campaign volunteer. Without question what all these interested parties in Peña's welfare, including Peña himself, had in common was a belief that as a municipal judge he would be able to earn a good salary for working reasonable hours while meting out justice. Peña would be perfect in the roles of judge and counselor to the working poor snared by traffic infractions, code violations, and teen misconduct.

An architect friend, Luis Viramontes, had recommended to Guerra that he go work for the Lila Cockrell reelection campaign. Guerra's extensive political work with the Jimmy Carter presidential campaign and union organizing work among the garbage collectors in Bexar County could help the mayor. Cockrell needed a person like Guerra, Viramontes told him, in her tough contest with John Monfrey. The idea intrigued him but he had a condition. He did not want to get paid for his political work on her behalf; instead he wanted Peña to be made a municipal judge. Guerra asked Viramontes about the viability of such an idea. He also contacted Joe Bernal, Pete Torres, Johnny Alaniz, Leo Alvarado, Arnold Flores, Willie Velásquez, and others for support for Lila if she appointed Peña as municipal judge. They agreed and she met with this other group to personally ask for their help and support. When Guerra met with Mayor Cockrell, he offered to work for her if she appointed Peña municipal judge. She had reservations but agreed in principle that nominating Peña would not be such a bad idea, but no deal. She told Guerra that she would not make deals for appointments in exchange for votes; besides, any appointments had to wait until after the election—no need to muddy the waters. Guerra said no, it must be done before the election. Nevertheless, Guerra continued to volunteer on the Cockrell campaign. As Lila was floating the idea of the Peña nomination between the first election and the runoff election, Alfonso Peeler, head of the Policemen's Association, learned of the machinations being orchestrated by various persons promoting a Peña-for-judge deal. Peeler felt he had to make that known to the membership and did. The police bitterly opposed the Peña nomination; he would be soft on crime and hard on cops, they felt. Peeler, a Mexican American, personally supported Peña, but his membership was opposed and he had to represent his group. Mayor Cockrell was hearing from all quarters on this matter, but she knew she had to put this to rest before the runoff. The police were against her anyway and were supporting Monfrey. New members on the council were waiting for her to make all kinds of nominations. The new members were ready to go to work and did not want to wait for her defeat or reelection.[13]

Cockrell did think about Peña's possible nomination. She had promised Flores as much on the eve of the runoff election. Shortly after that highly publicized meeting on television, she had sounded out her GGL confidants on the pluses and minuses of such a relationship, and what the Chicano labor supporters would want in return. Arnold Flores, Tino Guerra, and Leo Alvarado, each without telling the others, began a quiet lobbying campaign on Peña's behalf among the new council members, Ureste, Ortiz, Alderete, Webb, and Frank Wing in particular. Leo met again with Henry Cisneros, privately. Of all these new councilmen, Wing was particularly close to Albert Peña.[14] Peña had been a South Side resident for years, and Wing had worked on his campaigns and supported him in countless public protests. Peña's county commissioner precinct covered the South Side. He had been Wing's county commissioner. These five councilmen represented half of the entire city council. A sixth vote was needed, either Cockrell or Henry Cisneros. At the same time this lobbying and sounding out was going on, the city council was beginning to consider a governance process by committee in order to oversee the city manager's recommendations and proposals. That is to say, city business is complex and overwhelming to the individual council member; it is best handled by committees of council members focused on public safety, judicial affairs, parks and recreation, and streets and sanitation, for example. Councilman Wing cut his own deal with Mayor Cockrell over the Peña nomination. If she nominated Peña, he would forego any appointment to head a committee. She accepted the lopsided offer: one municipal judge in exchange for an additional committee chair from among the few GGLers on the council.

Tino Guerra, on his own initiative, had signed on to help the Cockrell campaign. He also asked her to nominate Peña before the final mayoral runoff election. A calculated risk she had to take, nominating Peña would not hurt her with her GGLers; she had already checked around. Only positive reinforcement in the form of Chicano votes from such a nomination would come her way if she did. And she did. Mayor Lila Cockrell described her political trauma at being asked to nominate Peña as municipal judge when she shared the platform with Presiding Judge Peña at the dedication of a building facility named in his honor at Mission County Park. She corroborated this account without mentioning specific names.[15]

PART 4

Second Career

CHAPTER 14

All Rise! Judge Peña Presiding

THE *SAN ANTONIO LIGHT* RAN A DOUBLE-SIZE FONT HEADLINE IN RED LETTERS announcing to San Antonio that Albert A. Peña Jr. was a new municipal judge.[1] After he was sworn in on April 22, 1977, Peña began to settle into a routine as before, reading the newspapers over coffee before he began seeing his court docket for the day; meeting briefly with Virginia Estrada and Benny Matias, his court staff, to review the case files, phone messages, or appointments they might have made for him; and donning his robe to hear cases. Once again, Peña had a regular salary, $32,000 a year, and a new retirement account for future use that augmented his pension from Bexar County.

The Workings of Municipal Courts

Municipal courts are an important part of city government across the country. These courts are the most familiar to residents because local ordinance violations that prompt citations by local police are a common occurrence (such as parking violations, speeding, failure to stop; domestic quarrels; housing, health, and safety violations) and regularly take place, particularly in large cities. In Texas, the eight largest cities (Houston, Dallas, San Antonio, Austin, El Paso, Fort Worth, Arlington, and Corpus Christi) account for 45.1 percent of all municipal filings in the state. The adjudicated cases also generate millions of dollars in revenue for the cities.[2] Revenue generated by the city courts of San Antonio from September 2002 to August 2003, for example, totaled $19,949,028.00.[3]

Typically, a person accused of a violation of a city ordinance is given a citation to appear in court on a specific date or pay a fine without the need to go to court. Many people just pay the fine by mail and avoid the effort of having to take time from work, travel to the downtown courthouse, and spend a day in the court building waiting for their court appearance. Others choose to contest the citation and do appear in court for their hearing on the violation. The contested cases are handled jointly by a prosecutor whose job it is to present the evidence of wrongdoing, and a judge and/or jury that hear the evidence in order to reach a legal conclusion on guilt or innocence. At this stage of the process, an agreement, often called a plea bargain, can be reached on the punishment and court costs. If not, then the case is set for trial and the actual hearing takes place before a judge and/or jury at the choice of the accused. If the police officer or city official that issued the citation does not appear at trial, the case is dismissed on the spot or continued to a later date when all parties are present and ready. At stake in these minor offenses are not only the monetary fines and court costs imposed but also a subsequent increase in auto insurance rates and the making of a criminal record for the accused, which can have grave consequences in the event of future citations and convictions. These minor offenses rarely result in confinement in jail, and then usually only when court orders are violated or contemptuous behavior is displayed in the courtroom. Ultimately the judge renders the decision and imposes a fine plus court costs.

With regularity the media will publish or report on abuses of the process in the municipal courts. The usual allegation is ticket-fixing by someone within the court administration, be it the prosecutor, clerks, judges, or even the police. While county commissioner, Peña recalled the exposé series on ticket-fixing run by the *San Antonio Express* in 1965, which involved his friend Charles Lieck, former district attorney for Bexar County. It was reported that Lieck had filed an injunction against the city, keeping them from impounding his car for failure to pay many traffic tickets. The newspaper reported that Lieck had paid less than the amount of the normal fine in each case in exchange for dropping his legal battle against the city. City council member Robert Jones brought the matter up in a city council meeting, adding fuel to the fire and more newsprint for the local media. The city council voted to investigate what they termed "bargain rates" afforded to repeat offenders with multiple citations pending.[4] This ticket-fixing scandal continued to appear in article after article from February to May 1965. The city council increased the number of judges and prosecutors, raised fines, began to computerize record keeping, and sought ways to stop the flow of cases with unfavorable outcomes for defendants being appealed to county courts. The city courts of San Antonio in 1965 were not courts of record, so that an appeal to county court basically was a delay in the case and very possibly a dismissal in the distant future. From the city council's view, this was not only a bad system of justice but a money drain on the city from uncollected fines and court costs.[5]

The Garbage Strike: SARCA

The most difficult time for Peña as municipal judge came within a year when the garbage collectors for the city went on strike, primarily over higher wages, and were arrested. They, 108 of them, had been fired by the city for demanding higher wages and the right to unionize. They called themselves the San Antonio Refuse Collectors Association (SARCA), and they had help from Tino Guerra and Arnold Flores. When arrested, the SARCA employees were sent to municipal courts for adjudication and Peña could end up with some in his court. This was the first local labor struggle, particularly a strike, that Peña had not joined on the picket line or gone to jail for protesting, as he had done with the San Antonio Savings and Loan Association boycott. He did manage to pass along some money and would meet "accidentally" with some of them at Mario's Restaurant off Frio Street, where the strikers held their meetings. And of course, he always told Flores and Tino what words of encouragement, advice, and legal points to pass along to the strikers.[6]

Rosa Charms Judge Peña

Rosa Gutiérrez, twenty-eight, was a clerk in the police department. Rosa had a wild, tempestuous look: slim, black hair, dark-skinned, outspoken, sensual, and young. Rosa would regularly visit the floor where the municipal courts were located. She noticed Judge Peña and, of course, Peña quickly noticed her and began his flirtatious behavior. Rosa was a youthful, olive-skinned version of Olga. She made friends with Virginia and Benny in the outer office to his chambers. Before long, Judge Peña began inviting her into his inner office for coffee and small talk. And not long after that, according to Virginia, Judge Peña began asking Virginia to hold his calls and prevent interruptions because he wanted to visit with Rosie, as he called her. Soon the rendezvous in chambers were not sufficient for spending quality time with Rosie; Peña began to leave the office early by mid-afternoon.[7]

Despite the developing affair between the judge and the police clerk, Peña was earning glowing praise from his colleagues on the bench, attorneys who appeared before him, and city auditors who checked fine revenue. He was doing an excellent job as municipal judge. Helping people was his forte and it came easy and naturally to him. Judge Peña frequently would be stopped along the way to his office by countless persons with pending matters to ask his advice and counsel. Attorneys would look for ways to have their case heard by Judge Peña; he was understanding, conscientious, and easy to work with toward a just and fair resolution. He fined people the least possible under the law, but since he handled more cases than any other judge, his total figures for fines and costs drew no attention.

Rosie was another matter. Peña was crazy in love with the young woman and her wild ways. Peña decided once again to marry another woman and asked her. Rosie and Judge Peña had an on-and-off marriage relationship for over a decade. Every time they would fight, they divorced, and later Albert would return to the relationship and remarry her—possibly as many as five times. The couple had a child, Cristina. Peña and Rosie's attempts to raise the child were not very successful; however, Cristina managed to attend school and graduate from Jefferson High School. Albert built the home on Vista del Sur off Frio Street for Rosa. During this time, Judge Peña was the target of a paternity suit from another woman, and he was convinced it was his child. A friend, Frances Guerra, later to be another wife of his, insisted he get legal help and ask for a paternity test. Tino Guerra became his attorney and prevailed in court, proving the child in question was not that of Judge Peña; rumors circulated about the old man still making babies and being with Rosie, off and on.

Presiding Judge Peña

As soon as the presiding judge, chief justice of the municipal courts, position opened, Peña was interested in being nominated. Of all the sitting judges, he had the best record and enjoyed wide popularity with his colleagues for his congeniality and willingness to help them with their dockets when necessary. And Peña, the consummate politician, began making calls—"feelers" as he called them. The usual political friends and admirers began to rally around Peña for presiding judge. The city council deliberated, and again Councilman Frank Wing, who was still head of the council committee over judges, got him the committee support. Wing made a strong recommendation for Peña before the council and he was the unanimous choice. He was named presiding judge of the municipal courts in 1983, and served in that capacity for nearly a decade until May 31, 1992. His salary went up to $42,898 and he received a car allowance of $275 per month. His financial condition vastly improved with this elevation in rank and increased his retirement account substantially as well.[8]

As presiding judge, Peña was more of an administrator and mediator than an actual sitting judge hearing cases. He would hear cases mostly when other judges had conflicts with parties in a case, or during vacation times when he was needed. He also relished the idea of continuing to be the *"consejero"* for people that came and sat in his lobby waiting for a chance to speak to him for "just one minute" about their problems or counseling needs. He could also manage his time any way he wanted, unlike when he was on docket call or hearing cases as judge.

Peña found himself attending more and more funerals and fewer and fewer political events. He was nearing seventy years of age. In early January 1987, he attended the funeral service for Maria Hernandez in Elmendorf, Texas, where she is buried in the Orden Hijos de America plot. Peña was fond of Ms. Hernandez and her husband Pedro, always at her side, for their decades of activism and struggle. He admired her.

With Peña's help in May 1987, Tino Guerra was appointed municipal magistrate. Guerra had asked Mayor Henry Cisneros for an appointment to the municipal bench and filed his paper application. Frank D. Wing still controlled the Judiciary Committee for the city at that time and went along with the nomination. When asked, Presiding Judge Peña told all he also strongly supported Guerra's appointment. Peña was not one to forget a favor or a person who, in his time of need, had helped him.

Purge of Municipal Judges

Eddie Matias, assigned to Peña as legal assistant, had access to the judge's signature stamp and, more importantly, the power to plea bargain with prosecutors and defendants/offenders. Peña was happy with that, even though Guerra advised him to stop the practice. Peña loved the contact with the public but not the grind of hacking out plea bargains and assessing fines and court costs. Besides, he was busy with Rosa and her frequent visits to his office.

Leticia Luna, daughter of state representative Gregory Luna, had also been appointed municipal judge. As presiding judge, Peña put her in charge of the Assault Docket, all cases involving assaults. Presiding Judge Peña moved her to the magistrate duty during the daytime. She had been the subject of many complaints by citizens alleging she was rudest to them. Judge Luna objected to the move and told her father how capricious Peña's actions had been. Frankie Boyd, another judge, taped Peña during a meeting of judges when he made known his decision on reassignments, and also made it known that they were to come to him and not go to the city council with their complaints. Magistrate Luna went public with the recording. These magistrates and some judges also resented the role Matias grew into as their supervisor in lieu of Albert Peña Jr. Matias would say, "Peña said this . . ." or "Peña said that . . ." when it was he who was making up the instructions. According to inner-sanctum court personnel, Matias had a rough edge to him and lacked social and communication skills.

Representative Luna introduced legislation to rotate the office of presiding judge and election of municipal judges. It was a local bill and easy to pass. Senator John Whitmire (D-Houston), chair of Governmental Affairs, handled the bill in the Senate. Magistrate Guerra on behalf of Peña spoke to him about killing it. Guerra made the case against the bill by pointing out that it was the city council members' responsibility and duty to follow the city charter dictating the process. Guerra also enlisted the support of Hank Brown and other labor leaders to lean on Senator Whitmire. Guerra even made a contribution to the senator's campaign. Senators Frank Tejeda and Cindy Krier cosponsored the bill in the Senate but were not members of the committee. Meanwhile, council member Frank Wing passed a resolution by the city council in support of the current plan and in opposition to the Luna bill. Guerra met with Peña about the growing problem the municipal courts were having with state policymakers. John Flowers, executive director of the State Commission on Judicial Conduct, was personally acquainted with Frank Wing from other business in years past. He called Wing and told him the commission had received complaints about Judge Peña. Wing invited Guerra and Peña to go with him and visit Flowers to learn about the allegations made against Peña.

The meeting went well in that Flowers made available a copy of the allegations to Peña. Guerra looked it over and stated that the allegations were defensible and not serious. The group returned to San Antonio and discussed the alternatives. Peña felt that resignation under the circumstances would ruin his reputation forever. He could not leave office under any cloud of misconduct. Wing expressed his concern that his attempts at reform of the municipal courts now had resulted in Peña's possible ouster. Wing had pushed Peña as presiding judge to implement reforms to make the courts more efficient and productive. Peña agreed with Wing's suggestions and had obliged by implementing many of those proposals. In so doing, Peña had incurred the wrath of his subordinate judges. Guerra was personally hurt that his colleagues had turned on Peña. His hero was wounded as a result of the unrelenting negative press and Representative Luna's legislation. The bill was killed in committee, but the negative press continued.

Media War against Judge Peña: 1988

Early in 1988 as presiding judge of the Municipal Courts, Peña got his first taste of a media sting involving allegations of ticket-fixing. The *San Antonio Light* began a series of articles on ticket brokers burrowed deep into the city courts. The scam reportedly was initiated by a bail bondsman, Jimmie Rizik, acting as broker for local attorneys. Rizik would for a fee refer the case to an attorney for dismissal or guilty plea at a reduced rate of fine and court costs. Quickly, Peña named a three-member panel to investigate the newspaper stories and report to him their findings within two days. The panel consisted of Judge Joe Pina, chief deputy prosecutor Luz Viesca, and Eddie Matias, Peña's legal assistant.[9] Peña wanted to nip this scandal in the bud.

Within days, Judge Peña called a news conference to report on the panel's findings. He prepared for that press conference as he used to when he was county commissioner and political leader of PASO by carefully reading the investigative report and recommendations made by the panel. He anticipated the reporters' questions, memorizing answers to the questions that were sure to come about his knowledge of the ticket-fixing practice by his subordinates. The day of the press conference he dressed conservatively in a dark suit with a white shirt, his trademark. Peña was always an immaculate dresser. Before the battery of microphones and reporters, Peña began reading the press release in a controlled, calm manner. His baritone voice resonated in the room above the din of the whispered talk of the audience as he finished reading. Careful to demonstrate that he was in charge of the court system by opening up for questions, he looked into the audience, reporters in particular, and announced that he was revamping the court's plea-bargaining system to stop the practice he called the two-for-one. The scheme was simple: an attorney or bondsman would take several tickets for processing and would ask to plea on one in exchange for a dismissal on the other(s). Peña estimated the loss of revenue to the city from this practice exceeded $600,000 per year. The reporters busily took notes as fast as Peña was voicing the reforms to be implemented. He also announced that he was referring this entire matter to the local Bar Association and the Bexar County Bail Bond Board for internal policing and investigation.[10] Peña wanted to spread the taint of corruption as widely as he could and bring in other parties to share in responsibility for this scandal. The press conference and question period left everyone pleased that Peña had addressed the issue squarely and was going to make changes to end the corruption.

In an independent move, the city council had authorized a program of placing traffic boots rendering a vehicle immobile on those with three or more delinquent tickets during the previous year. Revenue from collected fines reached an all-time high for the month, which undoubtedly included offenders who, fearful of being booted, paid delinquent fines.[11] The ticket-fixing scandal of 1988 subsided, and the reporters moved on to other issues on the political landscape.

Media War against Judge Peña: 1991

Councilman Frank Wing and others on the city council continued to press Judge Peña to exert more control and closer supervision of the municipal judges and magistrates. The city council had eliminated all part-time judges and magistrates and prohibited judges from having an outside law practice, as most part-time judges and magistrates were accustomed to having. The council even increased salaries. Peña had made some reforms and cracked the whip, but the judges only grew more resentful. They continued to take longer lunches and to come in late and leave early; yet they still clocked and billed for eight hours of work, even though they only sat on the bench a few hours a day. The backlog of cases increased and revenues dropped. Peña, as presiding judge, ordered individual signature stamps for each judge, and required a signature on each case processed either by trial, plea bargain, or dismissal. A record was going to be kept of work production by each judge and actions taken on each case. The judges' signature stamps turned into a nightmare for Peña and an embarrassment for the city. Both Arnold Flores and Tino Guerra advised him to go immediately to the city manager and lay out the problem before he became the major target. Peña did just that and even went before the city council to lay bare the facts surrounding this problem. At that meeting he made a speech. According to Arnold Flores, who accompanied him, Peña said,

> When I adjudicate a traffic citation I take into consideration the amount to be charged to the violator. Surely a $300 amount to H.B. Zachary is pocket change but a single mother on unemployment, a low wage worker it is the difference of paying their utilities or putting food on the table. When I accepted the appointment, it was on the basis of running a court of justice not a court of revenue. And I will not do so even if instructed by this council.[12]

The members of the council did not question Peña; only Councilman Van Archer, a very conservative member, got into a verbal confrontation with Peña. The councilman made serious accusations against Judge Peña. In stoic fashion, Judge Peña looked intently at Van Archer and responded to the diatribe with this comment: "I would like to say that while I have walked with Presidents and rubbed shoulders with royalty I have never become accustomed to being jostled by pygmies."[13]

To Peña's surprise, the city manager, Alex Briseño, ordered his own investigation of the city courts. Briseño told the press that his investigation was the fifth probe launched in the last decade. The scandal, however, widened very quickly to the State Commission on Judicial Conduct,[14] which also received complaints, and to the local district attorney, Steve Hilbig, who vowed to investigate once the city completed its internal investigation. Hilbig was concerned about bribery, perjury, and the illegal practice of law by non-attorneys such as bondsman Rizik.[15]

CHAPTER 15

The End of Public Life

THE MAJOR INFLUENTIALS WITHIN CITY GOVERNMENT SOUGHT A WAY OUT OF the growing media scandal over ticket-fixing. Peña had once before purged the courts of judges and now was being asked once again to clean house—or else he would be the one removed, with a successor doing the job. Peña, forever cautious of tarnish in his public affairs but oblivious to his private reputation, saw a silver lining in the proposition. He suggested to Councilman Wing that he be kept on until such time as he cleaned up the mess. Once assured that he would be given time, Judge Peña instituted reforms and made reassignments of personnel, including Eddie Matias, and quietly pressured some judges to resign. After a few months, after the media had quieted on this issue, Peña announced he would resign at age seventy-five and retire from public life.[1]

Frances Meets Albert

Frances Guajardo,[2] daughter of José Manuel and Felicita Guajardo, was born in 1947 at home. The Guajardos lived on Guadalupe Street in San Antonio's West

Side. Her father was an older man from Lampasas, Nuevo León, Mexico, who came to San Antonio's West Side when that section of the community was a series of unincorporated areas without water, paved streets, drainage, electricity, or adequate housing. He married Frances's mother, who was younger than him by twenty-three years. He died in 1985 at the age of ninety-six. Frances basically grew up with an older man in the home. He was a *notario* and very involved with his neighbors in making sure they paid their poll tax to vote, and attending public and civic meetings to press for improvements in the *colonias* of the West Side. Mr. Guajardo was an active Democrat and had been a Peña supporter all his adult life. Frances remembered the backyard "rallies" organized by Yolanda Ibarra for Albert Peña Jr. that her family would attend during his campaigns, when she was twelve years old.

Don José was an avid reader and forbade his children to speak English at home, but he stressed they read as much as they could in either language. He encouraged Frances and made it possible for her to join the Junior LULAC group sponsored by Council No. 2. He was a proud and learned Mexican.

Frances attended the public schools and graduated from Brackenridge High School, then attended San Antonio College, Incarnate Word College, and finally St. Mary's University her senior year. Her college years were during the tumultuous Chicano Movement days in San Antonio. She was fascinated with the Brown Berets and the young militants involved with the Mexican American Youth Organization (MAYO). She and her dad still would attend political rallies and meetings. She recalls that she worked in several of Albert Peña's political campaigns and those of Henry B. González. Albert Peña Jr. was her hero. She always admired him from afar for his strong presence and manner of public speaking, always getting to the point without many words.

While at St. Mary's University for her senior year, she met and married Jesse Guerra from Corpus Christi in 1969, and had a son from that marriage, which lasted until 1977. While married, the couple resided in Corpus Christi. Jesse helped run the family businesses, which were a chain of stores, Green's Jewelers. It was during that time that she became reacquainted with Albert A. Peña Jr. Frances recalls that Peña and an entourage of men would come next door to the family place and business where Arnold Flores had his union office, on Buena Vista Street.[3]

Many years later, after Peña had lost the commissioner's race, Frances and her husband were dining at Ship Ahoy, a local restaurant in Corpus Christi. She glanced around the restaurant's seating area, and to her surprise there was Albert Peña Jr. with his older son, Albert III, also dining. She excused herself from the table and asked her husband "if I could get up and say hello to them." He said yes, and Frances went over and greeted them. Later, Peña told her that when she left, his son Albert III asked, "Who is that lady?" And he said, "I don't know, but someday she is going to be my wife." Perhaps Peña did not want to admit he did know her, or forgot the many persons he had met; regardless, it was a prophetic statement. What was not prophetic was Albert Peña Jr.'s wish to associate himself in the practice of law with his eldest son in Corpus. Albert III and his associates did not extend an offer to join them, even though Peña had humbled himself and asked his son for a job.[4]

When Frances returned to San Antonio, by then a divorcée with a child, she immersed herself in work and politics. Many jobs involved politics, such as Project SER and the Mexican American Unity Council. She was instrumental in obtaining letters of support for a Manpower Program funded by the Department of Labor. She became the assistant director of that project under Dario Chapa. She volunteered for many political campaigns in which Henry Cisneros and Maria Berriozabal were candidates, among many others. She attended and joined the Democratic Women's Club led by Joyce Peters, who later became the Bexar County Democratic Party chair. Every second Tuesday of the month, the Democratic Women, five hundred or more, would meet at the downtown Gunther Hotel. She volunteered to help Willie Velásquez and his Southwest Voter Registration and Education Project. Time after time she would run into Albert A. Peña Jr., but she was afraid of him because she viewed him as a very powerful man and still always surrounded by a group of men. "I was afraid of him. I respected him, but I was afraid of him." But over time they became friends—platonic, but meeting from time to time for business or dining. Frances needed his advice in politics and help for her Manpower Program enrollees who had citations for traffic and other violations.

When he was a municipal judge, then presiding judge, Peña graciously received her in chambers. He was always courteous and helpful, she recalled. When they met for dinner for the first time, she was most impressed with his humor, knowledge, and passion for social justice. "I always respected him and I . . . he is quite a scholar; a brilliant man, brilliant man. And I guess that is why we finally got married." Having had an older man in her life as her father, Don José, the thirty-year age difference between her and Albert Jr. was never an issue. Frances had another weakness, she admitted: "If a man can make me laugh, I'll take my clothes off for him and jump in bed." Peña made her laugh.[5]

Albert and Frances were married on May 25, 1994, by District Judge Mike Machado in chambers. Her brother Tony Guajardo and an ex–River Side Cats friend, Carl Shubert, were witnesses. Over the next two years, the couple began a project, the Committee to Educate on Voting Rights and Procedures. Frances and former Judge Peña began encouraging citizenship drives among those eligible for naturalization. "What we do is we go to the swearing-in ceremonies, thanks to Judge Orlando García, the Honorable Orlando García, who allowed us to come in there," Frances explained. "I told Albert . . . we were having a hard time trying to get into Immigration," and Peña spoke to Orlando García, whom he knew from years past. García had been a state representative from the 1980s to 1991, then with Peña's help won election to the 4th Court of Appeals. In 1993 President Clinton nominated him for the federal bench, which position he had taken by March 1994. When Peña approached Judge García he said, 'I don't see a problem with it. They can come in there with their group and register them.'"[6]

The Peñas did not always have a honeymoon time together; as Peña got older he became more jealous and possessive of her. She organized a surprise birthday party for him in 1994 and invited some of his closest friends. Rene González, one of those close friends, had not committed. When Frances and Albert were out at a reception one evening, she excused herself from the table and rushed to meet Rene to inquire about his coming to the party. Rene kissed her on the cheek. Upon her return, Peña was furious and accused her of infidelity. It took two days to calm both of them down. At the party she had organized, he had a great time with his friends, but upon leaving he again brought up the subject of infidelity and said, "Don't think I have forgotten what you did with him because of this party." Frances claimed she was so furious she consulted friends about divorcing Albert. They reconciled, but Peña's insecurities began manifesting themselves in fits of jealousy and unbearable possessiveness. The couple managed to ride the bumps in the marriage.

Inner City Advocates

Albert Peña Jr. founded, with the help of Frances, one last organization: Inner City Advocates (ICA). The idea began with her efforts to make citizens out of resident persons. Peña arranged it so that MAUC would sponsor her work and his idea of a confederation of groups to hold politicians accountable. Frances wanted new citizens, upon reaching citizenship status, to register to vote. She wanted to combine naturalization and voter registration at the ceremonies held to swear allegiance to the United States and become citizens. She had learned that most new citizens did not fill out the voter registration card or mail it back. If she could register them on the spot, this would most assuredly continue to increase the voter rolls in Bexar County. Peña wholeheartedly agreed with this fantastic idea. Using the new committee, they set up as a base, they called on other organizations to join a federation, an umbrella group, to hold public officials accountable for their decisions and also have Frances do voter registration. That was the beginning of Inner City Advocates, with a seventeen-organization membership—Peña's last organizing effort.

Together, Frances and Albert under the aegis of ICA began holding public rallies in public parks across the city and county promoting voter registration and naturalization drives to make citizens of legal residents. Peña's favorite event was the annual one held on July 4th.

Words as Weapons

Most students learn to communicate well by the time they graduate from high school and attend college. All students must learn to speak, write, read, and listen in order to progress and ultimately complete their studies. The more education a person obtains, the more expansive are the communication skills expected of her or him. Writing and speaking figure prominently in the list of skills a graduate is to master. Peña was no exception; he wrote countless essays, term papers, research papers, letters, and subjective examinations in the pursuit of his education. In the early part of his legal training, he added to his writing ability by preparing case and appellate briefs, jury arguments, course outlines, and more subjective examinations. Public speaking is also a necessary skill for lawyers and politicians. Peña, the lawyer and aspiring politician, also learned to prepare, write, and compose press releases, speeches, formal letters, one-page flyers, radio and television political announcements, newspaper articles, letters to the editor, and persuasive commentary for use at press conferences or interviews with media representatives. He developed expertise in both languages, Spanish and English, but his dominance was in English.

Over the course of his long political career, I estimate that Peña wrote in excess of three thousand articles for which he sought publication. Undoubtedly, many of his writings were published but are not preserved. His many writings are found primarily in two sources: *La Prensa* and among his personal papers at the UTSA archives. The earliest published article was sometime in 1948, and it is doubtful a copy can be found, according to the publisher of the *Snap News* in San Antonio, Eugene Coleman. Peña's last article was published in *La Prensa* on December 20, 2002.

San Antonio has had two major Spanish-language newspapers over the last two centuries. *La Prensa* dating back to the early 1900s is not in existence. This first *La Prensa* was begun by Ignacio Lozano shortly after the Mexican Revolution when the family found refuge in San Antonio. The current *La Prensa* was started in 1989 by Florentino "Tino" Duran and his spouse.[7] The Durans relocated from Fort Worth, where they owned and published *El Informador Hispano*. Duran also had some connections with the Dallas newspaper *El Sol de Texas*, owned and published by Sara Suarez and Jesus Gutiérrez, both former residents of San Antonio. He was a journalist for the newspaper for a number of years after a stint in the U.S. Air

Force.[8] Duran apprenticed under Gutiérrez and Suarez at *El Sol de Tejas* until such time as he conceptualized a similar venture in neighboring Fort Worth, Texas.

But Duran yearned to return to San Antonio and start a bilingual newspaper there. In 1988, the Durans decided to return to San Antonio and begin a Spanish-language newspaper. As Tino began "pulsing the community," as he called it, for opinion about such a venture, he found more opposition than support. A local prominent media personality, Henry Guerra (aka "La Voz de San Antonio"), adamantly told him to forget the venture. "Open a *taqueria*, washateria, car wash, restaurant, but not a Spanish language newspaper. The people that read Spanish are buried in San Fernando 1, San Fernando 2 and 3, forget it." The reference to San Fernando 1, 2, and 3 was to Catholic Church–owned cemeteries where most persons of Mexican ancestry have been buried in the city.

By contrast, Albert A. Peña Jr. was in favor of the venture and encouraged Tino to begin publication. Peña's words, according to Tino Duran, were "Let's do it. Let's do it. I'll write for you." Tino wasted no time in recruiting Peña to become a columnist for the paper. When in Fort Worth, Duran had wished for an "Albert Peña" to include in his newspaper. Peña was good for reaction among the readers because he was always pressing issues dealing with social justice and was most involved with Democratic Party liberal politics.[9]

Duran had a column in the Fort Worth, Tarrant County, *El Informador Hispano* entitled "Pico de Gallo," which provided political commentary. Peña would have been a natural fit for this column. Now that Duran was opening in San Antonio, and Peña was opening the door to such a relationship, Tino seized the opportunity. Peña accepted the offer to write a timely column weekly: "By all means. You don't mind what I write about?" Tino told him he could write on "anything you want, just get it to me ahead of time." Duran meant on time every Wednesday, no later than 5 p.m., for the Friday publication date.[10] Peña never asked for a cent for his contribution and Duran never offered. Peña wrote his first piece for *La Prensa* within two weeks of the inaugural issue. Peña was too busy to make deadline for the first issue of July 5, 1989. But he rarely missed a column after that. Duran claims that only on rare occasions did he have to run a repeat column due to a missed deadline by Albert—maybe six times in thirteen years.

Duran's perspective on Peña's contribution was that his column would provoke reaction. Reaction is good in the newspaper business because it expands the reader base. An extensive readership will make for more advertising dollars, if you have a sales force. *La Prensa* grew to a staff of thirty-two employees under the Durans' leadership and Peña's weekly column. Peña was always on time and on point. "I got a lot of reaction from his columns," Duran said. The Peña articles did in fact provoke reaction, which in Duran's view was great. His editor once complained that he did not like Peña's writings. Duran admonished him by saying, "He provokes reaction and any reaction, good or bad, is good. Reaction makes for readership and readership increases circulation which drives advertising prices." Enthusiastic supporters and irate opponents regularly would call Duran's office only to be referred to Peña. Duran and Peña agreed that it was best to place his law-office number at the end of his weekly piece. Not only would such a move free up space in *La Prensa*'s "Letters to the Editor" but also get directly to him promptly. His column began to carry his phone number to avoid this runaround. Peña loved to talk to his critics. He would not only respond to calls from critics but would also call Duran to tell him how much he enjoyed talking to this person or another.

The Peña weekly article prompted Peña's *compadre* and subsequent electoral opponent Rubén Munguía to ask for a similar column by 1992. Duran was eager to oblige; more reaction meant more circulation. Duran credits Peña with being the person in public office to first learn the power of the print media to influence and get name recognition for the author. Peña's regular weekly column soon brought requests from other politicians, such as Congressmen Henry B. González and Albert Bustamante, Peña's nemesis. Henry B. first started writing a column for the *Westside Sun*, a subsidiary publication of the *San Antonio Express*. He was not interested in the Chicano paper at that time. A year after Peña's columnist debut, Henry B. called Duran for space when the *Sun* collapsed.

Duran is not sure whether the congressman actually wrote his columns or dictated thoughts, because his only contact was a man named "Saenz." He would call in Henry B.'s column or to make an excuse for a missed deadline. Congressman Albert Bustamante asked for space in 1974. Curiously, Henry B.'s son and successor in office, Charlie González, only wrote about three columns and stopped. Since Peña's debut, subsequent politicians, such as Congressman Henry Bonilla and U.S. Senators Kay Bailey Hutchinson and John Cornyn, have craved space in *La Prensa*.

Albert A. Peña's editorial opinion on immigration won a national award, the National Print Media Award, from the National Hispanic Journalists Association in 2001. He was the only politician-writer ever in the history of *La Prensa* to win such an award.[11] *La Prensa* owners and staff held a reception for Peña to present him with the award plaque given to him in absentia at Las Vegas, Nevada, where the journalists met.

Words That Influence: Speeches and Editorials

Words influence people.[12] Words influence those who utter or write them as their thoughts and ideas, and they influence those who hear or read them, either in agreement or opposition. Words communicate more than a verbal or literary message; they simultaneously carry values, culture, history, symbols, action, ideas, and emotions. Politicians and lawyers depend on words as tools of their vocation and profession, respectively. Albert A. Peña Jr. used words effectively as a politician and lawyer. He was good with words, spoken or written, and he learned both at an early age. He also had role models that used words *en Español* most effectively in the family environment and the work roles of his father: salesman in the furniture store and dance promoter and emcee.

Most assuredly, his private and public school training introduced him to the world of words. And his university and subsequent professional training as a lawyer honed his vocabulary, usage, meaning, and application during that time frame. It is in the public arena, however, that a wordsmith learns the usage of words and their effectiveness in the contexts of audience, issue, time, and situation. Albert learned to be twice as good, being bilingual.

As an organizer he learned to use words to interest, recruit, argue, inspire, persuade, and for envisioning a better future, a major goal in being perceived as a leader. As a politician, he learned to motivate and cajole, soft-sell and bargain tough, practice both diplomacy and the hard stance, negotiation and compromise, principle and point, succinctness in argumentation and verbosity for buying time, bluff and trade. Albert became a master wordsmith by his early thirties after his return from law school in Houston. A review of available materials shows that Peña gave no less than five major talks a week during his public life. Among his last memorable speeches while still presiding judge of the municipal courts were his remarks during the dedication of the Albert A. Peña, Jr. Pavilion at Mission County Park, San Antonio, Texas. In his later years, particularly after a head injury in 2003, Peña continued to make appearances and speak to audiences. Regular events he had helped found many years before include the Martin Luther King, Jr. March in San Antonio, reported to have grown into the largest in the nation, and the César E. Chávez March. Peña never missed being involved with the MLK March or the César Chávez March up to 2006, months before he died. His son Bill and friend Jaime Martinez would take turns being the wheelchair drivers for Peña so he could participate in both events.[13]

From the days he organized the Latin American Democrats to his last opinion-editorial piece in *La Prensa*, when he was confined to his home and almost bedridden, Peña still used words daily to influence public opinion and policy. He delivered more speeches than he wrote opinion editorials, as politicians are asked to speak more often than a weekly deadline for a column. Peña was always available to his various constituencies for a speech at political gatherings, meetings, rallies, and conventions. He also made himself readily available to groups for a speech aimed to inform and recruit. During his early days as the lead organizer in Texas and subsequently the Southwest, he delivered hundreds of motivational speeches to audiences in countless cities. Unfortunately, many of Albert A. Peña Jr.'s speeches were made during an era when tape recorders and video cameras were not yet in existence. These speeches are either lost or will be if not properly archived.[14]

Peña's writings are not completely lost, however, although many of them are. He began writing letters to the editor in 1948, but these are lost. He kept no copies, nor are there archival records for such writings that I could find. He wrote many other opinion pieces, but I was unable to find publication records. Some writings are in his archives. The bulk of these were found in weekly columns of *La Prensa* between 1989 and 2002. Averaging one column a week during this time, Peña must have written more than six hundred such opinion pieces in his lifetime, just for *La Prensa*.

Albert A. Peña Jr. never had a problem with topics for a speech or written piece. He had opinions and he wanted to influence the public and public policy. In a review of articles written by Peña from June 2, 1993, "I Remember Bobby," to August 19, 1998, "Viva Kennedy," no less than fifty-five pieces were on national politics; from February 1, 1995, "Election Reform," to July 19, 2000, "Who Are You?," no less than ten pieces were on state politics; and from December 9, 1992, "Greater Chamber," to May 5, 1998, "Term Limits," no less than forty-one articles were on local politics.[15]

Last Years as a Lawyer with Douglas Dilley

Douglas Dilley, a young lawyer from Laredo, remained in San Antonio to practice law after graduation from St. Mary's Law School in 1969.[16] In his early twenties, he had dated one of Peña's nieces, Linda, daughter of Peña's sister Belinda. Linda introduced her uncle to Douglas. Later, when Dilley began to practice employment law, he met Peña in the company of two United Auto Worker (UAW) union organizers, Roy Hernandez and Juan Díaz. The UAW had a small office near Mario's Restaurant where Interstate 35 dead-ends with Pecos Street in San Antonio. After his last term on the Bexar County Commissioners Court in the 1970s, Peña did consulting work for the UAW, and he had long been active with labor issues and organizing drives.

Dilley also did legal work from time to time for labor unions and reviewed labor contracts with management. He was involved as legal advisor with union efforts to win contracts with Creative Cabinets (now under the name of Cardell Cabinets), Dickey Clay Pipe Company, Structural Metals of Seguin, International Harvester, and the Fruehauf Company. In these unionization efforts, Dilley got to know Peña and his passion for the working class. Dilley observed that Peña was ever ready to help a worker with any legal case regardless of money. Peña was committed to the cause of labor as a movement to break the cycle of poverty, low wages, poor working conditions, and to improve employee benefits, according to Dilley.

Dilley tried to avoid handling municipal court cases, but nevertheless took on such matters for friends and family or important clients with other cases, particularly personal injury ones. He would run into Peña, before he was a municipal court judge, at the courthouse while representing a client. Peña, Dilley noted, was always trying to help someone and eager to serve. He was always courteous and a true gentleman, willing to listen to anyone approaching him. The other thing that Dilley noticed about Peña was his appearance, always dapper in his expensive suits, well-groomed, and calm.

Years went by, and Dilley was regularly reading Peña's columns in local newspapers as well as reading about Peña in those same newspapers. It seemed to Dilley that Peña had boundless energy and was always involved with one issue or another and making headlines. On other occasions, he would hear Peña's voice on radio or see him on television. There were weeks, Dilley recalls, that Peña was ubiquitous in making daily news with his comments and doings, not only in San Antonio but across the country.

Dilley did well in his practice and soon could afford to purchase prime real estate in San Antonio's prestigious and historic King William area—an older two-story mansion. He opened the Dilley Law Office at 629 S. Presa. He almost exclusively began to handle worker's compensation claims and personal injury cases. With time and a few profitable cases, Dilley opened a branch office in McAllen, Texas, and purchased another King William property next door to his office to handle more cases and house additional staff and attorneys. John Meade was one such attorney, with an office in the adjacent building that eventually also was to serve as Peña's last law office.

Arnold Flores called Douglas Dilley one day in 1994 after Judge Peña had retired from the position of presiding judge of the Municipal Court. His conversation was quick and to the point: "Judge Peña needs an office to practice law. Do you have space?" Dilley was just as quick and to the point and said, "Sure, tell him to come by." Dilley correctly guessed that Peña still had lots of energy and willingness to help people and was not sitting idly by at home contemplating his legacy. When Peña called about visiting with Douglas, Rosalinda "Rosie" Fernandez took the call and entered him into Dilley's appointment book. That day Peña showed up exactly on time, and Dilley recalled that the two discussed Peña's legal interests and what he needed in terms of space and help. Since the Flores call, Dilley knew what he was going to offer Peña, so he announced to Peña that he could have "free office, secretary, telephone, everything." Peña was gratified to hear Dilley's words; he felt appreciated and needed. The truth of the matter was that this offer was a one-sided deal. Dilley would bear the costs of having Peña in his building although Peña would contribute little to his practice. Peña assured him that all his referrals would be first to the Dilley Law Office and no other lawyer. Peña and Frances brought over his plaques, posters, photographs, licenses, and other memorabilia. The two decorated the office so that it looked like the Peña Museum of Chicano History.

Dilley estimates that in their time together, Peña referred an occasional case, perhaps a dozen. And only one of Peña's personal injury cases referred was lucrative enough for Dilley to share legal fees. The bulk of Peña's cases were on behalf of impoverished clients who needed a free lawyer. Dilley and Fernandez, the office receptionist, frequently joked with one another about the endless stream of persons, claiming they had voted for Peña in every election, who asked for his legal help. Some people Peña did help with his broad network of contacts and asking other lawyers to help out; others he handled as best he could himself. Dilley, like most other lawyers in San Antonio familiar with Peña, knew he was not well versed in the practice of law. Peña's forte was politics and helping people.

With Peña in the office next door, across from John Meade's office, the 7:30 morning ritual became a habit for Dilley and staff. In the basement of Dilley's office was the record storage area and the coffee bar with table and chairs. Peña would drive up in his banged-up Altima; he was having difficulty driving safely in his later years. He would sit in the car for a few minutes (for longer periods of time as he aged), gather his thoughts it seemed, then step slowly out of the car and walk ploddingly to the door. Within minutes he would make the descent to the basement for the coffee and conversation. Peña would instantly begin the morning lecture about something he heard or read or wrote the night before. He engaged everyone in political discussions, and he was humorous while recounting events and his experiences. From time to time he would repeat the same stories, but Dilley claims Peña told these stories with such relish and animation that everyone listening enjoyed them over and over.

Dilley recalls that a mangy, ugly, malnourished cat appeared one day at the Dilley Law Office, and both secretaries, Rosie and Connie Sanchez, were repulsed and afraid of the animal. A few days went by and the cat seemed to make the Dilley Law Office his home; he wouldn't leave. The cat also refused to come when beckoned or to even acknowledge them. It would scamper off when approached, except with Peña. They would just look at one another, the staff observed, and Peña would say, "Hello *gato*."

The question arose as to what to name the cat, now that he was part of the legal team. Peña came up with the best name, "Joe Berta," because it was impossible to ascertain the sex of the cat. Peña also pulled out a crisp twenty-dollar bill and asked the secretaries to buy some cat food for the animal. Peña took it upon himself to provide for the feeding of the cat, but the secretaries were actually the ones to buy and place the food by the door leading to Peña's office. The staff began to notice that Joe Berta would instantly spring into action when Peña pulled into the office parking lot, and wait for Peña to open the car door. Often Peña would sit in his car for what seemed an eternity to those watching from the office windows. Joe Berta would not move, and sat motionless waiting for Peña to exit. As Peña opened the car door and began to walk to the office, the cat would walk right behind Peña as if he were the assigned escort. Once Peña was inside the office, Joe Berta would curl up by the door until Peña came out again and would follow him to his car. As Peña drove away, Joe Berta would disappear behind the building until the next morning to wait and greet Peña again. The cat and Peña bonded; they looked out for one another.

The day Joe Berta was run over by a car in the street, Peña insisted on the cat being treated by a veterinarian. The cat had splints on his legs until they mended and he could walk once again. When the cat died, Peña was so sad and melancholy that he left early from the office. The only other time Peña left the office early was when he received a telephone call informing him of the death by suicide of Rubén Sandoval. Peña was inconsolable and haltingly narrated what he knew of the death and tried to eulogize Sandoval at the coffee bar. He couldn't. His voice would break; he would take deep breaths and sigh. Sandoval had been his sidekick in many protests and his lawyer during the San Antonio Savings Association (SASA) boycott.

As time went by, Peña saw less and less people in his office but spent more and more time writing his opinion editorials. His longhand writing, usually in pencil, was legible to Connie Sanchez, who typed most of his articles from 1994 to October 22, 2002, his last one while at the Dilley Law Office. This last piece was entitled "Racism and Murder" and was about his opposition to Attorney General John Ashcroft's immigration policy and lack of inquiry into the murder of an unarmed Mexican immigrant by a South Texas rancher. The man, Peña wrote, "stopped to ask the rancher for a drink of water from a leaking hydrant. The rancher refused. When the immigrant started to return to his way home, the rancher shot the immigrant in the back—a cold-blooded murder."[17]

Albert A. Peña Jr. had not been sickly during his life—an occasional cold or flu, nothing serious. When he did not show up for work for almost an entire week, Douglas called Frances to check on Peña. She told him he had been hospitalized. She also told him that Peña could not and would not be allowed to drive himself to work anymore. She asked that they help look out for him. The Dilley staff knew Peña's health was deteriorating, but they thought it was just the aging process. Peña did stumble often, and fell several times while walking from his car to the office front door. According to Frances, Peña had been diagnosed with Parkinson's disease. From then on, he had to depend on escorts and drivers to get around. He stopped going to Pico de Gallo restaurant on Saturday mornings before going to work at Dilley's. The restaurant was where the old politicos gathered to talk politics and recall events of yesteryear. Later when Peña was hospitalized and badly injured in 2003, he stopped going to the office altogether. One day Frances, Dilley assumed, came to the office after working hours and removed all of Peña's memorabilia. The office was empty and stripped of all the items Peña had on the walls, bookshelves, desk, and behind the door. The keys to the office were never returned to Dilley.[18]

CHAPTER 16

Who Caused the Injury or Assault?

An incident report dated "4/29/03, Case no. 03/276846, San Antonio Police Department" (SAPD) lists the victim as "Peña, Albert Judge LM" (for Latin Male perhaps) of age "87 yrs." The reporting person was "Peña, Frances LF 57 yrs." The address of the incident was entered as "214 Vista del Sur," a "Single Family House" with telephone number 224-6052. Peña was taken by ambulance to "Santa Rosa" Hospital in "undetermined condition" with "cut and bump on head" at 4:10 p.m. The reporting officer was G. Smith of SAPD. He wrote in the section for "Details of the Offense/Event" the following in his handwriting:

> I was dispatched to the location. Upon arrival I contacted both (R) and (C). [R is for Frances and C is for Peña.] (R) said that she came home to find (C) in bed with a cut to his head. (R) said (C) was very disoriented at first. (C) said that his head started hurting and when he touched his head it started bleeding. I asked (C) if he had been assaulted. (C) said "No." (C's) wallet and money was accounted for. No forced entry into the house and nothing was said to be missing from the home. I asked (C) if he had fell. (C) said no but it looks like that's what may have happened. EMS transported (C) along with (R).

Frances Peña, Albert's wife, had received an emergency distress call from a neighbor around mid-afternoon that the front door to their home at 214 Vista Del Sur, a small residential area, just blocks from the downtown campus of UTSA, was open. The neighbor was concerned because she knew that Peña was alone in the home during the day and she had not seen him outside or with his dog, Jack, that afternoon. Frances dropped everything she was working on at the insurance office on Buena Vista and rushed home. Upon arrival, she "found the front door wide open and called out for Albert" as she frantically surveyed the living room and kitchen area. She peered into the small backyard area, but no sign of Albert. Again, she screamed out his name as she raced upstairs to check the bedrooms. She found Albert in bed bleeding from what appeared to be a head wound. She knelt beside him and discovered that he was semiconscious and had a cut on the back of his head. Albert had been having trouble walking the past few months and often tripped on the carpeted floors, being unable to lift his feet while he stepped forward. "Rather than accept the use of a cane or his walker, Albert insisted on walking unaided around the two-story house, both front and back yards, and outside. He had fallen on occasion previously."[1] She was concerned he had fallen again and hurt himself badly this time. She ran down the stairs back to the car to search for her cell phone, but then realized the home phone was closer. She immediately and frantically called 911 for the police to report the emergency. After some calming by the police emergency receptionist, Frances reported what she had found and gave her name, phone number, and address. She also implored the police dispatcher to send an ambulance immediately to their home. The police and ambulance arrived within minutes. The paramedics tended to Peña while the police began their preliminary search for clues as to the incident. There was no apparent damage to the front door. There were no other visible marks on windows or the backyard entryway of any forcible entry. The police ruled out robbery or attempted burglary. Either Peña had left the door open or someone had entered and assaulted him, but nothing appeared to be missing. His wallet and money were all accounted for. The police then proceeded to question a very disoriented Albert A. Peña Jr. He told the police what had happened as best he could. His version was repeated in the police report.

Frances was asked about her whereabouts that afternoon and who might possibly have come to their home to visit. The police also asked her about any recent troubles with neighbors or transients in the area. The day labor center and St. Vincent de Paul shelter for the homeless were several blocks away, just north and to the west of UTSA. Frances could not recall any such episodes or sightings in the neighborhood. The investigating police officer, G. Smith, proceeded to knock on neighborhood doors asking the inhabitants for any information as to strangers seen in the area or at the Peña home. None reported any unusual occurrences that afternoon. It was ultimately surmised that Peña had probably gone outside for a moment and left the door open when he reentered the home. Jack, the dog, was still missing outside. Albert could not have forgotten to completely close the front door; he left it open for Jack. Once inside, as he made his way upstairs to his bedroom, he probably lost his balance and fell backward and hit his head, accounting for the nasty gash on the back of his head. The police, however, could not find any trace of blood on the staircase railing or wood frame by the nearest door to his bedroom.[2]

At the Santa Rosa Hospital, where Albert was taken for emergency care, the prognosis was not good. Albert had sustained a hard hit on his head and was in a semiconscious state. He could not relate what happened to him. The medical staff precluded any further questioning by police and other personnel about the occurrence. Albert remained in the hospital for days under intensive care. His brain was swelling from the trauma and the doctors had to perform surgery on his head. To relieve the pressure building from fluid in the brain, the doctors made two quarter-size penetrations into his skull to drain the extra fluid. Without that release of pressure, Albert could have suffered permanent brain damage and even death. For weeks after the surgery, Albert was comatose.

He finally recovered from the injury and surgery to the point that he was talking and even walking. His talk was slurred somewhat and came in spurts of words. He was coherent and logical but halting. His walk, however, was now worse than prior to the incident. He now shuffled more than ever. He could not lift his feet off the ground. His balance was radically affected. He needed to hold onto something as he shuffled from the hospital bed to the bathroom or anywhere he walked. His appetite remained as normal; Albert had always been a hearty eater.

After he was taken home, Albert continued to improve, but adjustments to his daily life, and that of Frances, had to be made. Albert needed adult daycare and could not be left alone. He needed to continue with rehabilitation to regain not only his balance and walking ability but also his speech. Within months Albert seemed back to normal, although with greater physical limitations than before the injury. The only reminders were the very visible scars on the top left side of his head where the doctors had bored holes into his skull. The indentations on that part of his head drew attention to the incident.

The cause of his injury remained a mystery to all. The police could find no evidence of a crime or perpetrator. Albert's daughters from Olga, however, suspected foul play and insisted that the police keep investigating the incident, but nothing conclusive was ever found to support such an allegation. The daughters also began legal proceedings to declare Albert incompetent and Frances unfit to care for him. The probate court, however, dismissed that effort as baseless in later months. Relations between Frances and the daughters continued to deteriorate and became more acrimonious. Because Frances had to keep close watch on Albert and restrict his movements, friends and relatives believed she was keeping them from him. Albert's daily life now was spent with a caregiver at the family home or at the insurance office with Frances in an upstairs apartment. Frances outfitted a loft space in her office on Buena Vista Street with Albert's memorabilia, such as plaques, posters, awards, diplomas, and other testaments from his achievements; a bed; and even his desk, complete with his nameplate, gavel, photos, and reading material. The "office" part of that apartment was surreal to visitors in that it seems as if retired Judge Albert Peña Jr. was still holding court and conducting business. To Albert, the apartment was the embodiment of his previous life as a doer and political activist; besides it also had a bathroom and television for him to watch his necessary news programs and talk shows. More importantly, he soon could go up and down the stairs, just with greater difficulty than before the injury.

When I visited Albert at the insurance office on various occasions in the spring of 2004, he was often downstairs, either singing, talking, flirting, or otherwise entertaining Frances's office assistant, Barbara de la Fuente, and his day nursemaid, Yolanda Rodríguez, another caregiver. Barbara recalled in a 2004 interview with me, "He did not talk, walk, just slept a lot. Slowly he recovered and began coming down the stairs to visit with me. He had a good singing voice and could do a dance, a gig." She had to remind him to walk. When they had to go to court fighting about his guardianship, he grew despondent. "He was on edge on court days. When those hearing were cancelled, he would light up and his despondency would stop."

Barbara was responsible for Albert when Frances was not in the office. She had to stop him from walking outside. "I controlled him when he was here, but he was persistent. Once he did walk out with a customer and she comes back hysterical because Albert was sitting down in the middle of Buena Vista Street on the ground." She coaxed him to get up and return to the office with the help of a policeman who stopped traffic so Albert could shuffle back across the street. He did not want help walking by himself, although it was increasingly a problem for him. He kept protesting to Barbara that he did not need watching and that this lady was following him. "Albert was like a baby again; needed space to be independent, but feeble." He would hold onto furniture to maneuver his way around the office, but chairs move, especially those on casters.[3]

On three occasions when I was in the insurance office, Albert fell again. Fortunately, he did not hurt himself other than a bruised ego. He still refused to use the walker or cane, insisting he could walk by himself. Regrettably, that was not the case. Peña had developed the habit of reaching for the next object, such as a chair or stand or furniture piece, as he shuffled to his destination, but not all the things he grabbed could hold his weight or maintain his balance. He would fall. Once, he fell coming from the bathroom as I waited by his bed. Upon hearing the thud on the floor, I jumped up from my chair only to find him sitting on the floor somewhat dazed, with his pants half down. Either he had failed to lift them up completely to his waist, or he did not fasten them securely before attempting to walk back to the bed. As I lifted him to his feet, he asked me to help him secure his pants but warned me not to touch him near his private parts because "I still don't care for that." We both laughed at his wonderful sense of humor, even in the worst of times and in distress. That was the quintessential Albert A. Peña Jr.

PART 5

The Final Years

CHAPTER 17

Second Retirement

ALBERT A. PEÑA JR. AND CÉSAR E. CHÁVEZ WERE CONTEMPORARIES. WHILE they are very similar in character, they diverged in their early life paths only to converge in their mature lives as leaders in the developing Chicano Movement of the late 1950s. Both Chávez and Peña were born in the United States during the early part of the twentieth century to Mexican immigrants. Both attempted public schooling, but only Albert A. Peña Jr. finished high school, went on to professional training, and became a lawyer. Chávez went to work in the agricultural fields. Both married young and fathered many children. Both joined the Navy during World War II. Again, only Peña utilized his G.I. Bill benefits to complete legal studies and purchase property. Chávez was content to earn meager wages the remainder of his life and owned no real estate. Chávez learned to organize within the framework of the Community Services Organization (CSO) and under the tutelage of Fred Ross, a protégé of Saul Alinsky. Peña and his peers taught themselves organizational politics in the barrios, but made important friends within the various unions of organized labor and the growing African American community of San Antonio. Peña quickly realized that while coalition politics with labor unions, white liberals, and black leaders were necessary, ultimately his role within that coalition and into the future rested on his leadership among his own people. Chávez reached the same conclusion: he left CSO to form a union of farm workers among Filipino and Mexican seasonal agricultural workers.

From that pivotal moment on, both Chávez and Peña rose to prominence in organizational politics of the Chicano Movement. Chávez became a labor leader and Peña an activist and politician. Both became icons in the Chicano Movement.[1] The history of the farm worker struggle in the United States is synonymous with Chávez. Important institutions such as the National Council of La Raza (NCLR), the Mexican American Legal Defense and Education Fund (MALDEF), the Southwest Voter Registration and Education Project (SVREP), and even San Antonio's Mexican American Unity Council (MAUC) are the legacy left by Peña as an activist in the Chicano Movement. As a politician he was successful in building the Viva Kennedy Club network across the country, but primarily in Texas, crafting a local coalition to join the Democrats of Texas (DOT) and taking the Political Association of Spanish Speaking Organizations (PASO) to regional, if not national status.

It was most appropriate that in San Antonio, as in other cities, contemporary Chicano activists joined with others to celebrate the spirit and vision of César E. Chávez, who died on April 23, 1993.[2] From that date forward, groups have sought to honor him by naming streets, parks, schools, buildings, and other places in his honor.[3] The United States Postal Service honored Chávez with a commemorative stamp in 2003. At the University of California–San Diego, his birthday, March 31st (1927) is a holiday, celebrated on the last Friday in March.[4] The City of Dallas has declared his birthday a holiday for city employees. The State of Texas honors his birthday with an optional state holiday for employees. Cities such as San Antonio and Fort Worth, for example, annually hold parades, marches, rallies, banquets, and/or celebrations to commemorate the man. There are many, many other celebrations held across the country in his honor. El Paso, for example, has a César Chávez *Marcha* on Wheels weeklong celebration. San Antonio celebrated in 2016 with their twentieth annual parade for Chávez, and Fort Worth is on their twelfth year. All of these groups and others are combining forces to create a national holiday in his honor.[5]

On March 23, 2004, at "The Legacy of César Chávez La Causa Awards" banquet held at San Antonio's La Villita Assembly Hall, honored these persons with lifetime achievement awards: Manuela Solis Sager, Willie Velásquez, Emma Tenayuca, and Judge Albert A. Peña Jr., the only one alive at eighty-eight years of age.[6] The annual event is a joint effort between the César Chávez March Foundation and the local League of United Latin American Citizens (LULAC) chapters and officers, and countless of unaffiliated supporters.

Albert A. Peña Jr. strode into the cavernous hall promptly at 6 p.m. escorted by his wife, Frances. Following closely behind were some of the grown children,

Bill, Sandy, and Olga, from the marriage to Olga Ramos Peña. The crowd enjoying the dinner noticed his entrance and many rushed to greet and congratulate him. Albert did not make many public appearances at his age. He struggled to walk and tired easily. His voice still projected and resonated but was halting and repetitious as he found the memory to fit the words. Albert labored mightily to make the long walk from the entrance to the head table at the front of the hall just below the stage. He shuffled as he walked and made a great effort to be erect and not stoop. Frances helped each step of the way. He was breathless by the time he reached the head table and was anxious to finally sit. He managed a feeble smile to those engulfing him with congratulations and other laudatory words. Albert seemed pleased but puzzled at all these people he did not recognize, or whose names he could not recall at that moment.

La Villita Assembly Hall was nearly packed by the time Peña arrived. Each table accommodated ten persons and most tables were full, with only three left empty by politicians who wanted to be known for their support but were not present. The volunteers from Fuerza Unida, LULAC, and college students from area universities had decorated the hall with United Farm Worker union memorabilia. Each table had a red tablecloth centered with a white circle with a hand-sewn black eagle, the UFW logo. The tables resembled the UFW flag. Atop each tablecloth was a cup centerpiece with two flags and a bound sheet of paper.[7] The two flags were of the UFW and the United States. Very much in the tradition of Chicano weddings, the guests took home the flags, centerpieces, and tablecloth center logo as souvenirs. This author did so as well.

After the welcome and invocation, the various personalities and dignitaries took turns expressing words of praise for Chávez and each of the four recipients of the lifetime awards. Judge Albert A. Peña Jr. was the first to be noted. An all-female *conjunto* sang their composition of "El Corrido de Alberto Peña." The judge was beaming with pride. Guests continued to come to his table and congratulate him. He made it to the podium to speak after Jaime Martinez introduced him and made the award presentation, but Peña only managed a few words. He said, "I would like very much to say that I am happy to be here with you . . . a wonderful crowd. I remember, I remember when you told me I had to go to a little town to meet our good friend . . . César Chávez. . . . He fought for many, many years . . ." The crowd didn't care if he could talk or not, if he made sense or not, if he said anything important or not; they poured out their love for their hero with a standing ovation that drowned his words out.

Jaime Martinez began the chant, "Viva Peña, Viva Albert Peña." The crowd responded with *Vivas* of their own. Others chanted "Si Se Puede, Si Se Puede." And the standing ovation evolved into a Chicano clap in cadence and unison.

The *conjunto* struck up the "Corrido de Alberto Peña" once more, and the crowd continued to cheer, clap, whistle, and chant.

The people closest to him over the years never really cared if Albert A. Peña Jr., their champion, won or lost; they remembered that evening that he would always fight for them. He was still feisty and tried mightily to recapture the Albert A. Peña Jr. of yesterday.

The other awardees had someone accept the presentation in their stead. It was very moving to hear from the grandson and niece of Emma Tenayuca and a former friend of Manuela Solis Sager. Manuela is not as well known as Emma or Albert, but nonetheless she is a heroic figure. Rafael, "Ralphie," youngest brother of Willie Velásquez, accepted for him. And as each of the other awards was presented, the crowd began to dissipate, as if they had really come just for Albert A. Peña Jr. It was a weekday night, and people had to go to work the next day and drive children to school and still make it through the day. Weekdays are not the time to stay up until midnight, and the program that evening was headed in that direction with the many speakers.

Albert A. Peña Jr. stayed to the very end of the night and walked back out the hall the same way he had entered. He took small steps, stayed erect, and held onto his wife's arm. He was proud and happy. The people that knew him best honored him that night. And, he was honored among those since departed that he knew best. He attended high school with Emma and supported Manuela's unionization work among women in the local fur and leather industry. He befriended Willie and the MAYO militants when they made their political presence known in the city, state, and country. Of the group honored, he was the last man standing. Briefly, he stood in the entrance hallway to shake hands with well-wishers. To some he pledged to see them at the César E. Chávez march the following Saturday. To others he promised to see them next year at the same event.[8]

On March 27, 2004, a dreary Saturday morning, Albert A. Peña Jr. arrived at the march by car with some of his family members promptly at 10. William "Bill" Peña, his second son, pulled out a wheelchair from the car trunk for his dad. Albert had to ride in this march commemorating Chávez. Albert had marched in both the Martin Luther King Jr. parade and César Chávez March for Justice in 2003, but not this one. Albert had tried to walk during the 2004 MLK parade and tired almost immediately. He was wheeled the rest of the way but was adamant about completing the march. This was vintage Albert A. Peña Jr.: Finish what you start. Never quit the fight.

The 2004 César E. Chávez 8th Annual March for Justice started at the corner of Guadalupe Street by the cultural center after a short program outdoors that featured speakers attempting to fire up the crowd for the long walk to the Alamo. The monitors lined up folks and proceeded down the street. As if riding in a parade car, Peña waved and smiled to onlookers and well-wishers while Bill pushed. Albert was happy to be involved and part of the march. He had never passed up an opportunity to join a march or protest—and still didn't.

Albert was concerned about being there at the march and not with his grandchildren, perhaps a reflection on advice he once gave to Arnold Flores. He said, "Arnold, I lost my kids because I was too busy. Never think that going to chicken-shit meetings is worth it. Your kids are more important than that."[9] Perhaps it was a lesson learned too late in life, but he learned it nonetheless.

Hardly a month had gone by when Albert heard his bosom buddy, Herschel "Herky" Bernard, age seventy-seven, was dying of cancer. He was beside himself and kept insisting that Frances arrange a meeting of his "guys." It never happened, not because of Frances but due to Herky dying unexpectedly on April 28, 2004. The outdoor memorial service was at the Bernard residence in Terrell Hills, a suburban community just north of San Antonio, held on May 2nd at 2 p.m. Albert went to pay his last respects to his decades-long friend along with his wife Frances, her sister Lupe, and me. Herky had been his counselor and lawyer, oftentimes coleader and organizer of the coalition they built in San Antonio, Bexar County, and in Texas.

Linda Wilson, the former wife of Richard Avena, former staffer of the U.S. Commission on Civil Rights, commented as she surveyed the crowd at Herky's farewell that if a bomb went off, that would be the end of liberalism in San Antonio. Her comment was prompted by the many, many distinguished liberals from years past that were present: Frank Herrera, Lou Fox, Joyce Peters, Les Mendelson, Robert Brischetto and spouse, Ernie and Oralia Cortes, Hank Brown, Juan and Elena Patlan, William Elizondo, Arnold Flores, Ignacio Pérez, and hundreds more. The memorial service was more of a party than a somber affair. The wine and refreshments flowed freely. Finger food was in the house. A huge canopy covered the musicians and the speaker's podium. Herky's son, Michael, welcomed the guests that kept arriving. Valet service out front was complimentary, and all the neighbors in a gesture of service permitted parking by the valets in their parking areas and street fronts. Just before the program began, Hank Brown, former head of the state AFL-CIO, leaned over to Albert and said, "We are the few left, Albert. I wonder when we will meet like this again." Albert gazed intently into Hank's face and while smiling said, "I sure don't want it to be me."

Around mid-afternoon, someone tinkled a glass rim as a signal that the program was to begin. Michael Bernard moved to the microphone and, as I recall, said:

> Welcome my friends. My father wanted it this way. He was adamant that no memorial service be held, but if we did then to make sure no eulogies were made, just parts of his

favorite music played, some poetry, lots of libations, and friendship. So enjoy each other for a while, then the musicians will play some of my dad's favorite pieces and Naomi Shihab Nye will read some poetry.

Several minutes later and after more people had arrived, a string quartet under the direction of Doris Norton began to play. The crowd was hushed for the entirety of the musical program. The music smoothly eased from one piece to another without interruption: "Sheep May Safely Graze" and "Air from Suite in D" by J. S. Bach; a piece from Vivaldi, "Largo" from *"Winter" Concerto*; Chopin's "'Raindrop' Prelude"; and Pachelbel's Canon. Naomi Nye then read some poetry. More music followed: "Amazing Grace," "Simple Gifts," "Waltz in A Minor," "Jesu, Joy of Man's Desiring," "Romanza" from *Eine Kleine Nachtmusik*, and "Prelude to a Te Deum." Michael thanked everyone again for coming and encouraged all to stay and enjoy each other longer, as his dad would have wanted. Herschel Bernard is interred at Sunset Memorial Park in San Antonio.

On the trip home, Peña, who downed three rather full glasses of wine at the service, was most talkative. He mused about the great times with Herky. He reminded Frances that he wanted full military honors at Fort Sam Houston when he died and was to be buried. She was surprised at the outburst. She asked him if he had changed his mind about cremation, but he ignored the question. Frances asked him if he wanted to have dinner with her and Lupe, if he felt up to it. Albert said he wanted more wine for me. Upon arrival at the family residence, Albert said to Frances, "I can't get out, help me." Frances moved around to his side and admonished him, "Don't say you can't. Try. If you've had too much wine, then no more for you." Albert, like a reprimanded little boy, sheepishly said, "OK. OK. Just checking on you; I am all right." He promptly made his way out of the backseat jerkily and shuffled his way into the house.

The following Friday after work hours, Frances had a *fiesta* for friends and clients at her place of business, Farmers Insurance Group, on 2502 Buena Vista. Albert had a great time being greeted and feted by those who dropped in to the event. He danced, or tried to, and sang his favorite tunes to Barbara, the office receptionist and pinch-hitting caregiver, and others. Days later, Albert showed up for his granddaughter Lili Dwyer's graduation party. Frances had to have help in order to bring him to the party. Lili had just received her bachelor's degree.

The party was held at a place in Northwest San Antonio that was owned and operated by Frances's brother, a two-story structure off Jefferson Street. It was ample and spacious, with a private swimming pool that was also rented for such occasions. The place had park-style benches in the shade and an almost Olympic-size pool. The Peña clan gathered there along with friends. Mary Peña (Albert Peña Jr.'s first daughter-in-law, formerly married to his first son, Albert Peña III) was there, as were her grown children and grandchildren. Albert IV was her firstborn. Her two other children were there also with wives and their children. Linda Wilson, formerly Avena, was there also. She was Mary's best friend when Albert III was married to Mary and they lived in San Antonio. Mary brought all her grown sons and daughter to Lili's graduation party. She had not divorced the Peña family. She still was a Peña. Mary resided in Laredo and operated a successful real estate business in that city. She also owned several expensive properties in San Antonio.

Food was plentiful and the mood was loud, with each family member meeting other Peñas whom they had not seen in a long time or ever. When Albert Jr. was escorted in after the party was well underway, he sat at the front table near the entrance, not because he was shy or reserved but because he couldn't make it any further into the crowd. Once he sat, the grandchildren and great-grandchildren were brought over to meet and greet Papa Peña. Great-grandfather Albert A. Peña Jr. was beaming. He hugged the children back and tried to kiss them. Belinda, his first daughter, and her mother brought him a Hawaiian lei, a colorful wreath, and placed it over his head and around his shoulders. Peña smiled his toothy smile. He glanced up and said to all, and yet to no one in particular, "I've been laid again." Those near him roared with laughter. Those further away wondered what the excitement surrounding this old man was about. They were too young to know they had Albert A. Peña Jr., dean emeritus of Chicano politics, in their midst. They had never read about him in their textbooks. They had never heard about the Chicano Movement from teachers. Hopefully they will be able to someday and follow in his footsteps. Until then, the country will have to wait for another Albert A. Peña Jr.; perhaps a great-grandchild, or someone else's grandchild or child, will take the leadership mantle and forge new opportunities for current and subsequent generations.

A week later on May 13, 2004, Albert showed up again on the arm of his wife, Frances, to attend the early-evening book premiere of the biography of William "Willie" Velásquez held at St. Mary's University, his old alma mater, and cosponsored by the publisher, Arte Público Press, with the support of Prudential Financial, Inc. The ceremony was well attended. The Velásquez family was there.[10] The author's family was there. Members of the press were there working overtime identifying the many luminaries present and jotting down names, comments, and the speeches that opened the reception. Photographers, amateurs and professionals alike, were taking aim, trying to capture a significant moment featuring an important person of their choice. And there were many such persons and moments there, beginning with Peña.

Old friends gathered around Albert to greet him. It was like déjà vu. Albert came to life. He was talkative, smiling, saying, "Good to see you," and hugging people back. Albert was enjoying himself. The program began with Dr. Charles Cotrell, president of St. Mary's University, welcoming everyone and proudly proclaiming how Willie was an alumnus of the university along with other MAYO members in the crowd: Ignacio Pérez, Flaco Rodríguez, Rosie Castro, and me. Dr. Cotrell reminded the audience of the importance of young men like Willie in changing the course of history for all Americans. President Cotrell introduced Henry Cisneros for remarks, who then introduced the author of the Velázquez biography, Juan Sepulveda.[11] The final speaker was Henry Ramos, senior editor with Arte Público Press (University of Houston). The crowd broke into intense applause at the conclusion of all the speeches, finished off the finger food available, and paid their respects to Albert, sitting by the exit door of Conference Room A of the new Student Center.

The event was an important moment for everyone, particularly Albert A. Peña Jr. He could not fathom why Willie had been taken from us at such an early age. Why did his friends die before him, like Herky? He turned to me and asked, "When is this book of yours going to be finished? Is it soon?—because I have to have it to go make presentations and go organize." He was referring to this book.

On Saturday May 22, 2004, at a noon luncheon held at the Asador de Leo, a restaurant near the intersection of Culebra, Bandera, and 24th Streets, several friends of Peña Jr. gathered to eat with him. Albert and Frances arrived as many were done eating and I had just made remarks on the status of the Peña manuscript. Peña was also saying goodbye and thanking many of those who had helped me with the research. Some present made check donations to the Center for Mexican American Studies at Our Lady of the Lake University. These funds were used to preserve the audio- and videotapes featuring Peña and others of his time, including copies of his many writings.

Albert and Frances joined those at the head table. He beamed with joy at being celebrated. He shook hands with everyone there: Dr. Charles Cotrell and wife Abby, Charles Lieck Jr., Leo Alvarado, Jaime Martinez, Rolando García and son Roberto, Laura Barberena Mendoza, and Patricia Mejia. I saw him for the last time that day and gave him an incomplete copy of the manuscript. I left San Antonio on May 28, 2004, after five months of research and writing about the life of Albert A. Peña Jr.[12]

The Icon Passed Away

At age eighty-eight, on July 3, 2006, Albert A. Peña Jr. passed away after a couple of weeks of lingering with various ailments until his body tired of functioning. The obituaries of local and area newspapers noted his passing. All the major organizations he had cofounded issued their own eulogies in the form of press releases to the media. Family and friends were called by his widow Frances and son Bill to help make arrangements for his interment at Fort Sam Houston, Texas; he was to be buried, not cremated as he once requested.

The church service was divided into two parts, with a rosary on Thursday, July 6, 2006, at 7 p.m. and the Mass the following day at noon. At the rosary service, Bill Peña gave a welcome and expressed appreciation for the outpouring of affection by those attending for his father on behalf of their families. Following the rosary, officiated by Rev. I. A. Blanco, the mourners were treated to a video presentation of a speech Albert A. Peña Jr. had made, and often, entitled "Why I Call Myself Chicano." The videotaped speech was presented by Gabriel Velásquez. Albert had made similar speeches on why he considered himself a Chicano in the latter part of his years. The crowd at the rosary was able to see and hear Albert A. Peña Jr. one last time in his notable oratorical style.

The turnout for both events was impressive, and with the church completely full, mourners spilled out into the street. Hundreds and hundreds tried to get into Immaculate Heart of Mary Church at 617 S. Santa Rosa Street for the Mass. Cars were parked everywhere. There were demonstrators, not against Albert A. Peña Jr. but for some upcoming event in support of a cause. Peña probably would have smiled in his coffin as he was taken into the church for his Mass if he had caught sight of the protestors across the street. The coffin was carried into the church by some of his grandsons: Albert A. Peña IV, Robert Francis Peña, Aaron Sandoval, Fred C. Kroger IV, Eric D. Wurts, and Anthony Montana. Honorary pallbearers were listed in the printed program: Leo Alvarado, Joe Bernal, Charlie Cotrell, Dario Chapa, Ernest Cortes Jr., Douglas Dilley, Tino Duran, Bill Elizondo, Arnold Flores, Richard Gambitta, Tony Guajardo, Tino Guerra, Ralph López, Juan Patlan, Gene Rodríguez Sr., Rodolfo (Rudy) Rosales, Andrew Sarabia, Gabriel Velázquez, and Frank Wing. Many of these honorary pallbearers were important figures in the political career of Albert A. Peña Jr.

Albert A. Peña Jr. probably frowned when he saw and heard Bishop John Yanta of Amarillo giving the quasi-eulogy and sermon and co-celebrating the Mass with Ignacio A. Blanco, CMS. Peña and Yanta, when he was a priest in San Antonio, had sparred and quarreled over the War on Poverty programs in the county years before. Yanta headed SANYO, the contract agency for youth programs. In essence, efforts by the Catholic Church with Yanta as head to establish and succeed in operating youth programs resulted in taking up all money allocations for these kinds of operations in Bexar County and starving other agencies and programs also serving youth.

The actual eulogy was given by Ernie Cortes with the Southwest Industrial Areas Foundation Network, an affiliate of Saul Alinsky's Industrial Areas Foundation. Bill Peña also made remarks on behalf of the Peña families, thanking all for their condolences and other contributions of affection for his father. Henry Cisneros, former mayor of San Antonio, also was given a moment to comment on the legacy of Albert A. Peña Jr. Key influentials in the city and current politicians were all in attendance, sitting next to union members, blacks, liberals, poor Méxicanos, and behind the Peña extended families.

It was not a long Mass service; then the funeral car procession meandered slowly past his last residence, the Municipal Courts building, then the Bexar County Courthouse, and through downtown streets that contained the memories of his actions, arrests, marches, demonstrations, protests, vigils, celebrations, and the like. The long caravan finally made it to the cemetery. The family was under a tent; the hundreds and hundreds of others who came to say a final "Bueno bye, Judge Peña" (one person held a poster with those words) stood in the sun. Peña probably took one last look at the military escort, comprised of Navy personnel, half of whom were women sailors. Had he been able to, Peña probably would have said, "I love these sailorettes." The soldiers with rifles fired their volleys on command. The draped United States flag was folded and delivered to Mrs. Frances Guerra Peña, and the ceremony ended. Some lingered to talk, not having seen each other in years. Funerals were becoming the gathering place for members of the Chicano Movement era.

After the funeral service, many retired to the MAUC building at 2300 W. Commerce Street where Olga Peña, and her daughters and son, held a reception. People ate and took photographs with each other; some made speeches in Albert's honor. Family members thanked everyone, and some remarked that "we ought to stop meeting this way." Within a year, Frances Guerra Peña also expired.[13]

Thank you, Albert A. Peña Jr., our leader, for always being there for us all!

APPENDIX 1

In Memoriam

SO MANY PERSONS WHO WERE DIRECTLY INVOLVED WITH OLGA AND ALBERT Pena Jr. in the empowerment of Chicanos in Bexar County, throughout the Southwest, and throughout the nation have passed. Among these are William "Bill" Peña, Richard Peña, Joséfina Herrera, Kay Turner Peña, Frances Guerra Peña, Claude Black, Leo Alvarado, Jesus and Virginia Múzquiz, Ramon and Enriqueta Palacios, Elvirita de la Fuente, Moises Falcon, Reynaldo Mendoza, Emma Tenayuca, Adela Navarro, Franklin "Tortilla" García, Guadalupe Youngblood, Ramon Pérez, Reymundo "Tigre" Pérez, Magdaleno Dimas, Warren Burnet, Rubén Munguía, Herschel Bernard, Willie Velásquez, Maria and Pedro Hernandez, Eleuterio Escobar, Rudy Esquivel, Lalo Solis, Albert Fuentes Jr., Pete Tijerina, Cesar and Helen Chavez, Antonio Orendian, Matt García, Ludevico "Lico" López, Mamie and Manuel López, César E. Chávez, Maclovio Barraza, Francisco "Pancho" Medrano, Pete Torres Jr., Paul Montemayor, Henry Santiesteban, Julian Samora, G.J. and Nelle Sutton, Ernesto Galarza, Eduardo Quevedo Sr., Mario Cantu, Bob Vale, Charles Albidress, Alfred J. Hernandez, Felix Salazar, Charles Grace, James De Anda, John Herrera, Felix Tijerina, Mario Obledo, Alonso Perales, Gabriel Tafolla, Cristobal Alderete,

Mike V. González, E. B. Duarte, Gus García, Martin Sada, Dr. Hector P. García, Ed Idar, Jake Johnson, Johnny Alaniz, Dr. Fred Logan, Rubén Salazar, Juan Patlan, Willie Velásquez, Henry Casso, Arnold Flores, Virgilio P. Elizondo, George Ozuna, Choco Meza, and Leo B. Leo.

APPENDIX 2

Note on County Government

TEXAS, INCLUDING MUCH OF WHAT WE KNOW TODAY AS THE UNITED STATES, was explored and colonized by Spain years before the "pilgrims" stepped foot on the Atlantic seashore. There are countless geographic places, rivers, mountains, valleys, canyons, and communities in 2016 United States with Spanish names. Valdez, Alaska, for example, is named after Spain's minister of the navy who commissioned the exploration several centuries back. San Agustin, Florida, and Santa Fe, New Mexico, are among the oldest Spanish settlements still in existence today. San Miguel de Guadalupe was the name for what came to be recognized after Anglo colonization as Jamestown. Numerous places such as the Rio Grande and Colorado Rivers; states of Colorado, Arizona, New Mexico, Florida, Texas, California; the La Sal Mountains in Utah, the Grand Canyon, and the Spanish Trail are current testaments to this Spanish America that once existed.[1]

Mexican Texas, after the insurrection by illegal residents from such states as Tennessee, Kentucky, Georgia, Alabama, Virginia, and North Carolina, became a republic in 1836.[2] A system of state and local government that was a double hybrid between Mexican and Spanish established forms, and between English and United States Anglo forms was instituted. The notion of county government in Texas, however, had origins in post-feudal England and was transported by name and initial function to the American colonies. For example, the titles of tax assessor-collector, bailiff, sheriff, and constable along with the duties of each office were copied from English government. The House of Lords in English parliamentary structure became the model for the United States Senate and was imitated in the states. No such entities ever existed in either Spanish or Mexican rule. The Mexican rule of law also incorporated elements of the Napoleonic Code, dating to the French occupation of Mexico in the 1860s.

Once the United States took form in 1789, as we know it today, states and territories were created and incorporated. Within states, county government became established by name, distinct geographical boundaries of each county, and similar forms of local government. As the population grew or political exigency required, new counties were created by taking land areas from existing counties. Texas became a state in 1845, and county government was the only unit of local government specifically authorized in the first state constitution. There were no provisions for cities, school districts, community college districts, water districts, and the like; all came much later when created by the state legislature. County government has remained unchanged in structure and responsibilities since then but for legislative mandates from time to time imposed on the local level.[3] The *Texas Almanac* for any given year contains a listing of all 254 counties in Texas with a map indicating cities and major roads, a history of development, demographic and statistical data on population, economic indicators, and origin of its name.

The various plural officeholders at the county level in twenty-first-century Texas are basically the same in title, job responsibility, and number as those of two centuries ago. It is a structure of plural executives, because there are various countywide elected officials with executive power, such as county judge, sheriff, tax assessor-collector, treasurer, county clerk, and district clerk.[4] Moreover these individuals seek office in partisan countywide elections. They owe their political position once elected to their voters and contributors, not necessarily to any other political officeholder. They have a budget for their office; they can hire and fire employees, except in counties with a civil service system; they set policy within the limits of the law; they have an individual office and identifiable physical space; they have a specific title for their office; and they have few overlapping duties with other officials. The sheriff, however, is the custodian of the courthouse and can assign office space to other officeholders at his or her discretion.

On the other hand, county commissioners with staggered terms have been elected from single-member districts named commissioner precincts in Texas since Texas became a state. Single-member districts are mandated in the Voting Rights Act of 1965 (VRA). In 1975 the VRA was amended, and its provision extended coverage to Texas and other states. The county judge, presiding officer of the Commissioners Court, together with the four commissioners form the executive branch of county government.[5] To set an agenda, effect policy, adopt a budget, or vote on any item of business, no less than three members must concur. Consequently, the activity on the Commissioners Court is based on a member seeking two other votes to get anything done. Partisanship and ideology must give way to compromise, trading, and negotiation among the members.

A member of the Commissioners Court has various duties. Primarily, a commissioner must make decisions affecting county government and provide services to the public. They each do this by exercising certain functions of the position: set tax rates and adopt a county budget each year; hear property owner appeals on value; supervise and control the courthouse and other facilities, except the jail, which is the exclusive responsibility of the sheriff; maintain county roads and bridges; award contracts; provide services, which vary by county, such as libraries, welfare, parks, hospitals, ambulance service, recreation, indigent relief, civil defense, and health; fill vacancies in elective and appointive positions; and represent the county.

The Commissioners Court is not a court in the judicial sense, but it does hear property appraisal appeals, sitting as an administrative court of equity in rural and some urban counties. Each county in Texas has four county commissioners; justices of the peace in varying numbers depending on population, but no less than one sitting at the county seat courthouse (usually four or more by legislative act); and four constables, chosen according to the same rules as justices of the peace. This is to say that each of the 254 counties in Texas is divided into four districts for election purposes of these officers in even- and odd-numbered years. The term of office is four years and staggered so only two commissioners, justices of the peace, and constables are up for election every two years, along with the countywide officials mentioned above.

The First Spanish-Surnamed County Commissioners in Texas

In 1837, two commissioners constituted the County Board in the Republic of Texas for Bexar County: José Antonio Navarro and Ignacio Chávez. The county judge was John R. Baker.[6] These two Spanish-surnamed Mexican county commissioners were the first and the last to serve as a majority of the court in Bexar County. By 1838 the three county board seats were all held by Anglo Texans. Beginning in 1839, one seat was allocated to a Mexican Texan, Miguel Arciniega; José Antonio Urrutia in 1840; and Nicolas Urbina in 1842. Mexican military forces under the direction of General

Woll attacked San Antonio in these years, and records are unavailable for the county board. Beginning in 1845 Texas became a state of the United States and adopted the four-person Commissioners Court, with a county judge as presiding officer.[7] From that period on, a majority of Anglos served and dominated the Bexar County Commissioners Court. In 1858 J. E. Mondragon was elected commissioner for Precinct Three; Lorenzo Cano succeeded him in 1860, as did José Antonio Navarro in 1864, and Martin Delgado in 1866. All of these commissioners represented only one precinct: Number Three.

In 1882 County Commissioner B. Quintana was elected in Precinct One and remained in office until 1890. For a brief two-year term, Antonio Herrera served as county commissioner in 1909 and 1910. Thereafter, for forty-six years, not one single person of Mexican ancestry or Spanish surname served as county commissioner until the election of Albert A. Peña Jr. in 1956. Peña defeated Dan F. Traugott in the May Democratic Primary.

Texas was a one-party dictatorship (Democrats) from Reconstruction in 1865 to the late 1990s, when the first Republican county commissioners were elected. Albert A. Peña Jr. was the lone voice and representative for Bexar County Mexicans from 1956 until 1972, when he was defeated in the May Democratic Primary election. His successor, Albert Bustamante, also was the only Chicano voice and representative on the Commissioners Court for a number of years.

Beginning in 1983 and into the present time, two persons of Mexican ancestry have been elected to the Commissioners Court from Precincts One and Two. Briefly in 1983, after the election of Albert Bustamante as Bexar County judge, and in 1984, three persons of Mexican ancestry, a majority, served on the five-member Commissioners Court.[8] Bustamante was the first and last county judge of Mexican ancestry elected in Bexar County up to the present time.

Comparative Note: City of San Antonio Officeholders

The first and only Mexican Texan to serve as mayor of San Antonio during the time period between September 29, 1837, when it was first organized as a city under the Republic of Texas, to April 18, 1842, was Juan Nepomuceno Seguin. He served barely one year and four months. Typically, the term of office as mayor was a year. Seguin, the real hero of the Battle of San Jacinto for persisting and leading the attack on the Mexican troops while they slept after the noon meal, as contrasted with Sam Houston, served from January 9, 1841, to April 18, 1842. After Seguin's brief one-year term, no other person of Mexican ancestry or Spanish surname served as mayor until the elections of Henry Cisneros in 1981, Ed Garza in 2000, and Julian

Castro in 2009 to 2014. Castro resigned to become secretary of Housing and Urban Development (HUD) in the second Obama administration.

Members of the San Antonio City Council from 1837 to the present time that can be discerned by Spanish surname follow a similar pattern as did Bexar County commissioners. Initially, from 1837 to 1841, an Anglo Texan was always mayor while the eight council members were predominantly Mexican Texans, if not overwhelmingly so. For example, the city council membership for 1837 was all Mexican. In 1838, one Anglo Texan was a member, W. E. Houth. The following year, two Anglo Texans, John W. Smith and George Dolson, were among the six other Mexican Texan members of the city council. In 1840, there were three Anglo Texans among the eight city council members: Cornelius Van Ness, George Blow, and John McMullen. When Juan Seguin was mayor, Francis Gilleau served as mayor pro tempore during Seguin's absence from August 17, 1841, to September 7, 1841, and six Anglo Texans were members of the council: L. Smithers, Bryan Callaghan, John R. Black, Diego A. Taylor, Antonio Lockmar, and J. L. Truehart. This council was comprised of sixteen members, the largest ever until the ward system was instituted in the early 1900s and single-member districts in the 1970s. The following year, 1842, the city council membership was reduced to eight once again, with only three Mexican Texans on board: Rafael Garza, J. A. Urutia, and C. Rivas. Mexican Texans became a numeric minority of the members of the San Antonio City Council at this time and continued to be so until the 1990s, when they reached majority member status once again. Also, between 1837 and 1842, the city administration included persons with Spanish surnames indicative of Mexican ancestry, but after that period only Anglo Texans and a token Mexican Texan administered the city until 1849. After 1850 no Mexican Texan is listed as an administrative official for the City of San Antonio, except for J. A. G. Navarro as collector, until December 31, 1858. Navarro reappears as assessor for the city in 1862.

On January 1, 1855, the only two Texas Mexican members of the San Antonio City Council left office: J. A. Urutia and J. A. Navarro. The first all-Anglo Texan city council was seated. An occasional Spanish-surnamed city council member is listed during the late 1850s, such as G. Soto in 1857, José Rodríguez in 1858, and J. M. Peñaloza in 1859 and 1861. In 1862 the city council was increased to eleven seats plus the mayor. And from 1863 to 1865 only two out of the eleven city council members were Mexican Texans: F. Casiano and José Martinez. Casiano continued to serve until he was replaced in 1867 by new members M. Yturri and A. M. Ruiz, each for one year. In 1867 the term of city council office was extended to two years, and J. M. Chaves was elected the lone Mexican Texan among fifteen members, the largest group ever. In 1872, Chaves was replaced with José Flores, again the lone Mexican Texan voice among nineteen on this council by this time. No other Mexican Texans served during these years. San Antonio adopted a four-ward system and a mayor beginning in January 19, 1875, for a two-year term. Each ward had four places for a total council of sixteen in 1875 to 1877, three places per ward in 1877 to 1879, and finally one place per ward in 1879; E. J. Chávez, from January 19, 1875, to January 19, 1877, was the last Mexican Texan to serve on the San Antonio City Council for many years to come.

The ward system was expanded to six wards, with one alderman per ward and four additional aldermen running at-large, beginning in 1887, and to eight wards and four aldermen at-large by 1889. The ward system remained in place until early in 1915, when San Antonio adopted the city commission form of government until 1952. The commission consisted of four members plus the mayor, with each commissioner responsible for a major service: taxation, sanitation, streets, and police and fire. During the ward system with alderman and alderman at-large positions, no Mexican Texan had been elected or appointed to serve. During the commission form of local government, similarly, no Mexican Texan was ever elected or appointed to serve.

When Albert A. Peña Jr. entered San Antonio/Bexar County politics in the 1950s, this had been the history of exclusion of Chicanos.[9] Mexican Americans were largely unrepresented in local government, county government, state government, and the federal government. Further, there were no members of Congress from the Southwest, except New Mexico, in the early 1900s. Since Lorenzo de Zavala was elected vice president of the Republic of Texas, no person of Mexican ancestry served in any statewide office until Governor John Connally appointed Roy Barrera Sr. as secretary of state in 1960.

In 1952 the city government again was changed to a council-manager form of government. The first person of Mexican ancestry in nearly seventy-five years was elected under this system: Rubén Lozano. Henry B. González was elected the following year, 1953. During 1955 to 1957, two persons of Mexican ancestry served on the eight-member city council, José Olivares and Henry B. González, but the latter only served his second term briefly. He resigned effective May 19, 1956, and Dr. José San Martin was appointed in his place. When Peña was finally elected county commissioner, there were only Councilmen González and San Martin in local government, no one else in Bexar County government, and only one person of Mexican ancestry in the state legislature, Eligio "Kika" de la Garza from State Representative District 38–3 in the Rio Grande Valley and resident of Mission, Texas. State representative districts were structured by places in the same district for at-large election, rather than creating three distinct legislative seats, as in the case of de la Garza running in Place 3. Even the border counties during these times were unable to elect a Mexican Texan to the legislature. Earlier, in 1918, José Tomas

Canales was elected state representative for the four counties of the Rio Grande Valley, but his one-term career was short. In that year the Company D of the infamous Texas Rangers and a unit of the U.S. Army murdered all male residents of Mexican ancestry over the age of fifteen of Porvenir, Texas. Representative Canales conducted hearings on these murders, only to receive daily death threats from Texas Rangers and his own committee chair. His supporters and family members escorted him in and out of the legislative chambers to protect his life. He did not seek reelection. The records of his hearings, eight boxes, are found at the Briscoe Center of Texas History in Austin, Texas, and his personal papers are at the South Texas Archives of Texas A&M University at Kingsville, Texas.

During the 1960s, two seats from among the eight city council seats were allocated by San Antonio's Good Government League (GGL) to Mexican Americans of their choosing. For example, George de la Garza replaced Dr. San Martin when he resigned on June 2, 1960, and Ray Padilla was elected in Olivares's place. Roy S. Padilla replaced Ray Padilla on the city councils of 1961 and 1963. George de la Garza resigned in January 7, 1965, and was replaced by Dr. Herbert Calderon. Felix B. Treviño was elected in 1965 instead of Roy S. Padilla.

The first non-GGL Chicano city council representative, Pete Torres Jr., was elected in 1967 and served for two terms. His election and reelection boosted the number of Spanish-surnamed members of the council to three. In 1973, resignations from the city council changed the names of the membership but not the numbers among the Mexican American representatives. The new faces were Richard Teniente replacing Leo Mendoza Jr., and Alvin G. Padilla replacing Felix Treviño; when Padilla resigned, he in turn was replaced by Dr. D. Ford Nielsen.

In 1970, with the advent of single-member districts in the air, Henry Cisneros, the last of the GGL-sponsored Mexican American candidates, won and joined Teniente as the only two Mexican Americans on the eight-person council.[10] Lila Cockrell was elected the first woman mayor of San Antonio in the 1975 election. The following round of municipal elections under ten single-member districts dramatically changed the makeup and numbers of minority officeholders on the council. A record four seats were won by Mexican American candidates: Henry Cisneros (District 1), Bernardo Eureste (District 5), Rudy C. Ortiz (District 6), and Joe Alderete Jr. (District 7). And when Cisneros ran and won as mayor, he had three other Mexican American council members, Maria Antonietta Berriozabal, Bernardo Eureste, and Joe Alderete Jr., on the council together with Frank Wing, an Asian American, and Joe Webb, an African American. Together, minorities held six of eleven seats on the city council.

Interestingly, in the County Commissioners Court no person of Mexican ancestry served as county judge until Albert Bustamante in 1978, and none since. As mayor of San Antonio, no person of Mexican ancestry served in that capacity, except for Juan Nepomuceno Seguin in 1841 for one year, until Henry Cisneros in 1981, Ed Garza in 2000, and Julian Castro in 2009.[11] With Mayor Castro's resignation from office to become HUD secretary, the city council voted 5 in favor of Ivy R. Taylor and 3 for Ray Lopez to fill the unexpired term as mayor. In a conciliatory move, Lopez withdrew and Ivy's selection was made unanimous. Mayor Taylor became the first African American woman to lead a major Texas city. She subsequently won election in her own right, defeating all challengers, which included former state senator Leticia Van de Putte, a local pharmacist and Mexican American. Ms. Taylor is from New York State and came to San Antonio for a position in the planning department before seeking election to the city council from District 2.

The Politics of Mexican Removal

The removal of Mexicans from public office and politics coincided with their loss of wealth—namely, land and possessions—beginning with the establishment of the Texas Republic. The review of officeholders with Spanish surnames from that era to the present time in San Antonio and Bexar County is indicative of that gradual to complete exclusion from politics until the advent of the Chicano Movement in the mid-1960s spawned by the civil rights activities of returning World War II veterans of Mexican ancestry. According to George Norris Green, conservative Anglos have dominated state politics in Texas since 1939.[12] The exclusion of Mexicans from public office and rise of Anglo hegemony began much earlier with the formation of political machines in South Texas and later the urban centers such as San Antonio, according to Evan Anders.[13] The Good Government League (GGL), under the direction of Jack White as mayor in the San Antonio municipal elections of 1953, was a direct beneficiary of the stranglehold conservative Democrats had on statewide public office and reflected the repression of Mexican political participation. The repression of Mexican voters and by extension candidates for public office rested largely on devices that tended to dilute the voting power of minorities and poor people in general, such as the poll tax, costly filing fees for partisan races, at-large elections, the White Primary, literacy tests, early voter registration periods, and majority vote for the primary election with runoff elections in early summer months. The dates for primary elections were in May, with runoff elections in June; this also diminished the voter turnout among Mexican Americans. They left the state in search of seasonal agricultural labor in northern states as early as March and returned in mid to late October to vote, if at all, for the only choice on a ballot among Democrats. The Republican Party fielded candidates to engage in presidential politics and token gubernatorial candidates up to the mid-1950s—none in down-ballot races. In the mid-1990s the Republican Party took control of state government and replaced the Democrats as the "one-party dictatorship."

Albert A. Peña Jr. was among those returning World War II veterans in the mid-1940s who sought access to political power in San Antonio. He and others formed the Latin American Democrats (LAD) for that purpose. At approximately the same time that the GGL was recruiting and sponsoring token Mexican Americans for city council positions in the early 1950s, other independents were organizing and recruiting Mexicans and blacks into a counterforce. Gus García, a brilliant attorney, won election to the San Antonio School Board along with G. J. Sutton, an African American, who won a seat on the community college district in 1948.[14] "For the first time the Westside stuck together on a Latin candidate. Hitherto it had been possible to split it into two factions."[15] Organized labor began to recruit Mexican Americans into their unions. San Antonio, with its extensive number of military installations and related defense industries, began to employ thousands of civilian employees, some of whom were Mexican Americans. The post–World War II economy was ripe for organizing employees.

Nationally, President Franklin Delano Roosevelt had won presidential contest after presidential contest because his campaigns rested on the traditional Democratic Party coalition of voters from important sectors ignored by the Republican Party: labor, liberals, and minorities, ethnic and racial. This same formula began to be applied at the local level to counter the conservative Democratic Party forces that opposed FDR and his policies and programs in Texas. At the local level, the leaders of these very same constituencies sought out one another for the building of a similar coalition. Liberal whites and organized labor teamed up with the nascent minority efforts in the West and South Side barrios and with blacks in the East Side. San Antonio's Mexican American voters were led by Albert A. Peña Jr., and the African American voters in East San Antonio were led by G. J. Sutton and later Rev. Claude Black.

San Antonio's Growth

In 1891 President Benjamin Harrison visited San Antonio, the first U.S. president to do so. During the tour around the city, he was informed that from 1870 to 1890 the population had jumped from 12,256 to 37,673. Business sales had jumped from $10 million in 1886 to $31 million in 1890.[16] The city was on the upswing and a boom town, the largest city in the state. Four decades later, by 1930, San Antonio had gained 178,000 residents, or a 335 percent increase. But it was not enough growth compared to other Texas cities, because San Antonio lost ground and status as the largest city to Houston and Dallas.[17]

During the first thirty years of the twentieth century, San Antonio quadrupled its size of population to nearly a quarter million persons. Those of Mexican ancestry made a fantastic jump of 840 percent, and rose from 25 percent of the total population to 35 percent.[18] In 1930 Mexicans were 82,373, a number almost 30,000 higher than San Antonio's total population in 1900.

The city's growth rate virtually stopped between 1930 and 1940 due to the economic ravages of the Wall Street stock market crash and subsequent Depression. During this decade, the rate of growth for the city was a mere 10 percent. However, the growth was among Méxicanos. Of the 22,000 new residents by 1940, about 21,000 were of Mexican origin.[19] From 1940 to 1950, the city once again experienced renewed growth to over 500,000 metro residents, a rate of over 60 percent. Promptly, city leaders declared this growth among Mexicans a "serious problem." They formed a committee to study the problem. The Public Service Company issued its own report, stating that "Replacement of 35% of the Latin Americans by an equivalent number of economically independent families would transform San Antonio, socially, politically, economically, and in health. It would raise the whole standard of living."[20]

Mexican children's deaths in San Antonio accounted for 64 percent of all infant deaths in 1946. This was the highest death rate for cities over 100,000 in the United States.[21] Heywood Broun called San Antonio the "worst in America." In 1950 San Antonio still had the highest concentration of juvenile delinquency, the most deaths from tuberculosis and infant diarrhea, the most cases of Aid to Dependent Children (state-sponsored public assistance), and segregated neighborhood areas consisting of 90 percent Mexican residents.

Part of the growth and economic mainstay of the city had been the military installations that were ubiquitous on the periphery of San Antonio in the early years. (In 2016, the military bases are well within the territorial limits of the city.) By 1964, San Antonio relied heavily on the military complex for jobs, payroll, expenditures, business, housing, and transportation. Military retirees began to make San Antonio home. And returning veterans, Chicanos in great numbers, were taking the vacated jobs and making payroll at the military bases and rapidly becoming the middle class in the city.[22] "The combined military civilian payrolls of the seven military installations totaled $303,000,000 in 1964."[23] But this payroll largely went to Anglo employees, not Mexican Americans, nationally and locally. The federal government, like state and local governments, discriminate against Mexican American job seekers. Earl Shorris found in the 1990s that nearly 80 percent of all federal jobs went to whites while only 5.1 percent of jobs were held by Mexican Americans. Yet, Mexican Americans in the 1990 enumeration by the U.S. Census Bureau constituted 9 percent of the nation's population.[24]

By 1970 the Anglo community had become a numeric minority of the population in the city. Their drop as a percentage of the total population had dramatically gone from 51.2 percent in 1960 to only 39.2 percent in 1970. Conversely, the Chicano population grew from a minority to become the majority of the population at 52.2 percent of all residents. The African American population in the city has hovered at 7.7 percent of the total since the 1930s, to 7.3 percent in 1980—not a significant numeric minority population, but enough to be necessary for any coalition or alliance with Anglos or Chicanos to be forged or prevented. In 1928, Chicano laborers and service workers plus those in other unskilled labor jobs constituted 56.9 percent of the work force. Within six decades, by 1980, Chicanos were 56.5 percent of those in skilled occupations and 29.5 percent of those in white-collar positions.[25] Richard A. García's work on the rise of the middle class among Mexican Americans of San Antonio during the period 1929 to 1941 aptly chronicles these ascending generations and the dramatic shift from the ranks of lower-working-class Mexicans to middle-class skilled and white-collar professionals.[26] The Peña families of Sr. and Jr. were typical of that emerging Mexican American middle class.

These dramatically changing times occurred during Peña Jr.'s lifetime. He rode the wave of demographic explosion and the rise to power, economic and electoral, of the emerging Chicano middle class after a long history of Mexícano exclusion and repression in the region and across the state.

Notes

PREFACE

1. See "Tejano Voices," the University of Texas at Arlington Center for Mexican American Studies, http://library.uta.edu/tejanovoices, for the sixty-two-page transcript of this interview and audio. The VHS video recording is available from Special Collections at the University of Texas–Arlington library.
2. See "Tejano Voices" for a description of the project and content of those interviewed between 1996 and 2006.
3. The holdings at the UTSA archives basically cover the period from 1952 to 1977 and consist of 33 boxes, some 16.5 linear feet. The largest series of materials are organized alphabetically in 17 boxes and contain the files on issues he was most concerned about: discrimination, poverty, hunger, education, and civil rights. The most important part of Peña's life, his voluminous writings on these subjects, are not there. His opinions expressed in speeches, opinion editorials, columns, essays, press releases, and notes primarily are found on microfilm and microfiche at the City Library and some, not many, at the offices of *La Prensa*, the local Spanish-language newspaper. See "A Guide to the Albert A. Peña, Jr. Papers, 1952–1977," UTSA Libraries Special Collections, http://library.utsa.edu for the guide to his papers at UTSA Archives.

INTRODUCTION

1. He was registered on his birth certificate as Albert A. Peña Jr., but as he progressed through life his name changed to Alberto, Al, and back to Albert. His middle name changed to Armendarez (sic) on his military discharge papers, and he often claimed to be an Armendariz. This book is written chronologically and to distinguish between Alberto Peña Sr. and Jr. I used those designations and, of course, Albert III for the firstborn son from Joséfina Herrera. Once the reader gets past Part 1, I simply use Peña Jr. or just Peña to refer to him. See birth certificate issued on December 22, 1917, by attending physician T. N. Haggard under Register No. 2276, issued by the City Board of Health, San Antonio, Texas.

2. Benjamin Márquez, *Democratizing Texas Politics: Race, Identity, and Mexican American Empowerment, 1945–2002* (Austin: University of Texas Press, 2014).

3. William S. Clayson, *Freedom Is Not Enough: The War on Poverty and the Civil Rights Movement in Texas* (Austin: University of Texas Press, 2010).

4. Ignacio M. García, *Hector P. García and the American G.I. Forum* (Austin: University of Texas Press, 2001); and Ignacio M. García, *Viva Kennedy: The Quest for Camelot* (Texas A&M University Press, 2002). For an earlier work on the American G.I. Forum, see Carl Allsup, *The American G.I. Forum: Origins and Evolution* (Austin: Center for Mexican American Studies, University of Texas Press, 1982); and a more recent effort by Henry A. J. Ramos, *The American G.I. Forum: In Pursuit of the Dream, 1948–1983* (Houston: Arte Público Press, 1998). For work on another organization, the League of United Latin American Citizens, see Benjamin Márquez, *LULAC: The Evolution of a Mexican American Political Organization* (Austin: University of Texas Press, 1993). An early biographical work on a LULAC founder is by Adela Sloss-Vento, *Alonso S. Perales: His Struggle for the Rights of Mexican Americans* (San Antonio: Artes Graficas, 1977).

5. Thomas H. Kreneck, *Mexican American Odyssey* (College Station: Texas A&M University Press, 2001).

6. Gilberto J. Quezada, *Border Boss: Manuel B. Bravo and Zapata County* (College Station: Texas A&M University Press, 1999).

7. Transactional leadership is based on exchange theory: the necessary transactions between follower and leader to accomplish desired outcomes. Transcendental or transformational leadership is the moving of followers to higher levels of awareness, interest, needs, and empowerment through persuasion, modeling, and daily actions. For a brief discussion of these two types of leadership, see William E. Rosenbach and Robert L. Taylor, *Contemporary Issues in Leadership*, 5th ed. (Boulder, CO: Westview Press, 2001), 1–3.

8. Kim Geron, *Latino Political Power* (Boulder, CO: Lynne Rienner, 2005), 13–14. Also, see my article "The Chicano Movement: Paths to Power," *Social Studies* 102 (2011): 25–32.

9. See Gordon K. Mantler for a focused analysis of the coalition of blacks and browns that sought economic justice during the 1960s and into the 1970s: *Power to the Poor: Black-Brown Coalition and the Fight for Economic Justice, 1960–1974* (Chapel Hill: University of North Carolina Press, 2013).

10. For a positive analysis toward a black/brown coalition, see Bill Piatt, *Black and Brown in America: The Case for Cooperation* (New York: New York University Press, 1977); for a counterview, see Nick Vaca, *The Presumed Alliance: The Unspoken Conflict between Latinos and Blacks and What It Means for America* (New York: Rayo Books, 2004).

11. José Angel Gutiérrez and Michelle Melendez, *Chicanas in Charge: Texas Women in the Public Arena* (Lanham, MD: AltaMira Press, 2007). García et al., *Politicas: Latina Public Officials in Texas* (Austin: University of Texas Press 2008). See also my coauthored article with Rebecca E. Deen, "Chicanas in Texas Politics," Julian Samora Research Institute Occasional Paper No. 66, Michigan State University, East Lansing, October 2000.

12. Ralph W. Steen published the first text in 1939 with Steck & Company (Austin), and in 1948 the second revised text, with a new title from the new Steck-Vaughn Company in Austin. I was in grade school during the 1950s, and this was the text assigned for the class on Texas history. In the state, there is a legislative mandate that all students seeking any degree, and teachers and professionals seeking a license to practice their trade take courses about both the history and government of the state.

13. John Staples Shockley, *Chicano Revolt in a Texas Town* (Notre Dame, IN: Notre Dame University Press, 1974); and Armando Navarro, *The Cristal Experiment: A Chicano Struggle for Community Control* (Madison: University of Wisconsin Press, 1998).

14. Douglas Foley, *From Peones to Politicos: Ethnic Relations in a South Texas Town* (Austin: University of Texas Press, 1977).

15. Arnoldo de Leon, *Mexican Americans in Texas* (Arlington Heights, IL: Harlan Davidson, Inc., 1993), 1.

16. Peter Matthiessen, *Sal Si Puedes: Cesar Chavez and the New American Revolution* (Berkeley: University of California Press, 1969); Richard Griswold del Castillo and Richard A. García, *César Chávez: A Triumph of Spirit* (Norman: University of Oklahoma Press, 1995); and Susan Ferris and Ricardo Sandoval, *The Fight in the Fields: Cesar Chavez and the Farm Workers Movement* (New York: Harcourt Brace, 1997). For Tijerina, see my translation and edition of the autobiography of Reies López Tijerina, *Mi lucha por la tierra* (Mexico City: Fondo de Cultura Economico, 1978), *They Called Me "King Tiger": My Struggle for the Land and Our Rights* (Houston: Arte Público Press, 2000), xviii.

17. Acosta, *The Autobiography of a Brown Buffalo* (1972; New York: Vintage Books, 1989); and *The Revolt of the Cockroach People* (1973; New York: Vintage Books, 1989). Ilan Stavans published a book about Oscar "Zeta" Acosta and his writings: see *Bandido: Oscar "Zeta" Acosta and the Chicano Experience* (New York: IconEditions, 1995).

18. See https://artepublicopress.com for a listing of the current catalog of publications available from Arte Público, and http://bilingualpress.clas.asu.edu for a listing of the current catalog of publications available from Bilingual Review Press.

19. Galarza, *Barrio Boy* (Notre Dame, IN: University of Notre Dame Press, 1971).

20. Larralde, *Carlos Esparza: A Chicano Chronicle* (San Francisco: R & E Associates, 1977), and *Mexican Americans: Movements and Leaders* (Los Alamitos, CA: Hwong Publishing Co., 1976).

21. Mazon, *The Zoot-Suit Riots: The Psychology of Symbolic Annihilation* (Austin: University of Texas Press, 1984). García, *Partido de la Raza Unida* (Los Angeles: Tlaquilo Press, 1976). This monograph is primarily focused on the development and events of the political party in California.

22. See Navarro's earlier works: *Mexican American Youth Organization: Precursor of Change in Texas* (Austin: University of Texas Press, 1995); *The Cristal Experiment: A Chicano Struggle for Community Control* (Madison: University of Wisconsin Press, 1999); and *La Raza Unida Party: A Chicano Challenge to the U.S. Two-Party Dictatorship* (Philadelphia: Temple University Press, 2000); as well as Ignacio García's *United We Win: The Rise and*

Fall of the Raza Unida Party (Tucson: Mexican American Studies and Research Center, University of Arizona, 1989).

23. Shorris, *Latinos: A Biography of the People* (New York: W.W. Norton & Co., 1992).

24. Gonzalez, *Harvest of Empire: A History of Latinos in America* (New York: Penguin Books, 2011). The book has now been made into a documentary by IMDb and is free to download at Snagfilms.com.

25. Previously, in 1989, Mario T. García had published two books that are biographical in nature about Mexican Americans in general and those residing in El Paso, Texas. See *Desert Immigrants: The Mexicans of El Paso, 1880–1920*, and *Mexican Americans: Leadership, Ideology, and Identity* (New Haven, CT: Yale University Press). For a subsequent and somewhat comparative book on Chicanos in El Paso, see Oscar Martinez, *The Chicanos of El Paso: An Assessment of Progress* (El Paso: Texas Western Press, 1980). For similar work about another Texas city, see Andres A. Tijerina, *The History of Mexican Americans in Lubbock County* (Lubbock: Texas Tech University Press, 1977). See also Mario García's *Memories of Chicano History: The Life and Narrative of Bert Corona* (Berkeley: University of California Press, 1994); his 1995 edited book on Rubén Salazar, *Border Correspondent: Selected Writings, 1955–1970* (Berkeley: University of California Press); *Luis Leal: An Auto/Biography* (Austin: University of Texas Press, 2000); and *Padre: The Spiritual Journey of Father Virgil Cordano* (Santa Barbara, CA: Capra Press, 2005) for additional works on leaders and leadership. Early in his career, Mario García published *The Making of a Mexican American Mayor: Raymond L. Telles of El Paso* (El Paso: Texas Western Press, 1998).

26. Mario T. García, ed., *The Gospel of César Chávez: My Faith in Action* (Lanham, MD: Sheed & Ward, 2007).

27. Gutiérrez, *The Making of a Chicano Militant: Lessons from Cristal* (Madison: University of Wisconsin Press, 1998).

28. Louise Ann Fisch, *All Rise: Reynaldo G. Garza, the First Mexican American Federal Judge* (College Station: Texas A&M University Press, 1996).

29. Almaraz, *Knight without Armor: Carlos Eduardo Castaneda, 1896–1958* (College Station: Texas A&M University Press, 1999).

30. Emilio Zamora, Cynthia Orozco, and Rodolfo Rocha, *Mexican Americans in Texas History* (Austin: Texas State Historical Association, 2000).

31. Juan Sepulveda, *The Life and Times of Willie Velásquez: Su voto es su voz* (Houston: Arte Público Press, 2005).

32. José Angel Gutiérrez, *We Won't Back Down! Severita Lara's Rise from Student Leader to Mayor* (Houston: Arte Público Press, 2005).

33. Gutiérrez, Meléndez, and Noyola, *Chicanas in Charge: Texas Women in the Public Arena, 1950–2004* (Walnut Hill, CA: AltaMira Press, 2007).

34. Paredes, *"With His Pistol in His Hand": A Border Ballad and Its Hero* (Austin: University of Texas Press, 1968).

35. Vernon E. Lattin, Rolando Hinojosa, and Gary D. Keller, eds., *Tomás Rivera, 1935–1964: The Man and His Work* (Tempe, AZ: Bilingual Review Press, 1988).

36. See, for example, the work of Luis J. Rodríguez, *Always Running: La Vida Loca; Gang Days in L.A.* (Willimantic, CT: Curbstone Press, 1993); Roy P. Benavidez and Oscar Griffin, *The Three Wars of Roy Benavidez* (San Antonio: Corona Publishing Co., 1986) about a Congressional Medal of Honor recipient; and Mona Ruiz with Geoff Boucher,

Two Badges: The Lives of Mona Ruiz (Houston: Arte Público Press, 1997) about a former gang member turned police officer.

CHAPTER 1. THE FAMILY AND YOUNG ALBERT JR.

1. Video interview with Madeline Peña Davila, January 27, 2004, San Antonio, Texas, in author's possession. The narrative is composed from her remarks about the family history.
2. Letter from Antonio Peña, Banning, California, to author postmarked August 2, 2005.
3. Eve Ball, *In the Days of Victorio: Recollections of a Warm Springs Apache* (Tucson: University of Arizona Press, 1970). See also Joséph A. Stout Jr., *Apache Lightning: The Last Great Battles of Ojo Calientes* (New York: Oxford University Press, 1974) for a description of the Chiricahua Apaches and Victorio, the heir apparent to the leadership of Mangas Coloradas after he passed away in 1863. Victorio merged his Mimbreño Apaches with the Mescaleros into a band of some three hundred warriors.
4. Interview with Jaime Martinez, May 17, 2004, San Antonio, Texas. He corroborated that his grandmother, also an Apache, lived in that area and also made mention of the massacre and forced march south by Mexican soldiers. She also told Jaime that she knew that *la ciega* (Mama Peña) also had made it to San Antonio from Nuevo Laredo.
5. Letter from Antonio Peña, Banning, California, postmarked August 2, 2005, to author.
6. The original house on Belvin and California Streets was torn down to make room for San Antonio Vocational and Technical High School, previously known as Main High School and today called Fox Technical High School.
7. The attending physician at Albert A. Peña Jr.'s birth listed the father's occupation as "elevator boy," with an age of twenty-one years, and the mother as fifteen years of age.
8. An important set of new books on the role of Catholicism and faith among Mexican Americans are Brett C. Hoover, *The Shared Parish: Latinos, Anglos, and the Future of U.S. Catholicism* (New York: New York University Press, 2014); Timothy Matovina and Gerald E. Poyo, eds. *Presente! U.S. Latino Catholics from Colonial Origins to the Present* (Maryknoll, NY: Orbis, 2000); Roberto Trevino, *The Church in the Barrio: Mexican American Ethno-Catholicism in Houston* (Chapel Hill: University of North Carolina Press, 2006); and Ray Suarez, *The Holy Vote: The Politics of Faith in America* (New York: HarperCollins, 2006). Timothy Matovina has a specific book on San Antonio's Catholics, *Guadalupe and Her Faithful: Latino Catholics in San Antonio, from Colonial Origins to the Present* (Baltimore: Johns Hopkins University Press, 2008), and a more recent publication, *Latino Catholicism: Transformation in America's Largest Church* (Princeton, NJ: Princeton University Press, 2012).
9. Madeline Davila video interview, January 23, 2004, San Antonio, Texas.
10. Author interview with Arnold Flores, San Antonio, February 12, 2004, tape 1.
11. Video interview with Antonio Esparza, April 25, 2004, San Antonio, Texas. Photo of "Peanuts" and the football team are in Mr. Esparza's possession.
12. Peña once mentioned to me that he would warn his sisters about the new book they brought home on Texas history, particularly the part on the Battle of the Alamo and how the author portrayed Mexicans. I assume it was Ralph W. Steen's *Texas: A Story of Progress* (Austin: Steck Co., 1942) or one of his earlier works, *History of Texas, Twentieth Century Texas.*

13. Arnold Flores interview, tape 1.
14. Chris Strachwitz with James Nicolopulos, *Lydia Mendoza: A Family Autobiography* (Houston: Arte Público Press, 1993), 57, 60.
15. Belinda and Bill Peña video interview, February 5, 2004, San Antonio, Texas.
16. "John K. Weber," Memorials, *Texas Bar Journal* 27, no. 9 (October 22, 1964): 841–45.
17. Romo, "The Mayor's Silk Underwear," *Texas Observer*, May 7, 2004, 6–18.
18. In 1926 Edith Abbott, Fay Cooper-Cole, Manuel Gamio, and Paul Taylor each began research into Mexican immigration to the U.S. See Manuel Gamio, *Mexican Immigration to the United States* (Chicago: University of Chicago Press, 1930). See also a recent work by Devra Weber, Roberto Melville, and Juan Vicente Palermo, *El inmigrante Mexicano: La historia de su vida* (Mexico D.F.: Porrua, 2002), of Manuel Gamio's interviews done during 1926–1927, which include several San Antonians such as José Leonides González, father of former U.S. congressman Henry B. González; Clemente Apolinar, hung in the Bexar County jail in 1923; José A. Valenzuela, consul general of Mexico in San Antonio in 1927; Elena de Leon, waitress at the Crockett Hotel; and dozens of others, 119–264.
19. See the Worley's *Miscellaneous Directory, 1934–1935*, San Antonio, published by John F. Worley Distributing Co., on microfiche at the San Antonio Public Library (main branch, 6th floor).
20. "Albert A. Peña," Memorials, *Texas Bar Journal* 26, no. 8 (September 22, 1963): 804.
21. *Consejos* is Spanish for "advice." In the traditional Mexican culture, a person with authority, real or perceived, was thought to be more judicious and experienced and was sought for advice, *un consejo*. Peña Sr., as a persuasive, assertive, charming salesman and dance promoter, probably was perceived as an experienced and knowledgeable "elder" by Mexican San Antonians.
22. *San Antonio Express*, January 1, 1939.
23. See "A Pictorial Supplement to the 1939 Annual Report" to the main report entitled *Housing in Our Time*, Housing Authority of the City of San Antonio, Texas, found in *The Explorer*, Texana/Genealogy Department, San Antonio Public Library 13 (2007): 39–45.
24. See Theo N. Picnot's address "Socio-Economic Status of Low Income Groups of San Antonio," in *The Explorer* 13 (2007): 58.
25. "Biographical Note," Papers of Maury Maverick, Sr., Center for American History, University of Texas, Austin, Texas.

CHAPTER 2. PEÑA, THE SAILOR MAN

1. Peña had married and lived apart, but he had not changed his mailing address from the family home where he grew up to his new residence.
2. Noonday lunch notes from March 3, 2004, during which Peña recalled wanting to go into the Navy and the arguments his mother made against that decision. Peña outlined them to me as written here: the values, the new family, and his logic in deciding to enlist.
3. There is confusion among the family, as in my mind, regarding the middle name for all three of the Alberto Peñas. Sometime after Alberto Jr. was introduced to his cousin Pedro Armendariz, he began claiming the A. in his middle name was for Armendariz. He told me this in his videotaped interview of January 22, 2004. Moreover, he used that middle name in the Navy. His discharge papers list him as Alberto Armendarez [sic] Peña

Jr. Younger brother Antonio "Tony" claims it is from a maternal grandfather and spells it Almendarez.

4. Telephone interview with Anthony "Tony" Peña on July 18, 2005. Tony was born on July 20, 1926, a year and a half after Richard's birth on January 11, 1925. Tony graduated from high school in San Antonio and studied to become an engineer. He graduated with that degree from the University of Texas and proceeded to enroll in night classes at St. Mary's Law School. He did not graduate; instead he relocated to California and sat for that bar examination in 1977. He practiced in that state for years. He is now retired and residing in Banner, California. Tony also wrote a letter to me with more information.

5. Moises Iglesias interview July 23, 2005. Iglesias was a chief petty officer in the U.S. Navy, having joined in 1980. He verified that basically the instructions to all sailors going on shore leave are still the same. The Shore Patrol personnel are trained and instructed to prevent disorderly conduct and public indecency; to maintain good relations with civilians, foreign and domestic; and to preserve and uphold proper military conduct, particularly that of the U.S. Navy, according to its heritage and tradition. Peña was more explicit and to the point on his "instructions and training" while a shore patrolman.

6. Albert A. Peña Jr. interview, January 22, 2004.

7. Conner Gorry, *Cuba*, 3rd ed. (New York: Lonely Planet Books, 2004), 388–96.

8. Spanish term for a female person of mixed Spanish and African descent.

9. Gorry, *Cuba*, 88.

10. See Evelio Grillo, *Black Cuban, Black American* (Houston: Arte Público Press, 2000) for a vivid description of this author's memories of a lector in an Ybor City, Florida, cigar-making factory.

CHAPTER 3. PEÑA JR., THE LAWYER

1. Belinda and Bill Peña, videotape, February 5, 2004.

2. The law school was founded in 1927 as the San Antonio School of Law and officially transferred to St. Mary's University and housed downtown at 112 College Street. Initially, only evening classes were offered at the downtown campus until 1936 when the day division was established. In 1968 the downtown campus was moved to the main campus off Culebra and Woodlawn Streets in West San Antonio; the evening program was discontinued in 1971 and restarted in 2007. See St. Mary's University, *Gold & Blue* (Fall 2006): 18.

3. See oral history interview with Albert Peña Jr., July 2, 1996, 9 of transcript.

4. See oral history interview, Olga Peña, August 23, 1997, 16–18.

5. Robert A. Goldberg, "Racial Change on the Southern Periphery: The Case of San Antonio, Texas, 1960–1965," *Journal of Southern History* 49, no. 3 (August 1983): 349–74.

6. On May 24, 1932, the State Democratic Convention passed a resolution that only white citizens could vote in the Democratic Primary, and registered voters had to sign a sworn oath as to their race. Any misrepresentation as to their racial background on this form could result in criminal penalties for false swearing and fraud. The U.S. Supreme Court ruled on April 3, 1944, in *Smith v. Allwright*, 321 U.S. 649, that this practice was unconstitutional. See Conrey Bryson, *Dr. Lawrence A. Nixon and the White Primary*, 2nd ed. (El Paso: Texas Western Press, 1974) for the story of the litigation spanning over a

decade of exclusion from the franchise.

7. Ibid. The material in this section is drawn from the transcript of her video interview. See also José Angel Gutiérrez, Michelle Meléndez, and Sonia Adriana Noyola, *Chicanas in Charge: Texas Women in the Public Arena* (Lanham, MD: AltaMira Press, 2007) for a chapter on Olga Ramos Peña, 17–26.

8. See Julie Leininger Pycior's *Democratic Renewal and the Mutual Aid Legacy of US Mexicans* (College Station: Texas A&M University Press, 2014) for a history of community-based mutual aid societies in the Southwest formed by persons of Mexican ancestry. San Antonio's Sociedad de la Union was the largest group of *mutualistas* in the Southwest during the twentieth century.

9. See oral history interview with Arnold Flores, tape 1.

10. Jeffery C. Adams, senior associate, Governor Bill and Vera Daniel Center for Legal History, State Bar of Texas, provided invaluable assistance in finding information about the Weber School of Law and bar memberships of the various Peña lawyers.

CHAPTER 4. FIRST SCHOOL DESEGREGATION CASES

1. For an excellent seminal work on the segregation faced by Mexican Americans, see Guadalupe San Miguel, *"Let Them All Take Heed": Mexican-Americans and the Quest for Educational Equality, 1910–1981* (Austin: University of Texas Press, 1987). See also Kenneth J. Meier and Joséph Stewart Jr., *The Politics of Hispanic Education: Un paso pa'lante y dos pa'tras* (Albany: State University of New York Press, 1991) for a policy perspective of the impact Hispanic elected officials have on the educational system post–Voting Rights Act implementation in Texas (1975).

2. An important point involved in this litigation is the fact that the intermediary appellate court stated that school segregation based on race was unconstitutional. On January 5, 1931, seventy-five Mexícano children were turned away from the door of Lemon Grove Grammar School on the outskirts of San Diego, California, by the school principal and told to go to "La Caballeriza," the name for the dilapidated two-room building that was the Mexican school and translates into horse shed. The parents obtained legal assistance from the Mexican consulate and successfully sued the school district. This case began to end school segregation based on race and the lack of ability to speak English in California. These cases predate the celebrated *Brown v. Board of Education of Topeka, Kansas* of 1954. See PBS documentary special *The Lemon Grove Incident*, produced by San Diego, California, KPBS-TV in 1980 for a reconstructed dramatization of the incident and subsequent court challenge. See also Robert R. Alvarez, "National Politics and Local Responses: The Nation's First Successful School Segregation Court Case," in *School and Society*, ed. Henry T. Trueba and Concha Delgado-Gaitan (New York: Praeger, 1988), 37–52.

3. San Miguel, *"Let Them All Take Heed,"* 32, 11, quoting the superintendent from *A Handbook of Information as to Education in Texas, 1918–1922*, 22–23. San Miguel's book is most useful for understanding the conditions and struggles for equal educational opportunity waged in Texas by Mexican Americans. See also James D. Cockcroft, *Latinos in the Struggle for Equal Education* (Danbury, CT: Franklin Watts/Grolier, 1995), for an analysis of unequal educational opportunity for Mexican Americans and other Latinos in Texas and the country.

4. Cockcroft, *Latinos in the Struggle for Equal Education*, 12–13.

5. For a compilation of articles on this significant case, see Michael Olivas, *"Colored Men" and "Hombres Aqui":* Hernandez v. Texas *and the Emergence of Mexican-American Lawyering* (Houston: Arte Público Press, 2006).

6. Lico López Greenbook, with several undated and/or untitled newspaper clippings, MSU Library Special Collections, Albert Peña Collection. One is entitled "$1236 FUND GI Forum Aids Court Fight," and the other, "Lulacs Plan 'Tamalada.'" A newsprint photograph from the *Forum News Bulletin* of November 1954, 4, features many of the prominent Mexícano attorneys affiliated with, or members of, the G.I. Forum.

7. José Andres Chacon, "Gus C. García Legal Genius," *San Antonio Express*, March 12, 1972.

8. San Miguel, *"Let Them All Take Heed,"* 123–26.

9. San Miguel, *"Let Them All Take Heed,"* 128–32.

10. For works on these organizations, see Benjamin Marquez, *LULAC: The Evolution of a Mexican American Political Organization* (Austin: University of Texas Press, 1993); Henry A. J. Ramos, *The American G.I. Forum: In Pursuit of the Dream, 1948–1983* (Houston: Arte Público Press, 1998); and Carl Allsup, *The American G.I. Forum: Origins and Evolution* (Austin: Center for Mexican American Studies, University of Texas Press, 1982).

11. Ignacio García has produced a biography of the Forum's founder, *Hector P. García: In Relentless Pursuit of Justice* (Houston: Arte Público Press 2002).

12. Radio station KEDA, aka Radio Jalapeño and also as *La Tejanita*, on the AM band is still operated under his sister's direction in San Antonio. It began broadcasting March 17, 1966. See also Carlos R. Guerra, "*25th Aniversario* at KEDA Radio Jalapeno," *La Prensa*, March 15, 1991, 12. For a work on the relationship between Lyndon B. Johnson and Mexican Americans, see Julie Leininger Pycior, *LBJ and Mexican Americans: The Paradox of Power* (Austin: University of Texas Press, 1997).

13. This narrative by Peña about the Hondo case is reconstructed from his comments, both written and stated. See "Hondo in the Fifties," *La Prensa*, February 1, 1991, 5; and Albert A. Peña interview, UTA Special Collections, Tejano Voices Project, July 2, 1996, San Antonio, TX, 5–8. See also interview with Peña conducted by Professor Rudy Rosales, UTSA, July 30, 1985, for another recollection of this case. The transcript and recording of this interview are at the Center for Mexican American Studies at Our Lady of the Lake University, San Antonio, and the original tape is in the possession of Prof. Rosales.

14. Peña, "Desegregation in Hondo and Lytle, Texas," *La Prensa*, March 29, 1991, and "Lytle in the 50's," *La Prensa*, June 21, 1991. Peña wrote several versions of these two cases for *La Prensa* and made frequent reference to these same events in other interviews cited above. The narrative is my reconstruction of events as gleaned from these interviews and his articles.

15. Peña, "Desegregation in Hondo and Lytle, Texas."

16. "Civil Rights," *La Prensa*, March 6, 1992, 4.

17. "Harvey Case Headed for Top Courts?," *San Antonio Light*, undated news clipping in Lico López Greenbook.

18. "Sutton, Garlington Jerome," *The Handbook of Texas*, Texas State Historical Association, https://tshaonline.org/handbook/online/articles/fsu11. .

19. Author interview with Rev. Black on March 23, 2007, San Antonio, TX, and also interview of Rev. Black by Sterlin Holmsley, May 26, 1994, Institute of Texan Cultures, San Antonio, TX.

20. Author interview with Herschel Bernard, San Antonio, Texas, February 19, 2004.

CHAPTER 5. BARRIO PRESIDENTIAL POLITICS

1. Ralph Cuaron from Los Angeles and a member of the Communist Party USA became the full-time national organizer for the "Amigos de Wallace" component of the campaign. In Texas the Amigos had support from Communist Party USA state chair Emma Tenayuca and her husband Homer Brooks, party secretary, both residing in San Antonio. See Eugene Buelna, "The Mexican Question: Mexican Americans in the Communist Party, 1940–1957," Center for Research of Latinos in a Global Society, University of Irvine, California, 1999, Paper WP14. See also the Papers of Henry Wallace, primarily speeches, at the University of Iowa Libraries, Iowa City, for mentions of Amigos de Wallace and a speech in Phoenix, Arizona, addressing Mexican Americans.
2. *Smith v. Allwright* (1944). The U.S. Supreme Court invalidated a Texas law denying blacks the right to vote in the Democratic Primary in the 1928 case *Nixon v. Herndon*. The legislature then turned the matter of eligibility to vote in a primary and runoff election over to the state Democratic Party. In *Grovey v. Townsend* (1935) the U.S. Supreme Court ruled that primary elections were not a "state action"; rather they were a private matter of a private group and as such could permit those who could vote in their private elections. See Conrey Bryson, *Dr. Lawrence A. Nixon and the White Primary*, 2nd ed. (El Paso: Texas Western Press, 1974).
3. Ms. Tenayuca's husband, Homer Brooks, was the state secretary of the Communist Party, Texas. Together they authored a critical analysis of the Mexican people, "The Mexican Question in the Southwest," *The Communist* (no date or volume available). A copy of this article is found in my archival deposit at the Julian Samora Research Institute, Michigan State University, under my name.
4. The names of elected officials and candidates, as well as election dates, poll-tax receipts, and election results data in this section are found in the annual publication by Belo Corporation, *Texas Almanac and State Industrial Guide*, for 1949–1950 on 447–76. *Texas Almanac* for 1947–1948 was also consulted for population, names of elected officials, and poll-tax figures, 336–404.
5. T. A. Sloane, *González of Texas: A Congressman for the People* (Washington, DC: John Gordon Burke Publisher, Inc., 1996), 2.
6. A similar account from Munguía's perspective as Peña's cohort is found in Rosales's interviews on June 9, December 10, and December 12 in 1984.
7. In May 1965 a master's degree candidate, Eugene Rodríguez Jr., in the Department of Government at St. Mary's University submitted a thesis entitled "Henry B. González: A Political Profile." Rodríguez has also been a staff member for Congressman González. His thesis was published ten years later in 1976 in basically the same form, but with an epilogue. See the published work with the same title by Arno Press, a New York Times Company. I relied on this work for details about the González family and Henry B.
8. The library at Main Avenue High School, now named Fox Technical High School, does not have school yearbooks for the high school years 1931–1935, nor do they have photographs of graduating classes. St. Mary's University does not have yearbooks for most of the years 1935–1941, when Albert Jr. attended the university and law school briefly. Henry first attended the University of Texas, but financial difficulties made him return home and attend St. Mary's, where he graduated from both the university and the

law school.

9. See Eugene Rodríguez Jr., *Henry B. González: A Political Profile* (New York: Arno Press, 1976), 42.
10. Adlai Stevenson, *Stevenson Speeches* (New York: Random House, 1952), 89–90.
11. Ibid.
12. Spanish persons of Mexican ancestry used the self-identifier of Méxicano, Chicano, and Raza for the larger group. Latin American was one of several ethnic identifiers used in English during the era to refer to the population of Mexican ancestry. Mexican American had not yet come into vogue, nor had Hispanic or Latino. A group prior to Loyal American Democrats was the Pan American Progressive Association (PAPA), organized by Henry B. González, but they did not seek to field candidates to public office; rather it was González's organizational vehicle for his own electoral activity.
13. For an early biography on Garner, see Marquis James, *Mr. Garner of Texas* (New York: Bobbs-Merrill Co., 1930).
14. Municipal reform reached its peak in San Antonio in the 1951 city election. The pro-reform group calling itself the Council-Manager Association elected one of their own as mayor, Jack White. By 1953 Mayor White had aligned himself with the anti-reform group and was reelected. During these two municipal contests, white businessmen began to organize themselves into the Good Government League (GGL). By 1955 the GGL had approximately three thousand members. The GGL continued to dominate municipal politics for decades to come into the mid-1970s.
15. The Mercado is now known as the Market Square, a tourist destination, but then it was a farmer's market with fresh produce and other goods for sale. Milam Square is also known and referred to as Santa Rosa Park because of the adjacent street and hospital name.
16. LAD at this time consisted of Albert A. Peña Jr., A. M. Ramirez, Hilario "Lalo" Solis, Hector M. Diaz, Charles R. Knopick, Joe A. Estrada, Alfred "Fred" M. Ramirez, George de la Garza, Roger T. Saldana, and Joe A. Tovares. At least these eleven members signed a very large commemorative hardcover book that contains photos of the Stevenson rally at Milam Square and newspaper clippings. The first page of this book reads "The Latin-American Story" with bottom caption of "San Antonio-1952." A newspaper article by Ed Castillo, "Adelaido Doesn't Make Jokes Even in Spanish," *San Antonio Light*, October 19, 1952, 15A, mentions other LAD officers as being involved with organizing the rally: Richard Casillas, Bill Maldonado, and Rubén Munguía.
17. "Forum News Bulletin" dated November 1954 in Lico López Greenbook, MSU Library Special Collections, Albert Pena Collection, 4, which has in addition to the Hernandez case lawyers, Albert A. Peña Jr., Al Hernandez from Houston, Frank Pinedo and David Loyosa from Austin, Homero López from Kingsville, and Leo López and William Bonilla from Corpus Christi, Texas.
18. Original poster in the possession of UTSA Prof. Rudy Rosales in green-colored album given to him by Lico López.
19. *San Antonio Light*, October 19, 1952, 1A.
20. State representative positions, seven for Bexar County, were all chosen by voters in at-large elections. Candidates ran by places for District 68. Henry B. and Albert did not run for the same position in the same place, only for the same position in that district.
21. José Olivares was the first recruited in 1955 for the GGL slate and became the first Mexican American since Juan Seguin elected to the San Antonio City Council. Henry

Cisneros was their last choice in 1971.
22. See flyer printed and posted throughout Bexar County featuring Maury Maverick Jr. endorsing both Peña and Semaan in the runoff election, copied from the Lico López Greenbook.

CHAPTER 6. *EL COMISIONADO*, OUR MAN DOWNTOWN

1. See Maury Maverick, Sr. Papers, University of Texas-Austin, Box 4K124.
2. See Lico López Greenbook, MSU Library Special Collections, Albert Pena Collection, 33.
3. See Lico López Greenbook, 35.
4. See *San Antonio Express* editorial, July 18, 1956, 4A, and more in Lico López Greenbook, 38.
5. Parenthesis in text. See Eugene Rodríguez Jr., *Henry B. González: A Political Profile* (New York: Arno Press, 1976), 75.
6. *San Antonio Light*, May 20, 1956.
7. *San Antonio Light*, November 7, 1956.
8. Antonio Navarro was appointed to the State Senate in 1846.
9. July 18, 1956, 4A.
10. July 20, 1956.
11. *San Antonio News*, August 26, 1956; *San Antonio Light*, August 26, 1956, 10A.
12. See Lico López Greenbook, 49, newspaper clipping titled "Winner Peña Tells Love for Politics," by John Ruckman.
13. See clipping dated "Wednesday Oct. 24, 1956" and entitled "Sen. Kennedy Raps 'Party of Opposition,'" in Lico López Greenbook, 53.

CHAPTER 7. THE COMMISSIONER YEARS, 1957–1960

1. See Lico López Greenbook, MSU Library Special Collections, Albert Pena Collection, 65.
2. See Gutiérrez interview with Marie and Pic Swartz, February 20, 2004, San Antonio, TX. Mimi Swartz was associated with *Texas Monthly* magazine.
3. See oral history interview with Herschel Bernard, February 19, 2004, San Antonio, TX.
4. See Lico López Greenbook, 55.
5. See Lico López Greenbook, 54 and 55, for those photos.
6. See Peña document dated January 7, 1957, in folder 57.
7. See Lico López Greenbook, 54.
8. See Lico López Greenbook, 58.
9. See Lico López Greenbook, 64.
10. See Lico López Greenbook, 54.
11. *San Antonio Light*, January 18, 1957, 4A.
12. See oral history interviews with Eugene Coleman and Rev. Claude Black, April 10, 2007, San Antonio, TX.

13. Ibid. These articles by Peña in this newspaper were lost to a fire. Coleman informed me that his building burned years ago.
14. For mention of this incident, see back page of Peña funeral program, July 6, 2006, and my interview with Rev. Claude Black and Eugene Coleman, April 10, 2007.
15. UTSA, Peña Archive, Box 38. Only one full year of "Monthly Pocket Appointment Calendars" is complete. The years 1969 and 1970 have some missing months and only January 1971 is intact. Some are badly deteriorated and illegible.
16. Bernard interview, February 19, 2004.
17. See oral history interview with Romulo Munguía Jr., April 2004, San Antonio, TX.
18. UTSA, Peña Archive. Some of these early writings are divided and indexed into several categories. Under Speeches and Addresses see Box 26; for Radio and Television Speeches see Box 27; for Writings see Box 28; and for other writings scattered in the archive see primarily Box 36, which contains Chicano newspaper articles and clippings, some of which contain Peña's comments or quotes. Regrettably the archival material is limited to early years from 1957 to 1971 and not complete. I have copied most of his opinion editorials found at this archival collection and the San Antonio City Library. *La Prensa*, which carried most of Peña's material, also had a fire in which they lost years of back copies. The award-winning article by Peña was also lost, and even the plaque given *La Prensa* for that award was not among those displayed in the current offices of the newspaper. The photographs that are available are found in Box 38 and some of his audio recordings are in Box 39. The UTSA Guide to the Peña Papers for Box 39 has this: "(NOTE: Tapes are brittle and dirty. All are reel to reel with the exception of four cassettes. all [sic] tapes are stored in labeled acid-free envelopes.)" Approximately fifteen audiotapes on reel and three cassettes with dates of 1969, 1970, and 1971, plus nine of these are undated. I could not financially afford to pay for the archive to transfer these tapes to modern digital technology, nor did the archive have the equipment from that era to play and hear the content, assuming they would have given permission for same in that the tapes could be destroyed completely at first playing.
19. Meeting on May 4, 1957, copy in folder 57.
20. Flores interview, March 24, 2007, tape 1.
21. Radio speech written copy dated February 5, 1958, in folder 58.
22. Radio speech KEXX dated March 8, 1958, folder 58.
23. UTA interview with Richard Davila, March 28, 1998, and interview with Madeline Peña Davila, January 23, 2004, San Antonio, TX.
24. For a brief historical account of the development of the Democratic Party in Texas, see The Handbook of Texas Online at https://tshaonline.org/handbook.
25. See oral history interview with Gail Beagle, May 28, 2004, San Antonio, TX.
26. Bernard interview, February 19, 2004.
27. See Lico López Greenbook, 68.
28. Ibid.
29. The Metropolitan Water Board turned over management of the lake and its 1,350 acres of land to the San Antonio River Authority, which has now expanded this facility into a 4,900-acre recreational area. The idea behind this manmade lake was to build electricity-generating power plants for the city, and to use some of the discharged water from the power plants and waste water effluent from the city to also supply water. San Antonio water was handled by the City Public Service Board.

30. See oral history interviews with Jake Johnson, December 9, 1997, April 16, 2003, and July 9, 2005, Round Rock, Texas. See also the Albert A. Peña Jr. interviews. There is a discrepancy in the Braunig Lake story as retold by Peña and recalled by Johnson, but only on the point of breaking the lock and driving up to the cabin. And, Johnson claims he and Peña did not drink that much or that often together.

31. This story as narrated by Jake Johnson has a great ending. Mr. Braunig met the young woman, a Mexican American, and romanced her. They married and eventually she became his widow, for he was much older than she. Braunig Lake, located in southern Bexar County, is open to the public.

32. Radio KEXX broadcast of March 15, 1958, in Spanish, Gutiérrez folder 58.

33. Radio KEXX broadcast of August 29, 1958, in English with brief Spanish translation, Gutiérrez folder 59.

34. Radio KEXX broadcast of September 6, 1958, in English with brief Spanish translation, Gutiérrez folder 58.

35. Emphasis in article. September 11, 1958, Gutiérrez folder 58.

36. See articles in Gutiérrez folder 58.

37. This restrictive practice continued until 1975 with the extension of the Voting Rights Act to cover Texas. See Article 5.11a in *Texas Election Laws, 1970–1971* (Austin, TX: Steck-Warlick Co.), 71, for an actual example of the wording. This process was not only restrictive but also preventive of enthusiasm among potential voters when coupled with the filing deadline for county, state, and federal offices in February. In other words, persons had to pay their poll tax and register to vote before they knew exactly who was running for office in any given position.

38. In 1988 Lloyd Bentsen also benefited from the LBJ law in that he was running for reelection to the U.S. Senate and running as vice president on the national Democratic ticket.

39. See Lico López Greenbook, 66.

40. Gutiérrez folder 59.

41. July 9 and 16, 1959, Gutiérrez folder 59.

CHAPTER 8. VIVA KENNEDY CLUBS

1. Ethnic identification began to shift across the country from Latin American and Mexicano to Mexican American in 1960. Peña also adopted new self-descriptive jargon, calling himself Mexican American and subsequently Chicano, a term he kept until his death. Accordingly, I have changed the descriptor from Mexicano to Mexican American and Chicano in the narrative.

2. See Thomas H. Kreneck's *Mexican American Odyssey: Felix Tijerina, Entrepreneur and Civic Leader, 1905–1965* (College Station: Texas A&M University Press, 2001), 264–65, for a masterful job on the life of Felix Tijerina and an account of this convention and Peña Jr.'s role.

3. Ibid., 265.

4. See article written by Kathleen B. Voigt, "Voigt Reports on Demo Meet," with handwritten notation that suggests it was published in *La Prensa*, May 18, 1960, Gutiérrez folder 60.

5. This opinion piece is dated July 5, 1960, Gutiérrez folder 60.
6. Allan O. Kownslar, ed., *Texas Iconoclast: Maury Maverick, Jr.* (Fort Worth: Texas Christian University Press, 1997), 241, 244.
7. Charles Ashman, *Connally: The Adventures of Big Bad John* (New York: William Morrow, 1974), 73–77.
8. See Robert Dallek, *An Unfinished Life: John F. Kennedy, 1917–1963* (Boston: Little, Brown and Co., 2003), 239, for mention of the Kennedy Club strategy in various states.
9. Ignacio M. García, *Viva Kennedy: Mexican Americans in Search of Camelot* (College Station: Texas A&M University Press, 2000), 43–44. García's book is the first work to flesh out the organization, campaign, leadership, and role of the Viva Kennedy Clubs during the John F. Kennedy presidential campaign. I relied heavily on García's work for details about Peña Jr.'s involvement in this effort.
10. See oral history interview with Bill Peña, February 5, 2004.
11. García, *Viva Kennedy*, 47–48.
12. García, *Viva Kennedy*, 45.
13. Written commentary entitled "Speech" dated September 23, 1960, with handwritten notation at top "Weekly Dispatch–9/30/60," Gutiérrez folder 60.
14. Folder 23, MSU Library Special Collections, Albert Peña Collection.
15. "County Comment," by Commissioner Albert Peña Jr., with no date but has "Coleman" handwritten at top right, in Gutiérrez folder 61.
16. See Eugene Rodríguez Jr., *Henry B. González: A Political Profile* (New York: Arno Press, 1976), 111 n. 11, referencing a speech Henry B. gave to Young Democrats at Incarnate Word College, December 15, 1964.
17. March 31, 1961, Gutiérrez folder 61.
18. Author interview with Herschel Bernard, February 19, 2004.
19. Faxed notes from Arnold Flores to author, December 7, 2007. See Gutiérrez folder 07.
20. Peña interview, July 4, 1996, San Antonio, TX.
21. Author interview with Herschel Bernard.
22. UTA interview with Peña, July 4, 1996.
23. Faxed notes from Arnold Flores to author, December 7, 2007. See Gutiérrez folder 07.
24. James McCrory wrote several articles on this election, as did other reporters; see "González Is the Winner," *San Antonio Express*, November 5, 1961; Dick Balmos, "Backers Celebrate: Victory Sweet to González," *San Antonio Light*, November 5, 1961; Victor Panfeld under pen name Don Politico, "Record Vote Turnout," *San Antonio Light*, November 5, 1961.

CHAPTER 9. PASO AND CRISTAL'S LOS CINCO CANDIDATOS

1. "County Comment," April 28, 1961, and August 25, 1961; also speech during a dinner held in his honor, August 19, 1961, Gutiérrez folder 61.
2. "County Comment," May 26, 1961, and June 16, 1961, Gutiérrez folder 61.
3. Most history books covering Chicano politics of the time make brief mention of PASO and of the California counterpart, the Mexican American Political Association

(MAPA), in April 1960 by members of the Viva Kennedy Clubs in Texas and California, respectively. See, for example, Juan Gomez-Quinonez, *Chicano Politics: Reality and Promise, 1940–1990* (Albuquerque: University of New Mexico Press, 1990), 67, for reference to MAPA; and John Shockley, *Chicano Revolt in a Texas Town* (Notre Dame, IN: Notre Dame University Press, 1974), for analysis of PASO's direct-action work in the electoral arena in South Texas.

4. U.S. 811. Argued January 11, 1954. Opinion announced May 3, 1954. See *United States Law Week* 22, no. 42 (May 4, 1954), Section 4: "Texas jury commissioners' systematic exclusion of persons of Mexican descent from jury service deprived murder defendant, who was member of that class, of equal protection of laws; Fourteenth Amendment is not solely against discrimination between Negro and white races, but prohibits discrimination against any group which community treats as separate class." See also the Texas Court of Criminal Appeals decision that affirmed the exclusion of Mexicans from the jury in this case by the trial court at 251 S.W. 2d 531. For a summary of the key points in the opinion written by Chief Justice Earl Warren, see also *Hernandez v. Texas*, in F. Arturo Rosales, *Testimonio: A Documentary History of the Mexican American Struggle for Civil Rights* (Houston: Arte Público Press, 2000), 207–10.

5. Gus García, "An Informal Report to the People," n.d., n.p. Copy in the possession of Rodolfo Rosales at UTSA.

6. The Office of Management and Budget, officially in Directive 15 issued May 1977, fixed ethnicity for all persons with origins from a Spanish-language country residing in the U.S. as being Hispanics. All national-origin peoples with that commonality were lumped into one category, eliminating other choices such as Chicano or Mexican American. See Emily B. Gratton and Myron Gutmann, "Hispanics in the United States, 1850–1990: Estimates of Population Size and National Origin," *Historical Methods* 33: 137–53, but specifically 143, table for the estimated number of Mexican-origin persons in the United States in 1960.

7. Published material on PASO and MAPA is scant. More research is needed. A history of each organization is long overdue. PASO ceased to exist in Texas in the 1980s, with only a Houston-based chapter remaining in the 1990s. MAPA continues to exist in California in 2016. The material presented in this section is from many documents in Gutiérrez folder POS taken from the UTSA Archives of the Peña Papers, namely Box 22, folders 1–9. These records cover the time frame of 1962 to 1972.

8. Regrettably, the oral history interview I did with Lydia Camarillo, vice president, Southwest Voter Registration Education Project, San Antonio, Texas, has not been digitized by Special Collections, University of Texas Arlington Library for my Tejano Voices website and therefore cannot be cited accurately. This library does have the audio and video interview within this collection. In this interview, Ms. Camarillo traces the historical attempts to place members of their group in transition teams for the Carter and Clinton presidencies, with little success.

9. March 17, 1961, Gutiérrez folder 61.

10. Letter of four pages from Ed Idar, signed "Executive Secretary, PASSO," dated February 21, 1962. Folder 50, MSU Library Special Collections, Albert Peña Collection.

11. Gutiérrez folder POS, UTSA Archives, Peña Papers, Box 22, folder 1.

12. José Angel Gutiérrez, *The Making of a Chicano Militant: Lessons from Cristal* (Madison: University of Wisconsin Press, 1998), ch. 5, "Texas A&I," 78–96.

13. Letter from Robles to Peña, dated February 13, 1962, and single sheet without date or

origin indicating dues received from these three cities. Folder 50, MSU Library Special Collections, Albert Peña Collection.

14. Speech delivered by Peña and reprinted in "County Comment," December 28, 1962, Gutiérrez folder 62.
15. "County Comment," December 28, 1962, Gutiérrez folder 62.
16. Two-page written statement dated February 25, 1963, Gutiérrez folder 63.
17. March 8, 1963, Gutiérrez folder 63.
18. "County Comment," March 29, 1963, and April 12, 1963, Gutiérrez folder 63.
19. This section is my recollection of events and persons involved as I was a participant, observer, or involved in many of them, plus in later years recounting, recalling, and retelling of these events with Albert Peña Jr., Moises Falcon, Natividad Granados, Reynaldo Mendoza, Elvirita de la Fuente, Enriqueta Palacios, Albert Fuentes, Hershel Bernard, Arthur Gochman, Emmett Tuggle, George Ozuna, Juan Cornejo, Virginia Muzquiz, John Shockley, Armando Navarro, Douglas Foley, and many others. The academic works by Shockley, Navarro, Foley, and myself all contain varying interpretations of these events from 1962 to 1967. In 1969 I returned to Crystal City and organized the second revolt known as the walkout of 1969 and founding of La Raza Unida Party in Texas.
20. In addition to the story making its way into area newspapers and those of larger cities in the state the next day, over the next few days, and up to six months after the election, national and international media, newspapers, and magazines also ran the story. See local coverage in the *Texas Observer*, April 18, 1963, 10; *Dallas Morning News*, April 13, 1963, and May 7, 1963, 1; *Valley Morning Star*, May 12, 1963; *Corpus Christi Caller*, May 19, 1963, 2B, and June 16, 1963; *San Antonio Express*, April 7, 1963, and May 2, 1963, 7D; and *Laredo Times*, April 29, 1963. For national reports and stories, see *Time*, April 12, 1963, 25; *Look*, October 8, 1963, 68–72; *Newsweek*, April 29, 1963, 26; *Life*, June 4, 1963; *New York Times*, April 14, 1963, 49, May 5, 1963, 83, and again September 21, 1963, 21; *National Observer*, April 22, 1963, 1; *Los Angeles Times*, May 27, 1963, 1; *Wall Street Journal*, September 18, 1963; and Mexico's *Mañana*, September 14, 1963, 20–33.
21. Shockley, *Chicano Revolt in a Texas Town*, 1.
22. Ibid., 259.
23. Gutiérrez folder 63.
24. Peña Papers, UTSA Archives, Box 22, folder 2; and Gutiérrez folder 63.
25. "Peña, Ploch Trade Oral Jabs over Crystal City," *San Antonio Express*, and "Peña Discounts Censure: As Hiding Something More Important," *San Antonio News*, both May 10, 1963.
26. Gutiérrez folder 63.
27. Lyndon B. Johnson Library, John May Collection, Box 450, "Peña, Albert, Jr., Ethnic folder."
28. Patrick Carroll, *Felix Longoria's Wake: Bereavement, Racism, and the Rise of Mexican American Activism* (Austin: University of Texas Press, 2003).
29. Peña Papers UTSA Archives, Minutes dated February 14, 1964, Gutiérrez folder POS. The list of those in attendance for the convention that followed the executive meeting is impressive. Labor leaders such as Raleigh Mull, Ray and Louis Shaffer (*sic*), Henry Muñoz, and Paul Montemayor; Mayors Juan Cornejo from Crystal City and Leo. J. Leo of La Joya; prominent attorneys such as Bob Sanchez, Filemon Vela, and

Charles Albidress; ministers and priests; and Dr. R. Casso, among many others from throughout the state, were appointed to various committees.

30. Gutiérrez folder 64.

31. "Peña Defends Policeman's Association," *San Antonio News*, September 18, 1963.

32. Letter signed by Peña as co-chair along with three other co-chairs of the Texas Democratic Coalition, Hank S. Brown, W. J. Durham, and Franklin Jones Sr., addressed to the President of the United States, dated December 7, 1963, Lyndon B. Johnson Library, White House Control File, Box 119.

33. *Texas Almanac, 1968–1969* (Dallas: Belo Corporation 1969), 560 and 563.

34. *Texas Almanac, 1972–1973* (Dallas: Belo Corporation, 1973), 525.

35. Peña Papers, UTSA Archive, Gutiérrez folder POS; two-page written speech is dated August 9, 1966.

36. Lyndon B. Johnson Library, White House Control File–Name File, Box 119, "Peña, Albert A., Jr. Ethnic folder." Peña's letter to González is dated May 21, 1964, and Valenti's note to Moyers is dated May 27, 1964.

37. Peña Papers, UTSA Archives, Gutiérrez folder POS, five legal-size-page speech.

38. Peña Papers, UTSA Archives, Gutiérrez folder 65, speech dated August 27, 1965.

39. Lyndon B. Johnson Library, White House Control File–Name File, Box 119, "Peña, Albert A., Jr. Ethnic folder."

40. "Bexar Hospital District Hit by Peña on Representation," *San Antonio Express*, June 30, 1964, 4D.

41. Peña Papers, UTSA Archives, Gutiérrez folder POS, four-page booklet.

42. Peña Papers, UTSA Archives, Gutiérrez folder 65.

43. Letter of reply from Ralph A. Dungan, Special Assistant to the President, dated March 9, 1964, Lyndon B. Johnson Library, White House Control File, Box 119.

44. In Texas by 1965–1966 the self-descriptive ethnic term gaining favor was Chicano rather than Mexican American. The youth and laborers increasingly referred to themselves as Chicanos, particularly when involved in protests and labor strikes.

45. Lyndon B. Johnson Library, John May Collection, Box 450, "Peña, Albert, Jr. Ethnic folder." Interestingly, the address on the letter was not that for Hernandez but Peña's, "423 Sharon, San Antonio, Texas."

46. "PASO Chairman Gets Support on GOP Issue," *San Antonio Light*, January 24, 1966.

47. Gutiérrez folder 65, documents dated September 15, 16, and 19, 1965. Luis Avila's three-page statement is dated September 15, 1965, and the three-page press release Peña issued has no date.

48. PASO Sees 'Mental Terrorism,'" *San Antonio Light*, and "PASO Unit Claims School Politicking," *San Antonio Express*, both dated January 26, 1966.

49. Author interviews with Henry Casso, Albuquerque, NM, June 24, 2004, and Juan Patlan, San Antonio, TX, March 22, 2005.

50. Lyndon B. Johnson Library, White House Control File–Name File, Box 119, "Peña, Albert A., Jr. Ethnic folder." The note is on González congressional personal stationary with his photo dated "1-30-67," and press clipping is from the *San Antonio Light*, dated January 25, 1967, entitled "Peña Asks Probe of End to Migrant Project." I assume Peña did not know of González's handwritten note nor of the offensive slur because it was

never mentioned in interviews by him or anyone that I was able to find. Peña never asked, or had someone request what documents under his name were housed at the LBJ Library at the University of Texas in Austin.

51. The first White House staff person who identified himself as Chicano was Henry M. Ramirez in the Nixon administration. See his self-published book, *A Chicano in the White House: The Nixon No One Knew*, 2014, and my book review of this first-person narrative in the online journal, *Somos Primos*, April 2016 at http://www.somosprimos.com/.

52. UTA Interview with Vicente Ximenes, Albuquerque, NM, June 25, 2004. See www.libraries.uta.edu/tejanovoices/vicenteximenes/. Currently, Prof. Michelle Hall Kells, University of New Mexico, is working on a manuscript on Ximenes.

53. Copy of letter sent to me by Ximenes, which is his memo to Louis Martin dated February 15, 1965; see Gutiérrez folder 65. Louis Martin was the first black official in the White House and served six different presidents in various capacities. See Alex Poinsett, *Walking with Presidents: Louis Martin and the Rise of Black Political Power* (Lanham, MD: Rowman & Littlefield, 2000), first published by Joint Center for Political and Economic Studies (Washington, DC, 1997).

54. Lyndon B. Johnson Library, White House Control File–Name File, Box 119, "Peña, Albert A., Jr. Ethnic folder." See telegram sent by Marvin Watson, Special Assistant to the President, with list of invitees to this ceremony dated June 7, 1967, and request to confirm attendance.

55. See oral history interview with Vicente Ximenes, June 25, 2004, Albuquerque, NM.

56. Lyndon B. Johnson Library, White House Control File–Name File, Box 119, "Peña, Albert A., Jr., Ethnic folder." The North note is dated October 19, 1967.

57. Mary Margaret McAllen Amberson, "'Better to Die on Our Feet, Than Live on Our Knees': United Farm Workers and Strikes in the Lower Rio Grande Valley, 1966–1967," *Journal of South Texas* 20, no. 1 (Spring 2007): 12–17, has a detailed account of events of the farm labor organizing that led to the strike and hearings.

58. *Valley Evening Monitor*, June 12, 1966.

59. *Dallas Morning News*, September 1, 1966.

60. UTA interview with Francisco Pancho Medrano, Dallas, TX, 1996.

61. See *Allee et al. v. Medrano et al.*, 416 US 802 (1974). Case was argued by Texas attorney general John Hill with Gilbert Peña, Joe Dibrell, and Lang Baker representing the state, and Chris Dixie representing Medrano et al.

62. See oral history interview with Joe Bernal, San Antonio, TX, April 2004.

63. Flores interview, March 24 and April 18, 2007, tapes 1 and 2.

CHAPTER 10. THE COMMISSIONER YEARS, 1965–1972

1. *Texas Observer*, April 15, 1966, 5.

2. Telephone interview with Maurice A. Lawrence by Pamela Clayton, Southwest Texas State University, San Marcos, Texas, dated November 16, 17, and 19, 2006, and transcribed at https://www.eeoc.gov/eeoc/history/35th/voices/oral_history-maurice_lawrence-by_pamela_clayton.wpd.html.

3. *Texas Observer*, April 15, 1966, 5.

4. Julie Leininger Pycior, "From Hope to Frustration: Mexican Americans and Lyndon Johnson in 1967," *Western Historical Quarterly* 24 (November 1993): 469–94, has an excellent account of events leading up to the EEOC Walkout and the El Paso hearings of November 1967.
5. Letter from Watson to Temple, dated August 23, 1965, Lyndon B. Johnson Library, White House Control File, Box 119.
6. Richard Graham was a deputy to Sargent Shriver while administering the Peace Corps program before becoming a founding commissioner of EEOC. Later he helped found the National Organization for Women. He died at age eighty-six, October 2007. See *Time* magazine, "Milestones," October 15, 2007.
7. Lyndon B. Johnson Library, John May Collection, Box 450, "Peña, Albert, Jr. Ethnic folder." The letter is dated November 1, 1966, and was sent from Riverside, California, by Flores to James C. Falcon at the White House.
8. Ibid. See letters from Jake Jacobsen, Legislative Counsel to the President, dated September 3, 1965, responding to Congressman González; from John B. Clinton, Staff Assistant to the President, to Peña, dated June 16, 1966; and from Mike Manatos, Administrative Assistant to the President, to Senator Yarborough, dated November 15, 1966. From the content in this latter communication, it is apparent the White House quickly decided to accede to the Albuquerque Walkout demands by accepting the idea of a White House Conference on the Spanish-Speaking for the following year, but declining to accept the twenty-one names of Texas Mexican Americans nominated as invitees from Senator Yarborough. The letter states in part, "The planning sessions of the White House Conference were already in progress. However, we are interested in securing the opinions and advice of a broad spectrum of leaders in the Mexican-American community, and appreciate your calling your constituents to our attention."
9. See oral history interview with Vicente Ximenes, Albuquerque, NM, June 25, 2004.
10. Ibid., 52–55.
11. Ibid., 53–55.
12. Ibid., 39.
13. Lyndon B. Johnson Library, White House Control File–Name File, Box 119, "Peña, Albert A., Jr. Ethnic folder." See telegram sent by Marvin Watson, Special Assistant to the President, with list of invitees to this ceremony dated June 7, 1967, and request to confirm attendance.
14. Author interview with Vicente Ximenes, June 25, 2004, Albuquerque, NM.
15. Author interview with Henry Casso, Albuquerque, NM, June 24, 2004, and Juan Patlan, San Antonio, TX, March 22, 2005.
16. Lyndon B. Johnson Library, White House Control File–Name File, Box 119, "Peña, Albert A., Jr. Ethnic folder." The note is on González congressional personal stationary with his photo dated "1-30-67," and the press clipping is from the *San Antonio Light*, dated January 25, 1967, entitled "Peña Asks Probe of End to Migrant Project."

CHAPTER 11. MALDEF: PEÑA'S OR TIJERINA'S?

1. In 2004, I requested from MALDEF in San Francisco a copy of any document containing the history of the organization and was sent two documents. One document, a

thirty-five-page report, is entitled "Diez Años"; the other is an eighteen-page report written by Alicia Maldonado and Diane Palmiotti entitled "MALDEF: The First Twenty Years, 1968–1988," cited hereafter as "Diez Años" and "First Twenty."

2. For additional information on MALDEF and the history of the founding, particularly the San Antonio office as first headquarters, see oral history interview with Al Kaufman, January 15, 1998.
3. For the interviews I conducted with these persons, see http://library.uta.edu/tejanovoices. Greg Luna is deceased. The interview with Henry Casso, no longer a Catholic priest and also deceased, was conducted on June 26, 2004, in Albuquerque, NM, where he resided.
4. Albert Peña, "MALDEF," *La Prensa*, July 19, 1998, 2A.
5. Ibid.
6. "Diez Años," 4; and also "Comentarios: The Birth of MALDEF," *La Prensa*, January 29, 1991, 2A.
7. "Comentarios: The Birth of MALDEF," *La Prensa*, January 29, 1991, 2A.
8. "Diez Años," 3, 9.
9. Ibid., 10.
10. List of all participants at this meeting held on March 14, 1968, provided to me by Gordon K. Mantler, Durham, NC, January 16, 2006. Gutiérrez folder 68. See also Siobhan O. Nicolau and Henry Santiestevan, "Looking Back: A Grantee-Grantor View of the Early Years of the Council of La Raza," in *Hispanics and the Nonprofit Sector*, ed. Herman E. Gallegos and Michael O'Neill (New York: The Foundation Center, 1991) for a description with analysis of events and key players in the formation and evolution of the National Council of La Raza, which includes mention of Peña and other persons featured in this manuscript.
11. Gordon K. Mantler, *Power to the Poor: Black-Brown Coalition and the Fight for Economic Justice, 1960–1974* (Chapel Hill: University of North Carolina Press, 2013), 108–12.
12. For an account of this protest march and the written manifesto ("The Del Rio Mexican American Manifesto to the Nation") composed by various MAYO members and written by Rev. Jorge Lara-Braud, see Armando B. Rendon, *Chicano Manifesto* (New York: Macmillan, 1971), 332–36.
13. For the only scholarly work on MAYO, see Armando Navarro, *Mexican American Youth Organization: Avant-Garde of the Chicano Movement in Texas* (Austin: University of Texas Press, 1995).
14. The material for this section is from my recall as a participant observer and organizer of several of these protests in Del Rio that culminated in the Palm Sunday March, and from the UTA oral history interview with Mike V. Gonsález, January 13, 1998.
15. Navarro, *Mexican American Youth Organization*, 160–71.
16. Ibid., 153–57.
17. Information on these cofounders of MAYO and the second tier of leadership is from my personal knowledge and recollection. I was the first statewide chair of MAYO, followed by Mario Compean. Carlos Guerra and Alberto Luera also became statewide MAYO leaders after I began organizing the Raza Unida Party; Efrain Fernandez headed the Rio Grande Valley MAYO chapters and was most visible during the Pharr, Texas, police riots; Patlan headed MAUC; and Velasquez began organizing the Southwest Voter project.
18. The biographical material on Cortes is taken from various sources, including "Social

Justice—Ernesto Cortes, Jr.," *Fast Company* magazine, November 30, 1999, at https://www.fastcompany.com/39208/social-justice-ernesto-cortes-jr; and an interview with Cortes by Chris Flores and Robin Johnson dated April 12, 2002, for the Texas Legacy Project (Austin: Conservation History Association of Texas). See also Mark R. Warren, *Dry Bones Rattling: Community Building to Revitalize American Democracy* (Princeton, NJ: Princeton University Press, 2001) for a book on the organizing efforts by Cortes and the Industrial Areas Foundation that he joined after leaving the Chicano Movement, MAYO, and MAUC.

19. See Navarro, *Mexican American Youth Organization*, 151–53, 155; and José Angel Gutiérrez, *The Making of a Chicano Militant: Lessons from Cristal* (Madison: University of Wisconsin Press, 1998), 107–11 for narratives on these Raza Unida issues conferences and the many school walkouts MAYO members organized across the state.

CHAPTER 12. LOSS OF POWER

1. Angela Y. Davis has published several books. The material in this text is from *Angela Davis: An Autobiography* (New York: International Publishers, 1974). See also her *If They Come in the Morning* (1971); *Women, Race and Class* (1983); and *Women, Culture and Politics* (1989). See also the entry under her name in *Africana: The Encyclopedia of the African and African-American Experience*, ed. Kwame Anthony Appiah and Henry Louis Gates Jr. (Philadelphia: Running Press, 2003), 170.

2. See oral history interview with Albert Bustamante, San Antonio, Texas, May 9–10, 2004. Reies Lopez Tijerina also supported Angela Davis in her attempts to get bail and a fair trial. See her autobiography, *Angela Davis*, 167. At the New Politics Convention held in Los Angeles, California, Angela was in the company of James Forman, Stokely Carmichael, Bobby Seale, Ron Karenga, Rap Brown, and Reies Lopez Tijerina.

3. Albert Bustamante interview with author, May 9–10, 2004.

4. *San Antonio Express-News*, April 16, 1972, 4H.

5. *San Antonio Express-News*, May 16, 1972, 15C.

6. Rosales interview with Treviño, San Antonio, TX, March 6, 1985.

7. See oral history interview with Juan Patlan, San Antonio, TX, May 1, 2004.

8. *San Antonio Express-News*, April 16, 1972.

9. See oral history interview with Tino Guerra, San Antonio, April 10, 2005.

10. The issue of excessive use of the county telephone for personal calls first came to light in an *Express-News* article on August 31, 1972, and again on December 27, 1972, just days prior to Peña's last appearance before the Commissioners Court with Olga at his side. The couple's photograph also was published in that edition.

11. "Collisions, Rollover Accidents Leave 4 Dead," *Albuquerque Journal*, February 17, 1998.

CHAPTER 13. POLITICS OF THE PALACE

1. Oral history interviews with Albert A. Peña III, Corpus Christi, TX, September 6, 2007, and Arnold Flores with comment added by Walter Martinez dated December 7, 2007. See Gutiérrez folder 07.

2. *San Antonio Light*, March 4, 1977, 16A.
3. For pioneering work on the impact of the Voting Rights Act, particularly the 1975 extension, see Henry Flores, *Latinos and the Voting Rights Act: The Search for Racial Purpose* (Lanham, MD: Lexington Books, 2015). In a related book about Latinos and the law, see Richard R. Valencia, who traces the litigation history of Chicanos seeking educational equity, *Chicano Students and the Courts: The Mexican American Legal Struggle for Educational Equity* (New York: New York University Press, 2008).
4. *San Antonio Express*, March 18, 1977, 16D.
5. Ibid., 1.
6. *San Antonio Express*, April 5, 1977, 1B; and *San Antonio Express*, April 7, 1977, 1B.
7. *San Antonio Light*, April 9, 1977, 1A.
8. Oral history interview with Juan Patlan, San Antonio, TX, May 1, 2004.
9. Oral history interview with Arnold Flores, San Antonio, TX, February 12, 2004.
10. *San Antonio Light*, April 7, 1977, 2A.
11. *San Antonio Express-News*, April 17, 1977, 1A; and *San Antonio Light*, April 17, 1977, 1A.
12. Oral history interview with former state representative Leo Alvarado, San Antonio, TX, March 22, 2004.
13. Oral history interviews with Tino Guerra, Frank Wing, Leo Alvarado, Arnold Flores, and Herschel Bernard. See interview list in bibliography for dates.
14. See oral history interview with former city council member Frank Wing, San Antonio, TX, May 7, 2004.
15. VHS tape of the dedication of the Albert A. Peña, Jr. Pavilion, at which she spoke about the politics of that appointment. I wish to thank Arnold Flores for obtaining a copy of this event for my use.

CHAPTER 14. ALL RISE! JUDGE PENA PRESIDING

1. April 19, 1977. For an insightful analysis of the impact of the Voting Rights Act when applied to Texas after 1975, see Jerry L. Polinard et al., *Electoral Structure and Urban Policy: The Impact on Mexican American Communities* (Armonk, NY: M.E. Sharpe, 1994).
2. See "Caseload Trends in the Municipal Courts: Analysis of Activity for Year Ended August 31, 2003," in *Annual Report of the Texas Judicial Council, 2002–2003* (Austin, TX: Texas Municipal Courts Education Center, January 2004).
3. See "Municipal Courts Summary of Reported Activity from September 2002 to August 2003," in *Annual Report of the Texas Judicial Council, 2003–2003*, http://www.txcourts.gov.
4. "Ticket Bargain Rate Probe Due," *San Antonio Express*, February 12, 1965.
5. See articles "Traffic Law Crackdown Set," in *San Antonio Express*, March 11, 1966, 6F; James McCory, "Inside Story on Kicking Parking Ticket Addiction," *San Antonio Express*, March 13, 1965; "Bargain Basement Ticket Settlement Hit by Mayor," *San Antonio Express*, March 17, 1965; "Ignoring Traffic Tickets Due to Stop," *San Antonio Express*, March 26, 1965; and Leo Cardenas, "Judge Says Citizens Swindled" and "Sleuths Put Lid on Case," *San Antonio Express*, May 5, 1965, 1A, 14A.

6. This issue began in July 1978 and continued into 1979. See mention in *San Antonio Light*, September 8, 1978; *San Antonio Express*, October 1, 1978, 1G.
7. See oral history interview with Virginia Estrada, San Antonio, TX, February 9, 2004.
8. *San Antonio Light*, May 23, 1983, and October 1, 1983.
9. Kevin Johnson, "Ticket Brokering Faces Probe by Judge's Panel," March 15, 1988, Bl.
10. Kevin Johnson, "Ticket Brokering Probe Leads to System Changes," *San Antonio Light*, March 19, 1988, A1. See also his article "Group Asked to Investigate Ticket Brokering," *San Antonio Light*, April 2, 1988, B3.
11. See "Fines Situation Solution? Just Threaten to Collect," *San Antonio Light*, April 7, 1988, B1.
12. Arnold Flores fax notes to author, December 7, 2007.
13. Arnold Flores interview, February 18, 2004.
14. A request was made to the State Commission for a copy of their report on these allegations. The request was denied on April 15, 2004, in a letter from senior commission counsel/public information officer Tom Broussard to me. The denial letter basically invoked confidentiality of records and cited various Texas Rules of Judicial Administration. Letter is in my possession.
15. Jim Price and Ed Lane, "DA Waits for Word on Fixing of Tickets," *San Antonio Express-News*, I28. See Frances Peña interview, July 4, 1996, for these and additional details of her life and involvement in politics.

CHAPTER 15. THE END OF PUBLIC LIFE

1. *Express News*, May 6, 1992, 1A, and May 31, 1992.
2. See oral history interview with Frances Guerra Peña, San Antonio, TX, July 4, 1996, and also February 5, 2004.
3. See oral history interview with Albert Peña III, Corpus Christi, TX, September 8, 2007.
4. Frances Peña interview.
5. Ibid.
6. Frances Peña interviews.
7. See oral history interview with Florentino "Tino" Duran, March 23, 2004, San Antonio, TX.
8. See oral history interview with Jesus Gutiérrez, Tejano Voices, UTA Special Collections, General Libraries, December 23, 1996.
9. Duran interview, March 23, 2004.
10. Ibid.
11. Ibid.
12. See José Angel Gutiérrez, Richard Jensen, and John Hammerback, *War of Words: Chicano Protest in the 1960s and 1970s* (Westport, CT: Greenwood Press, 1985) for a first work on Chicano rhetoric. Since then Hammerback and Jensen each have continued to write on Chicano rhetoric by specific leaders.
13. Time Warner Cable San Antonio videotape of 2004 Martin Luther King Jr. March, January 19, 2004; and author interview with Jaime Martinez, San Antonio, TX, January 28, 2004.

14. Several of his speeches, debates, and interviews were deposited in his archive at the Institute of Texan Cultures (San Antonio), but these may perish if not reproduced in a contemporary format. See www.libraries.uta.edu/tejanovoices/.
15. On January 3, 1998, *La Prensa* suffered a major loss in that a fire destroyed the archives and building. Peña's material is also found in the city library and at UTSA Peña Archives.
16. See oral history interview with Douglas Dilley and Connie Sanchez, San Antonio, TX, September 25, 2007.
17. In author's possession and JSRI archival material on Peña.
18. See oral history interview with Douglas Dilley, San Antonio, TX, September 24, 2007.

CHAPTER 16. WHO CAUSED THE INJURY OR ASSAULT?

1. Frances Peña interview of July 5, 2004.
2. See double-sided incident report filed under No. 03/276846 dated 4/29/03 by G. Smith of the San Antonio Police Department, San Antonio, TX.
3. See oral history interview with Frances Peña, San Antonio, TX, February 18, 2004. Barbara de la Fuente was interviewed while waiting for Mrs. Peña to arrive for the appointment.

CHAPTER 17. SECOND RETIREMENT

1. The governments of Mexico and the United States have honored Chávez. In 1991 he was the recipient of the most prestigious award given to a non-Mexican, El Premio Aguila Azteca, by the Mexican president. In 1994, President Bill Clinton awarded Chávez the Presidential Medal of Freedom. President Barak Obama dedicated his gravesite at La Paz, near Keene, California, as a National Historic Landmark and Monument on October 8, 2012, and with congressional approval this place and other Chavez/UFW–related sites may become part of a national park.
2. There are many sources of biographical information on César Estrada Chávez. Any Internet search engine will produce sites loaded with information. The farm-worker union Chávez founded can be accessed at www.ufw.org, and the foundation at www.cesarechavezfoundation.org.
3. The University of California at Los Angeles has the César E. Chávez interdisciplinary Institute in Chicana and Chicano Studies. San Francisco State University also has a César E. Chávez Institute for Public Policy; see https://cci.sfsu.edu. Arizona State University also has a Leadership Institute named for Chávez. There is also a highway named after Chávez in Kent County, Michigan, near Grand Rapids.
4. See "Holidays," Blink, UC San Diego, http://blink.ucsd.edu/HR/benefits/time-off/holidays.html.
5. Efforts were made by Colorado activists and by a union local in Illinois.
6. "Premio 'La Causa' a Peña, Duran, y Rosales," *La Prensa*, March 24, 2004, 4.
7. The bound single sheet of paper was a copy of a page with some biographical notes on one of the recipients.
8. César Chávez Foundation Banquet program in author's possession, San Antonio, Texas,

March 23, 2004.

9. Arnold Flores interview of February 18, 2004, 2nd tape.

10. Notably absent was George Velasquez, Willie's brother and a former MAYO member as well. Younger brother Ralph Velasquez explained to me that George boycotted the event because he was most displeased with the author's final product and published reviews of the book in the press. Ralph himself walked out of the presentation when Henry Cisneros was introduced and returned only when the speakers had finished making their remarks. See also the rebuttal to John MacCormack's book review of the Sepulveda book on Willie Velásquez by Ralph Velasquez, "Activist Had No Use for Indifference," *San Antonio Express News*, April 4, 2004, 4H.

11. *The Life and Times of Willie Velásquez: Su voto es su voz* (Houston: Arte Público Press, 2004). Since the release of the hardback edition of the book, many articles and reviews have been published. For an example, see Alejandro Perez, "Requiem for a Working-Class Hero," *San Antonio Current*, February 19–25, 2004, 13–14.

12. Albert A. Peña Jr. claimed the A in the middle of his name stands for Armendariz. He also claimed to be the second male child with this name, and that is why his name ends with Junior. I could find no evidence that this is the case. If his parents followed traditional Mexican custom, there is no Junior in Spanish names; he is in fact Alberto Peña Lopez. His maternal name is Lopez, not Armendariz. His firstborn son, Alberto III, is not a III either but an Anthony. His name is Albert Anthony Peña. I believe Albert Jr. really was named Alberto Antonio Peña like his father and his firstborn son was named Albert Anthony Peña. Later in life Albert Jr. just substituted the Antonio for Armendariz.

13. Frances died November 9, 2006, in San Antonio and was buried in Corpus Christi on November 20, 2006. See also San Antonio Police Department incident report no. 60944874.

APPENDIX 2. NOTE ON COUNTY GOVERNMENT

1. These facts and much more are to be found in Felipe Fernandez-Armesto, *"Our America": A Hispanic History of the United States* (New York: W.W. Norton & Co., 2004).

2. Jesus F. de la Teja's *San Antonio de Bexar: A Community on New Spain's Northern Frontier* (Albuquerque: University of New Mexico Press, 1995) is one of the few good texts on the history of San Antonio from 1700 to 1800. A couple of additional histories of colonial San Antonio to consider are Gerald E. Poyo and Gilberto M. Hinojosa, *Tejano Origins in Eighteenth-Century San Antonio* (Austin: University of Texas, 1991), and for a Spanish academic's perspective on basically the same period, Maria Esther Dominguez, *San Antonio, Texas, en la epoca colonial (1718–1821)* (Madrid: Ediciones de Cultura Hispánica, 1989).

3. While the civil appellate court in the 1952 court case of *Harrison County v. City of Marshall* (253 SW2d 67) held that although counties are corporate entities and enjoy that status, they are still creatures of the Constitution and state statutes passed by the legislature. See also Section 71.001 of the Texas Local Government Code for the corporate status of counties, and the Texas Election Code for qualifications of candidates for the various county positions.

4. See Ann Van Wynen Thomas's article "Tracing Sheriffs and Shire Reeves" (*Texas Lawman* 75, no. 3 [Summer]: 27) for a description of the origins of the public title in England.

5. See Article V, Section 15–18 of the Texas Constitution for description of authority and responsibilities of this office, the highest official in county government. Any standard state and local government text on Texas usually contains a chapter on local government, such as chapter 4, "Local Government in Texas," in *Texas Politics: Individuals Making a Difference*, 3rd ed. (Boston: Houghton Mifflin, 2007), of which I am coauthor.
6. Records obtained courtesy of Bexar County commissioner Tommy Adkisson, Precinct Four.
7. This county form of government is found primarily in Southern states below the Mason-Dixon Line. In some western states the county commissioners are called supervisors and the county judge is called the county executive. The functions remain very similar.
8. In 1982 two additional Spanish-surnamed persons of Mexican ancestry were elected county commissioners and took possession of their office in January 1, 1983: Leo Mendoza Jr. and Paul Elizondo. For more information on Albert Bustamante, see Albert Bustamante Papers, 1980–1992, MS 91, UTSA Archives, Library, University of Texas at San Antonio.
9. In the 1920s two publications made mention of the term "Chicano" and its use among working-class persons of Mexican ancestry residing in the United States. The first was published in 1928 by Daniel Venegas, ed., and issued by Arte Público Press (Houston) in 1998 under the title *Las aventuras de Don Chipote, o cuando los pericos mamen*; and the second was an article by Douglas O. Weeks, "The Texas Mexican and the Politics of South Texas," *American Political Science Review* 24, no. 3 (August 1930): 606–27. Among the emerging middle-class members of this same community, the favored term in the first half of the twentieth century was "Latin American," and later "Mexican American" by the 1960s.
10. See Kemper Diehl and Jan Jarboe, *Henry Cisneros: Portrait of a New American* (San Antonio: Corona Publishing Co., 1984) for a most favorable public relations piece on the up-and-coming Henry Cisneros, the GGL selection to be the leader of the Mexican Americans in San Antonio.
11. See Sharon Navarro, *The Latino Mayors: San Antonio Politics and Policies*, JSRI Research Report No. 52 (East Lansing: Julian Samora Research Institute, Michigan State University, 2015).
12. See George Norris Green, *The Establishment in Texas Politics: The Primitive Years, 1938–1957* (Norman: University of Oklahoma Press, 1979) for a detailed review of the rise of conservative Democrats during those decades and the brief challenge by Ralph Yarborough and liberals.
13. See Evan Anders, *Boss Rule in South Texas: The Progressive Era* (Austin: University of Texas Press, 1982) for a critical examination of several political machines in that region, long the historical base for the Mexican population: Parr, Guerra, Lassiter, Brooks, Kleberg, and Martin.
14. See José Andres Chacon, "Gus C. García, Legal Genius," in a series of profiles in the *San Antonio Express*, no date or page on the loose clipping in Lico López's Greenbook.
15. *San Antonio Light*, April 4, 1948.
16. Boyce House, *City of Flaming Adventure* (San Antonio: Naylor Co., 1949), 171–73.
17. U.S. Census, Fifteenth Census of the U.S.: 1930. Pop. II, 974. See also Michael Phillips, *White Metropolis: Race, Ethnicity, and Religion in Dallas, 1841–2001* (Austin: University of Texas Press, 2006), for a recent historical account of the city's growth and relations within its population; and Marguerite Johnston, *Houston: The Unknown City, 1836–1946*

(College Station: Texas A&M University Press, 1991), for a comparable history of growth and its population during similar times.

18. Cited in Eugene Rodríguez's master's thesis at St. Mary's University, "Henry B. González: A Political Profile," 23 n. 32, as American Public Welfare Association, Public Welfare Survey of San Antonio, Texas (Chicago: APWA, 1940), appendix A.

19. Cited in Rodríguez, "Henry B. González: A Political Profile," 22 n. 31, and see also the Seventeenth Census of the United States: 1950. Population, II, 203–4.

20. Public Service Company, "An Economic and Industrial Survey of San Antonio, Texas," 1942, 123.

21. Rodríguez, "Henry B. González: A Political Profile," 21 n. 27; Green Peyton, *San Antonio: City in the Sun* (New York: Whittlesey House, 1946), 120.

22. The term Chicano as a self-description and label for group identity among persons of Mexican ancestry, particularly youth, came into popular use and was in vogue during the 1960s to the 1990s, when the term waned in acceptance and use giving way to Hispanic and Latino. See Herb Hirsch with Armando Gutiérrez, *Learning to Be Militant: Ethnic Identity and the Development of Political Identity in a Chicano Community* (San Francisco: R&E Associates, 1977), 42–56.

23. Rodríguez, "Henry B. González: A Political Profile," citing the City of San Antonio, 1964, "Economic Base Study of San Antonio, Texas," 70.

24. Earl Shorris, *Latinos: A Biography of the People* (New York: W.W. Norton & Co., 1992), 477. Blacks were 12.1 percent of the population in 1990 and held 17.8 percent of the federal jobs—a huge disproportion and disparity that remains to this day in terms of underrepresentation of Hispanics in federal jobs vis-à-vis all other minority groups.

25. See Rodolfo Rosales, citing various U.S. Census reports of population and economic studies in his book *The Illusion of Inclusion* (Austin: University of Texas Press, 2000), 11, tables 1 and 2.

26. Richard A. García, *Rise of the Mexican American Middle Class, San Antonio, 1929–1941* (College Station: Texas A&M University Press, 1991).

Bibliography

ARCHIVES

Bexar County Courthouse. Office of the County Clerk. Marriage Records. San Antonio, TX.

Center for American History. Papers of Maury Maverick, Sr. University of Texas. Austin, TX.

Institute of Texan Cultures. Albert A. Peña, Jr. Archives. San Antonio, TX.

Lyndon B. Johnson Library and Museum. White House Central File–Name File and John May Collection. Austin, TX.

Our Lady of the Lake University. Mexican American Studies Program. Albert A. Peña, Jr. Archive. San Antonio, TX.

San Antonio Public Library. Newspaper Collection. Microfilm. San Antonio, TX.

Southwest Texas State University. Oral History Project. San Marcos, TX.

State Bar of Texas Archives. Austin, TX.

Texas A&M University. Mary and Jeff Bell Library. Special Collections and Archives Department. Hector P. García Papers. Corpus Christi, TX.

Texas A&M University. James C. Jernigan Library. South Texas Archives and Special Collections. Carlos F. Truan Collection. A2000-036. Kingsville, TX.

University of Texas. General Libraries. Special Collections Department. Tejano Voices Archive. Arlington, TX.

INTERVIEWS CONDUCTED BY AUTHOR

Alvarado, Leo. San Antonio, TX. VHS tape, March 3, 2004.
Beagle, Gail. San Antonio, TX. VHS tape, May 28, 2004.
Bernal, Joe. San Antonio, TX. 2 VHS tapes, April 17, 2003.
Bernard, Herschel. San Antonio, TX. VHS tape, February 19, 2004.
Biery, Fred. San Antonio, TX. CD-ROM, March 2007.
Black, Claude. San Antonio, TX. CD-ROM, March 2007.
Bustamante, Albert. San Antonio, TX. VHS tape, May 9, 2004; VHS tapes 2 and 3, May 10, 2004.
Coleman, Eugene. San Antonio, TX. CD-ROM, March 22, 2007.
Casso, Henry. Albuquerque, NM. VHS tape, June 24, 2004.
Davila, Madeline "Mary Magdalene." San Antonio, TX. VHS tape, January 23, 2004.
Davila, Ricardo "Guero Polkas." San Antonio, TX. VHS tape, July 4, 1996.
de la Fuente, Barbara. San Antonio, TX. VHS tape, February 18, 2004.
Dilley, Douglas. San Antonio, TX. CD-ROM, October 2007.
Duran, Florentino "Tino." San Antonio, TX. VHS tape, March 23, 2004.
Dwyer, Belinda. San Antonio, TX. VHS tape, April 25, 2004.
Elizondo, William. San Antonio, TX. VHS tape, March 3, 2004.
Esparza, Antonio. San Antonio, TX. VHS tape, April 25, 2004.
Estrada, Virginia. San Antonio, TX. VHS tape, February 9, 2004.
Flores, Arnold. San Antonio, TX. VHS tape, February 12, 2004; VHS tape, February 18, 2004; Super 8 digital tape, March 24, 2007; Super 8 digital tape, April 18, 2007.
Gonsález, Mike V. Del Rio, TX. VHS tapes, January 13, 1998.
Guerra, Carlos. San Antonio, TX. VHS tape, August 21, 1996.
Guerra, Tino. San Antonio, TX. VHS tape, April 18, 2004.
Gutiérrez, Ed. San Antonio, TX. VHS tape, November 3, 1997.
Gutiérrez, Gabriel. Austin, TX. CD-ROM, May 26, 2014.
Gutiérrez, Jesús. Dallas, TX. VHS tape, December 23, 1996.
Gutiérrez, José Angel, and Joaquin Jackson. Abilene, TX. VHS tapes 1 and 2, August 1, 1996.
Johnson, Jake. Round Rock, TX. VHS tape, July 9, 2004.
Kaufman, Albert. San Antonio, TX. VHS tape, January 15, 1998.
Luera, Alberto. Laredo, TX. VHS tape, June 10, 1996.
Medrano, Francisco "Pancho." Dallas, TX. VHS tape, July 16, 1997.
Munguía, Romulo, Jr. San Antonio, TX. Notes, April 7, 2004.
Muzquiz, Virginia. Crystal City, TX. VHS tapes, September 24, 1996.
Patlan, Juan. San Antonio, TX. VHS tapes, May 1, 2004.
Peña, Albert, Jr. San Antonio, TX, 1 VHS tape, July 4, 1996; 1 VHS tape, December 9, 1997; VHS tapes 3 and 4, April 16, 2003; VHS tape 5, January 22, 2004.

Peña, Albert Anthony, III. Corpus Christi, TX. CD-ROM, September 8, 2007.

Peña, Belinda, aka Belinda Degene. San Antonio, TX. VHS tape, February 5, 2004.

Peña, Belinda, and William "Bill" Peña. VHS tape, February 5, 2004.

Peña, Frances Guerra. San Antonio, TX. VHS tape, July 4, 1996; VHS tape, February 18, 2004.

Peña, Olga Ramos. San Antonio, TX. VHS tape, April 14, 1997; VHS tape, August 23, 1997; VHS tapes 3 and 4, May 13, 2004.

Peters, Joyce. San Antonio, TX. VHS tape, May 4, 2004.

Teran, Frances. San Antonio, TX. VHS tape, December 9, 1997.

Truan, Carlos. Corpus Christi, TX. VHS tapes, June 17, 1998.

Uriegas, José. Austin, TX. CD-ROM, May 26, 2014; CD-ROMs 2 and 3, September 29, 2014.

Wing, Frank D. San Antonio, TX. VHS tape, May 7, 2004.

Ximenes, Vicente T. Albuquerque, NM. VHS tapes, June 25, 2004.

Yzaguirre, Raul. San Antonio, TX. VHS tape, June 6, 1998.

Zamora, Aguinaldo. San Marcos, TX. VHS tape, January 16, 1998.

Zamora, Cristina. San Marcos, TX. VHS tape, January 16, 1998.

OTHER VHS TAPES OF EVENTS

"A Tribute to Arnold Flores." San Antonio, TX, November 4, 2006.

César Chávez Foundation Banquet. La Villita Assembly Hall, San Antonio, TX. VHS tape, March 23, 2004.

Dedication of Albert A. Peña, Jr. Pavilion. Mission County Park, San Antonio, TX. VHS tape, n.d.

Martin Luther King, Jr. March. San Antonio, TX. VHS tape by Time Warner Cable San Antonio, January 19, 2004.

INTERVIEWS CONDUCTED BY RODOLFO ROSALES

Alaniz, John. San Antonio, TX. CD-ROM, July 20, 1986.

Esquivel, Rudy. San Antonio, TX. CD-ROM, n.d.

Flores, Arnold. San Antonio, TX. CD-ROMs, February 23, 1993.

Peña, Albert, Jr. San Antonio, TX. CD-ROMs, July 30, 1985.

Munguía, Rubén. San Antonio, TX. CD-ROM, December 10, 1984; CD-ROM, December 12, 1984; CD-ROM, June 9, 1985.

Murillo, Gil. San Antonio, TX. CD-ROM, March 7, 1985.

Treviño, Felix. San Antonio, TX. CD-ROM, March 6, 1985.

PUBLISHED SOURCES

Acosta, Oscar Zeta. *The Autobiography of a Brown Buffalo*. New York: Vintage Books, 1989.

———. *The Revolt of the Cockroach People*. New York: Vintage Books, 1989.

Allsup, Carl. *The American G.I. Forum: Origins and Evolution*. Austin: University of Texas Press, 1982.

Almaraz, Felix. *Knight without Armor: Carlos Eduardo Castaneda, 1896–1958*. College Station: Texas A&M University Press, 1999.

Alvarez, Robert R. "National Politics and Local Responses: The Nation's First Successful School Segregation Court Case." In *School and Society*, ed. Henry T. Trueba and Concha Delgado-Gaitan, 37–52. New York: Praeger, 1988.

Amberson, Mary M. McAllen. "'Better to Die on Our Feet, Than Live on Our Knees': United Farm Workers and Strikes in the Lower Rio Grande Valley, 1966–1967." *Journal of South Texas* 20, no. 1 (Spring 2007): 12–17.

Anders, Evan. *Boss Rule in South Texas: The Progressive Era*. Austin: University of Texas Press, 1982.

Ashman, Charles. *Connally: The Adventures of Big Bad John*. New York: William Morrow, 1974.

Ball, Eve. *In the Days of Victorio: Recollections of a Warm Springs Apache*. Tucson: University of Arizona Press, 1970.

Benavidez, Roy P., and Oscar Griffin. *The Three Wars of Roy Benavidez*. San Antonio: Corona Publishing Co., 1986.

Bryson, Conrey. *Dr. Lawrence A. Nixon and the White Primary*. 2nd ed. El Paso: Texas Western Press, 1974.

Carroll, Patrick. *Felix Longoria's Wake: Bereavement, Racism, and the Rise of Mexican American Activism*. Austin: University of Texas Press, 2003.

Clayson, William S. *Freedom Is Not Enough: The War on Poverty and the Civil Rights Movement in Texas*. Austin: University of Texas Press, 2010.

Cockcroft, James D. *Latinos in the Struggle for Equal Education*. Danbury, CT: Franklin Watts/Grolier, 1995.

Dalleck, Robert. *An Unfinished Life: John F. Kennedy, 1917–1963*. Boston: Little, Brown and Co., 2003.

Davis, Angela Y. *Angela Davis: An Autobiography*. New York: International Publishers, 1974.

del Castillo, Richard Griswold., ed. *World War II and Mexican American Civil Rights*. Austin: University of Texas Press, 2008.

del Castillo, Richard Griswold, and Richard A. García. *César Chávez: A Triumph of Spirit*. Norman: University of Oklahoma Press, 1995.

de la Teja, Jesus. *San Antonio de Bexar: A Community on New Spain's Northern Frontier*. Albuquerque: University of New Mexico Press, 1995.

de Leon, Arnoldo. *Mexican Americans in Texas: A Brief History*. Arlington Heights, IL: Harlan-Davidson, Inc., 1993.

Diehl, Kemper, and Jan Jarboe. *Cisneros: Portrait of a New American*. San Antonio: Corona Publishing Co., 1984.

Dominguez, Maria Esther. *San Antonio, Texas, en la epoca colonial (1718–1821)*. Madrid: Ediciones de Cultura Hispánica, 1989.

Fernández-Armesto, Felipe. *"Our America": A Hispanic History of the United States*. New York: W.W. Norton & Co., 2004.

Ferris, Susan, and Ricardo Sandoval. *The Fight in the Fields: Cesar Chavez and the Farm Workers*

Movement. New York: Harcourt Brace, 1997.

Fisch, Louise Ann. *All Rise: Reynaldo G. Garza, the First Mexican American Federal Judge.* College Station: Texas A&M University Press, 1996.

Flores, Henry. *Latinos and the Voting Rights Act: The Search for Racial Purpose.* Lanham, MD: Lexington Books, 2015.

Foley, Douglas. *From Peones to Politicos: Ethnic Relations in a South Texas Town.* Austin: University of Texas Press, 1977.

Galarza, Ernesto. *Barrio Boy.* Notre Dame, IN: University of Notre Dame Press, 1971.

Gallegos, Herman E., and Michael O'Neill. *Hispanics and the Nonprofit Sector.* New York: The Foundation Center, 1991.

Gamio, Manuel. *Mexican Immigration to the United States.* Chicago: University of Chicago Press, 1930.

García, Ignacio M. *Hector P. García and the American G.I. Forum.* Austin: University of Texas Press, 2001.

———. *Hector P. García: In Relentless Pursuit of Justice.* Houston: Arte Público Press 2002.

———. *Partido de la Raza Unida.* Los Angeles: Tlaquilo Press, 1976.

———. *United We Win: The Rise and Fall of the Raza Unida Party.* Tucson: Mexican American Studies and Research Center, University of Arizona, 1989.

———. *Viva Kennedy:* Mexican Americans in Search of Camelot. College Station: Texas A&M University Press, 2000.

———. *White but Not Equal: Mexican Americans, Jury Discrimination, and the Supreme Court.* Tucson: University of Arizona Press, 2008.

García, Mario T. *Desert Immigrants: The Mexicans of El Paso, 1880–1920.* New Haven, CT: Yale University Press, 1981.

———. ed. *The Gospel of César Chávez: My Faith in Action.* Lanham, MD: Sheed & Ward, 2007.

———. *The Making of a Mexican American Mayor: Raymond L. Telles of El Paso.* El Paso: Texas Western Press, 1998.

———. *Memories of Chicano History: The Life and Narrative of Bert Corona.* Berkeley: University of California Press, 1994.

———. *Mexican Americans: Leadership, Ideology, and Identity.* New Haven, CT: Yale University Press, 1999.

———. *Luis Leal: An Auto/Biography.* Austin: University of Texas Press, 2000.

———. *Padre: The Spiritual Journey of Father Virgil Cordano.* Santa Barbara, CA: Capra Press, 2005.

García, Richard A. *Rise of the Mexican American Middle Class, San Antonio, 1929–1941.* College Station: Texas A&M University Press, 2000.

Geron, Kim. *Latino Political Power.* Boulder, CO: Lynne Rienner, 2005.

Goldberg, Robert A. "Racial Change on the Southern Periphery: The Case of San Antonio, Texas, 1960–1965." *Journal of Southern History* 49, no. 3 (August 1983): 349–74.

Gómez-Quiñonez, Juan. *Chicano Politics: Reality and Promise, 1940–1990.* Albuquerque: University of New Mexico Press, 1990.

Gonzalez, Juan. *Harvest of Empire: A History of Latinos in America.* New York: Penguin Books, 2011.

Gorry, Conner. *Cuba*. 3rd ed. New York: Lonely Planet Books, 2004.

Green, George N. *The Establishment in Texas Politics: The Primitive Years, 1938–1957*. Norman: University of Oklahoma Press, 1979.

Grillo, Evelio. *Black Cuban, Black American*. Houston: Arte Público Press, 2000.

Gutiérrez, José Angel. *A Chicano Manual on How to Handle Gringos*. Houston: Arte Público Press, 2003.

———. "The Chicano Movement: Paths to Power." *Social Studies* 102 (2011): 25–32.

———. *A Gringo Manual on How to Handle Mexicans*. Houston: Arte Público Press, 2000.

———. *The Making of a Chicano Militant: Lessons from Cristal*. Madison: University of Wisconsin Press, 1998.

———. *We Won't Back Down! Severita Lara's Rise from Student Leader to Mayor*. Houston: Arte Público Press, 2005.

Gutiérrez, José Angel, Michelle Meléndez, and Sonia Adriana Noyola. *Chicanas in Charge: Texas Women in the Public Arena*. Lanham, MD: AltaMira Press, 2007.

Gutiérrez, José Angel, Richard Jensen, and John Hammerback. *A War of Words: Chicano Protest in the 1960s and 1970s*. Westport, CT: Greenwood Press, 1985.

Hirsch, Herb, with Armando Gutiérrez. *Learning to Be Militant: Ethnic Identity and the Development of Political Identity in a Chicano Community*. San Francisco: R&E Associates.

Hoover, Brett C. *The Shared Parish: Latinos, Anglos, and the Future of U.S. Catholicism*. New York: New York University Press, 2014.

House, Boyce. *City of Flaming Adventure*. San Antonio: Naylor Co., 1949.

James, Marquis. *Mr. Garner of Texas*. Indianapolis: Bobbs-Merrill, 1930.

Johnston, Marguerite. *Houston: The Unknown City, 1836–1946*. College Station: Texas A&M University Press, 1991.

Kaplowitz, Craig A. *LULAC, Mexican Americans, and National Policy*. College Station: Texas A&M University Press, 2005.

Kennedy, Caroline, ed. *Profiles in Courage for Our Time*. New York: Hyperion, 2002.

Kownslar, Allan O., ed. *Texas Iconoclast: Maury Maverick, Jr*. Fort Worth: Texas Christian University Press, 1997.

Kreneck, Thomas H. *Mexican American Odyssey: Felix Tijerina, Entrepreneur and Civic Leader, 1905–1965*. College Station: Texas A&M University Press, 2001.

Lakoff, George. *Don't Think of an Elephant: Know Your Values and Frame the Debate*. White River Junction, VT: Chelsea Green Publishing Company, 2004.

Larralde, Carlos. *Carlos Esparza: A Chicano Chronicle*. San Francisco: R & E Associates, 1977.

———. *Mexican Americans: Movements and Leaders*. Los Alamitos, CA: Hwong Publishing, 1976.

Lattin, Vernon E., Rolando Hinojosa, and Gary D. Keller, eds. *Tomás Rivera, 1935–1964: The Man and His Work*. Tempe, AZ: Bilingual Review Press, 1988.

León, David, and Rubén O. Martinez., eds. *Latino College Presidents: In Their Own Words*. Bingley, UK: Emerald Group Publishing, Ltd., 2013.

Mantler, Gordon K. *Power to the Poor: Black-Brown Coalition and the Fight for Economic Justice, 1960–1974*. Chapel Hill: University of North Carolina Press, 2013.

Márquez, Benjamin, *Democratizing Texas Politics: Race, Identity, and Mexican American Empowerment, 1945–2002.* Austin: University of Texas Press, 2014.

——— . *LULAC: The Evolution of a Mexican American Political Organization.* Austin: University of Texas Press, 1993.

Martinez, Oscar. *The Chicanos of El Paso: An Assessment of Progress.* El Paso: Texas Western Press, 1980.

Matthiessen, Peter. *Sal Si Puedes: Cesar Chavez and the New American Revolution.* Berkeley: University of California Press, 1969.

Matovina, Timothy. *Guadalupe and Her Faithful: Latino Catholics in San Antonio, from Colonial Origins to the Present.* Baltimore: Johns Hopkins University Press, 2008.

——— . *Latino Catholicism: Transformation in America's Largest Church.* Princeton, NJ: Princeton University Press, 2012.

Matovina, Timothy, and Gerald E. Poyo, eds. *Presente! U.S. Latino Catholics from Colonial Origins to the Present.* Maryknoll, NY: Orbis, 2000.

Mazon, Luis. *The Zoot-Suit Riots: The Psychology of Symbolic Annihilation.* Austin: University of Texas Press, 1984.

Meier, Kenneth J., and Joseph Stewart Jr. *The Politics of Hispanic Education: Un paso pa'lante y dos pa'tras.* Albany: State University of New York Press, 1991.

Momayezi, Nasser, W. B. Stouffer Jr., David M. Billeaux, José Angel Gutiérrez, Eric Miller, Barry L. Price, and Carol Waters. *Texas Politics: Individuals Making a Difference.* 3rd ed. Boston: Houghton Mifflin, 2007.

Morehead, Richard. *50 Years in Texas Politics.* 2nd ed. Burnet, TX: Eakin Press, 1982.

Navarro, Armando. *The Cristal Experiment: A Chicano Struggle for Community Control.* Madison: University of Wisconsin Press, 1999.

——— . *Mexican American Youth Organization: Avant-Garde of the Chicano Movement in Texas.* Austin: University of Texas Press, 1995.

——— . *Mexican American Youth Organization: Precursor of Change in Texas.* Austin: University of Texas Press, 1995.

——— . *Mexicano Political Experience in Occupied Aztlan.* Walnut Creek, CA: AltaMira Press, 2005.

——— . *La Raza Unida Party: A Chicano Challenge to the U.S. Two-Party Dictatorship.* Philadelphia: Temple University Press, 2000.

Navarro, Sharon. *The Latino Mayors: San Antonio Politics and Policies.* JSRI Research Report No. 52. East Lansing: Julian Samora Research Institute, Michigan State University, 2015.

Olivas, Michael, ed. *"Colored Men" and "Hombres Aquí": Hernandez v. Texas and the Emergence of Mexican-American Lawyering.* Houston: Arte Público Press, 2006.

Orozco, Cynthia. *No Mexicans, Women, or Dogs Allowed: The Rise of the Mexican American Civil Rights Movement.* Austin: University of Texas Press, 2009.

Paredes, Américo. *"With His Pistol in His Hand": A Border Ballad and Its Hero.* Austin: University of Texas Press, 1968.

PBS Home Video. *A Class Apart: A Mexican American Civil Rights Story.* DVD. Public Broadcasting Service, 2009.

Peyton, Green. *San Antonio: City in the Sun.* New York: Whittlesey House, 1946.

Phillips, Michael. *White Metropolis: Race, Ethnicity, and Religion in Dallas, 1841–2001.* Austin:

University of Texas Press, 2006.

Piatt, Bill. *Black and Brown in America: The Case for Cooperation.* New York: New York University Press, 1977.

Poinsett, Alex. *Walking with Presidents: Louis Martin and the Rise of Black Political Power.* Lanham, MD: Rowman & Littlefield, 2000.

Polinard, Jerry L., Robert D. Wrinkle, Tomas Longoria, and Norman E. Binder. *Electoral Structure and Urban Policy: The Impact on Mexican American Communities.* Armonk, NY: M.E. Sharpe, 1994.

Poyo, Gerald, and Gilberto M. Hinojosa. *Tejano Origins in Eighteenth-Century San Antonio.* Austin: University of Texas Press, 1991.

Pycior, Julie Leininger. *Democratic Renewal and the Mutual Aid Legacy of US Mexicans.* College Station: Texas A&M University Press, 2014.

———. "From Hope to Frustration: Mexican Americans and Lyndon Johnson in 1967." *Western Historical Quarterly* 24 (November 1993): 469–94.

———. *LBJ and Mexican Americans: The Paradox of Power.* Austin: University of Texas Press, 1997.

Quezada, Gilberto J. *Border Boss: Manuel B. Bravo and Zapata County.* College Station: Texas A&M University Press, 1999.

Ramos, Henry A. J. *The American G.I. Forum: In Pursuit of the Dream, 1948–1983.* Houston: Arte Público Press, 1998.

Rendon, Armando B. *Chicano Manifesto.* New York: Macmillan, 1971.

Rodríguez, Eugene, Jr. *Henry B. González: A Political Profile.* New York: Arno Press, 1976.

Rodríguez, Luis J. *Always Running: La Vida Loca; Gang Days in L.A.* Willimantic, CT: Curbstone Press, 1993.

Rosales, Arturo. *Testimonio: A Documentary History of the Mexican American Struggle for Civil Rights.* Houston: Arte Público Press, 2000.

Rosales, Rodolfo. *The Illusion of Inclusion.* Austin: University of Texas Press, 2000.

Ruiz, Mona, and Geoff Boucher. *Two Badges: The Lives of Mona Ruiz.* Houston: Arte Público Press, 1997.

Salinas, Lupe. *U.S. Latinos and Criminal Injustice.* East Lansing: Michigan State University Press, 2015.

San Miguel, Guadalupe. *"Let Them All Take Heed": Mexican Americans and the Quest for Educational Equality, 1910–1981.* Austin: University of Texas Press, 1987.

Sepulveda, Juan. *The Life and Times of Willie Velásquez: Su voto es su voz.* Houston: Arte Público Press, 2005.

Shockley, John Staples. *Chicano Revolt in a Texas Town.* Notre Dame, IN: Notre Dame University Press, 1974.

Shorris, Earl. *Latinos: A Biography of the People.* New York: W.W. Norton and Co., 1992.

Sloan, T. A. *González of Texas: A Congressman for the People.* Washington, DC: John Gordon Burke Publisher, 1996.

Stavans, Ilan. *Bandido: Oscar "Zeta" Acosta and the Chicano Experience.* New York: IconEditions, 1995.

Steen, Ralph W. *Texas: A Story of Progress.* Austin: Steck Co., 1942.

Stevenson, Adlai. *Stevenson Speeches*. New York: Random House, 1952.

Stout, Joséph A., Jr. *Apache Lightning: The Last Great Battles of Ojo Calientes*. New York: Oxford University Press, 1974.

Strachwitz, Chris, with James Nicolopulos. *Lydia Mendoza: A Family Autobiography*. Houston: Arte Público Press, 1993.

Suarez, Ray. *The Holy Vote: The Politics of Faith in America*. New York: HarperCollins, 2006.

Texas Election Laws, 1970–1971. Austin: Steck Co., 1971.

Tijerina, Andres A. *The History of Mexican Americans in Lubbock County*. Lubbock: Texas Tech University Press, 1977.

Tijerina, Reies López. *They Called Me "King Tiger": My Struggle for the Land and Our Rights*. Translated and edited by José Angel Gutiérrez. Houston: Arte Público Press, 2000.

Trevino, Roberto. *The Church in the Barrio: Mexican American Ethno-Catholicism in Houston*. Chapel Hill: University of North Carolina Press, 2006.

Vaca, Nick. *The Presumed Alliance: The Unspoken Conflict between Latinos and Blacks and What It Means for America*. New York: Rayo Books, 2004.

Valencia, Richard R. *Chicano Students and the Courts: The Mexican American Legal Struggle for Educational Equity*. New York: New York University Press, 2008.

Vento, Adela Sloss. *Alonso S. Perales: His Struggle for the Rights of Mexican Americans*. San Antonio, TX: Artes Graficas, 1977.

Warren, Mark R. *Dry Bones Rattling: Community Building to Revitalize American Democracy*. Princeton, NJ: Princeton University Press, 2001.

Weber, Devra, Roberto Melville, and Juan Vicente Palermo. *El inmigrante mexícano: La historia de su vida*. Mexico D.F.: Porrua, 2002.

Weeks, Douglas O. "The Texas Mexican and the Politics of South Texas." *American Political Science Review* 24, no. 3 (August 1930): 606–27.

Zamora, Emilio, Cynthia Orozco, and Rodolfo Rocha. *Mexican Americans in Texas History*. Austin: Texas State Historical Association, 2000.

Index

A

Affirmative Action, 161
Alaniz, Johnny: early career, 86, 113–14, 120, 123, 135, 153; later career, 145–46, 151, 170, 200; participation in Crystal City elections, 128–29
Albert A. Peña, Jr. Pavilion, 201, 222
Albidress, Charles, Sr., 145
Albuquerque Walkout, xx, 149, 153, 159–60, 280n8
Alderete, Joe, Jr., 197, 201
Allee, Alfred Young, 129, 131, 152–53
Almendárez, Marcella, 3
Alvarado, Leo, 197–201, 244, 245
American G.I. Forum (AGIF), 33, 36–37, 48, 109, 132–33, 160–61
Anderson, Charles W., 10, 47, 67, 70–71, 73–75, 146
Archer, Van, 212–13
Armendariz, Albert, 169
Avila, Carlos, 144–45
Avila, Luis, 144–45, 153

B

Bailey, John, 140
Ball, Eddie, 29
Ballinger, Valmo, 76, 181
Barraza, Maclovio R., 160
Barrera, Roy, xxi
Beagle, Gail, 85
Bellinger, Harry, 42
Bennett, Sam C., 72, 74–75, 80–81, 85, 87
Bernal, Joe, xiii, 152–53, 165, 169–70,

■ 299

186, 187, 200, 245
Bernard, Herschel, 43, 58, 70, 78, 81–82, 88, 93, 105, 113, 132, 177; death of, 241–42; in 1970s, 188, 192; PASO and, 120; on Peña's organizing skills, 86
Bernard, Michael, 241–42
Berriozabal, Maria, 217, 255
Bexar County Democratic Coalition (BCDC), 113, 123, 126, 134–36
Black, Claude, 40, 42–43, 65, 76, 123, 154–55, 192; Davis petition and, 180
Blakley, William, 111–12
Blanton, Annie Webb, 34
Bonilla, William, 132–33
Bonilla, Tony, 132
Boyd, Frankie, 210
Boyd, G. D., 73–74
Bracero Program, 11, 141, 162
Braunig, Victor, 87–89, 274n31
Briscoe, Dolph, 182
Briseño, Alex, 213
Brooks, Homer, 270n1, 270n3
Brown, Hank, 43, 58, 90, 102, 114, 120, 152, 210, 241
Burnet, Warren, 166, 175
Burns, Harry, 42
Bustamante, Albert, 181–83, 185, 221

C

Cadena, Carlos, 35, 41, 56, 142, 169
Calderon, Fermin, 174
Callaghan, Alfred, 62, 63, 66
Cantinflas, 115
Cantu, Benny J., 36
Cardenas, Antonio, 127–28
Cardenas, José Angel, 154, 169
Carrillo, Henry X., 142
Carter, Jimmy, 143, 200

Casillas, Richard, 35, 49
Casso, Henry, 146–47, 164, 165, 169
Castillo, Lionel, 132
Castillo, Martin, 164
Catholic Council for the Spanish Speaking, 65
Centeno, Eloy, 115
Chapa, Dario, 191, 194–95, 197, 217, 245
Chávez, César, xxiv, 119, 152, 162, 171, 237–40, 285n1
Chávez, Dennis, 106
Chicano politics: biographies on, x, xix–xx, xxiii–xxv; lack of research on, xix–xx, xxii–xxiii; women and, 122, 126, 176, 217
"Chicano" self-description, 245, 271n12, 274n1, 276n6, 278n44, 287n9, 288n22
Churchill, Winston, 22, 23
Cisneros, Henry, 189, 191, 197, 198–99, 201, 209, 217, 24, 244, 246
civil rights issues, xix, 40, 42–43, 53, 77; at 1960 convention, 101–2, 105–6, 108; during 1960s, 141, 165–66, 168, 170, 172
Cockcroft, James D., 34
Cockrell, Lila, 190–97, 198–201
Coleman, Eugene, 26, 40, 42, 76–77, 181, 219
Commissioners Court, functions of, 251
Compean, Mario, 163, 171, 175
Connally, John, xxi, 58, 106, 109, 122, 131, 134; governorship, 136, 138–39, 147, 149, 151–52, 163
Cornejo, Juan, 127, 128, 131, 153
Corona, Bert, xxiv, 119, 158–59, 160, 169, 171
Cortes, Ernesto, Jr., 175–77, 182, 241, 245

Cortez, Frank G., 46, 47
Cotrell, Charles, 244, 245
"coyotes," 83, 90–92
Crystal City: election in, xxiii, 123–34, 144; school walkout in, 152, 277n19; violence in, 144–45, 153

D

Daly, Henry, 130
Dancy, Oscar, 132
Daniel, Price, 64, 68, 84–85, 105, 111, 122
Daniels, John, 123
Davila, Manuel, 8, 37, 83, 115
Davila, Richard, 83
Davis, Angela, 179–81, 282n2
Davis, Bond, 49, 56
de la Fuente, Barbara, 232, 242
de la Garza, Eligio, 145, 164
de la Garza, George, 35, 48, 49, 52
de Leon, Arnoldo, xxiii
Delgado v. Bastrop, 36
Del Rio, police brutality and march in, 171–75
Del Rio Independent School District v. Salvatierra, 34
Democratic Women's Club, 217
Democrats of Texas (DOT), 80, 81, 85, 94, 99, 108–9, 112, 134, 140, 238
Díaz, Hector, 49
Díaz Ordaz, Gustavo, 136, 150, 162
Díaz Peña, Ignacio, 21–23
Dilley, Douglas, 223–27, 245
discrimination, 11, 26, 27, 29, 35, 51, 78, 157–58, 276n4; job, 76, 101, 121, 141, 147, 150–51, 154, 159, 166–67. *See also* segregation
Duarte, E. B., 183–85
Duarte, Kay, 182–86, 197

Duran, Florentino, 219–20, 245

E

Economic Opportunity Development Corporation (EODC), 146–48
Eisenhower, Dwight D., 49, 52, 55, 64, 101, 114
Equal Employment Opportunity Commission (EEOC), xx, 148–49, 157–61, 164
Escobar, Eluterio, 34
Esparza, Antonio, 7
Esquivel, John A., 36
Esquivel, Rudy, 129, 152
Estrada, Joe E., 49
Estrada, Virginia, 205, 207
Evans, Rowland, 158

F

Falcon, Moises, 123–24, 127–28
Fernandez, Efrain, 175, 281n17
Fernandez, Rosalinda, 224–26
Finklestein, Mike, 169
Flores, Arnold, xxii, 43, 70, 82, 128, 185, 212, 224, 243, 245; background, 153–55; Cockrell campaign and, 192–97, 199–200; SARCA strike and, 207
Flores, Augustin A., 158–60
Flores, Oscar, 7
Flores, Richard A., 160
Flowers, John, 210
Ford Foundation, 167–70
Fuentes, Albert, Jr., 36, 70, 72, 76, 78, 81–82, 86–88, 113–14; PASO and, 120, 129–30, 132, 135–36, 139, 141, 143–44

G

Galarza, Ernesto, xxiv, 119, 162
Galvan, Salvador, 126, 130
García, Alex, 36
García, Gustavo, 27, 35–37, 43, 46, 51, 118; 1952 election and, 56
García, Hector P., xix–xx, 36, 37, 56, 101; Felix Longoria incident and, 104, 134; PASO and, 121, 132–33; Viva Kennedy clubs and, 109; Ximenes and, 161
García, Hipolito F., 142, 143
García, Ignacio M., xix–xx, 108
García, Johnny, 66, 70, 78, 81, 86–87, 114
García, Martin, 128, 131
García, Matt, 86, 154
García, Orlando, 217–18
Garner, John Nance, 54–55
Garza, Al, 154
Garza, Augustine, 8
Garza, Reynaldo, 64, 142
Gatti, John, 190
Geron, Kim, xxi
Gochman, Arthur, 128, 131–32
Gonsález, Mike, 166, 172, 173–75
Gonzales, Manuel C., 51
Gonzáles, Rodolfo ("Corky"), 153, 162, 171
González, Antonio, 151–52
González, Arturo, 173
González, Henry B., 48, 49, 50–52, 58, 65, 68, 82, 92–93, 106; congressional race and term, 113–16, 135, 137–38, 145, 148, 152, 160–64, 170, 189; gubernatorial race, 84–85, 124–25, 136; ingratitude toward Peña, 116, 148, 161, 181, 278n50; journalism, 221; senatorial races, 63–64, 110–12, 116, 128; Viva Kennedy clubs and, 108–9
González, Rene, 218
Good Government League (GGL), 55–56, 59, 135, 140, 147, 256; during 1970s, 181, 188–97, 201; origin of, 48, 52, 271n14
Goode, John, 114
Grace, Charles, 136, 141, 146
Graham, Richard A., 159–60
Granados, Natividad, 127–28
Greenburg, Jack, 167–70
Guerra, Carlos, 175, 177
Guerra, Henry, 220
Guerra, Tino, 186, 197–201, 207–10, 212, 245
Gutiérrez, Rosa, 207–8, 209

H

Hart, Tim, 62, 66–67
Hernandez, Alfred A., 158, 160
Hernandez, Joe L., 142–43, 187
Hernandez, Maria, 34, 209
Hernandez, Mario, 128
Hernandez v. State of Texas, xx, 35–36, 56, 118
Herrera, John, 35, 56
Herrera, Joséfina, 15–16, 19, 21, 23–24, 25–26, 28–29, 51; post-divorce years, 35
Hilbig, Steve, 213
Hoffa, Jimmy, 130, 132
Holcomb, Luther, 158, 160
Hoover, Sam, 29
hospital districting, 95, 117–18, 140–41, 177–78

I

illiteracy, 91, 126, 136, 137

Inc. Fund (NAACP Legal Defense Fund), 166–69
Inman, John, 40
Inner City Advocates (ICA), 218–19
Inter-Agency Committee on Mexican American Affairs, 150, 161–62, 164

J

John Birch Society, 117
Johnson, Jake, 87–89, 113–14, 129
Johnson, Lyndon B., xi, 37, 46, 56, 58, 68, 81, 82–83; 1960 presidential election and, 93–94, 99, 101–7, 109–10; presidency, 134, 136, 138–39, 143, 149–50, 157, 160; vice-presidency, 113–16, 142; Ximenes and, 149–50, 161–64
Jordan, Barbara, 152, 189
Jorrie, Sam, 67, 70–71, 73–75, 87, 118, 146

K

Kelly Air Force Base, 16, 24, 26; job discrimination at, 147, 151, 154
Kennedy, Edward, 151, 183
Kennedy, John F., 67–68, 94, 101–2, 106–10, 118–19, 123, 137, 142; assassination of, 131, 134
Kennedy, Robert F., 93, 106–8, 185
King, Martin Luther, Jr., 171
Knight, Jimmy, 49, 55, 57
Knopick, Charles R., 49
Kreneck, Thomas, xx, 101
Krueger, Robert, 189

L

League of United Latin American Citizens (LULAC), xx, 33, 34–37, 39, 48, 65, 139, 238–39; after Crystal City election, 132–33; during 1960 election, 99–101, 103–4, 109; Tijerina and, 35, 168
Leal, Manuel, 83
Lieck, Charles, Jr., 50–60, 65, 72, 81, 85, 90, 206, 244
Liga de Defensa Pro Escolar, La, 34
Little School of the 400, xx, 100
López, Antonio, 3–4
López, Arnold, 130–31
López, Dolores (née La Chapelle), 3–4, 6
López, Ludevico, 56, 67, 70, 78, 81, 154
López, Manuel and Mamie, 193
López, Rodolfo, 4, 9
Loyal American Democrats (LAD), 42, 49, 51, 54–58, 66, 80–81, 123, 271n16
Lozano, Rubén, 48, 52
Lucero, Ed, 146
Luera, Alberto, 175
Luna, Gregory, 165, 169, 175, 209–10
Luna, Leticia, 209–10

M

Maldonado, Bill, 49
Maldonado, Jesus, 128, 144–45
Maldonado, Manuel, 127, 130–31
Márquez, Benjamin, xix
Martin, Louis, 149, 279n53
Martinez, Cecilio ("Snuffy"), 189
Martinez, Jaime, 239, 244
Martinez, Walter, xiv, 189
Matias, Benny, 205, 207
Matias, Eddie, 209–11, 215
Maverick, Maury, Jr., 12, 41, 52, 55, 58, 59–60, 65, 102, 111–13, 140
Maverick, Maury, Sr., 12–13, 58, 62, 111
McAllister, Walter, 146–47, 190
McClure, Janice, 89–90, 93

McCormick, Carlos, 107–8, 110
McCrory, Jim, 72, 113–14
Medrano, Francisco ("Pancho"), 43, 114, 152
Mendoza, Lydia, 8
Mendoza, Reynaldo, 128, 130
Mexican American Legal Defense and Education Fund (MALDEF), xx, 165–70, 175, 189, 238
Mexican American Political Association (MAPA), 119, 276n7
Mexican American Students Organization (MASO), 176
Mexican American Unity Council (MAUC), 8, 170, 175, 177, 193, 195, 238, 246; Frances and, 217, 218
Mexican American Youth Organization (MAYO), xxiii, 146, 152–53, 162–63, 165–66, 170–77, 216, 240; leadership of, 281n17
Mireles, Irma, 194
Monfrey, John, 190–97, 200
Montemayor, Aurelio, 173–74
Montemayor, Paul, 43, 114
Montez, Eddie, 59
Moore, Carlos, 127, 128, 130–31
Mull, Raleigh, 58, 114, 182–83
Munguía, Marta, 48–49
Munguía, Romulo, Jr., 50, 79
Munguía, Rubén, 46, 48–49, 55, 57, 62, 65–66, 67, 192–93, 221; during Peña's commissionership, 78, 81, 87, 120
municipal courts, functions of, 205–7
Muñiz, Ramsey, 175
Muñoz, Henry ("The Fox"), 81–82, 86–87, 114, 128, 134, 158; later career, 192–93, 195
Murray, Mabel, 8

Mussey, Harold, 62, 63, 66, 70, 76, 86
Myrdal, Gunnar, 118

N

National Council of La Raza (NCLR), xx, 170, 175, 183–84, 238
Navarro, Adela, 81, 85
Navarro, James, 151–52
Nixon, Richard M., 92, 108, 164, 185
North, David, 150, 151
Novak, Robert, 158

O

Obledo, Mario, 188
Ochoa, J. B., 166, 175
O'Daniel, W. Lee, 85
Olivares, José, 56, 100, 271n21
Olivarez, Lorenzo, 128
Ortiz, Rudy, 191, 197, 201
Ozuna, George, 131

P

Padilla, Roy, 168–69
Pan American Progressive Association (PAPA), 48, 49–50, 51, 56, 271n12
Panfeld, Peter, 72
Paredes, Américo, xxv, 100
PASO (Political Association of Spanish Speaking Organizations), xx, 48, 113, 117–46, 157, 176, 238, 276n7
Patlan, Juan, xxii, 146, 175, 177, 192–93, 195, 200, 241, 245
Peeler, Alfonso, 191, 200
Peña, Albert A., Jr.: family background and youth, 3–9, 12, 13, 50–51; final years and death, 222, 225–27, 229–33, 238–46; judicial career, xxi, 196, 198–201, 205–13, 215, 217; on liberalism, 94; married life, 16, 26,

28–29, 35, 51, 65, 67, 101, 134, 137, 142, 182–86, 192, 208, 217–18, 243; media relations, 71, 72, 76–77, 80, 83, 90–92, 112, 113–14, 150–51, 211; money attitudes, 36, 78, 82; name changes, 6, 262n1, 266n3, 286n12; Navy career, 15–24; personal traits, 16, 27, 48, 77, 86, 88, 149, 176, 184–85, 211, 218, 233; religious observance, 6, 182; writings of, 77, 80, 91, 92, 104, 114, 133, 135, 219–23, 226

COMMISSIONERSHIP: xxi, 42, 61–67; during 1957–1960, 69–95, 99–101, 104; during 1961–1964, 113–14, 117, 121, 132, 134–35, 137–40; during 1965–1972, 146–48, 157–62, 171, 177, 181–83, 194, 201, 206; loss of 1972 reelection, 181–86; parks focus, 70, 79, 82, 87–89; support for Davis, 181

LEGAL CAREER: background for, 26, 29–30, 51; early activities, 34–37, 40–41, 48; labor cases, 43–44; later practice, 70, 78, 82, 86, 101, 166–67, 181, 186, 187, 192, 197–200, 217, 224–27; school desegregation cases, 37–40, 65–66, 100, 124, 167

POLITICAL CAREER: aspirations for, 26–27, 40–41, 44, 51, 58–60, 64–65, 67; boycotts, demonstrations, rallies, etc., xxi, 34, 49–50, 55–58, 92, 115, 145–46, 151–52, 207, 241; coalition-building, xxi–xxii, 49–50; during 1970s, 188–89; 1977 mayoral election, 192–97; presidential elections participation, 42, 46–47, 49, 55–59, 90, 94, 99–110, 118

Peña, Alberto Antonio, Sr., 4–9, 19, 24, 25–27, 50, 62; Jorrie on, 75; legal career, 10–13, 34–35, 37, 82

Peña, Albert Anthony, III, 19, 23–24, 25–26, 35, 65, 67; later life, 187–88, 216–17, 242–43; name, 286n12

Peña, Antonio (brother), 5, 6, 8, 12, 13, 267n4; Navy career, 15, 19

Peña, Antonio (grandfather), 3, 4

Peña, Belinda (daughter), 24, 25–26, 35, 65, 67, 231–32, 243

Peña, Belinda (sister), 5, 6, 7–8, 12, 13, 29

Peña, Dolores López, 4–9, 12, 16, 19, 121

Peña, Gregory, 142

Peña, Frances Guerra, xxii, 208, 215–18, 226–27, 230–32, 238, 241–46; death, 286n13

Peña, Lorenzo, 3

Peña, Madeline, 5, 6–8, 12, 13, 37, 83, 115, 188

Peña, Mary, 242–43

Peña, Mary Magdalene, 67

Peña, Olga (daughter), 67, 231–32, 239

Peña, Olga Ramos, xxi, xxii, 26; background, 27–30; commissionership elections, 61–62, 63, 65–68, 86, 93; commissionership years, 78, 80, 81, 134–35; divorce, 182, 185; later life, 193–94, 246; at 1960 convention, 104–7; other political activities, 37, 39, 47, 48–49, 58–60, 185, 187; PASO and, 120; White House visit, 148–50

Peña, Richard, 5, 6, 8, 12, 13; legal career, 29, 30, 34–35; Navy career, 15, 19

Peña, Sandra Frances, 30, 67, 105, 107, 239

Peña, William Albert ("Bill"), 29, 67,

105, 107; later life, 193, 239, 240–41, 245–46
Perales, Alonso, 153–54
Perez, Ignacio, 175, 241, 244
Peters, Joyce, 86, 217, 241
Pina, Joe, 211
Pincus, Bill, 168–70
Ploch, A. J., 67, 72, 73–75, 80, 132, 146
poll taxes, 27, 45, 47, 48, 58–59, 60, 61–62, 82–83, 92–93, 136–37, 154, 216; calls to eliminate, 108, 133, 134, 137–38; Crystal City and, 124–26
Prensa, La, 50, 219–20, 285n15; Peña's contributions to, 66, 80, 219–23, 269n14, 273n18
presidential elections: of 1944, 47; of 1948, 45–47; of 1952, 49, 52–59; of 1956, 59, 60, 64, 68; of 1960, 42, 81, 90, 93–94, 99–110; of 1964, 140

R

Ramirez, A. M., 49
Ramirez, Eugene, 35, 36
Ramirez, Fred M., 49
Ramirez, Henry M., 164, 279n51
Ramos, Rudy L., 160
Rayburn, Sam, 68, 81, 103–6
Raza Unida Party, 163, 171, 175, 187–88, 194
Reyna, Julio, 26
Rio Grande City strike, 151–52, 176
Rizik, Jimmie, 211, 213
Rodríguez, Eugene, Jr., 63, 270n7
Roosevelt, Eleanor, 12–13
Roosevelt, Franklin D., 45–46, 53, 257
Roosevelt, Franklin D., Jr., 158–60
Roybal, Edward, 106

S

Sager, Manuela Solis, 238, 240
Salas, Mario, 171, 181
Saldana, Roger T., 49
Samora, Julian, 149, 162
San Antonio, history of, 252–54, 257–59
San Antonio Refuse Collectors Association strike, 207
San Antonio Savings and Loan Association boycott, 207, 226
Sanchez, Connie, 225–26
Sanchez, George I., 37, 149, 160, 162
Sanchez, J. M., 64
Sandoval, Rubén, 187, 226
San Martin, José, 48, 190–93, 195
Seeligson, Frates, 52, 59–60
segregation, xx, xxi, 26, 34; in boxing, 40–41; in businesses, 77; in Crystal City, 126; in schools, 33–34, 36–40, 124, 145–46, 268n2
Sepulveda, Frank, 192
Sepulveda, Juan, 244
Shafer, Ray, 43, 120, 124, 126–28, 130–31
Shapiro, Ed, 131–32
Shivers, Allan, 49, 54–56, 59, 84–85, 111
Shockley, John, xxiii, 131
Shriver, Sargent, 119, 149
Smith, Preston, 136, 171, 174–75
Snap News, 26, 219; Peña's contributions to, 77
SNCC (Student Nonviolent Coordinating Committee), 171, 180–81
Soledad Brothers, 179–80
Solis, Hilario ("Lalo"), 48, 49, 63,

65–67, 81, 84, 109, 112
Southwest Voter Registration Education Project, xx, xxiv, 194, 217, 238
Sprague, George S., 137–38
Steen, John, 190–91, 195
Steen, Ralph W., xxii, 263n12, 265n12
Steinert, Sturge, 60, 62, 65, 70
Stevenson, Adlai, 49, 52–59, 60, 64, 68, 111, 118; 1960 election and, 102, 107, 110
Stevenson, Coke R., 46, 49, 54
Strickland, R. L., 60, 73, 109
Sutton, G. J., 27, 40, 41–42, 46, 48, 51, 55, 65; Davis petition and, 180; during 1970s, 192; during Peña's commissionership, 76–77, 87, 94, 99, 102, 104, 106, 154–55
Swartz, Marie, 70, 76, 77–78, 93

T
Telles, Raymond, xxi
Tenayuca, Emma, 13, 46, 238, 240, 270n1
Texas Institute for Educational Development (TIED), 175, 177
Texas Rangers, intimidation and violence by, 126, 129–31, 132, 151–53, 255
Thompson, Paul, 113
Thurmond, Strom, 46, 47
Tijerina, Felix, xx, 100, 101
Tijerina, Pete, 35, 120, 165, 167–71
Tijerina, Reies López, xxiv, 153, 162, 171, 282n2
Torres, Peter, 186, 199, 200
Tovares, Joe, 49
Tower, John, 111–12, 139–40, 144, 147

Traugott, Dan, 59–60, 62, 64, 66, 67, 69–70
Trejo, Martin E., 59–60
Treviño, Albert, 63, 66–67
Treviño, Felix, 181–82, 190
Truman, Harry S., 46–47, 53
Tuggle, Emmett, 131–32

U
Ureste, Bernardo, 191, 194, 197, 201

V
Velásquez, George, 286n10
Velásquez, Ralph, 286n10
Velásquez, Willie, 163, 175, 177, 186, 199, 200, 217; posthumous honors, 238, 240, 243–44
Viesca, Luz, 211
Viramontes, Luis, 200
VISTA (Volunteers in Service to America), 170, 173–74
Viva Kennedy clubs, xx, 43, 107, 108–10, 112, 118–20, 238
Voigt, Kathleen, 81, 86, 93–94
Voting Rights Act, 188–89, 250–51

W
wage complaints, 44, 129–30, 137, 141; minimum wage, 53, 101, 136, 138, 140, 151–52
Wallace, Henry A., 45–47, 118, 270n1
War on Poverty, xix, 137–40, 146–47, 149, 172–73, 245
Webb, Joe, 191, 197, 201
Weber, John Kelly, 9–10, 11
Whitmire, John, 210
Williams, Judson F., 162
Wilson, Linda, 241, 243

Wing, Frank D., 191, 197, 201, 208–10, 212, 215, 245
Winter Garden Project, 177
Wolfe, Umhau, 165–66
Wurzbach, Ollie, 85, 118

X

Ximenes, Vicente, 148–50, 161–64

Y

Yanta, John, 146, 147, 245
Yarborough, Don, 122, 136
Yarborough, Ralph W.: early career, 56, 59–60, 63–64, 80, 81, 85, 86, 111; later career, 133–34, 142, 145, 147, 150–52, 160
Yzaguirre, Raul, 183–85